RICHARD III
THE MALIGNED KING

In memory of Isolde Wigram,

gallant co-founder of the present day Richard III Society,
and champion of the standpoint that the 'princes in the Tower'
were not murdered there, nor killed by Richard III.

'The purpose and indeed the strength of the Richard III Society
derives from the belief that the truth is more powerful than lies
– a faith that even after all these centuries the truth is important.
It is proof of our sense of civilised values that something as
esoteric and as fragile as a reputation is worth campaigning for.'

HRH The Duke of Gloucester, KG, GCVO, Patron

RICHARD III
THE MALIGNED KING

ANNETTE CARSON

The
History
Press

Also by Annette Carson
Flight Unlimited (with Eric Müller)
Flight Unlimited '95 (with Eric Müller)
Flight Fantastic: The Illustrated History of Aerobatics
Jeff Beck: Crazy Fingers
Welgevonden: Wilderness in the Waterberg
Richard III: A Small Guide to the Great Debate
*Finding Richard III: The Official Account of Research by the Retrieval
and Reburial Project* (with J. Ashdown-Hill,
D. Johnson, W. Johnson and Philippa Langley)
Richard Duke of Gloucester as Lord Protector and High Constable of England
Camel Pilot Supreme: Captain D.V. Armstrong DFC
Domenico Mancini: de occupatione regni Anglie

As Publication Project Manager:
Arthur Kincaid, ed., *The History of King Richard the Third by Sir
George Buc, Master of the Revels (1619)* 3rd edn

First published 2008
This revised and updated edition first published 2023

The History Press
97 St George's Place, Cheltenham,
Gloucestershire, GL50 3QB
www.thehistorypress.co.uk

British Library Cataloguing in Publication Data.
A catalogue record for this book is available from the British Library.

ISBN 978 1 80399 183 2

Typesetting and origination by The History Press
Printed and bound in Great Britain by TJ Books Limited, Padstow, Cornwall.

MIX
Paper from
responsible sources
FSC
www.fsc.org   FSC® C013056

Trees for Life

Contents

List of Illustrations

23. Richard III falls at Bosworth, stained glass by Christopher Webb
24. Richard III as warrior king, statue by James Butler RA
25. Richard III armed and mounted, model by Roy Gregory
26. The Great Seal of Richard III
27. Richard III's full achievement of arms (Andrew Stewart Jamieson www.andrewstewartjamieson.co.uk)

Text illustrations

Cover illustration

Probably the earliest surviving version (*c.*1510) of a portrait from life. Distortions were added to all known portraits, including the grimly clenched mouth overpainted on this before restoration in 2007. (Society of Antiquaries of London ref. LDSAL 321)

All images not otherwise attributed are © Geoffrey Wheeler, whose invaluable picture research is gratefully acknowledged.

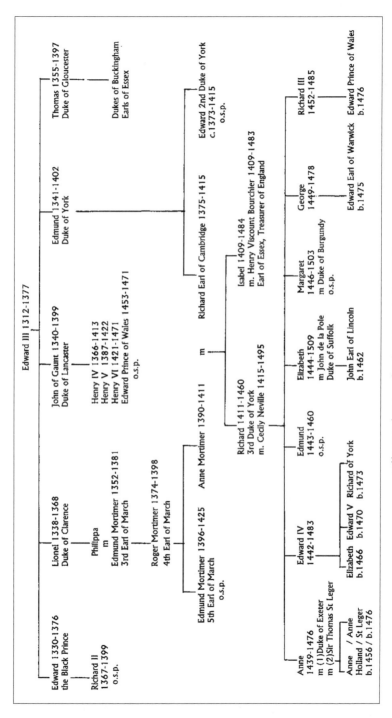

Table 1: Royal Houses of York and Lancaster (simplified)

Preface

This book is not a biography of Richard III. It is a highly personal analysis of the more controversial events of that king's reign, starting with the death of his predecessor and brother, Edward IV, in 1483.

At the outset my aim was to research, not to vindicate. However, in the course of my progress many surprising things became evident. Among them was the determination of most historians to place negative interpretations on Richard's actions, while applauding the career of deceit and underhandedness that characterized his nemesis, Henry VII.

Thus, the thrust of my writing gravitated towards Richard's defence. I do not claim to have found unequivocal answers; but I have delved as deeply as possible into particular topics that seem to need exposure to the clear light of day, seeking for a kernel of truth under layers of misinformation. Sometimes I offer conjectures, mine and other people's, that disturb long-established comfort zones. I offer them in support of a truth too often overlooked: we do *not* know as much as we are led to *think* we know. Context is everything, especially with equivocal events – for example speculation around Edward IV's death and its date. I see a clear parallel with the way theorists have interpreted historical records over the centuries to build their case against Richard III.

Although my main interests lie in the oft-ignored nooks and crannies of history, let me emphasize that this book is written for the ordinary reader – anyone who knows a little about King Richard III of England and would like to know more. A strand of narrative runs through it all which ensures that we keep following the story of Richard III's reign as it unfolds.

Above all you will find none of the sweeping judgements so loved by historians (good, evil, prudent, ambitious, pious, hypocritical, etc.). Richard was a man of his times and a king of his times, concerned with matters beyond the experience of any twenty-first century commentator.

Current academic orthodoxy concedes that Richard III was probably not the monster of Tudor mythology, but assumes the rationale behind his seizure of the crown must have been a fiction; that being a usurper, he must have had his two nephews murdered because that was what usurpers did; and that their murder was, on balance, confirmed by the bones inurned in Westminster Abbey by Charles II. These are, *inter alia*, assumptions that I challenge in these pages.

Those who cast Richard III as an unprincipled usurper have done so because they have made judgements and drawn conclusions: no concrete evidence exists to convict him. But academic orthodoxy is a tough nut to crack, and is passed on to each new generation of scholars.

If Richard III is to be assessed, let it be on his overall conduct as a sovereign. When it comes to matters in which he had some control, such as legislation brought before Parliament, his record has been recognized over the centuries as significant and enlightened. By contrast with kings before and after him, he indulged in no financial extortion, no religious persecution, no violation of sanctuary, no burning at the stake, no killing of women, no torture or starvation and no cynical breach of promise, pardon or safe-conduct in order to entrap a subject. Anyone who has been led to believe that Sir Henry Wyatt was tortured by Richard III is recommended to read my comprehensive refutation of that myth (see www.richardiii.net/downloads/wyatt_questionable_legend.pdf).

After Richard's death the story of the murderous, tyrannical king was fostered by his killers and became part of English legend. Encouraged by a climate of Court approval, chroniclers vied with each other to heap venom on his memory and devise horror stories to add to his constantly growing list of crimes. In their ignorance they jeered at his physical form and heaped on him an assortment of grotesqueries, believing that an ill-formed body was the outward manifestation of an evil mind. This fictitious Richard III became the subject of one of Shakespeare's most alluring melodramas. Shakespeare had little need for invention: he found the entire artifice already crafted to perfection by the Tudor chroniclers.

By contrast, the scant information dating from pre-Tudor times is generally found in letters and jottings, cursory government records, or a few isolated narratives. The unreliability of the latter is amply demonstrated in the works of John Rous, a Warwickshire priest who fancied himself a chronicler. Rous generously left to posterity two opposite views of Richard III: the first, composed during his reign, admiring and complimentary; the second, composed after his downfall, hostile and vituperative.

The example of Rous illustrates how important is familiarity with the source material when it comes to forming an independent opinion. Here, therefore, you will find an unusual approach: an Appendix is provided which contains a list of the principal sources used, together with notes about factors which may be relevant to the credibility of the writers. These include dates; partisanship; motivation; whether answerable to a patron; whether facts were accessed at first hand and, if at second hand, the reliability of the likely informants. The notes are mine, taking into account analyses by historians and academics.

In the last resort the issue of credibility is a matter for the individual to determine, and I cannot substitute my judgement for yours. Nor is it my intention to provide scholarly analyses of sources. As an author I have made choices as to which are reliable enough to be quoted in evidence, and which are, to a greater or lesser extent, dubious. If a source is so biased that it must, in my opinion, be read with inordinate care and circumspection, or if written by a person too far distant in time or location from the events he purports to describe, then it will be mentioned only if there is some exceptional reason for doing so – and then with a health warning attached.

I have taken as my main sources two narratives that were written by people who were present when most of the events they describe took place. The first is an intelligence report produced for his foreign master by an Italian cleric, Domenico Mancini, after visiting London in 1483. The second is also probably the work of a cleric, an anonymous Englishman this time, who in 1485–6 related his version of recent secular affairs while contributing to the ongoing Chronicle of the Abbey of Crowland; a man who seems to have enjoyed a degree of intimacy with the centres of political power. Even these sources are marred by identifiable errors and partisanship, but they are undoubtedly the best we have.

A third important writer, Polydore Vergil, produced a gigantic history of England in the early sixteenth century at Henry VII's behest. Vergil's treatment of Richard suffers from the same drawbacks, with a few new ones into the bargain: he writes at a distance of over two decades after the events; he is an Italian with no personal knowledge of Richard III's England, so his material is gleaned through informants; plus he always has to keep an eye on the interests of his patron.

Nevertheless, Vergil made manful efforts to get factual information, both written and oral. Regrettably, commentators have given equal credence to writers of his century with far less claim to credibility, whose fantastic stories have been believed and retold in all seriousness. In this book the reader will find scant place for such works of imagination, into which category Thomas More's *History of King Richard the Third* is firmly relegated.

Though written more than a generation after the event, and crafted as a literary piece with an underlaying didactic message, More's apologue is still trusted and quoted by experts up to the present day. Unfortunately, because so much of popular tradition about Richard derives from More, it has not been possible to ignore him altogether. In this connection it is instructive to consider who might have been his informants (see Appendix).

Such evaluation of sources is at the heart of all scholarship, and routinely gives rise to disagreements among historians. Unsurprisingly, opinions are polarized as to the relative value of Thomas More's imaginative 'history'. At one end of the scale we have David Starkey of television fame, who places utter faith in it as the work of a reliable historian – give or take a few blunders – while at the other end is Alison Hanham, author of an illuminating survey of Richard's early historians, who labels it a 'satirical drama'. See also a seminal paper, 'influential in the development of a critical trend', by Arthur Kincaid, 'The Dramatic Structure of Sir Thomas More's History of King Richard III', *Studies in English Literature 1500–1900:*

Elizabethan and Jacobean Drama (Rice University, Houston, Texas), Vol. XII, No. 2, spring 1972, pp. 223–242, twice anthologized.

Of course, professional historians tend to see it as their own peculiar and especial prerogative to evaluate sources. Charles Ross, in his 1981 biography of Richard III, speaks for many of his colleagues when he denigrates 'revisionists' for picking and choosing which portions of sources they believe. 'For example,' he says in his Introduction, 'Polydore Vergil, as a Tudor author corrupted by [Archbishop John] Morton, cannot be relied upon, and yet becomes an acceptable authority when he reports a general belief that the princes were still alive.'

Nevertheless Ross reserves for himself exactly this right to pick and choose. He thoroughly approves of Domenico Mancini (thereby dismissing observations on the reliability of Mancini by several noted historians, including Rosemary Horrox: see *Richard III: A Study of Service*). However, when dealing with reportage concerning Edward IV's execution of his brother Clarence, Ross actually prefers Thomas More's accusation that 'Richard was privately not dissatisfied', while discounting Mancini who claims that Richard was grieved by it. He takes the same line in his biography of Edward IV, not only discounting Mancini's report, but dismissing Polydore Vergil and the Crowland chronicler as well, both of whom, he admits, 'lay the blame firmly on the king [Edward] and do not mention Richard at all'.

While Professor Ross has every right to discriminate between the conflicting possibilities offered in various sources, his preference for More as opposed to all the others is surprising. But, if Ross can choose what he wants to believe then so, too, may lesser mortals.

In writing this book I have made use of Charles Ross as well as innumerable other writers and historians down the years whose painstaking researches have provided a fund of knowledge about Richard III, his life and his times, ready to be plundered by the likes of me. If I take issue with some of their pronouncements it is in a spirit of professional cut-and-thrust, and does not diminish my appreciation and respect for their work.

I have also consulted many advisers who have kindly found time to encourage and guide me through the many pitfalls that await the unwary.

Chief among them I must thank the late John Ashdown-Hill, our foremost authority on Lady Eleanor Talbot. I am indebted to him for allowing me to read a pre-publication manuscript of

Eleanor, the Secret Queen, and for his kindness in reading my own manuscript and suggesting improvements, all of them valuable. My thanks also go to Marie Barnfield for much appreciated advice for the 2009 paperback edition.

I am equally indebted to Geoffrey Wheeler for suggestions and encouragement, for his tireless work on illustrations and for meticulous research and advice concerning the architecture of the Tower of London.

My thanks go also to Richard E. Collins, whom I regret I have not been able to trace. Whether or not his research into the death of Edward IV contains a germ of likelihood, it certainly opens up vistas of interesting conjecture.

I have received unfailing help and support whenever I have requested it from members of the Richard III Society, without whom this book would not have been possible.

Finally, a personal thank you to David Baldwin, Rebekah Beale, Lesley Boatwright, Carolyn Hammond, Peter Hammond, William E. Hampton, Lt-Col. Bernie Hewitt, Keith Horry, Edward Impey, Michael K. Jones, Philippa Langley, Joanna L. Laynesmith, António S. Marques, Wendy Moorhen, Piet Nutt, Geoffrey Parnell, Adrian Phillips, Sandra du Plessis, Pauline Harrison Pogmore, Christine Reynolds, Jane Spooner, Phil Stone, Jane Trump, Carolinne White, William J. White and Andrew Williams. It goes without saying that I take entire responsibility for what lies within these pages; I have attempted to keep successive editions amended where flaws have been found, and updated to include new material as it emerges, including my own new translation and analysis of Domenico Mancini's crucial report *de occupatione regni Anglie*.

Chapter 13 of the 2013 edition added the discovery of Richard III's lost grave and the rescue of his mortal remains for dignified reburial, a project in which I was privileged to participate.

In this latest edition of 2023 we now have a new chapter 15, thanks to the dedicated work of Philippa Langley leading an international team of researchers in her Missing Princes Project. So far we have just two documents from a potential treasury of probative resources in overseas records, hitherto ignored because of historical certainties that the sons of Edward IV inevitably died a murderous death. Given that it was as long ago as 2008 that I first published my suggestions about the princes' likely survival, it is gratifying to know they still stand today.

I

Poisoned?

In the spring of 1483, King Edward IV of England was no longer the man he had been. His figure, once magnificent, was now corpulent – so much so that he could no longer ride at the head of his troops.

An outstanding military leader in his youth, he had intended personally to command a great campaign against the Scots in the summer of 1481, but when the time came to lead his army northwards, his fitness failed him. He then resolved to command an invasion in 1482. Eventually he abandoned the effort.

Edward had become a glutton, a drinker and a carouser in wanton company. In the censorious words of the chronicler of Crowland Abbey, he was 'a gross man', 'addicted to conviviality, vanity, drunkenness, extravagance and passion', 'thought to have indulged too intemperately his own passions and desire for luxury'.

However, although unfit and overweight, Edward was not a sick man. Historians were led to believe his health was deteriorating by an apparently contemporaneous report to the city fathers of Canterbury in 1482, but this has been identified as an editorial interpolation.[1] Indeed, the Crowland chronicler's observations of Court revelry that last Christmas, with the king cutting a dash in clothes of a brand new fashion, indicate nothing of any sickness.

In a recent parliamentary session he had also committed himself to a war of retribution against France: not the action of someone who felt his health was failing. In this context the Crowland chronicler describes him as a 'spirited prince' and 'bold king'.

Yet soon after Easter, Edward suddenly died a few weeks short of his 41st birthday. We hear details of his death from a wide variety of writers, few of whom are reluctant to offer ideas as to the cause. Writers after about 1500 are unlikely to be reliable; some of their wilder suggestions include over-indulgence in wine, an excess of vegetables, an ague brought back from France, and an attack of melancholy or chagrin.

According to the Crowland chronicler, mentioned above, the king took to his bed about Easter. He was affected 'neither by old age nor by any known kind of disease which would not have seemed easy to cure in a lesser person'. This cleric, writing in 1485, is the most authoritative source we have, being an official who was involved in Edward's government. Easter Sunday fell on 30 March; however, his date of death cannot be known with certainty. It was given out, apparently, as 9 April, but no one could have known the true date aside from those present at his deathbed: probably his wife, her London-based family, and members of their inner circle.

The Italian cleric Domenico Mancini, a visitor to London in 1483, said the king died from catching a chill while in a boat on a fishing trip. Mancini did not enjoy the Crowland chronicler's inside knowledge, nor, presumably, did he speak English. He had been sent to report on events in England by his patron, Archbishop Angelo Cato, a man of influence in the Court of Louis XI of France.

A different opinion was offered by another of Louis's courtiers, Philippe de Commynes, writing probably in the 1490s: Edward fell ill and died soon afterwards, he said, 'some say of a stroke'.

With these and a multitude of other theories to choose from, no one was sure what caused the death of this bloated but otherwise healthy king.

Then in 1996 Richard Collins of the University of Cambridge published a short treatise outlining his suspicions that Edward IV might have been poisoned.[2]

In his view, Edward's death had been too easily accepted as inexplicable. Writing from a substantial medical background, Collins considered the cause of Edward's death ought to be recoverable: 'I take it as self-evident that death occurs invariably through an assault on a mechanical organism with predictable results; and that, after it has happened, the cause of death may be deduced from that pattern of results.' He therefore set about investigating what was known about the patient, and the manner and circumstance of his demise.

Examining the story of the chill while boating, Collins observed: 'since the king certainly couldn't have indulged in such frivolity during Holy Week, the latest this trip could have taken place was 22 March … If true, it means he hung around in a fever for ten days, without treatment, which is a very unlikely state of affairs. Edward did not die of Mancini's chill.'

There is no reason to suppose Philippe de Commynes was better informed than anyone else, being a foreigner who would have relied on hearsay, but his idea of a stroke seems feasible at first glance. However, he was writing soon after his own king died of a stroke, so he might easily have made a subconscious connection.

Collins notes that if a person dies of a single stroke (apoplexy or CVA), he will do so within a matter of minutes. Or, having survived it, he may die from a second stroke, which might indeed occur some 10–12 days later. But strokes were events that would have been well known to mediæval physicians. By contrast, given the reactions of the people at the time, Edward's death seems to have come as a complete surprise – and Collins finds it quite impossible to believe that no one anticipated Edward might succumb to a second stroke if he had already suffered a first.

That people were taken by surprise again militates against Mancini's chill, whose symptoms would have been obvious and worrying as they worsened until he died (says Mancini) on 7 April, at least sixteen days after the fishing episode. Crowland asserts a more likely illness of less than ten days. Both were probably present in London at the time but the latter was close to the centre of power, which was then wielded by the queen and her Woodville family. Clearly the official story gave no cause of death, merely a date of 9 April; thus it is possible the announcement was delayed while arrangements were made for administration of the realm.

Collins finds the bewilderment over Edward's death in itself indicative in an age when no doctor was at a loss for a diagnosis, however far-fetched. The Crowland chronicler is assumed to be a learned cleric and high-ranking government official and, Collins suggests, probably had some education in medicine as part of his background training; yet despite his knowledge and likely access to the physicians attending the king, he was unable to venture a guess at what the fatal disease might have been.

Even Polydore Vergil, the historian favoured by Henry VII, writing his *Anglica Historia* some twenty-five years later but having full access to most of the State papers of the time, could not be more specific than to say he 'fell sicke of an unknowen disease'; though Vergil also reported 'ther was a great rumor that he was poysonyd'.

This is often discounted on the grounds that by the time Vergil was writing, sudden deaths in noble or princely families often gave rise to suspicions of poisoning. However, this scarcely seems a convincing argument. Poisoning was not, after all, a sixteenth-century invention.

Edward was not immune to assassination attempts. One at least is recorded, from which he escaped thanks to a warning given at supper by Sir John Ratcliffe, later Lord Fitzwalter. Whatever the source of the poisoning rumour, Vergil himself did not leap to it as a conclusion: his view was that the cause of death was unknown.

Yet another writer from France, Jean de Roye (misnamed Troyes), whose date of writing (1480s) means that he was commenting on contemporaneous events, believed that Edward died of 'une apoplexie' or perhaps, as some people said, he was 'empoisonné du bon vin', given to him by Louis XI. We encounter the poisoning theme again in the writings of the English Tudor chronicler Edward Hall, published in the mid-sixteenth century, which contained an agglomeration of material mostly culled from other writers. Hall ran through a number of possibilities: Edward's sickness was due either to melancholy, anger at the French King, a surfeit, a fever, a 'continuall cold' or, as some suspected, poisoning.

In his examination of the few known facts, Richard Collins takes into account this surprise and general bewilderment. Thus he rules out slow-building effects such as those of debauchery (e.g. venereal disease), or drink or obesity, to which the chroniclers make reference. Edward was still a very active and hard-working king, and although his fitness was beginning to be over-taxed by his habits of excess, he appears to have shown no characteristic signs of gradual mental or bodily degeneration. Mancini describes him as 'a tall man and very corpulent, though not to the point of disfigurement', so there is no suggestion that he was morbidly obese. Indeed, Mancini adds that he was fond of 'displaying how impressive he was' to onlookers.

We know that, in accordance with tradition, his body was displayed in an almost naked state to the view of the nobles and clergy. Since nothing untoward was noted, Collins eliminates violence or infectious diseases that would have left outward signs, any non-infectious conditions that also mark the body, and diseases that cause noticeable wasting of tissue. Appendicitis is also dismissed: given the diet of the time, this is 'so remote as to be almost impossible'.

One suggestion that crops up regularly is pneumonia, whether in its common or more exotic forms, or as an attendant illness or complication. The problem with pneumonia is that this lung infection, with its tell-tale signs of congestion, fever, and coughing up of characteristic sputum, would have been recognized from long experience and given cause for severe alarm. It does not square with the Crowland chronicler's comment about 'no known disease'.

In the course of eliciting opinions from some thirty colleagues in the large provincial hospital where he worked at the time, Richard Collins was careful to disguise the identity of the patient. He received no suggestions that fitted the case, except one: poisoning by arsenic, dispensed not as a series of small doses over time, but as an isolated dose or possibly two (arsenic is tasteless and odourless). This was put forward by no fewer than three highly experienced individuals. Collins found the theory convincing:

> Heavy metals such as arsenic, antimony and mercury when administered cause death either slowly or quickly, according to the dose. They leave no signs that would be obvious to the men of 1483; and you would, of course, be perfectly healthy up to the time you swallowed the first dose. Poisoning fits; and I would suggest that, out of all the possible causes of Edward IV's death, it is the only one that fits all the known facts.

As soon as one has a poisoning theory, of course, one needs a murder suspect or conspiracy. Most people would not immediately leap to suspect Edward's consort, Queen Elizabeth (née Woodville): it would appear foolhardy in the extreme for a queen to do away with a powerful and successful king, especially when he had been her family's principal meal-ticket for nineteen years. However, there are two considerations that work in favour of the hypothesis.

First, after nearly twenty years of marriage (and being already five years older than Edward), Elizabeth would undoubtedly have lost many of her charms for the king. Her place in the lustful Edward's bed was frequently supplanted by mistresses, and as a mediæval forty-five-year-old having survived ten pregnancies, it would not be surprising for her to fear being relegated to a position of obscurity. Her latest matrimonial humiliation had come at the hands of Elizabeth Lambert (Mistress Shore, later erroneously named 'Jane'), who occupied a position of particular favour at Court. For a neglected and probably disgruntled wife, the end of her influence with the king might have been staring her in the face.

Although there is sweetness in revenge, a more practical motive on Elizabeth's part might have been to remove the crown from the head of a dangerously bored husband and place it on that of a doting son. The twelve-year-old Prince of Wales, Edward, had been brought up as a Woodville, surrounded by Woodville handlers at his residence of Ludlow Castle in the Welsh Marches, and governed and educated by his mother's brother Anthony, Earl Rivers. Elizabeth was a woman of character who had built an empire for herself and her family since marrying the king: she certainly had the prescience to instil in her son the right attitude of family loyalty. By precedent, government by a protectorate and council would be expected while he was too young to rule; but during these last years of his minority he might, at a stretch, start participating in his own reign, in which the queen and her family could look forward to considerable influence.

Though evidence is lacking, unsurprisingly, for a relationship grown cool, Paul Murray Kendall suggests that in Edward's deathbed codicils he replaced Elizabeth as an executor of his will. By contrast, in 1475 he had loaded this in her favour, appointing her his foremost executor and not only ensuring that her personal property remained at her own disposal, but also giving her powers to divide his chattels between herself and their sons.[3] In 1483, far from being foremost, she was not even mentioned on the list of executors who met to prove the king's will.

There is other evidence that things in early 1483 were not proceeding in a way that would benefit Elizabeth's best interests. There was the threat of more expensive and distracting wars with Scotland, for example; a bottomless pit into which the royal treasury was being emptied. Not for nothing was she one of the leading opponents of the Scottish campaigns. And now, in his latest Parliament, Edward had announced his intention to embark upon an even more expensive war against France, for which the entire kingdom would bear a heavy financial burden.

Meanwhile, the successful outcome of the Scottish military actions had established Edward's younger brother Richard, Duke of Gloucester as the man of the hour, bringing him closer to the king's heart and heaping on him ever more rewards and powers. These would certainly increase as he assumed control of the French campaign. There was a danger here for the Woodville menfolk, since their intimacy with the king relied on consorting in his pursuits of the flesh, of which Richard's disapproval was well known.

Edward was doubtless proud of his two little boys, but at the ages of nine and twelve they were clearly too young to be his companions or equals. Nor could they be outstanding military commanders, as was Richard of Gloucester, who could be relied upon to carry out the king's orders and wishes with absolute loyalty and, it would seem, conspicuous success.

Born on 2 October 1452, the youngest of the late Duke of York's sons, Richard was Edward's last living brother. He would later ascend the throne as Richard III, and it is about this Richard that our story revolves.

Their father had successfully claimed the throne as his rightful inheritance during the civil unrest under the Lancastrian King Henry VI which came to be known as the Wars of the Roses, but had not lived to be crowned. There had been two other sons who reached adulthood: after Edward came Edmund, Earl of Rutland, killed in battle as a teenager; and after him came George, Duke of Clarence, done to death in the Tower of London five years ago after being convicted of treason. Popular Edward, the eldest, was seemingly endowed with all the necessary gifts to make him the strong and successful ruler that England needed when he ascended the throne in 1461.

Twenty-two years on, Edward IV no longer possessed the astonishing strength and virility that had impressed the world during the first dozen or so years of his reign. Young and vibrant, and over 6ft 2in in height, he had been described as the most handsome prince of his generation.

Richard, ten years younger, was shorter of stature, brown of hair and lean of face. In 1484 two visitors actually described him in writing: the Scottish ambassador complimented him on 'so great a mind in so small a body', [4] and the visiting Silesian Niclas von Popplau observed that he was 'three fingers taller than himself, a little slimmer and not so thickset, much more lightly built and with quite slender limbs'.[5] Niclas's own physique is unknown, but we may perhaps conclude that Richard was sinewy rather than strapping.

The recent dramatic discovery of his grave reveals that he was strong and well muscled, with good teeth. He could have stood 5ft 8½in but for the uncertain effects produced by what we now know was a lateral curvature of the spine (scoliosis) which made his right shoulder higher than his left – giving the lie to Thomas More who said the opposite. Developing after puberty, it would have become visible only gradually, and could scarcely have been striking when clothed or Niclas would surely have noted it. The curvature of scoliosis would manifest as uneven shoulders but not a hunched back (kyphosis). Nor, evidently, did it affect Richard's famed prowess as a fighting soldier. These realities, together with his sound and straight limbs, must once and for all debunk Shakespeare's monstrous shambling creature with hunched back and withered arm.

Richard was credited with a keen intelligence; he placed a high value on loyalty and seems to have been capable of inspiring it. Above all else he was his brother's trusted general. In an age when military achievement was the jewel in the aristocratic coronet, when virtues of chivalry, valour and loyalty were pearls beyond price, Richard gave his brother good reason for pride.

This is not to pretend he was without failings. Undoubtedly he was headstrong in a number of ways, aggressive in pursuit of his own ends, and as acquisitive as any other mediæval younger brother. Perhaps more so in view of his elevation to a royal estate for which he inherited no means of support.

Though modern sensibilities may recoil at the thought, these were times when land, income and status were frequently derived from the downfall of an opponent, often entailing forfeiture by that opponent's wife and children. Marriages were also routinely contracted with material advantage in mind. Richard had done well for himself on both scores, having been highly rewarded for his services to the king and having made an excellent match with a famous heiress, Anne Neville, daughter of the Earl of Warwick ('the Kingmaker').

Through his wife's inheritance he was fortunate to hold estates in the north of England, in addition to his favourite castle of Middleham which he and Anne made their usual residence. Edward had established Richard, while in his early twenties, as the principal potentate in the unruly north, giving him powers equal to those of a viceroy. Richard adopted a policy of consolidating his holdings there, which speaks of wholehearted commitment and perhaps an affinity for that region. The records of the time also indicate that he worked assiduously at carrying out his powers and responsibilities, pursuing the interests of the local citizenry when petitioned, and adjudicating fairly in disputes even if it meant giving judgement against one of his own employees.

When Edward IV died, Richard was residing in his northern estates. Though he attended the Court when state business required, his duties and home life were concentrated in the North. Some have suggested his absence was due not only to a dislike of the politicking and sensual excess practised at Court, but also to his revulsion at the fate of his brother Clarence, famously executed for treason in 1478 by (supposedly) drowning in a butt of malmsey wine.

The death of Clarence appears to have been a turning-point in many ways, so this is an appropriate moment to examine it here. According to Mancini, Clarence had started off on very much the wrong foot with his in-laws 'publicly and vehemently inveighing against Elizabeth's obscure origins, and by making it known that the king, who should have married a virgin, had acted against custom by taking to wife a widow'.

Such accusations, if made, did no more than give voice to a widely-held grievance about Edward's choice of queen. Elizabeth was a subject and a commoner who brought no financial and strategic advantage as might have been gained by an alliance with foreign royalty. No king since the Conquest, with the sole exception of Henry I, had sought a wife within England. Moreover,

Elizabeth's family had fought against the house of York. Clarence might well have added further objections to Edward's headlong rush into wedlock, such as its secrecy without consultation or proper formality, and the fact that Edward continued to conceal it for more than four months in the full knowledge of diplomatic approaches being made for marriage into some of Europe's leading royal families. The deception was still remembered as late as 1483 when Isabella of Castile, one of Edward's putative brides, declared that she had not forgiven the insult at his hands nearly twenty years earlier.

Much has been made of Elizabeth's unsuitability as a royal consort, and much has been written saying that she performed her job well, carried out acts of benevolence as befitted her station and was beautiful and fertile into the bargain. These were qualities that suited Edward well, and he certainly made it clear that his wishes were what counted. For most people it was a nine days' wonder that scarcely affected their lives.

Nevertheless, there were some for whom the *mésalliance* was keenly felt, and Clarence was one of them. Also among them was their mother, Cecily ('Proud Cis'), Duchess of York. Cecily's rage was such that she is reported by Mancini to have denounced Edward as no son of his father and unworthy of the throne. Mancini's story may or may not be reliable, but as Michael K. Jones comments: 'In an age when the niceties of position were all-important and the rituals of their observance paramount, Cecily refused to allow the new upstart queen to outrank her. In a startling act of royal one-upmanship, she devised a title of her own and now styled herself Queen-by-Right.' This was within months of Edward's marriage being announced.[6]

But Clarence was not only disliked for sharing these views. Shakespeare's phrase, 'false, fleeting, perjur'd Clarence', aptly describes his career of relentless self-advancement, which involved marrying against Edward IV's wishes and cementing an alliance with the king's enemies – both English and French – in the bold expectation of replacing him on the throne. Though temporarily reconciled, Clarence started behaving with extraordinary high-handedness in 1477 and challenging the king's justice. Edward's tolerance ended abruptly and he had his brother arrested, tried and condemned for treason.

Domenico Mancini tells the story juicily in his intelligence report; he appears to give us an insight into Woodville thinking when he relates the downfall of Clarence as follows:

> The queen, mindful of the insults ... that according to established custom she was not the legitimate wife of the king, deemed that never would her offspring by the king succeed to the sovereignty unless the Duke of Clarence were removed; and of this she easily persuaded the king himself. ... Accordingly, whether the charge was fabricated or a real crime brought to light, the Duke of Clarence was accused of purposing the king's death by means of magic spells and sorcerers. On being brought to judgement, he was condemned and executed. At that time Richard, Duke of Gloucester, his feelings moved by anguish for his brother, was unable to dissimulate so well but that he was heard to say that one day he would avenge his brother's death. Thereafter he very rarely went to court, but remained in his own province. By his good offices and dispensing of justice he set himself to win the loyalty of his people, and outsiders he attracted in large measure by the high reputation of his private life and public activities. Such was his renown in warfare that whenever anything difficult and dangerous had to be done on behalf of the realm it would be entrusted to his judgement and his leadership. With these arts Richard obtained the goodwill of the people and avoided the hostility of the queen, from whom he lived far distant.

Later in his report Mancini refers again to the Woodvilles being guilty of Clarence's death, in fact he makes two further such references. In the first he says, 'They had to suffer the accusation by all, of responsibility for the Duke of Clarence's death.' In the second he claims the Woodvilles feared that if Richard 'became the sole head of government, they who suffered the accusation of Clarence's death would either undergo capital punishment or at least be ousted from their high degree of prosperity'. Throughout his report, their guilt in the Clarence affair is a given.

Interestingly, the Crowland chronicler writes that during that fatal year of 1477 Clarence also started refusing to accept food and drink at Edward's palace. Taking this with the narrative from Mancini, it is hard to avoid the conclusion that it was from his Woodville in-laws that Clarence perceived the threat.

We need not give credence, by the way, to Richard of Gloucester's supposed vow of vengeance, said by Mancini to have been overheard (by an unknown source) in 1478. Mancini did not hear it himself, nor would it have come from Richard's circle: even Clarence's biographer, the staunchly anti-Richard Michael Hicks, maintains it is clear from Mancini's text that he knew none of those around the duke.

Perhaps it was a story whispered by those who witnessed Richard's dismay at his brother's demise, but frankly we have no evidence to tell us that Richard's inner feelings were anything but amicable towards the Woodvilles. In his capacity as an administrator and arbitrator, they asked him on occasion to act as executor or to adjudicate in a dispute, which would form a normal part of his workload. One might view the various members of royalty as co-directors of a company, where personal feelings have no relevance. Richard's sense of loyalty to the king would preclude behaving unprofessionally, and so would a lively sense of self-preservation.

The views of historians who believe Richard did hold the Woodvilles responsible for eliminating Clarence may be coloured by hindsight; for although there is corroboration that he had reached this conclusion in September 1484, he had by then occupied the throne for more than twelve months during which he would have learnt many previously unknown truths. He revealed his knowledge in overtures of friendship to the Anglo-Irish Earl of Desmond. In doing so, he drew a remarkable parallel between Clarence's death and that of the earl's father, the 7th Earl, who had been executed in suspicious circumstances during the reign of Edward IV. In Richard's written briefing to the ambassador who carried his letter, he not only stated in unequivocal terms that the late earl's fate amounted to murder under the pretence of law, but also proffered an invitation to Desmond to seek punishment for whomsoever was responsible. One can scarcely miss the implication that Richard felt the same perpetrators were involved in both executions.

The relevant part of the briefing document reads as follows (it is addressed to the ambassador and refers to Richard and Desmond in the third person; the emphasis is mine):

> … albeit the Fadre of the said Erle, the king [Richard] than being of yong Age, was extorciously slayne & murdered by colour of the lawes within Irland by certain persones then havyng the

governaunce and Rule there, ayenst alle manhode Reason & good
conscience, Yet notwithstanding that *the semblable chaunce was
& hapned sithen within this Royaulme of England, aswele of his Brother
the duc of Clarence, As other his nighe kynnesmen and gret Frendes*, the
kinges grace alweys contynuethe and hathe inward compassion of
the dethe of his said Fadre, And is content that his said Cousyne,
now Erle, by alle ordinate means and due course of the lawes when
it shalle lust him at any tyme hereafter to sue or attempt for the
punysshement thereof.[7]

In 2005, further support was published in research by John
Ashdown-Hill and myself into the mystery surrounding the
execution of the 7th Earl of Desmond, Thomas Fitzgerald,
which occurred in 1468.[8] Desmond, a close friend and ally of
Edward IV and his father, was charged with treason on flimsy
grounds by the then Lord Deputy of Ireland, John Tiptoft, Earl
of Worcester. The arrest, verdict and execution all took place in
Drogheda within the space of eleven days, ensuring he had no
time to appeal for clemency. The king later pardoned Desmond's
two co-accused who were lucky enough to escape and make
their way to England, which lends credence to the supposition
that had the earl managed to appeal in the same way, the king
would have done no less for the man who was his family's
staunch friend.

A number of sources vouch for Edward's surprise and
chagrin when he learned of Desmond's execution, and generous
reparations were subsequently made to the late earl's family.
Other sources add evidence that two of Desmond's young sons,
both aged under thirteen, were gratuitously executed by Tiptoft
at the same time as their father.

The most controversial aspect of the case is one which,
understandably, seems to have been less widely known at the
time. It was the belief of the Fitzgerald family that the 7th Earl's
fate was brought about by Queen Elizabeth through Tiptoft as
her agent; her motive being that Desmond, when pressed by
Edward IV for a reaction on the occasion of his marriage, had
insulted her by stating his view that the king had 'too much
abased' his princely estate 'in marrying a lady of so mean a house
and parentile'. Seeking his head in retribution, the queen sent
letters of instruction directly to Tiptoft arranging Desmond's

arrest. A supporting document states that the earl's fate was intended as a warning to others who would speak slightingly of the queen – a telling point, since it answers the important question of how knowledge came to his family that she was behind it all. She wanted them to know.

This knowledge had evidently reached Richard's ears, because the briefing he gave to his ambassador in 1484 indicates that he knew who had engineered the atrocity: those who had the 'governance and rule'. With the present earl now given the opportunity to pursue the perpetrators, obviously this could refer neither to Edward IV, who was many months dead, nor to John Tiptoft, who was many years dead. Who else had governance and rule in 1468? And who also had the power to arrange the destruction of Clarence in 1478?

Some commentators claim that Richard's words to his ambassador constitute mere compliments and platitudes, which is a reading my co-researcher and I would challenge: on the contrary, they are remarkably frank and decidedly controversial.

Then there is Richard's strange reference to a similar fate suffered by 'other nigh kinsmen and great friends', which may perhaps be dismissed as the kind of meaningless tautology seen in formal communications of the time. However, it must be remembered that this document was not itself a formal letter to Desmond; it was strictly a briefing document expounding to Richard's ambassador the gist of what he wanted him to convey by word of mouth. It could be that in the course of dictation Richard called to mind other deaths which for us, after many intervening centuries, have lost all significance but which perhaps seemed to him to smack of Woodville contrivance. For example, has anyone ever queried the whereabouts and circumstances of the death of his young cousin, George Neville, which for reasons of inheritance had an enormously negative impact on Richard's prospects? Or the death of Henry, Earl of Essex and Treasurer of England, which interestingly coincided with that of Edward IV? And if there is any truth in the assassination theory which opened this chapter, might Richard not even have had his brother Edward in mind? After a gap of 500 years, such questions cannot be answered, yet this is no reason for dismissing them out of hand.

The Politics
of Power

After Clarence's death it was remarked that Edward IV underwent a change of character, growing more bitter, avaricious and despotic. Matters worsened when in 1482 England's ancient enemy, France, coolly reneged on a treaty of seven years standing. Doubtless Edward's wrath was felt by all those around him.

If Edward's relationship with his queen had soured, that with his powerful Lord Chamberlain, William, Lord Hastings, may have gone the same way.

Hastings had been a councillor and intimate companion of the king for the past twenty years. A decade older than Edward, he was about the same age as other senior councillors such as Thomas, Lord Stanley, or Richard, Earl of Warwick ('the Kingmaker') who had helped him win the throne. A leading courtier and commander of the Calais garrison, Hastings had shared Edward's triumphs and adversities over the years, and equally had shared and encouraged his vices. In return he had been showered with rewards and offices, not the least being his appointment as Captain of Calais in 1471.

From this appointment a dispute blew up between Hastings and the Woodville family, since Elizabeth's brother Anthony, Earl Rivers, had been appointed to that same office in June the previous year. Edward, with typical insensitivity, failed to understand its significance to Anthony whose father and grandfather had held it before him. Not only was it the sole conspicuous office ever held by his Woodville forebears prior to his sister's elevation, it had now become, for the second time, a cause of Woodville humiliation. The first time was in 1460 when the Lancastrian Woodvilles had been tasked by Henry VI with recapturing Calais from the house of York. Instead they had been bested and held there as helpless captives while the Earl of Warwick and his cousin Edward, Earl of March, publicly berated and belittled them as upstarts and social parvenus. Now, exactly ten years later, that same Edward of March was King Edward IV and had calmly removed the Calais office from Anthony and given it to Hastings.

Long before Hastings began feuding with the Woodvilles, his relationship with Elizabeth predated her marriage to Edward in May 1464 and suggests his involvement in bringing it about. On 13 April 1464 – eighteen days before the king's notorious secret wedding – Hastings entered into a contract with her which promised, *inter alia*, one of her two sons in marriage to a daughter or niece of his. This was in return for his intercession to ensure those sons inherited certain lands which her late husband's family, the Greys, were contesting. The fact that she turned to Hastings for help, rather than Edward, reinforces the notion that no expectation of marriage with the king existed even as late as mid-April.

One cannot help wondering what possible interest the king's powerful chamberlain could have had in allying his family with Elizabeth and her sons. Although the Woodvilles were well-connected gentry, the boys were merely the offspring of a recently-made knight and the grandsons of a baron. Was it Edward's idea? Was he attempting to buy his way into her bed with a marriage alliance that would bring her family right into his inner circle, with all the patronage that entailed? If so, he doubtless underwrote Hastings's side of the bargain with the promise of a handsome payoff.

That Hastings was not entirely enamoured of the arrangement is suggested by the hard bargain he struck, and by the fact that in August that year, before Edward was prepared even to acknowledge Elizabeth as his wife, he granted Hastings the wardship of her elder son, Thomas. This smacks of an attempt to kill two birds with one stone: compensating his chamberlain for services rendered while simultaneously covering up the marriage, since no one would expect Edward to give away the wardship of his own stepson. The right of wardship under feudal law conferred control of a minor heir – and his income – until he came of age; often also included was the right of marriage which allowed influence as to whom the heir would wed.

Of course, once Elizabeth was revealed as Edward's queen, all of this was stood on its head: the marriage into the Hastings family never materialized, and doubtless Edward found a way to replace the modest income from the wardship. But the early connection between Hastings and Elizabeth is tantalizing.

At this rate we may reasonably take the supposition further, and ask ourselves whether one of Hastings's uses was perhaps as Edward's procurer. A man in the king's position had less freedom of movement than any of his subjects and less opportunity to make his own conquests. Was it Hastings who arranged private meetings with suitable ladies when Edward was still a bachelor, and did that role continue after he was married? If so, was it an arrangement the queen deeply resented, or did she tolerate it in the knowledge that it was the price she had to pay?

Hastings has usually been portrayed as a bluff military man, loyal to Edward through thick and thin, in wartime his trusted general, in peacetime hunting, carousing and wenching at his side. Mancini tells us that, even in his latter years, 'in carnal lust Edward indulged to an extreme', and that Hastings was 'an accomplice and participant in his private gratifications'.

He was, however, a great deal more cunning and self-serving than this suggests. For example, from 1461 he received an annual pension of 1,000 crowns from Charles, then heir to the Duke of Burgundy, for reasons unknown. Maybe it is significant that it was Hastings who helped cement England's alliance with Burgundy by negotiating Charles's marriage, in 1468, to Edward's sister Margaret of York. He was still receiving the same annuity when he accepted a 2,000-crown pension from Charles's enemy, Louis XI of France, in 1475. Hastings's adroitness in arranging that this pension be 'deniable' was admired even by Louis and his councillor, Philippe de Commynes.

Hastings showed himself very much his own man when, between March 1477 and January 1480, he took reinforcements to Calais against Edward's express orders. This was in response to a call to Edward for help by his sister Margaret, recently widowed on the death of the Duke of Burgundy; an appeal to chivalry which was refused by Edward but apparently accepted by Hastings and Richard of Gloucester. This action, and Richard's support in it, would have greatly enhanced Hastings's military reputation in the eyes of the Calais garrison. It might indeed have elevated his position to such an extent that Edward perhaps began to suspect Hastings of having his own agenda, together with the means to pursue it, in the foreign and domestic politics of the day.

A relationship may easily go sour when a subject appears to have a will of his own, especially when he shames the king and shows him wanting in chivalry. Did Hastings feel disillusioned by the king's actions of late, and had he felt the sting of his tongue too often? Did Edward resent Hastings's continued abilities as a military commander at age 50, when the king at 38 was too gross (or 'otherwise engaged') to take horse at the head of his troops?

Hastings's feud extended to the queen's eldest son Thomas, Marquess of Dorset, one of three Woodvilles detested as being the king's 'panders who aided and abetted his lustfulness', says Mancini, who adds that Hastings 'was estranged and at mortal enmity [with Dorset] on account of the mistresses they had abducted or seduced from each other'. Mancini attributes an important factor in the turbulent events that followed 'to have derived its origin in the quarrel of these two'. It even embarrassed the king himself in 1482 when Hastings crossed a line by intimidating a man named John Edward to make false accusations against Rivers and Dorset. The king assembled and personally presided over a very full Council meeting where John publicly confessed and recanted.

Perhaps Edward lost patience with Hastings and his feuds, or perhaps he was somewhat sickened by the unedifying spectacle of his ageing chamberlain vying with Dorset for the favours of youthful paramours. Maybe Hastings even overstepped the mark with some mistress that Edward considered his own property. The patronage of kings is notoriously capricious.

The significance for Hastings of a once-great friendship gone bad would have had far-reaching consequences. As the king's Lord Chamberlain, he was a natural channel for the demands made on royal patronage; he was in an ideal position to strike lucrative bargains in return for his influence. Now imagine if Edward began to refuse Hastings's requests. Perhaps there were words exchanged which signalled an end to their days of intimacy. At that rate his career would soon be over, and maybe he had made promises which he was now, embarrassingly, unable to fulfil.

If Edward had grown hard to deal with, this might have pointed to a decline in faculties and an increase in Woodville dominance; yet they might not have been alone in profiting from a new regime. Hastings had spent years as administrator of many of the Prince of Wales's extensive lands and as one of his councillors and tutors charged with his development until age 14; the boy knew and trusted him as his father's close and valued friend. Further, when England had a minor king the established custom was a protectorate, with the young king's royal uncle as Lord Protector: in this case Gloucester. If the Woodvilles were set to gain the ascendancy, he seems to have viewed Richard as a potential future ally. As shown in reports after Edward IV's death, Hastings would greet Richard's prominence with joy.

As for the Woodvilles, despite their accumulated wealth they enjoyed only fair-weather political support. Holding no permanent national offices, they were dependent on the Prince of Wales and future king. Whereas Hastings, long established at the heart of court and government, was one of the strongest magnates in England, with power to command not only the stronghold of Calais but also many more thousands of his own retained men. Bold enough to have feuded openly with the king's in-laws, he seems to have nurtured a sense of his own invincibility.

From his point of view he would feel equally sure of his position with Richard of Gloucester, a dutiful young man who would respect his years and his status. Hastings doubtless thought of him as the ever-faithful younger brother who had grown into a useful sidekick, who always deferred to Edward and would similarly defer to Hastings. Whatever the régime after the death of Edward IV, Hastings's military strength would be needed at the heart of it.

* * *

The Crowland chronicler tells us that as Edward lay dying he added several codicils to his will. Although no documentary evidence exists, most historians accept that in one of these codicils he named his brother Richard as Lord Protector of England during the young King Edward V's minority. Presumably the prospect of abandoning England to a child-king was not something Edward had anticipated since he last bore arms in 1475; with death staring him in the face, he felt urgently constrained to do something about it.

If he was minded to change his executors, common sense indicates that he must also have named a protector, in line with recent precedent: what could concern him more than support for his son in the government of the kingdom? So if Richard was not allocated the role of protector, who was? There is no suggestion that any of the Woodvilles were named; indeed, according to the Crowland chronicler, a body of opinion believed (and stated outright) that they were an unsuitable influence.

Let us briefly examine the role of protector. A babe in arms could inherit the English throne, as did Henry VI only sixty years previously. The government meanwhile would be in adult hands: in a mediæval kingdom, a single strong leader as regent was the obvious choice. The Lords in Council in 1422 set aside Henry V's desire for this, opting for a three-fold solution: they themselves would govern; the custody and care of the king would rest with a separate group of nobles; and the office of Protector of the Realm was invented with the specific role of protecting the kingdom against internal and external threat. This formula was echoed, with the Council and Parliament still paramount, for the protectorates in the 1450s. By then the governing council had failed to keep opportunistic magnates in check, and the result was a king easily manipulated by those who hungered for power or reward, leading the realm and its finances into chaos.

With Edward IV's policy of strong personal rule, it is most unlikely he wanted a regency council for his son, especially with antipathies festering between several individuals and factions. The protectorship fell by right to the strong and able Richard, his sole adult heir, as duly recorded in the writings of John Rous: 'brother of the deceased king and by his ordinance protector of England'. As a turncoat who vilified Richard after his death, there was no element of special pleading in Rous.[1]

Others confirmed the same, although foreign writers failed to understand that a 'Protector' in England was not a 'Regent'. The

French-employed Italian Domenico Mancini recorded his idea of opinions in the council: 'one was that the Duke of Gloucester should head the government, because Edward in his will had so decreed'. And elsewhere: 'In the same will, according to report, he appointed as Protector of his children and realm his brother Richard, Duke of Gloucester' (a report favourable to Richard which, uncharacteristically, Mancini never claimed was false). Of course, no protector in England was given sole charge of the government, nor of the king's person or family.

There was a similar report – and similar misconception of his role – from another Italian, Polydore Vergil, whose writings reflected the later Tudor antipathy to Richard. Anything in Vergil that supports Richard's legitimacy cannot be ignored, and here we learn 'that the king at his death had commyted to him onely, wyfe, chyldren, goodes, and all that ever he had'. Richard's appointment was also confirmed, and equally misunderstood, by Henry VII's French-born Court Poet and official biographer, Bernard André, in his Tudor-authorized *Life of Henry VII* [23, 24]. André, like Vergil, claimed that Richard was 'styled and named Protector of the Realm by his brother'.[2]

Finally, there occurred later an event that supports all the other sources that claim Edward nominated Richard as protector: he was officially confirmed as such by the King's Council in session by 8 May.[3] It was an appointment which Domenico Mancini, despite his general negativity towards Richard, reports was entirely to the liking of the people, who had already shown their approval by supporting him 'openly and vocally': 'having previously favoured the duke in their hearts from their belief in his integrity … it was commonly said by all that the duke merited the right to head the government'.

In the words of the modern historian Charles Ross: 'Not to have appointed him was a recipe for disaster… Equally, the Woodvilles could be expected to oppose any attempt to deprive them of control of the princes.'[4]

★ ★ ★

The protector's full title was Protector and Defender of the Realm and Church in England and Principal Councillor of the

King. The office was instituted in the minority of Henry VI by authority of the peers of England acting as the King's Council, a body of advisers comprising the leading aristocracy and some senior prelates, which in the 1420s took over the administration. In charge of the realm's security, the protector's task was not an onerous one at that time, but much more so later in the century when having to combat unrest and maintain law and order.

While the protector exercised such powers in the name of the king, his office was only 'at pleasure' and could be terminated by the King's Council or Parliament without overturning the structure that kept the monarchy functioning. Despite Richard's royal blood, which afforded him higher status than any other adult in the land, he was fully aware of the ambitions of the Woodvilles and their influence on the king. As well as constantly watching his back, as his father had learned while protector during Henry VI's mental infirmities, he also had to balance the conflicting self-interests of England's nobility, who were always scheming for advancement for themselves and their adherents. The very nature of the office, dealing with unrest and opposition, acquired enemies and courted danger.

Lessons could also be learned from the fate of two previous royal uncles. Humphrey, Duke of Gloucester, appointed royal protector during Henry VI's childhood, had been eliminated as soon as his power waned. Worse still, the previous Duke of Gloucester, Thomas of Woodstock, had met an even stickier end. He had been one of the Lords Appellant who briefly exercised a protectorate-like control of the realm when the young Richard II provoked resentment through his arbitrary personal rule. His reward, when the king felt ready to strike, was to be taken to Calais and murdered.

Dukes Thomas and Humphrey had seen the effects of untrammelled power wielded by the dangerous combination of an unreliable child-king and a faction-ridden council, and had paid the price when they tried to control the situation.

In 1483, the appointment of a protector certainly represented a significant stumbling-block to those who planned to be the power behind the boy-king; but it simultaneously delivered a poisoned chalice to the protector himself. If the lad, as seemed likely, remained a creature of the Woodvilles, then once he assumed full power the career of Richard of Gloucester would be ended – and probably also his life.

* * *

We have mentioned the feuding factions that gave concern to Edward IV at his death. However, it would not be unfair to say that Edward was himself at the root of much of the trouble, having allowed his wife's Woodville family to acquire great power which engendered deep unpopularity in certain quarters. This was exacerbated by their undistinguished bloodline and their record of fighting for the Lancastrian cause.

Even though their mother, Jacquetta de Luxembourg, daughter of a European count, was at one time married to the Duke of Bedford, none of Bedford's blood flowed through her children's veins. Elizabeth and her dozen siblings were fathered by Jacquetta's second husband, the handsome Richard Woodville, Lord Rivers, who had started as a knight and later acquired a baronage. (In the order of English nobility a baron ranked lowest.)

When Elizabeth became queen, she and Edward busily set about the promotion of her many relatives by arranging advantageous marriages. The haul included three dukedoms and three earldoms, together with a further earldom to which Lord Herbert was raised after his Woodville marriage.

Elizabeth's father was created Earl Rivers in 1466, and soon began to enjoy a series of glittering appointments. His heir, her elder brother Anthony, received numerous grants and offices. When her youngest brother Lionel was old enough he was provided with a career in the Church; he would later become Bishop of Salisbury. The queen's elder son, Thomas, soon sported the marquessate of Dorset and a betrothal to a richly endowed infant bride.

Not a few lifelong Yorkists saw how their loyalty in their king's cause, often entailing the suffering and death of fathers and sons, earned paltry recognition compared to the rich inheritances bestowed on these Lancastrian upstarts.

The principal and most disastrous damage caused by such actions was the offence they gave to Edward's ambitious cousin, Warwick the Kingmaker, who had laboured long and hard in support of Edward and his father before him. To add insult to injury, the king's secret Woodville wedding occurred at a time when Warwick had, with Edward's full authorization, set up negotiations with Louis XI for a marriage to Bona of Savoy, the French king's sister-in-law.

To rub salt into the wound, a number of the matches arranged for the queen's relatives represented a direct affront to the dignity and cupidity of Warwick's family, the Nevilles. One example was that of the young nonentity, John Woodville, to the senior of the two Dowager Duchesses of Norfolk, Warwick's elderly and fabulously wealthy aunt. Another such match was that of Thomas of Dorset to the infant Holland heiress, in the process rescinding her pre-existing betrothal to Warwick's nephew.

Then there were the marriages of Elizabeth's sisters to leading members of the nobility, especially that of Catherine Woodville to the 2nd Duke of Buckingham, the foremost peer of the land outside the king's immediate family. The marriage prospects of Warwick's heirs, his two daughters Isabel and Anne Neville, were blighted as suitable candidates were picked off for the Woodvilles. Only the king's brothers, the Dukes of Clarence and Gloucester, remained as fitting husbands for the Neville sisters, and Edward persistently refused to allow any such matches.

Thus, Warwick was entitled to feel not just unappreciated, but humiliated and alienated, as Edward must surely have expected. His underestimation of Warwick's enmity, however, proved to be Edward's greatest political blunder, since it produced three years of turbulence in the form of the Kingmaker's armed insurrection and revolt. The Woodvilles themselves paid a high price for Warwick's humiliation, with two of them being peremptorily beheaded in the course of his 1469 rebellion.

On the evidence we have to hand, there seems to have been no purpose or policy in Edward's choice of queen. His nature was lustful, and his age was twenty-two; it was simply an act of headlong folly. Indeed, within a few years there were rumours circulating that the king, who had ridden unaccompanied to a secret tryst at her home on the last day of April, emerging a married man on the first day of May, had actually been seduced into the whole thing by witchcraft. We will return to this very interesting topic in chapter 7.

As regards Elizabeth personally, her unpopularity has possibly been exaggerated by historians over the ensuing centuries; but a letter from Lord Wenlock to Jean de Lannoy, written in Reading on 3 October, hard on the heels of the revelation of the marriage, stated that it caused 'great displeasure to many great lords, and especially to the larger part of his council'.[5]

This displeasure was notorious enough to reach the ears of foreign diplomats. A Milanese envoy reported on 5 October 1464 that the 'greater part of the lords and the people in general seem very much dissatisfied', and another stated that the marriage had 'greatly offended the people of England'. Other accounts carried the same overall tone: the Burgundian Jean de Wavrin gave it as the royal council's opinion that Elizabeth 'was not [King Edward's] match, however good and however fair she might be, and he must know well that she was no wife for a prince such as himself'.[6]

The Danziger, Caspar Weinreich, also reported in 1464 that Edward's marriage was 'against the wish of all his lords' and Elizabeth's coronation was 'against the will of all lords'. Later, in 1469, he recorded Edward's ingratitude to the Earl of Warwick and others who had helped make him king, while he 'had the queen's friends and brothers live with him and made great lords of them' despite the fact that 'they or their knights ... had been traitors to the king'.[7]

We may excuse Elizabeth's motives in these matters: she was not a royal princess, schooled in diplomacy and the significance of dynastic marriages. Nevertheless she was by no means a fool and certainly knew enough about attitudes and mores to realize that offence was caused. But it was Edward IV who made the choice to exercise his feudal prerogatives in ways that flouted the normal disposal of estates which his loyal liege-men expected to enjoy in times of peace and prosperity. It undoubtedly did him harm in the eyes of his subjects, and unknowingly built up a bitter legacy for his son and heir.

★ ★ ★

Returning to the matter of Edward IV's unexplained death, it will be evident that the queen and her family occupied a considerable power base but that equally there were significant factions ranged against them. The Crowland chronicler notes that in the interim council meetings in April, 'The more foresighted members ... thought that the uncles and brothers on the mother's side should be utterly forbidden to have control of the person of the young man until he came of age.'

Richard Collins, while casting around for perpetrators in Edward's murder, does not name the queen as his prime suspect. He does, however, point the finger at the Woodville family and says that 'it would be most odd – not to say downright discourteous – if the others decided to kill him without at least consulting her'.

In particular, Collins's spotlight falls on one of the Woodvilles who behaved in a uniquely suspicious manner. While the entire Court and council were caught unawares by Edward's death, this individual had taken all the right steps, at least three weeks before Easter, to ensure his personal position was legally watertight and that machinery was in place for defensive or offensive action if circumstances demanded. This person was the queen's brother Anthony, Earl Rivers.

Rivers had been appointed in 1473 as 'governor and ruler' of the household of the heir to the throne. For nearly ten years he had enjoyed unfettered power to act on Prince Edward's behalf in Wales and the Welsh marches, where he was the prime mover in the prince's council and had the right to raise men for military actions. Nevertheless, Rivers suddenly decided on 8 March 1483 to write to his London agent, Master Andrew Dymmock, requesting copies of the letters patent that granted him the governorship of the prince and the right to raise troops.[8] This is all the more odd, Collins comments, 'as only a week before [Rivers] had been in London himself, attending the Parliament, and could well have requested and obtained them there'.

Another step, taken earlier that year, had even further reinforced Woodville control of the Prince of Wales, by issuing regulations that 'nothing was to be done by the prince' without the advice of three people who by then had a virtual monopoly on his actions: Earl Rivers, the prince's governor; Richard Grey, Elizabeth's younger son by her former husband; and John Alcock, the Bishop of Worcester, president of the prince's council and the boy's tutor. Again this might have been laying the groundwork for a planned Woodville takeover.

Finally, that same letter to Dymmock contained a third and even stranger instruction, which was to hand over Rivers's authority as Deputy Constable of the Tower of London to his nephew Thomas Grey, Marquess of Dorset.

'Edward had a rather clever policy in his appointments to sensitive positions,' Collins observes.

> He often chose someone who, whilst pleased to receive such public recognition of his value, was entirely unable to use it. Hence the Constable of the Tower was Lord Dudley, an old and infirm man quite incapable of doing the job. The Constable of Calais was Lord Hastings, who as Lord Chamberlain was permanently tied up in London. And Rivers was Deputy Constable of the Tower, despite being two hundred miles away in [Ludlow]. Thus a chain of command was established whereby those on the ground had no authority to act, and those who had authority could not use it.
>
> To transfer his authority thus to Dorset was to put active power into the hands of someone able to use it, and quite against the spirit of the appointment. But there is something even more irregular. The appointment was made by the king, and it was not in Rivers's gift in any sense.

Presumably they were doubtful that such an arrangement, if broached as an outright request, would receive Edward's consent. The Tower, after all, was the king's principal royal palace, of key importance militarily and strategically, and home to the state treasury and the mint which produced England's coin of the realm.

As events turned out, all three of the special powers mentioned above would be used by the Woodvilles in an attempt to resist the protectorship which the king, in his last hours, conferred on Richard, Duke of Gloucester.

Before leaving the subject of suspicious activities that took place *before* Edward's death, we have the curious matter of the false alarm.

On 6 April 1483, three days before it was officially made public, a report reached the city of York that the king had died.[8] A dirge was held for him in the minster the next day, Monday, and a Requiem Mass on the Tuesday.

The event cannot help but be suspicious, and no one has yet found any recorded reason. There are two ways of looking at it. (1) The king actually died several days before 9 April, and whoever sent word northward was unaware that the fact was to be withheld until convenient for those who were ordering matters. Or (2), it fits with Collins's theory of poisoning: it was, he suggested, a first attempt that failed. That being so, Collins felt he could establish roughly when the attempt took place:

> Because of the time necessary … for the news to be carried from London to York, we may say that it arrived no later than the evening of 6 April; and therefore that it was sent no later than the morning of 2 April. Indeed, unless the 'posting-system' used to carry dispatches from Richard in the North was still in operation, it was probably sent no later than Tuesday 1 April in the morning (to allow five full days for carriage). So the poison cannot have been administered later than the evening of Monday 31 March, the day after Easter … Hence we can deduce that Edward was taken ill by Monday 31 March, was ill for at least twenty-four hours, and then recovered enough to appear out of danger.

There is now an interesting correlation with the Crowland chronicler's date for the onset of the illness. Also, for the king to have been sufficiently in crisis that his death appeared certain on 1 April fits well with the timing of the Requiem Mass, which was normally offered, if not on the day of the funeral, then on the seventh or thirtieth day afterwards. Tuesday 8 April was seven days after Tuesday 1 April.

A failed first attempt is not uncommon, according to Collins, even today. 'If a dose is too small, obviously it will not kill: but if a dose is too large, the irritant effect on the stomach is so great that it is likely to be vomited straight out again, leaving a dose far too small to kill' (arsenic works by entering the bloodstream and reacting with haemoglobin).

There was no real tradition of poisoning in England at the time, and murder is, as de Quincey tells us, a fine art rather than a science; it is therefore quite likely that the dose was miscalculated, and that Edward voided it quickly. He would have been very sick, all the same, easily ill enough to prompt a message to York; but recovery to the out-of-danger stage would have been equally fast, followed by several days of weakness and malaise. Now the physicians would take over: and for once, the normal treatment would have been relatively effective. With a diagnosis of gastro-enteritis ('flux') the remedy would be a light diet, mainly barley water progressing to gruel, and emetics to purge the humours – coincidentally purging also the arsenic. Within a week, Edward would be back to his old self, with just a trace of weakness and nausea remaining.

'Certainly by Tuesday 8 April,' Collins deduces, 'he would be well enough to spend a quiet evening with close friends and family. And this is precisely when, I suggest, a second attempt was made. This time, they got it right.'

3

Plot and Counter-Plot

At the time of Edward IV's death the Woodvilles were well set up with key powers consolidated in their hands. Earl Rivers had moved to confirm his legal right to be in charge of the new king's person and to raise troops, which looks as if he anticipated objections.

He was not wrong: when an escort of some thousands of men was mooted for the king's journey from Ludlow, it became a topic of vigorous argument in council. The Crowland chronicler reported that 'the more foresighted members of the council' were of the opinion that the guardianship of the king should be utterly forbidden to his mother's relatives, and there was concern about such an armed force descending on London.

Lord Hastings put a swift end to the matter by issuing an ultimatum in which he threatened resorting to force unless the size of the escort was limited. A compromise of 2,000 men was quickly agreed. Were the members of the council taken aback by the hubris of the Woodvilles in proposing to march in force on the capital? If all was above board, why did they anticipate resistance?

It now became clear that the Woodville family had seized the initiative. The Marquess of Dorset, holding keys to the treasury as Deputy Constable of the Tower, appropriated State funds in accordance with the governing cabal's decision to equip and man a fleet.[1] Ostensibly to counter French harrying in the Channel, this also secured potential control of Calais. Such steps were a clear insult to the authority of Richard of Gloucester, Admiral of

England. In fact, once he took charge as protector he pursued the opposite course and wisely opted for negotiations with France.

Dorset lost no time in taking advantage of his new-found power by appointing his uncle, Sir Edward Woodville, as commander of the fleet. Mancini reports the common belief that the late king's treasure was now 'divided between the queen, the marquess and Edward', for which corroboration has been found in Financial Memoranda prepared during Edward V's minority.

Edward Woodville then coolly seized another £10,250 in English gold coin from a carrack lying in Southampton Water 'on the grounds that it was forfeit to the crown'. In return he thoughtfully provided an indenture, doubtless in the name of Edward V. Nothing more is known of the fate of this vast amount of coin.[2]

The question of what became of Edward IV's treasure is one that calls for a book of its own, or at least a scholarly treatise; regrettably it is beyond our scope here. The purse-strings should have been controlled by the Treasurer of England, the Earl of Essex, and one could be forgiven for finding it a suspicious coincidence, despite his advanced years, that the earl had met his death on 4 April 1483, very close to that of Edward IV.

The Crowland chronicler claimed it was all squandered away by Richard III. In reality, from the moment he arrived in London he was actually contributing to the cost of government: 'he received no payment for his attendance on the young king and he also paid £800 towards the king's expenses, including the cost of the royal household'.[3]

Confirmation for the disappearance of Edward IV's fabled treasure is found in the problems encountered by his executors, meeting on 7 May at Baynard's Castle, the town home of the late king's mother, when it was deemed there were insufficient funds to discharge the terms of his will. They met again on 23 May to find means of defraying the funeral expenses of £1,886.

I would suggest that although there remained plenty of Edward IV's personal assets to be inherited by his heirs, this is not incompatible with the likelihood that ready cash went missing. The queen probably accessed the chamber coffers for her own use, and the crown treasure (under Dorset's control in the Tower) was cleaned out by Dorset and his seafaring uncle, ending up, as we shall see, lining the pockets of rebels and traitors.

In the council meanwhile the Woodville party quickly secured an early coronation on 4 May. But they stirred up opposition on trying to deny Richard the protectorship, proposing government by 'many persons' among whom Gloucester would merely be supposedly 'numbered the foremost'. With Edward already in their hands, added to their long-held dominance of the council, if next they took the protector out of the equation the three-fold Henrician balance would be destroyed (see p. 34). In 1454 Henry VI's queen Margaret had similarly tried to consolidate all powers in her own hands but was refused by Parliament. In the council of 1483 Mancini reported voices supporting Richard's protectorate, 'because Edward in his will had so decreed, and because according to law it would fall to him to head the government'.

Their stand was reinforced when a letter to the council was received from Richard urging the law and Edward IV's known wishes, mentioning his long record of loyalty and service at home and abroad, and warning that 'it would not be possible, without doing wrong, to pronounce anything contrary to law and his brother's wish'. Mancini reported its contents and noted that the public, 'having previously favoured the duke in their hearts from their belief in his integrity, now mounted support for him openly and vocally'.

Nevertheless, the Woodvilles' strength was such that their proposal against the protectorship was carried when put to the vote. They also began arranging the collection of certain taxes, which was legally beyond their prerogative. The young marquess, flushed with success, could not help bragging to his friends; Mancini even reports him verbatim: 'We are so important that even without the king's uncle we can make and enforce these decisions.'

Yet there still existed in the council a residual movement to curb the all-encroaching power of the queen dowager's family. Would these anti-Woodville voices have been so brave, in the power vacuum that followed the king's death, had the Woodvilles been the only game in town? Rather it seems beyond doubt that those who were in opposition, including Hastings, were relying on Richard to stand as their champion. He could not have been unaware of their expectations resting on him.

The chronicler of Crowland comments that Hastings had his own axe to grind: 'He was afraid that if supreme power fell into the hands of the queen's relatives they would then sharply avenge the alleged injuries done to them by that lord.' He agreed the compromise of 2,000 men because 'he was confident enough, so it seemed, that the Dukes of Gloucester and Buckingham, in whom he had the greatest trust, would bring with them no less a number'.

This is the first mention we have of the involvement of Harry Stafford, 2nd Duke of Buckingham, who seems to have taken virtually no part in political life hitherto. Buckingham, like Hastings, had suddenly started corresponding with Richard in the aftermath of Edward IV's death, and would soon play a major role against the Woodvilles.

A great deal of to-ing and fro-ing of messengers must have occurred during that momentous month of April. Remembering that news of Edward's death reached York as early as 6 April, one can scarcely imagine Richard content to sit in his northern castle wondering what was happening. So couriers would have sped to Westminster and back. Accordingly, a plan was devised which entailed Richard and Buckingham riding separately to Northampton where they would rendezvous with the Ludlow party and escort the young king the rest of the way to London.

There is a point here that cannot be stressed too strongly: Hastings, as Edward IV's closest confidant, certainly knew the late king had placed the protectorship in Richard's hands, and through Hastings Richard certainly knew it too. So Richard's entire outlook and strategy, from before he even left Yorkshire, was based on the knowledge – supported by long-established precedent – that this was now his function. For twenty years his brother's word had been law, which Richard had loyally obeyed. He did not expect anyone to question it any more than he did. This was not an age of democracy, and the king's sole adult male heir of the blood royal did not expect to submit his status to somebody's vote. What he expected was a suitably prompt and deferential submission of the king's contingent into his charge as Protector and Defender of the Realm as well as High Constable of England. Though apprised that actions in London sought to undermine his authority, he would be wary but confident that right was on his side.

How Buckingham became involved we have no idea. Of a similar age to Richard, he was one of the greatest land-owners in the country and directly descended from Edward III's youngest son, Thomas of Woodstock. Most historians agree he nursed a bitter resentment of the Woodvilles for sullying his bloodline with their inferior stock: Mancini says he 'had been forced to marry the queen's sister, who earnt his scorn as a wife on account of her mean parentage'.

Perhaps we may reconstruct Harry of Buckingham's involvement by supposing that at the death of the king he probably sought out Hastings to offer his aid in resisting any seizure of power by the Woodvilles. As soon as the dowager queen's family started pushing their wishes through the council, Hastings would have reckoned a show of strength was needed, and this was the role in which he evidently cast Richard with Buckingham in support. Hastings himself presumably had to hold the ring in the capital, but Buckingham could betake himself to join Richard on the road, thus providing a larger force than Richard could raise on his own at short notice.

There is no report of Queen Elizabeth communicating in any way with Richard, not even to advise him of Edward's death; but we do know (from Crowland and Mancini) that his first concern on hearing the news was to write letters of condolence to the queen and council with promises, as the Crowland chronicler informs us:

> to come and offer submission, fealty and all that was due from him to his lord and king, Edward V. ... He therefore came to York with an appropriate company, all dressed in mourning, and held a solemn funeral ceremony for the king, full of tears. He bound, by oath, all the nobility of those parts in fealty to the king's son; he himself swore first of all.

Amid the bustle of preparation Richard would now have to come to terms with the reality of his brother's death, while at the same time wondering about its circumstances. These would be his last few days of normality; of living out the life of a northern magnate, known and respected by the common people, assisted by a loyal, industrious household, and supported by a wife and family who occupied a revered place in the community. From the moment he made his way southwards, he set in motion an undertaking that would forever change his fate, and with it the fate of England.

At this point, with events taking a dramatic turn, we are faced with the problem of sifting through stories from various sources: the serious clerics of the day (Mancini, Crowland), the amateur and professional chroniclers of Tudor times and the later embellishers whose concern was merely to tell a stirring tale.

Thus we hear that when Richard departed from York on or about 23 April 1483 he was accompanied by some 300 gentlemen, and that Buckingham, probably aware of the Woodvilles' intentions, wanted Richard to arrive with more strength, offering a force of 1,000 men himself. But Richard, perhaps still dubious about how serious the situation really was, requested Buckingham to bring a number similar to his own 300. Of the contemporaneous chroniclers, only Mancini notes the combined number of persons accompanying the two dukes, which he puts at 500. Whatever the exact figure, it was a fraction of the king's party.

At Ludlow, Edward V's first extant letter signed as sovereign was dated 16 April. Thereafter everything went quiet until eight more days had passed. Many writers have sought to explain why Rivers did not move his entourage towards London until around 24 April: the earl himself stated that he stayed in order to celebrate the Rites of St George on 23 April. But why not make more haste? Richard Collins believes his reason was to keep the new king 'away from Richard, the council, and preferably anyone else, until the very last moment, to prevent tampering with the plan'.

Equally possible is that the Woodvilles failed to weigh the possibility of serious resistance ('We are so important that … we can make and enforce these decisions'). Thinking their plans were working perfectly, they would have conveyed this impression when writing to Ludlow. Thus Rivers may have thought that the initiative lay entirely on his side.

Earl Rivers was a man of letters and of discourse. He evidently had some regard for Richard of Gloucester, having but a month previously referred a business dispute to the arbitration of his Council of the North. On the other hand, being twelve years Richard's senior, and having spent much time in the company of the extravagantly macho Edward IV, he was undoubtedly one of those who viewed Richard as the plucky young sidekick whose talent lay in carrying out orders. Although in younger days the earl had been a renowned jouster, his experience of warfare was limited.

As he approached their meeting point, Rivers doubtless believed the Woodvilles were impregnable given their control of the king, the fleet, the Tower and the treasure, allied to their substantial support in the council and elsewhere. Moreover, his outriders would have informed him that neither Richard of Gloucester nor Buckingham travelled with more than a few hundred men.

As to the modest entourage on which Richard insisted, the obvious conclusion to be drawn is that he harboured no aggressive intentions and expected no underhand dealings. Hastings would have taken the elementary precaution of forewarning him that the king was accompanied by an army of 2,000. Thus it seems evident that Richard expected a peaceful meeting.

The Crowland chronicler names the place and date of the rendezvous as Northampton on 29 April. Mancini confirms that the king's party had already gone on ahead by the time Richard and Buckingham arrived. There ensued a very interesting conversation between the two dukes.

Buckingham's marcher estates in Wales and the west of England were intimately connected with the council that governed from Ludlow Castle in the name of the hitherto Prince of Wales, now king. So he would have kept reliable informants at Ludlow. He also maintained a position at Court in Westminster; and being married to the queen's sister, Catherine, no doubt he gleaned much intelligence concerning activities in the Woodville camp, whether by means of the unguarded word or the intercepted letter.

It is likely that Buckingham and Richard knew each other only superficially, but Hastings would have provided the gel that bonded both parties, having assured them they had the same interests at heart. Perhaps there were already rumours at Court that the circumstances of Edward IV's death were suspicious, and if so, Buckingham would then have been in a position to pass on his view of the matter. Richard's subsequent actions – compared to his measured and statesmanlike behaviour of the past week – could take on new meaning if viewed in the light of suspicions about his brother's death.

Paul Murray Kendall paints a vivid word-picture of the situation:

> Precisely what was happening in the capital he could not tell; precisely what attitude Earl Rivers and his 2,000 men would take at Northampton he did not know. He did know that the authority of the protectorship was rightfully his, and he trusted to his abilities and to the will of the realm to make good that authority. There is something at once naive and formidable about Richard's rigorous confidence, in the face of opposition so aggressive and a political situation so complex and explosive.[4]

Of our two fifteenth-century reporters, Mancini gives the more detailed and reliable account, doubtless provided by the only source he names, i.e. Edward V's physician, John Argentine. The king and his escort, commanded by Rivers, high-handedly ignored their agreed rendezvous with the two royal dukes at Northampton on 29 April and instead moved south to the locality of Stony Stratford, 15 miles nearer London, with the evident intention to outrun the two dukes and arrive before them. Rivers meanwhile rode to attend their presence, citing Northampton's unsuitability for their meeting with the king (despite its being a strongly fortified town, already prepared for the royal visit, and important enough to have hosted Parliaments). Buckingham then arrived overnight, ready with details of the Woodville-dominated council's rejection of Edward IV's will for Richard to be appointed as Lord Protector.

In security terms this meant a child-king, uncrowned, on the road overnight at or near an unfortified township. Responsible under Edward IV's ordinances for the safe-conduct of the king, Rivers was presently in Northampton having abandoned his charge, and was promptly arrested by Richard who was now acting with his authority as Lord High Constable of England. To reach the king and take control of his security he was now forced to make hasty arrangements for his and Buckingham's party to rise at dawn and ride directly south for some three hours along a road far less well-surfaced than Watling Street. Where, to his surprise, he encountered a contingent newly up from London led by the queen's son Richard Grey. This raised more suspicions as it coolly exceeded the 2,000 cap set by the council on the king's Woodville escort. He took Grey and others into custody charging conspiracy against his life, a charge confirmed by Crowland, though the term 'ambushes' (*insidias*) used by Mancini remains untested as this Latin word is open to various interpretations and can mean a trap of unspecified nature.

These events were examined in an article by Gordon Smith who showed that if planning a confrontation the Woodvilles, by the ploy of pressing on to Stony Stratford, enjoyed the advantage of forcing Richard along the road from Northampton through their Grafton home estates where he suggested they could have set armed men.[5]

His strategy of pre-emptive arrests was a sound one since his combined force was outnumbered four-to-one. But it seems there was no resistance anyway from the main body of foot-soldiers as they made their morning preparations to depart for London. Instead they were sent home. Assuming they were unaware of the arrests of their leaders, which Mancini confirms were carried out swiftly and secretly, it is likely the men simply presumed Richard had terminated the Woodville arrangements and taken over escort duties.

The Crowland chronicler rather disingenuously claims that the king sent Rivers 'to submit everything that had to be done to the judgement of his paternal uncle, the Duke of Gloucester'. But as Smith points out, this is inconsistent with events in London, 'where the royal council under the Woodvilles had circumvented Gloucester's protectorship. … The notion that Rivers went to consult the dukes therefore looks unlikely.' Indeed, if Mancini knew the Woodvilles were bragging about being more important than Richard then the Crowland cleric, who probably attended council meetings, certainly knew their attitude was far from one of submission.

Of the leaders arrested, just three were detained in custody. They included the two men of greatest influence in young Edward's life: his uncle, 'governor and ruler' Earl Rivers and his half-brother Sir Richard Grey. The third was Sir Thomas Vaughan, his chamberlain, who had concurrently held the significant position of treasurer of Edward IV's chamber.

It has been said that among those arrested was 'Sir' Richard Haute (or Hawte), presumably that untitled Richard Haute who was a relative of the Woodvilles and controller of the Ludlow household. If so, he certainly was not executed for he lived to rebel against Richard III in October 1483. Sir Richard Haute, a loyal supporter knighted by Richard, was a different individual.

In relation to this incident the reader will be interested to note a subtle distortion of fact which appears in Mancini. The company of 2,000 men accompanying the king are described as 'a large number of companions brought from Wales', while Richard and Buckingham, with a combined escort that Mancini himself estimates at 500, have 'a large force of soldiers'. Polydore Vergil, the Tudor historian, indulges in a similar distortion by describing Edward V as having 'a small train' for the journey while Richard 'gathered no small force of armed men'.[6]

The Crowland chronicler is dismayed at these arrests; but on the other hand he has reported only a few lines earlier that men felt it best to forbid the guardianship of the king to his mother's relatives (who were even now running the council). He acknowledges they are not universally trusted; and he knows they have already seized control of events before Gloucester can reach London. Our cleric thereby makes his allegiance abundantly clear: he is a partisan of the dowager queen. His stance from this point becomes strongly antagonistic to Richard.

Indeed, if one examines his personal comments relating to Elizabeth Woodville, it is easy to discern his point of view. His earliest such comment says: 'the royal marriage was praised and approved, solemnly, by the earl [Warwick] himself and by all the prelates and great lords', with no mention of the condemnation that we know was expressed in high places. His next reference characterizes Elizabeth as 'the benevolent queen, desirous of extinguishing every spark of murmuring and unrest', when she is forced by the council to limit the number of troops escorting the new king to London.

The writer was entitled, of course, to be a Woodville partisan if he thought they were the proper group to be running the affairs of state; but the reader needs to be aware of his partiality.

* * *

Leaving aside the rather revolutionary suggestion of Edward IV's murder raised earlier, there has always been debate as to whether there ever was a 'Woodville plot'. That they intended to prevent Richard from exercising his powers as Lord Protector cannot be denied, although whether they planned to ambush him is disputed. Theoretically, they might have expected him to find their dispensations acceptable: it is possible to construct a hypothetical scenario where Richard, having made his home far away and being averse to life at the Court, would return happily to his family as soon as the coronation put a welcome end to his involvement.

What works against this theory is the reality of the times. There was a strong antipathy to the Woodvilles' exercise of control over the boy king, which went as high as the council and which we may well assume was shared by Richard. There were appeals from important magnates for him to take over and curb the Woodvilles' ambitions. After so many years as lord of the north, he must surely have been regarded as a formidable opponent. To quote Professor Michael Hicks (himself by no means pro-Ricardian): 'Undoubtedly in control of his own affairs, which he extended to embrace the whole of the North, Richard's forcible interventions elsewhere were not to be ignored. Nobody should have supposed that they could determine the minority government of Edward V without his participation.'[7]

Having conspired to prevent a protectorship, first in council and then by calling a hasty coronation without a Parliament, clearly the Woodvilles' intention was to rule through a twelve-year-old puppet king, leading England into whatever fate might befall it during the boy's vulnerable minor years.

To act this way was to embark on a risky venture, as Professor Hicks has pointed out. Richard was a seasoned general and had access to substantial military strength as controller of the wild Scottish border. Given that the Woodvilles knew his exclusion would challenge and antagonize him, was their large armed escort intended to neutralize Gloucester before he had time to marshal a sizeable force? Why else did they need such a large army?

In this context, it is surprising to read comments such as those of Professor Colin Richmond, a few pages after Professor Hicks's remarks quoted above. Leaving out any right of input on the part of Richard, Richmond's view is: 'The former King's advisers concurred with his last will (… was it destroyed by Richard?) that the young Edward should be crowned promptly and that there should be neither regency nor protectorate.'[8]

Agreed, the will is missing and there is no evidence of what its codicils said, yet the reports quoted earlier clearly indicate that a protectorate under Richard was known to be Edward IV's wish. To the best of my knowledge, there are no reports giving Professor Richmond's version of his wishes. Moreover, the will itself had long been in the hands of the late king's council before Richard of Gloucester arrived on the scene, and was passed to the custody of his executors. What would Richard achieve by destroying it after all this? And if Edward was so set against a protector, why did the council so appoint him?

Let us look at the words of the Crowland chronicler, that insider, writing safely after Richard's death, and under a régime that is antagonistic to the defeated king. Our chronicler is much given to hand-wringing and tut-tutting in disapproval of Richard's actions; surely you would expect him to mention this dreadful overthrow of the late king's will? Yet his report of Richard's protectorship appointment by the council is utterly matter-of-fact, and everyone thereafter 'hoped for and awaited peace and prosperity in the kingdom'.

Professor Richmond contends that Edward IV, after publicly recognizing the bitter feuding among his family and advisers, 'evidently hoped that around the crowned and anointed Edward V … would group all those, or almost all of those, who had served his father', an optimistic hope if ever there was one. Nor had the crown sat peaceably on Edward's own head. In the last couple of years there had been disturbances against him in Northumberland and the Duchy of Lancaster, and the Mayor of Canterbury had been told by Hastings that another revolution was possible.

It is not difficult to conclude that, drawing on the bitter experience of Henry VI's reign, many people realized that a child was a thoroughly undesirable option as England's next king. The Woodvilles were not the only candidates lined up ready to get their noses in the trough; there was still a formidable lust for power and wealth on the part of other ambitious magnates who would not hesitate to take advantage of any monarch's weakness. And outside the country's borders there were yet more threats to consider. The rule of a child king offered England's long-standing foreign enemies the perfect opportunity to make trouble – or, in the case of France, to escalate the trouble already in the making.

In addition, another distant threat was biding its time across the English Channel in the person of Henry Tudor, who represented one of the last few dregs of hope for dissident Lancastrians.

★ ★ ★

Henry Tudor was then twenty-six, and as he grew to manhood he had seen the house of York enjoy increased security on the throne of England. His mother, Lady Margaret Beaufort, Countess of Richmond, was proud of her aristocratic blood and Henry himself harboured lofty ambitions. The problem, which must have infuriated Margaret all her life, was that despite her descent from John of Gaunt, third surviving son of Edward III, there was a flaw in her bloodline (see Table 2).

John of Gaunt, Duke of Lancaster, whose son seized the throne in 1399 to become Henry IV, was Margaret's great-grandfather. But Margaret's grandfather, John Beaufort, was Gaunt's second son, born a bastard from the duke's adulterous relationship with his children's Flemish governess, Katherine de Roët, wife of Sir Hugh Swynford. Gaunt subsequently made Katherine his third duchess and successfully petitioned Parliament to legitimate their offspring in 1397, announcing in the Act of Parliament that the pope had already done likewise; but their legitimation never granted them any right to the Lancaster title or inheritance, and the surname Beaufort was invented for them.[9]

There was also a special taint that attached itself to John, the eldest of four bastards by Katherine, since he was believed to be the product of a double adultery, being conceived while both parties were still married to other spouses. Was he a Beaufort or a Swynford? Indeed, after John's birth in 1372 Gaunt went on to father two legitimate children by his second wife, Constance of Castile, before the affair with Katherine was resumed and the remaining three bastard children were born.

Legitimated they may have been, but there was no place for Henry IV's Beaufort half-siblings in the succession according to Henry's stance. This was not merely because he produced four lusty sons; it was because (in the view of established historians,

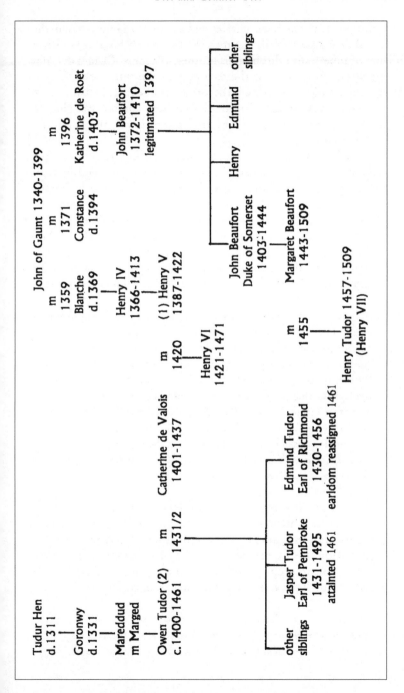

Table 2: Houses of Tudor and Beaufort

although this has been challenged recently) Henry based the hereditary aspect of his claim to the throne on his alleged direct line of inheritance through his mother, Blanche of Lancaster, not his father. Blanche was the sole heir of Edmund Crouchback, second son of Henry III, who according to the Lancastrian version of history was actually that king's first-born son but was cheated of the throne. If hers was the true blood royal, the Beauforts shared none of it.[10]

So when in 1407 Henry IV's half-brother John Beaufort requested a copy of the Letter Patent confirming his legitimation, the king made absolutely sure the Beauforts would be barred from the succession by inserting an interlineated additional clause, *excepta dignitate regali* (except to the royal dignity). The interlineation, in a later hand, was incorporated in Henry IV's 1407 confirmation and exemplification of this charter (see *Excerpta Historica*, pp. 152–3). Arthur Kincaid, in his 2023 edition of Sir George Buc's *History of King Richard the Third*, summarizes thus:

> Although *Excerpta Historica* mentions that Henry IV could not legally interpolate a Parliamentary statute, Kendall [in *Richard III*] comments that 'Whether, in the light of present-day constitutional studies, he had the right so to alter an act of Parliament matters little; most people of the fifteenth century took it for granted that the legitimating patent barred the Beauforts from the throne', and Mortimer Levine, 'Richard III – Usurper or Lawful King?' *Speculum*, XXXIV (1959), 391n, says, '… it is questionable that Richard [II]'s legitimation could extend to the crown in the case of bastards born while their parents' lawful spouses were living'. In any case, no one challenged it and Henry VII ignored it.[11]

Another light is thrown on the subject by the wording of the 1397 act of legitimation. In their biography of Margaret Beaufort, the authors Jones and Underwood observe that whereas the legitimation itself specified no limiting conditions, nevertheless when it came to property, office and noble rank, the Enabling Act specified (and limited) exactly what was conferred:

> Although it accorded the right to dignities it conferred no royal interest or right and title to the throne. Here the language of the act was significant. It used no words of empire, majesty or

sovereignty, such as 'regnum', 'summa potestas', 'corona' or 'maiestas' that would enable a man to be an heir of a kingdom ...

At the end of 1406 a detailed discussion of the issue of succession had seen the designation by statute of the crown on the king's sons and the heirs of their body. No mention was made of any remainder to the Beauforts, and continued emphasis was laid on a sense of legitimate succession, *suis de ipsius corpore legitime procreandis*. [It was perhaps in pursuance of this very topic that] ... a desire for a clarification of his position led to John Beaufort petitioning the king in February 1407, requesting an exemplification 'of the tenour of the enrolment' of the letter patent dated 9 February 1397 providing for his legitimation. The royal response was the confirmation of the original letters, with the insertion of the clause, after the enablement of honours and dignities, *excepta dignitate regali*.[12]

This crucial clause was never intended to be a resumption of rights accorded to the Beauforts by the original act of legitimation. The insertion was made on the patent roll, and the wording of the act on the roll of parliament was left in its original form. It was a refinement of the act of 1397, made on the king's initiative, though it did not carry a binding power on his successors.[13]

The Beaufort legitimation has exercised historians and constitutionalists for centuries, for two principal reasons: first, although Henry IV made his decision clear, the form in which he did so was questionable; second, Henry was later declared a usurper, therefore his enactments were open to challenge. To the lay person, however, the following seems obvious: (a) the circumstances of the Beauforts' birth, especially those of the eldest, John, were so irregular as to exclude them from any normal inheritance of parental honours or titles. This is confirmed by (b) the necessity to legitimate them, invent a surname and marquessate, and *bestow on them* a right to receive certain dignities and titles of a limited nature together with permission to pass these on to their heirs. Moreover (c) they were never identified as scions of the house of Lancaster, the honour acquired by Gaunt via his first wife, Blanche.

As to acts of legitimation, and tamperings with same to clarify the succession, it is true that these might be open to challenge once their instigator was named as a usurper and his line set aside.

By this logic, enactments by the Lancastrians for their heirs to succeed them had been challenged by Richard, Duke of York, and set aside by Parliament in 1460. The test, of course, depended on a challenge being made. If not, the normal precept in law is that the *status quo* is deemed to have been accepted. Significantly, no one, least of all the Beauforts, ever challenged Henry IV's provisions in the matter of debarring them from succession to the throne.

Even in 1484, after Henry Tudor had attempted an invasion and was being touted as a contender for the crown of England, Richard III did not see any necessity to place before his Parliament any enactment, whether new or interpretive, to ensure the Tudor's disqualification. A missed opportunity, perhaps, but evidently he felt it was already sufficiently covered. Indeed, Richard's later proclamations against the pretender, who 'encrocheth and usurpid upon hym the name and title of royall astate of this Realme of Englond', say clearly that in such royal estate 'he hath no maner interest, right, title, or colour, as every man wele knoweth'.

This view was emphatically shared by his sister, Margaret of York. After Tudor eventually seized the crown, she wrote to the pope protesting that although the new king pretended to be of the blood of Lancaster, he knew full well that he was illegitimate on both sides.

The double illegitimacy allegation certainly held water since Henry Tudor's paternal ancestry was also questionable. After the direct male heirs of John Beaufort (or John Swynford Beaufort) died out, only Lady Margaret Beaufort remained as their senior descendant. In 1455 she married Edmund Tudor, Earl of Richmond, and it was the Tudor marriage that introduced the second illegitimacy. Edmund was the product of a liaison of dubious legality between Henry V's widow, Catherine de Valois, and the Welshman Owen Tudor, said to have been either a servant in her chamber or a member of her household involved in managing her Welsh estates. The relationship produced four children, but did not become common knowledge until Catherine's death at the beginning of 1437.

Owen came from a family of some significance, though not ranked as nobility. However, there was far more at stake than merely his lineage. Henry VI's council had recognized the problems that might be created by the dowager queen marrying one of her late husband's subjects, and a statute was passed by the Parliament of 1427–8 prohibiting anyone from marrying a queen dowager without the express permission of the king, given only after he had reached years of discretion (at the time of the supposed marriage he was scarcely ten years old). The penalty if such a marriage took place without permission was that the husband 'should suffer forfeiture of his lands and other possessions during his lifetime, though it was implicitly recognized that the children of such a match would be members of the royal family and should not themselves be punished'.[14]

A clue as to date may perhaps be found in the actions of the Parliament of 1432 which gave Owen the rights of an Englishman, enabling him to marry legally, 'releasing him from the embarrassing provisions of Henry IV's statutes against Welshmen'.

Not surprisingly, after Catherine's death those who had drawn up the statute of prohibition pursued Owen and clapped him in gaol. He was pardoned eventually and taken into the household of his step-son, Henry VI. No evidence of legal marriage is known, but evidently it was thought better to recognize it retrospectively rather than degrade the king's mother. And Henry could have regularized the position if it ever became necessary.

The two eldest sons, Edmund and Jasper, were born in 1430 and 1431 respectively. Certainly in the case of Edmund there is doubt whether any legal marriage took place between his parents before his birth since it would have violated two statutes. Owen paid the penalty and was pardoned, but such stains were long remembered.

Edmund Tudor and his brother Jasper were ennobled by their half-brother King Henry VI in 1452. This was no ordinary ennoblement, since the titles they received – Earls of Richmond and Pembroke respectively – were royal titles formerly held by the king's uncles. The newly created earls were given a special position among the English nobility, with precedence over all other noblemen below the rank of duke. Entirely without justification they started using the royal arms with marks of cadency.

The king's largesse was quite extraordinary, but perhaps not so very surprising since his party was at the time beleaguered by civil unrest and he needed every ounce of support he could get. Moreover, Henry had a heart that was easily susceptible, and was doubtless touched by the plaints of the Tudors.

It has been suggested that this perhaps reflected the king's concern at having no heir, but any such idea must be seen as highly dubious, principally because they were not of the Lancaster bloodline. They were in fact sons of the French royal line through their mother, coupled with a relatively obscure Welsh sire who might or might not have been her husband. Nor did Henry make any move to establish their legitimacy despite the widespread doubts that must have existed. In any case, there were still at that time legitimate descendants of the Lancaster blood in the offspring of John of Gaunt's two daughters by Blanche of Lancaster, namely Philippa and Elizabeth (see Table 4). In the 1450s the senior heir was Philippa's grandson, Afonso V of Portugal. Elizabeth's heir in this period was the very conspicuous Henry Holland, Duke of Exeter.

That the Lancastrian claim through Blanche was taken seriously is illustrated by Philippa's daughter Isabel who attempted to claim the English throne on the death of Henry VI. Despite the existence of male heirs in her own family, presumably she considered her proximity to Blanche more important.

A little over two years after Edmund and Jasper received their earldoms, they were given the wardship and marriage of the wealthy ten-year-old heiress Lady Margaret Beaufort, whom twenty-six-year-old Edmund married in 1455. Again there has been a suggestion that Henry intended to fill the vacancy for an heir by nominating Edmund Tudor in the right of Margaret, but again the arguments of descent apply. Despite his bestowal of royal largesse, the king knew perfectly well that the Beauforts were not of the Lancaster line any more than were the Tudors. Nor could he have been unaware of his own grandfather's determination to disallow the Beauforts a place in the succession. The plain reason behind the granting of the wardship was obviously to provide for his recently ennobled half-brothers without depleting the dwindling royal coffers.

It was a few weeks after Edmund's early death from the plague that Margaret Beaufort gave birth to Henry, her only son, in January 1457. When Edward IV came to the throne the Tudors suffered for their Lancastrian sympathies in his Parliament of 1461. Although Margaret retained her title of Countess of Richmond, Jasper Tudor was attainted and his and Edmund's lands 'parcelled out to supporters of the new regime.

Henry Tudor, a minor, [was] degraded from the earldom of Richmond'.[15] The Richmond lordship was given in 1462 to young Richard of Gloucester but was subsequently transferred to George of Clarence. It reverted to the crown on Clarence's death. Nevertheless Henry Tudor continued to style himself Earl of Richmond, in open defiance of the king.

Henry had fled with his uncle Jasper to Brittany in 1471, and remained there in exile while his mother tried to secure his prospects at home. At some unknown time a draft pardon from Edward IV to Henry was 'written on the dorse of the [1452] patent of creation of Edmund Tudor as Earl of Richmond'. In 1482, now married to her fourth husband Lord Stanley (of whom more later), Lady Margaret obtained Edward IV's agreement that her son might receive a number of estates if he made certain concessions in return; principal among the latter was that he must return from exile 'to be in the grace and favour of the king's highness'.[16]

Yet although the king was inclined to be conciliatory, Henry Tudor rebuffed all inducements to return and take up his inheritance (and resume his allegiance).

With Henry stubbornly clinging to his exiled status, Edward's councillors would have been acutely aware of the recalcitrant Tudor cloud hovering across the sea in Brittany, acting as a possible magnet for disaffected Lancastrians and compounding other threats that lurked during a minority monarchy. Those with hard heads as well as wise would have no difficulty realizing that what England needed was a strong protectorship in the hands of a grown man, proven in war and in powers of administration.

★ ★ ★

Returning to the events of 30 April in Stony Stratford, both the Mancini and Crowland reports state that the Dukes of Gloucester and Buckingham explained their actions to the young king with all courtesy, pointing out that the men who had been arrested were part of a conspiracy to deprive Richard of the protectorship and of his life. Mancini adds a lengthy exposition on the part of Richard, saying that these same people had contributed to Edward IV's demise by ruining his health; they must not be allowed to inflict the same disservice on the new king.

Though caution must be exercised when reading any account of events, my new translation and analysis gives me considerable confidence in Mancini's report of this episode, written as it was just a few months afterwards. I have the strong impression that his account came from someone who had been present in the king's entourage, probably Edward V's talkative physician, Argentine. It is obvious from Mancini's and Crowland's hostile assessment of Richard of Gloucester that they spent no time seeking an account from the point of view of his circle; even so, making allowance for this, the details given by Mancini sound credible. And supporters of the Woodvilles like Argentine were doubtless soon relating their version of the episode to anyone who cared to listen.

To be plain, we do not know what was said. But bearing in mind the views of the 'more foresighted members of the council' in advising against further Woodville influence on the boy, it is obvious that both Mancini and Crowland are correct in reporting Richard's declared intent that corrupting influences must no longer be tolerated around the young king. As Mancini says, certain men had impeached his brother's honour and 'brought his health to ruination'; they must not be allowed to 'play the same game with the son ... [and] should be removed from his side'.

Did Richard have the right to arrest Rivers and company? Certainly he did as Lord Protector, the position he knew was his by right and which Hastings would have told him he must fill. Certainly he did in his specific capacity as High Constable of England, an office to which he had been appointed for life. This is discussed further in chapter 4.

Did he intend to execute them? Very probably not. Since we know they *were* later condemned to death, it is easy to assume their execution was intended from the start. However, as a military commander Richard would have known the advantage of keeping them in custody as hostages for the future behaviour of the Woodvilles. As events transpired, they were thus held for a total of eight weeks. The estates of Earl Rivers were seized shortly after, but this did not preclude their return should a suitable agreement be reached.

Mancini tells us of the first violent response of Elizabeth and her eldest son, Thomas of Dorset, to the news from Stony Stratford, which was to attempt immediately to raise an army. This was ostensibly for defence, but in reality – having made no attempt to negotiate or conciliate with Richard of Gloucester – it was a bid to wrest the king from his control. In this enterprise her party found itself totally without support: '... they perceived that all men's hearts were not only irresolute but deeply inimical to themselves'.

While adherents of the Woodvilles tried unsuccessfully to gather forces at Westminster, those of Lord Hastings took up their position in London. Knowing he was the late king's greatest confidant, many nobles must have turned to Hastings for information and leadership. They had misgivings certainly, not least about Hastings's personal agenda, but were evidently satisfied with his position of support for the royal dukes.

Elizabeth's next move was one of sheer perversity, but was calculated to gain maximum possible sympathy: she betook herself to the Sanctuary at Westminster Abbey, accompanied by her brother Lionel (then Bishop of Salisbury) and most of her children; but not before she had gathered all her goods from Westminster Palace.

Retreating to sanctuary was a course of action which she had taken before. But that was in 1470 when her husband had been ousted from his kingdom, the streets of London were thronged with rioters and looters, and she was eight months pregnant. Ordinarily the right of sanctuary existed as a last resort for those who were at peril of arrest or execution. Thus, her move in May 1483 sent out a clear message that she felt mortally threatened by the protector, an egregious insult to him.

Why would she do such a thing, when her status as mother of the king entitled her to an honoured place at Court? The Plantagenets had no history of violence towards women for political acts. Furthermore, it was a strangely short-sighted policy. Her menfolk might quietly slip away, as indeed they did, but how long did she suppose she and her children could remain there? And on what conditions did she plan to come out? She could scarcely expect an uprising of the people in her favour.

In the event, her stay in Westminster Sanctuary lasted nearly a year: not because she was forced to remain there, nor for want of encouragement to emerge. One is led to the inevitable conclusion that there was something very serious that weighed on Elizabeth's mind, and not just the matter of the appropriated treasure. Did she fear that Richard harboured suspicions about his brother's death? Or did she fear the exposure of a different secret, known to a certain bishop, that would indeed shortly come to light?

Messages meanwhile kept the protector apprised of events in the capital, and by 2 May, prior to setting out for London, he had doubtless heard enough about the transfer of the Tower to Dorset, the plundering of the treasure, the illegal collecting of taxes, and other high-handed Woodville actions in his absence. At this point, perhaps having waited for just such confirmation, he sent the arrested hostages to his northern castles to be held respectively at Sheriff Hutton, Middleham and Pontefract.

In an act of particular astuteness, he now wrote a letter in the king's name to the senior prelate of the land, the Cardinal Archbishop of Canterbury Thomas Bourchier. In this letter he courteously requested the cardinal to perform two duties: he was to see to the safekeeping of the Great Seal until the king's arrival, and he was to safeguard the Tower of London together with 'the treasure being in the same'.[17] This clearly signalled Richard's knowledge of what was really going on, and sent an unmistakable message that questions would be asked upon their arrival.

A similarly astute move was his decision, conveyed in a letter to the mayor and aldermen of the city, that their king would enter London in two days' time on Sunday 4 May. Thus, wasting no words on argument, Richard simply timed the king's arrival so as to effect an automatic postponement of the planned coronation.

Meanwhile, it appears that Richard and Edward became better acquainted. Edward revealed he had a favourite chaplain at Ludlow named John Geffrey, and together they found a way to reward him.

A scrap of parchment has survived from this time, on which the autographs of the king and the two dukes appear for no apparent reason other than that they were perhaps comparing signatures. Maybe Gloucester and Buckingham were inviting Edward to practise his new signature as king, and to consider what his motto would be. Richard's signature appears neatly under his best-known personal motto, 'Loyaulté me lie' ('Loyalty binds me'). Buckingham's signature, large and full of flourishes,

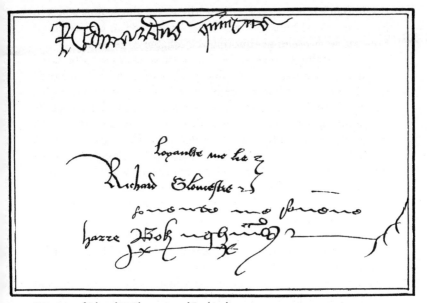

Signatures of Edward V, Gloucester and Buckingham

is surmounted by his motto, 'Souvente me souvene' (usually rendered as 'Remember me often' or, less convincingly, 'Often I recall').

All appeared to be well as the royal party entered London, officially greeted by the mayor and aldermen to the accompaniment of cheering crowds. If there was a jarring note amid all this jubilation it was the presence of four wagon-loads of weapons 'bearing the devices of the queen's brothers and sons', flanked by criers whose function was to proclaim that this warlike equipment had been amassed by Richard's enemies as part of their plan to ambush him.

This was quite a large consignment of arms, not inconsistent with provisions for an army the size of Rivers's now-dispersed troops from Ludlow. So the weaponry was not particularly significant in itself. Rather its display was a way of visibly symbolizing the Woodvilles' taking up of arms against the protector, the truth of which anyone might have seen for himself had he witnessed their abortive efforts at mustering an army two days previously. Which raises a point of some relevance to the Italian's reportage: are these the exact allegations asserted by those criers? Now that the scene has moved to the streets of London, he is no longer quoting the reliable Argentine.

Mancini alleges that 'many knew these charges to be false' because the equipment on display was known to have been stored near London long before the old king's death, as provision for warfare with Scotland. However, even assuming that our cleric was standing listening in the crowd, given his lack of English he could have recorded only what he was told. In particular, he could have had no personal knowledge of England's supposed intentions towards the Scots (with whom a treaty had been agreed nine months previously), and indeed, one wonders who in his acquaintanceship could be privy to such sensitive intelligence as the location and purpose of war stores. Mancini's allegation falls short on two further counts. First, why did the weaponry carry those Woodville bearings? And second, why should matériel for a war with Scotland be stored several hundred miles short of where it was needed? Historians have assumed Mancini believed this argument because he failed to realize the border was so far distant.

There is a further comment by Mancini that the exhibition of weapons 'immensely increased distrust' of Richard and made people suspect he had designs on supreme power. This editorializing is obviously coloured by hindsight because Mancini's claim of mistrust is not supported by his own narrative, according to which the general populace approved of Richard and appeared entirely satisfied with the turn events had taken. Mancini's problem, writing six months afterwards, was to reconcile the observations he had made *in situ* with his later conclusion that Richard had ambitions to rule England from the moment of Edward IV's death – a once common conclusion which is discounted by most authorities today.

The Crowland chronicler records that a council meeting now took place over several days, underlining his intimate knowledge of council proceedings at that time (there is a noticeable decline in the quality of his information once Richard takes the reins of power). After mentioning the pride and joy with which the new king's subjects took their oath of fealty, our chronicler moves on to business; the first item being a discussion about where the lodgings of the new king should be. Hitherto he had been staying at the Bishop of London's palace, while Richard of Gloucester had taken up residence in his rented town house of Crosby Place in Bishopsgate (the great hall of the latter was relocated in 1908–10 to Chelsea and is now known as Crosby Hall).

The council soon decided that Edward should reside at the Tower of London. This was an obvious choice: since time immemorial it had been the custom of the sovereign to process from the Tower along a well-established route to be crowned at Westminster Abbey.

In 1483 the Tower was not the horrid place of torture and captivity it later became when filled with state prisoners in the reigns of the Tudors and Stuarts. In the fifteenth century, it was the principal royal palace and fortress containing the sovereign's menagerie, the treasury, the armoury for London and the royal mint. As well as comfortable royal apartments in the Lanthorn Tower, the palace complex also contained council chambers where the King's Council met on a regular basis.

The Crowland report of the council's deliberations continues with Richard receiving 'that solemn office which had once fallen to Duke Humphrey of Gloucester who, during the minority of King Henry, was called protector of the kingdom. He exercised this authority with the consent and the good-will of all the lords, commanding and forbidding in everything like another king, as occasion demanded.' The coronation was fixed for 22 June, and everyone looked forward to peace and prosperity for the kingdom.

'However,' the cleric adds, 'a great cause of anxiety, which was growing, was the detention in prison of the king's relatives and servants and the fact that the protector did not show sufficient consideration for the dignity and peace of mind of the queen.'

With this last remark we see that Richard has now acquired blame for the fix that the Woodvilles have got themselves into. A different commentator might have deplored the fact that Edward's queen tried to seize power for her family, and when thwarted, ran for cover after unsuccessfully attempting an armed insurrection. But the Crowland chronicler finds fault with Richard on grounds that he is inconsiderate of Elizabeth's dignity and, by implication, a threat to her security.

What remedy could the protector offer for the dowager queen's dignity, given that the lady had gone into hiding of her own accord? Indeed, what course of action – compatible with the dignity of the crown and protectorate – was he expected to take? We know that he initiated negotiations with her at an early date, at least by 23 May according to the minutes of the Court of Common Council,City of London Corporation,[18] yet she refused to leave sanctuary until the following spring. It seems perverse to blame Richard for this.

4

A Shadow over the Succession

Having taken charge of King Edward V and separated him without violence from the Woodvilles, Richard as protector proceeded to set up the administrative council. Had his motives been dishonest or his status questionable, he would certainly have needed to bring his own supporters into the King's Council to counteract opposition. Instead he continued with essentially the same group of advisers, while also retaining the vast majority of the late king's household men.

Richard's councillors included Bishop John Alcock, personal tutor to the young king and president of his council at Ludlow, who presumably accompanied him to London. Thomas Rotherham, the old Archbishop of York who owed his career to Woodville favour, was replaced as Lord Chancellor of England but still remained in the council. The new chancellor was John Russell, Bishop of Lincoln, a particularly interesting appointee since he was not by any means a place-man of the protector and reportedly evidenced reluctance in the job.

The council's first concern on convening in early May was not to quibble with Richard of Gloucester's status as protector but to confirm him in the position. Those who have tried to characterize Richard's conduct as a *coup d'état* are therefore wide of the mark, since his position was entirely constitutional. No dissent was heard from the magnates of the land, and Lord Hastings was reported in the Crowland chronicle as:

bursting with joy over this new world ... asserting that nothing had so far been done except to transfer the government of the kingdom from two blood-relatives of the queen to two nobles of the blood royal, moreover he asserted that this had been accomplished without any killing and with only so much bloodshed in the affair as might have come from a cut finger.

This seems to have the ring of authenticity, especially when quoted by one who is usually censorious of Richard. No doubt these words of triumph were etched in the mind of our clerical chronicler, because Hastings's elation was so soon to be cut short by the dramatic events that followed.

Meanwhile, with new coins to be minted, coronation ceremonials, robes and festivities to be arranged and a Parliament to be summoned thereafter, the council was faced with a massive workload. The chancellor started work on his oration for the opening of Parliament: essentially a manifesto setting out the recommendations of the council. Here again we have proof of confidence in the protector since the main burden of the speech, while emphasizing a climate of harmony and obedience, was that the council wished the protectorship to continue *even after* the coronation.[1] There was every reason to want this extension, given the youth of the boy, and if anything it tends to confirm Richard's commitment to the role of protector rather than a headlong desire for the crown.

Plainly the Woodville party had been thoroughly discredited, as Michael Hicks observes:

first in the extension of Richard's protectorate beyond the coronation, agreed about this time, and second in Lord Chancellor Russell's commendation of the 'surety and firmness' of lords and noblemen against the tempestuous Rivers and his praise for Richard's 'great puissance, wisdom and fortunes at this recent execution of the defence of this realm as well against open enemies as against the subtle and faint friends of the same'. This was in the sermon he drafted for Edward V's Parliament.[2]

Other urgent business to be despatched included the matter of Sir Edward Woodville. As noted by Louise Gill, his behaviour was giving the council cause for concern:

As admiral of the fleet he had been sent against [the French] with a force some two thousand strong, and within days appeared to be menacing the south-east coast [of England]; as Dorset may also have had up to a thousand men in his charge doubtless the council came quickly to rue its commission.[3]

Accordingly on 10 May he was ordered to disband the fleet or be declared an enemy of the State. Given the promise of pardons and other inducements, the crews of all save two ships eventually brought their craft back to England, but Woodville himself fled to Brittany where the Lancastrian recusant Henry Tudor was based.

The Tudor camp would have seen this as a golden opportunity. From a position of enforced inaction for so many years, suddenly they now had potential allies bearing undreamed-of funds from the plundered treasury. Given that Henry would be ready as early as the end of September to attempt an invasion of England – a breathtakingly audacious venture that required several months of planning – Edward Woodville's defection in May was clearly the spark that ignited the Tudor conflagration.

There can be little doubt that these individuals were driven by a desire for power that placed their personal ambitions far higher than the good order of the kingdom and the peaceful conduct of its subjects' lives. While the protector and the council strove to proceed according to established norms, the Woodvilles were concerned only to cement alliances with any dissident who happened to be handy.

Mancini's report, harping back to the allegations of *insidiae* (plots of ambush or treachery) that pervade his story, claims that Richard tried to persuade the council to condemn Rivers and his associates to be punished 'as guilty of treason itself'. This supposed incident occurs only in Mancini, who says the council refused on the grounds that Richard at the time 'was neither *administratorem* [head of the government] nor did he hold any other public office'.

Mancini is in error on several counts in this passage. First, Richard's public offices at the time of Edward's death included Great Chamberlain of England, High Constable of England, Lord High Admiral of England and Lieutenant General of England's land forces. For years, his position in the realm had placed him as the principal source of authority after the king. As senior royal male he was entitled to consider himself *in loco protectoris* from the moment of Edward IV's death, as that king's will provided. Even in Mancini's own report, when the council had proposed 'government by many' (*administratio per plures*), they had already appointed Richard their chief. No public office, indeed!

Second, the Italian's understanding of the workings of England's government and justice system was seriously at fault. Mancini evidently thought that the council had powers of summary judgement and conviction: he states that Richard wanted punishment, by decree of the council, inflicted on those whom he had taken into his custody, for 'plotting ambushes or rather as guilty of treason itself'. On the contrary, Charles Ross tells us that the King's Council was not that kind of tribunal in terms of enforcing the law: 'it did not initiate actions itself ... generally it merely referred complaints for action to the proper common-law authorities'.[4] The council might investigate reports of treasonable conspiracy, but having examined the accused (under oath), would send them for trial in the appropriate court. Above all, it could not impose the death penalty.

On the other hand, Richard himself as Constable of England had the right and power to bring about not merely a charge but a conviction and sentence for treason in a court of his own. That was the nature of the job.[5] Louise Gill summarizes it as follows:

> authorized to act summarily against those *suspected of treason*, he was able to pronounce sentence without appeal. The position carried with it not just formal obligations but in the event of a crisis such as the king being killed in battle, or if his power were deemed to be tyrannical, the constable was empowered to take over the reins of government. [My emphasis.]

Rosemary Horrox adds that in Edward IV's reign, Richard's role as constable seemed to become yet broader, even being tasked with looking into more general forms of treason and disaffection.[6]

A snub by the council, as alleged by Mancini, was both unlikely and uncharacteristic. What is more striking is that the supposed rebuff is mentioned nowhere by the Crowland chronicler, who was in a position to record it, and with some satisfaction.

Thus, if Mancini (uniquely) heard of objections to the case put by Richard, just as with the wagons of Woodville weapons, it is more likely that they emanated from his informants than from the council.

We have mentioned the special Constable's Court before, and we shall encounter it again in a later chapter, so the following summary by Ross is germane; he says the court during Richard's tenure was used:

> when the security of the realm was threatened by treason and insurrection as well as general disorder ... It was a summary court, acting without indictment and without benefit of trial by jury, and it employed a law other than the common law of England ... The king could 'record' a verdict based upon his knowledge of notorious treason without further justification.[7]

Given the prevailing unrest around the capital, with conflicting factions calling men to arms, the situation called for firm control on the part of Richard as protector/constable. But still he stayed his hand. The hostages remained in custody with their fate in the balance for a full eight weeks while Elizabeth and her family continued jeopardizing them by their activities against the new régime.

* * *

During the rest of May the council continued working at full tilt, sometimes dividing itself into subcommittees to concentrate on specific projects, while Richard of Gloucester doubtless spent long hours acquainting himself with matters of domestic and foreign policy. Yet however unprepared he might have been to assume the role of protector, nothing could have prepared him for the next bombshell that was to be dropped in his path.

It concerned an accusation that the marriage between the late King Edward IV and Queen Elizabeth was not only clandestine but also bigamous. This had far-reaching implications for the legitimacy of their offspring, notably the boy Edward V and his right to the succession.

As reflected in the records of the time, the story went as follows: some time before his secret marriage in 1464 to Elizabeth

Woodville, Edward had entered into an equally secret marriage with the high-born Lady Eleanor Butler, née Talbot, elder daughter of the 1st Earl of Shrewsbury by his second wife, Lady Margaret Beauchamp. (To preserve consistency we will adhere to maiden names.) Lady Eleanor's identity is confirmed, *inter alia*, by the Crowland chronicler and by official parliamentary records which were later suppressed.

To flesh out these bare bones, let us add the additional details that have subsequently come to light:[8] first let us dispose of the allegation that Lady Eleanor was a mistress of Edward IV in her youth. Born in 1436, she was already married to Thomas (later Sir Thomas) Butler in 1450 when Edward was eight years old. John Ashdown-Hill is the author of her definitive biography, *Eleanor, the Secret Queen*, and he asserts that her husband had met his death by early 1460, quite possibly fighting for the house of Lancaster: 'She seems to have been noted for her piety,' he comments. 'We know little of Eleanor's character or appearance, although she is reputed to have been both beautiful and virtuous. The fact that she attracted the attention of Edward IV is sufficient, perhaps, to vouch for the former, while both her insistence on marriage and her later life style could be considered evidence for the latter quality.'[9]

The circumstances of how they met are unknown, but it seems to have been at some time after March 1461. Dr Ashdown-Hill observes that, to the best of his knowledge, no one has ever denied the existence of a relationship between them. 'Edward seems to have played out with her a similar scene to the one he was later to enact with Elizabeth Woodville,' he comments. To assist this comparison, we have the Mancini report to thank for the prevailing story current in the 1480s of Edward's wooing of Elizabeth: 'that when Edward put a dagger to her throat to make her submit to his lust she remained unperturbed and determined to die rather than live unchastely with him.' Mancini's original editor, C.A.J. Armstrong, commented that such a story had been known at an early date in North Italy, possibly soon after 1464, and had reappeared later in sixteenth-century sources.

Force, unfortunately, was not unusual in the relationships of mediæval men with their women, whether of high or humble rank; the fact that this was a common story shows that, true or not, it was believable of the young Edward IV. Knowing this, it might even have been put about by the Woodville clan in order to enhance Elizabeth's standing. Another clue to Edward's character is given by Mancini: it was said he had been 'most insulting to many women after he had possessed them'. Mancini also claims that he took none by force, somewhat contradicting his own titbit about the wooing of Elizabeth Woodville. In any case, there is no way Mancini could have known the truth of it.

Whether or not coercion was involved with Lady Eleanor, we have a statement in the *Memoirs* of Philippe de Commynes that he 'promised to marry her, provided he could sleep with her first, and she consented'. De Commynes further volunteers that Edward made this promise 'in the Bishop [of Bath and Wells]'s presence. And having done so, he slept with her'.[10]

The *Memoirs* of Philippe de Commynes are discussed elsewhere (see Appendix). Although it was his business to be particularly well-informed on foreign affairs, he was not necessarily reliable in matters of detail. Hence we may accept his identification of Robert Stillington, Bishop of Bath and Wells, as the cleric who was the custodian of this remarkable secret, while noting inaccuracies in incidental facts. He even claims that Stillington actually married them, although this is not confirmed as there is no recorded evidence of the marriage. Stillington (a canon at the time) might have been no more than a witness, although given the secrecy of the event it seems doubtful there would have been very many clerics in attendance.

Referring again to information provided by John Ashdown-Hill, we learn that Robert Stillington held a number of appointments in 1461, including that of Keeper of the Privy Seal. Edward favoured him towards the end of that year with the award of an annual salary of £365. His elevation to the bishopric of Bath and Wells came in early 1465, a few months after Edward had made public his Woodville marriage. One might conclude that the two events were not unconnected. Later in his career he became Edward's Lord Chancellor (1467–70 and 1471–73), an ambassador to Brittany, and a key figure in Edward's extensive trading activities, which perhaps enabled the bishop to augment his already considerable wealth.

Dr Ashdown-Hill has noted that Lady Eleanor, whose income in widowhood was not substantial, somehow acquired holdings in her own right in Wiltshire whose documentation is singularly lacking in legal formalities. Could they have been a gift from the king? Other members of her family are also recorded as receiving royal favours around the time of Edward IV's Woodville marriage and its revelation (1464–5).[11]

Lady Eleanor's first marriage produced no children, and there is no evidence of her bearing a child with Edward as the father. Evidently his interest in her soon waned, perhaps hastened by her predilection for religion: in the 1460s she became closely involved with the Carmelite Friary in Norwich, of which she became a lay associate, perhaps a *manumissa* or a *conversa*. Little more is known of her life, and she died on 30 June 1468 at the early age of 32.

At this point in our story we encounter something that is crucial for readers to bear in mind: a massive division exists between those historians and commentators who have a good opinion of Richard III and those who do not; and that division tends to reside in whether the precontract with Lady Eleanor Talbot is considered true or merely a fabrication. It is from this starting point that the two opposing views diverge. This is the reason why so much space in this chapter will be devoted to examining it.

It must be emphasized that no proof now exists that the prior marriage did or did not take place, and reactions were mixed even in 1483 (we need not concern ourselves with the speculation of later chroniclers, who were in no position to have an informed opinion). It is logical, of course, that people of intelligence would be both incredulous and sceptical at such an unheard-of revelation, and fearful of its import. This might result in disapproval, as expressed by Mancini, and possibly opposition as in the *Crowland Chronicle*, but disapproval and opposition do not in themselves constitute evidence that the claim was spurious. The fact is that whereas the existence of the precontract is confirmed for all to see in an Act of Parliament, no report exists, nor does any documentary evidence survive, of any argument refuting it.

Thus it is important to bear in mind that the widespread dismissal of the precontract by traditional historians is not based on solid proof, but on mere supposition: it seems too opportune, it seems incredible, and some of the written records are censorious; therefore they choose to view it cynically. Yet it should be noted that James Gairdner, that most traditional of historians whose anti-Richard views reigned supreme for three-quarters of a century, nevertheless believed in the existence of the precontract with Lady Eleanor.

* * *

To examine the case as it was viewed in 1483, we must now discuss the significance of this precontract of marriage. The word 'precontract', by the way, which is often misunderstood to mean 'betrothal' or perhaps 'preliminary contract', is actually a precise term used to signify a *previous marriage* when alleged as a challenge to a subsequent marriage.[12]

First, therefore, we have to look at the mediæval view of what constituted a marriage. The following observations are taken from Mary O'Regan:[13]

> A valid marriage could be formed by the simple exchange of consents. No ceremony, or witnesses, or priest, were needed. What was necessary was that these vows should be in the present tense – *sponsalia per verba de praesenti* – 'I do marry you'.
>
> What we would call 'solemn betrothal' is referred to in mediæval canon law as *sponsalia per verba de futuro*. In such espousals, some such words as 'I promise I will marry you' were exchanged between the parties. This did not form a binding contract in itself ... But if intercourse took place between the betrothed pair this had the effect of validating and completing their marriage.

If the precontract was an exchange of consents *per verba de praesenti*, and if (as Philippe de Commynes tells us) Robert Stillington claimed to have been a witness, then O'Regan asserts, 'His sworn evidence before the proper court would probably have been sufficient to prove the fact of the marriage, both parties being dead.'

If it was a case of *verba de futuro*, it was the subsequent act of intercourse (which we can scarcely doubt took place) that 'would have converted the formless contract *de futuro* into a valid

marriage'. Thus, Edward IV already had a wife when he married
Elizabeth Woodville in 1464.

Viewing the situation from a modern standpoint, some writers
maintain that Eleanor's death in 1468 rendered the Woodville
union valid after that date. This would mean that Edward V
and his brother were legitimate, since they were born in 1470
and 1473 respectively. This claim has been refuted by Professor
R.H. Helmholz, a leading authority on mediæval canon law, who
has pointed out that in fact the opposite was the case: 'Under
mediæval canon law, adultery, when coupled with a present
contract of marriage, was an *impediment* to the subsequent marriage
of the adulterous partners' (my emphasis). There were conditions
under which this harsh impediment was capable of being set aside,
but they would depend upon facts which would need to have been
proved, and never were. In any case further debate 'is rendered
unnecessary because of the clandestine nature of the marriage
between Edward and Elizabeth'.[14]

True, clandestine marriages were considered valid and
binding, even though they were sinful and subjected the parties
to penance. However, according to Helmholz, 'It does not
follow that the legitimacy of the children was not affected by
the fact of clandestinity.' In fact it was very seriously affected.
To summarize: although there were circumstances under which
the children of the Woodville union might have been deemed
legitimate under canon law, those circumstances would apply
only if their parents had contracted marriage according to
the laws of the Church (i.e. *in facie ecclesiae*). It was precisely
the clandestinity of the marriage that ensured the offspring
remained illegitimate.

Another point sometimes raised is the public recognition of the
marriage by the highest authorities of Church and State over an
extended period. Once again Professor Helmholz shows that the
clandestinity of the marriage was the aspect that prevented any
such grounds for presumption of a valid marriage with legitimate
children, which he explained could exist only where the marriage
had been contracted *in facie ecclesiae*.

Finally he addressed the argument that once the parties to the
precontract had died it was too late to dredge the matter up again.
On the contrary: 'canon law specifically allowed the question
of bastardy to be raised after the death of the parents in order to

determine questions of inheritance. ... The mediæval canon law allowed the matter to be raised when it was.'

In Helmholz's view, therefore, there was a 'legitimate cause of action' in the matter of whether the Woodville marriage was invalid and its offspring illegitimate. We may also safely assume that Bishop Stillington, a doctor of canon law himself, would have known the precise canonical position.

There is one more legal aspect that remains to be discussed, and this is a subject on which experts tend *not* to speak with one voice. It concerns two sides of the same coin: succession to the throne. On the one side there is the civil law regarding bastardization and inheritance, and on the other there is the question of whether, and to what extent, such legal principles were applicable to the succession of the sovereign.

Mary O'Regan examines both these matters in the article quoted above, and her conclusions are (briefly) as follows:

(a) Civil law had an important role to play in matters of inheritance. 'Hence, decisions as to general bastardy – whether the parents' marriage had ever taken place or was a lawful marriage – were given by the bishop's court, and questions of special bastardy, related to succession, descent and inheritance, were triable "by the country".'

(b) In the debate whether the monarchy is governed by the laws of hereditary descent, O'Regan feels it is not clear that the crown is regarded as 'real property', even though it may happen for the most part to follow the conventions of feudal inheritance. 'If the rules of real property succession did apply unchanged to the crown, then not only Richard but "many of our mediæval kings, as well as all those after 1689, would be usurpers".[15] The pertinent example is Henry VII, whose sole claim to the throne was by right of conquest.'

In this aspect, therefore, O'Regan concludes that 'the crown is neither real property nor a peerage, but *sui generis* – unique – and that its descent need not follow the rules customary in either of those things'.

'As to inheritance and succession to the crown by Prince Edward,' she observes, 'these were triable "by the country", and Parliament, being the court of final appeal, had the right to decide the issue.' She adds a cavil as to whether the 1484 Parliament gave reasoned consideration to the matter; but

Dr Anne Sutton assures us that it was indeed thoroughly debated by Richard III's Parliament of January 1484 (see chapter 12).

It is as well to bear in mind the unique nature of the crown when considering the sometimes dogmatic assertions of historians, many of whom take the narrow, feudal view. When one regards the sovereignty of England as *sui generis*, considerations are admitted which may be of more importance than direct bloodlines.

Professor Michael Hicks offers this summary: 'A king's title had three parts: hereditary right; election or acclamation of the people; and conquest.' He regards the hereditary aspect to be paramount ('the hereditary title had to be made out first'), although title by inheritance 'was not precisely defined'. Illegitimacy and kingship, he claims, were not incompatible: 'Even if Edward's sons were bastards, William the Conqueror was not the only bastard to be a mediæval king.'[16]

But here Hicks has reversed his own criteria. William's claim to the throne on grounds of heredity was contested: he won it purely by conquest. Henry Tudor, of bastard stock specifically barred from the throne, won it by the same means. They both extinguished the rightful line. If comparisons are to be made, better would be a case where a choice existed between a bastard son and a deceased king's younger brother. This was precisely the position with the Duke of Monmouth whose illegitimacy was a fatal barrier to succeeding his father Charles II, who like Edward IV produced no legitimate heir. In 1685 the brother was preferred, as in 1483.

With Edward V the obstacle was not merely the illegitimacy but the age of the child. Had he been a grown man, proven in judgement, leadership and valour, perhaps he might have made good his claim to rule. But the boy had no qualification to undertake the mighty burden of mediæval sovereignty save that he was son to a king, and if that sole qualification was flawed, he would always be open to challenges.

This view is underlined by David Baldwin who states:

> primogeniture was only one factor (and not necessarily the determining one) in the succession ... There had been four occasions between the Conquest and the end of the twelfth century – in 1087, 1100, 1135 and 1199 – when a deceased ruler

had been succeeded by a claimant other than his nearest blood relative; ... the precedent that a reigning king should be succeeded by his eldest son (or, alternatively, his eldest grandson) had been established by 1400.[17]

Baldwin suggests, 'if the revolution of 1399 had not taken place and Richard II had died from natural causes after reigning a year or two longer, the peers would almost certainly have turned to Gaunt's son, Henry of Derby, who was in his mid-thirties and enjoyed a reputation as a man of action,' rather than the youthful Edmund Mortimer, even though the latter was descended from Gaunt's elder brother Clarence. 'A child who was nearest in blood to the late king could not expect to prevail against the claims of a more distant but potentially more able candidate.'

The position of a child heir had never been secure, as G.M. Trevelyan observed when discussing the claim of Harold Godwinson against the boy Edgar the Atheling in 1066:[18] 'England had never observed a strict law of hereditary succession; the passing over of minors was quite usual though not obligatory.' Trevelyan also emphasized that 'in Europe all monarchies were, within certain limits, originally elective'.

To conclude this debate, B.P. Wolffe argues that although there was in the fourteenth and fifteenth centuries 'a strong predilection' for primogeniture,

usurpation by the strongest and ablest male member of the larger royal family became almost the norm. From 1399 special 'inauguration ceremonies', by which the king performed every kind of royal act prior to his coronation, were designed to convert usurpation into a valid authority. The office of king was a very exacting one. Its holder had to be physically tough, able to win battles and campaigns, with a commanding presence and integrity; able to inspire loyalty, service and confidence.[19]

★ ★ ★

Before we continue with the events that followed Bishop Stillington's astonishing revelation, readers will perhaps be interested to examine Lady Eleanor's position in all this. Why did she hold her peace after being bedded and discarded by the king? Why did she not come forward and claim her rightful place as Queen of England?

Muriel Smith maintains she might have had no wish to be Edward's wife: 'It is possible that she had taken a vow of chastity, as was not particularly uncommon for a widow.' Eleanor's reason for submitting to Edward's advances may simply have been that he would not accept her repeated refusals, 'and in the end she yielded to the threat of force'.[20]

'There is here,' she continues, 'a point of canon law. The decretal of Alexander III (1180) provides that a bride may enter religion within the two months following the marriage if it has not been consummated, and once she has taken the habit the bridegroom is automatically free to marry again. The question then arises whether a marriage is, technically speaking, consummated by a forced act of intercourse.' After quoting various opinions, Smith concludes that most authorities concede 'the bride is not deprived, by forced intercourse, of her canonical right to use her option during the first two months. This, then, might lead to a situation in which Eleanor regarded herself as not married, and Edward was in honest doubt whether he was married or not, and dared not ask in case he was.'

As for the two months option, John Ashdown-Hill makes the valuable point that Lady Eleanor's choice was a lay association with the Carmelites, rather than actually taking the veil, which 'could perhaps be seen as evidence that she was not free to become a nun because she had a living husband'.

In another article[21] he discusses her deed of gift of land holdings, a few weeks before her death, to her sister Elizabeth. He suggests this was perhaps because a will would have needed to name a husband, if living, and indicate his consent. However, a deed of gift was fairly routine in the 1460s – and it, too, required a husband's agreement, as did a testament, which she also drew up. So although there is nothing to disprove Dr Ashdown-Hill's suggestion, these arrangements are equally compatible with Eleanor acting as a widow.

Although Eleanor had powerful family connections, they may well have advised silence as the best policy. One does not lightly attempt to enforce one's rights against a resistant king. Indeed, such an idea became fraught with difficulty, if not danger, once Edward married his new wife and the Woodville family entered the fray.

Eleanor's father, the illustrious Old Talbot, was dead by then, but she was a niece by marriage of the Kingmaker and first cousin to the Neville sisters, Isabel and Anne, who later married Edward IV's brothers, the Dukes of Clarence and Gloucester. It is possible that members of her family, including her mother, the Dowager Countess of Shrewsbury, knew of the episode with Edward. Indeed, Ashdown-Hill suggests that 'perhaps Edward's failure to do anything to resolve the long-standing Berkeley inheritance dispute, in which the countess was involved, was an act of deliberate policy on his part, since while the matter remained unresolved it gave him a hold over the countess'.

In his view, given Eleanor's family relationship to Richard's wife Anne, 'It is doubtful … whether Richard would have chosen deliberately to bring her name into the public eye as he did, had the allegation been unsubstantiated.'

Another factor to remember is that Warwick the Kingmaker, who could have learned something about it, had a private agenda of his own. Throughout the period of his insurrection (1469–71) he was claiming that Edward IV was illegitimate while promoting the Duke of Clarence as heir to the throne with his own daughter Isabel as consort. If he secretly suspected the Woodville marriage was invalid and its offspring potentially tainted, perhaps he was hugging this knowledge to himself ready to reveal it if his first line of attack proved unsuccessful. After all, those offspring did not become a significant factor until a male heir arrived in late 1470. Unfortunately, by then his star witness (Eleanor) had died. Warwick himself was killed in April 1471.

It is just possible that Warwick decided to tell Clarence so as to ensure the secret did not die with him. Would he entrust explosive knowledge of this sort to such a loose cannon? Quite conceivably he covered the eventuality by asking Bishop Stillington, in case of his death, to tell Clarence at some opportune moment; which Stillington probably put off for as long as he could.

In relation to Clarence, John Ashdown-Hill argues that Warwick's *protégé* and son-in-law did become aware of the precontract 'and this fact,' he suggests, 'explains both some of Clarence's behaviour and his execution'. One of the official treasons for which Clarence was condemned in 1478 was that he had kept an exemplification of an undertaking under the seal of Henry VI making him heir to the throne if Henry and his son died without male issue. Thus there is little doubt that he was still clinging to some deluded idea of disinheriting and replacing Edward, even at so late a date.

We know for a fact that Bishop Stillington, once Edward IV's chancellor, was committed to the Tower by Edward in 1478 (hard on the heels of Clarence's execution), denounced for something 'prejudicial to the king and his estate'. He was released soon afterwards (certainly by mid-April when he was appointed to a Berkshire Commission of the Peace) and in June secured a pardon after paying a heavy fine. It has been suggested that the link between Stillington's 'prejudicial act' and Clarence's treason was that, at some point during the 1470s, the bishop informed Clarence of the precontract, upon which the latter started secretly rebuilding his hopes of supplanting his brother. Stillington had been close to Clarence for many years: his diocese lay in the heart of the duke's land holdings, and he was among those who persuaded Clarence in 1470 to return to his family allegiance. The suggestion that, possessing this information, Clarence was put to death at the insistence of the Woodvilles has been postulated by eminent writers and historians including Sharon Turner, James Gairdner, Sir Clements Markham, and Paul Murray Kendall.

Muriel Smith, in the article quoted above, addresses the knotty question of why Edward IV took no steps to regularize the situation by arranging a subsequent public marriage to Elizabeth. She explains that a sacrament, if valid, cannot actually be repeated. 'In case of doubt, the safer course must be taken and [the marriage] be repeated *sub conditione*, conditionally.' Unfortunately the king could not afford to admit of such doubts himself. He might overcome the problem by consenting to be 'publicly rebuked for the clandestinity of his marriage' – but certainly not by one of his own subjects. This would have been a matter for the pope.

The difficulty here was the available time-frame in which to get any such procedure carried out. It could have been attempted only after Eleanor's death in 1468 and before Edward's queen produced a male child. After the latter, of course, no possible doubt must be cast on the royal marriage.

As Smith points out, 'Rome never hurries'. Edward was doubt-less pondering the problem when the Lancastrian conspiracies started brewing in the second half of 1468, culminating in arrests and trials that continued through to early 1469. Rebellions in the north ensued in the spring and summer of 1469, quickly followed by Warwick's July insurrection in which Edward was captured and held prisoner. From that moment until he recovered his throne, in May of 1471, he could do nothing further in the matter of the marriage. Meanwhile, his first son had been born in November 1470.

We have spent some time examining the precontract revelation, but the digression is a necessary one because of the heated disputes that surround it. To Ricardians it is perfectly plausible that Edward, a known womanizer, should have played the game of entering into a secret marriage to secure a reluctant lady's sexual favours. To traditionalists the story is totally bogus, a red herring, and far too conveniently produced at the very moment when it suited Richard to make a play for the crown.

At least we know, from experts in canon law, that given the existence of the precontract, it was a perfectly good conclusion on canonical grounds that Edward's Woodville children were illegitimate. The question must now be asked, why was this case not subjected to canonical court review?

Over the centuries, much has been made of the allegation that Richard and his supporters leapt to assume the new king was debarred from the throne by reason of bastardy, without putting the case to the test of an ecclesiastical court. This is cited as proof that they knew their story would not stand up to scrutiny.

However, Richard is known to have had an informed understanding of the law, so he was doubtless well aware that it was not his place to assert the charge of precontract. He was last in the chronological list of people who had been let in on the secret, he had heard it at second hand twenty-two years after the event and probably had the least proof at his disposal. More importantly, he was not one of the principals in the case.

As John Ashdown-Hill explains,

the onus of bringing the matter before an ecclesiastical court properly belonged ... to one of the parties to the dispute – and the only living parties in 1483 were Elizabeth Woodville and her children – and not to Richard who was not directly involved in any way in the point of canon law which was at issue.

The strict legal position was that any person who had knowledge of a matter that invalidated a marriage must come forward, or become an accessory. At the time of the Woodville marriage this onus applied to Stillington, to Eleanor's family, and to anyone else who knew about the precontract (Lord Hastings being a prime candidate). However, because this second marriage took place in secret, the parties to it conveniently avoided the possibility of any such impediment being made public at the time of the wedding.

Now, some twenty years later, the outcome of Edward IV's recklessness resulted in a very serious dilemma for those whose task it was to govern the country and uphold the rule of law. Was the present king legitimately entitled to wear the crown?

Professor Helmholz explains the legal position: although legitimacy of birth was a matter that mediæval canon law decreed should be tried by the Church, nevertheless:

> rights of inheritance, the canon law conceded, belonged to secular determination ... Therefore, under a specific decretal of Pope Alexander III, the proper procedure was to suspend the secular trial whenever a question of legitimacy was raised, and refer the matter to the proper ecclesiastical tribunal, which would determine the limited question of bastardy and certify its answer to the secular court. The secular court could, in turn, finish the case.

In this instance it was not so referred, but instead was decided by Parliament.

What we can say, with Helmholz, is that when it came to deciding who should rule England, urgency was paramount. 'To have opened the case up to the exigencies of litigation would have invited delay of a quite intolerable sort. Affairs of state had to prevail over full exploration of the issues. This is not a dilemma our own age has solved.' Allied to this is a political question of some significance: what mediæval kingdom would wish to have the succession decided (essentially) by Rome?

Nevertheless, although it is true we have no report of the matter being discussed by the Church, this does not preclude some such discussions having taken place.

In the British Library Harleian record of items that passed under Richard's personal seal or signet, there is a writ dating to about 16 May 1483. In it King Edward V, via the protector, calls upon Thomas Bourchier, Archbishop of Canterbury, to summon at St Paul's a convocation of the southern clergy to consider 'certain difficult and urgent matters closely concerning us and the state of our realm of England and the honour and benefit of the English Church'. Further matters are to be raised at the time of the meeting.[22]

Dr Pamela Tudor-Craig, among others, has suggested that this reference to 'difficult and urgent matters' was not a normal convocation mandate, but an indication of crisis and an attempt to find a responsible solution. The conclusion may be correct, but the premise on which it is based does not, however, withstand scrutiny. Comparison of the Latin text reveals that it closely follows the standard form used in other convocation mandates of similar date. There is a difference in that this document twice uses the phrase 'honour and benefit of the English Church', rather than emphasizing security and defence of the kingdom, but the distinction is a small one. [23]

Neither Edward V's writ nor any resultant convocation is recorded in Archbishop Bourchier's register: the section relating to convocations ends suddenly and much earlier (in 1481) at folio 30v. Afterwards, pages seem to be missing. At first sight this appeared suspicious, but further research has now revealed that, although two convocations were called early in the year, none at all took place in 1483, despite what one would assume was a pressing royal need for the tax known as the clerical 'tenth'. (A convocation called earlier by Edward IV is supposed, by many experts, to have taken place on 18 April, but this is not supported by the Bishop of Lincoln's register and is contra-indicated by the date itself – being that of Edward's own funeral. Another salutary reminder not to rely on secondary sources!)

Previous editions of this book have suggested that it may have been Richard's first instinct to seek advice from convocation on the question of the precontract. Certainly a convocation was called, and must later have been cancelled. Perhaps it was felt that such explosive matters were best discussed by a more discreet private gathering of clerical experts on canon law.

★ ★ ★

To pick up the threads of our original narrative, we now find ourselves somewhere in late May/early June of 1483, with Richard having heard Stillington's precontract story. He was aware that Bishop Stillington's reason for raising the matter was that he knew it put the succession in jeopardy; the bishop's sworn testimony as witness to the marriage was sufficient proof for any ecclesiastical body. Richard would doubtless also have obtained second opinions from other lawyers, and the picture was beginning to look decidedly gloomy for the offspring of Edward IV. A dark cloud of doubt surrounded the succession, and as soon as word got out it would be sufficient excuse for uprisings, rebellions and the settling of old scores.

The obvious next step was to investigate every aspect of the precontract, trying to discover what was known and who knew it. When all possible information had been uncovered, an official meeting of the foremost dignitaries of the realm was necessary to consider these developments. This is widely held to have taken place on Monday 9 June, an event which was reported in a letter of the same date from Simon Stallworth to William Stonor. Stallworth was well placed to hear the news in London, being in the household of John Russell, Bishop of Lincoln, currently Lord Chancellor. In this letter, having remarked that the queen was still in sanctuary (with Bishop Lionel Woodville and others), Stallworth reported: 'My lorde Protector, my lorde of Buckyngham, with all othyr lordys as wele temporale as spirituale wer at Westminstre in the councelchamber from 10 to 2 butt there wass none that spake with the Qwene. There is gret besyness ageyns the Coronacione wyche schalbe this day fortnyght as we sey.'[24]

Clearly this four-hour meeting had weighty business to consider – and it should be noted that although it took place in the council chamber, Stallworth actually describes the participants as 'the lords temporal and spiritual'. This is not a normal way of referring to the members of the King's Council, and indeed this phrase is usually found referring to the Upper House of Parliament. Here it very likely indicates a meeting of the Great Council. Certainly this was a more significant assembly than would routinely be called, and reveals an occasion of uncommon consequence.

Stallworth also felt it significant enough to mention that no one spoke with Elizabeth Woodville. We know negotiations with the queen dowager had been in progress since at least 23 May, so obviously there had hitherto been contact with her on a regular basis. Perhaps those councillors who kept a foot in both camps were in the habit of visiting nearby Westminster Abbey to update her on council discussions, or perhaps a formal deputation was occasionally sent. Either way, the absence of contact was unusual enough to be remarked upon, which chimes with the likelihood that there were sensitive matters under discussion which concerned her closely.

Such an augmented Council must have deliberated on weighty matters; but it was not yet time to reconsider the coronation, and Edward continued signing warrants as king until at least 18 June.

It is difficult to resist the conclusion that this was the occasion when Stillington's news of the precontract was aired; in which case the meeting must have been summoned several days earlier to ensure that participants from outlying districts would have sufficient notice to allow them to reach Westminster. On this basis, I would challenge the widespread assumption that Stillington revealed the precontract story to Richard only the previous day, on Sunday 8 June, whereupon it was immediately blurted out to a meeting of the nobility. Much more likely is that a thorough process of checking and evidence-gathering needed to be undertaken on a twenty-year-old incident, as well as the seeking of legal and clerical opinions.

The Tudor publisher Richard Grafton in his *Chronicle at Large* (1569), elaborating on Hall's *Chronicle*, depicted Richard bringing in 'authentic doctors, proctors and notaries of the law, with depositions from divers witnesses'. We need not suppose Grafton had any special knowledge of what happened in 1483, although this helpfully recounts for modern eyes the kinds of procedures he thought would have been involved. Since the precontract was indeed accepted as fact by the government of the realm, and later enshrined in law, even the most cynical commentator must concede that some depositions and witness statements were heard. The groundwork for all this would have occupied several weeks before it could be concluded that a case needed to be put to the foremost lords of the land. This places Stillington's revelation no later, surely, than the middle of May.

The next information we have about Richard's actions is that on 10 and 11 June he suddenly decided he needed the support of troops from home. Entrusting messages to one of his most loyal lieutenants, Sir Richard Ratcliffe, he wrote urgently to his northern city of York and to Lord Neville of Raby. To the men of York, his staunch allies, Richard wrote:

> We hertely pray you to come unto us to London in all the diligence ye can possible aftir the sight herof, with as mony as ye can make defensibly arraied, their to eide and assiste us ayanst the Quiene, hir blode adherentts and affinitie, which have entended, and daly doith intend, to murder and utterly distroy us and our cousyn the duc of Bukkyngham, and the old royall blode of this realme, and as it is now openly knowen, by their subtill and dampnabill wais forcasted the same.[25]

We will return to 'forecasting' in chapter 7.

The sum total of troops that eventually reached London, as we know from various chronicles, numbered in the region of 4,000. Richard, who had left Yorkshire less than two months previously, certainly had an accurate idea of what numbers were available, so presumably a force this size was adequate to quell any actions against the governing party – a show of strength to let the Woodvilles know he was prepared to act decisively.

Richard identifies those enemies as 'the queen, her blood adherents and affinity', who had presumably reacted immediately and furiously as soon as they got wind that the precontract had been revealed. It need hardly be stressed that in the turbulent times of the fifteenth century, a network of spies and informants was vital to the survival of any magnate. Edward IV, his queen and her Woodville family would have controlled the most extensive and sophisticated of such networks. The Woodvilles had amassed considerable power over the years, as Mancini confirms. They were also well provisioned from the late king's and dowager queen's wealth which had accompanied her into sanctuary. From this we may conclude that even now they had trusty eyes and ears at their disposal.

Whether through informants or, more likely, from personal knowledge, Elizabeth would have known all about Bishop Stillington's revelation long before its official disclosure at the meeting on 9 June. Her need to silence Clarence in 1477 suggests prior knowledge of the precontract; if so the mere hint of Stillington's private audiences with Richard, and the probable comings and goings of messengers, could have alerted her to this threat.

Consequently her party would have had time to engage in planning their counter-move during the entire period that Richard's agents were seeking evidence to verify Stillington's story. Which explains why their machinations were sufficiently advanced for Richard to learn of them (through his own spies and intercepts) as a full-blown conspiracy by 9 or 10 June; by which time he realized he must look to his personal safety.

5

Battle Lines are Drawn

As Mancini moves forward with his narrative, he describes two events in June 1483 that did not occur in the order in which he relates them. Despite the disbelief of historians, it is obvious to me that it must be through Mancini's mistake that the majority of later chroniclers made the same error.

The first occurrence chronologically was one of the most incredible episodes of that dramatic year, when the protector without warning arrested several council members.

It was on Friday 13 June that the life and career of William, Lord Hastings came to an end after a council meeting at the Tower of London. We have seen that in the days immediately following the assembly of lords on 9 June, when the precontract was probably discussed, Richard sent urgently to his northern supporters citing an armed threat from the Woodvilles.

Thanks to Vergil, it is widely believed that Hastings had allied, surprisingly, with the queen. This foreign chronicler, brought to England two decades later by Henry VII, misrecorded the facts as reported by Mancini and Crowland: Vergil claimed there was a movement under Hastings's leadership that threatened to wrest the new King Edward from the protector by violence. On the contrary, the *Crowland Chronicle* had Hastings 'bursting with joy' at the turn of events: when the Woodvilles attempted to raise armed forces in early May, 'there were partisans of one side and of the other … taking this side or that. Some collected their associates and stood by at Westminster in the name of the queen, others at London under the protection of Lord Hastings.' So at that time he was a focal point for supporting Richard.

Much later there are explicit references to intrigues in the summer of 1483 aimed at taking possession of Edward IV's royal children, which we will return to consider later: among the sources are the *Crowland Chronicle* and the Tudor antiquary John Stow. There is evidence that perpetrators of plots were apprehended. Probably all such attempts in mid-1483 resulted from Woodville conspiracies set in train after Richard's accession, aimed at restoring the deposed Edward V to the throne. But Hastings's treachery on 13 June was much earlier, spearheading a small group of malcontents in a precipitate attempt on Richard's person. Arrested as their leader, for treasonously entering the protector's presence bearing concealed arms, Hastings was summarily executed. Since preparations were still in progress for Edward V's coronation, we must find earlier reasons for their actions.

This episode is the single incident in Richard's career that most perplexes historians. A few, of course, attribute it merely to a ruthless ambition that does not balk at eliminating even his brother's oldest friend (and his own erstwhile supporter). However, those who delve into these matters more deeply are concerned to seek reasons. Even a man of ambition, however ruthless, does not risk committing a wanton act of destruction, especially of a widely esteemed and powerful magnate – and in front of witnesses – unless with very good cause. And Richard seems not to have been taken unawares. So why had Hastings turned against the protector?

Though several co-conspirators were later rounded up, Hastings was the instigator when it came to the physical attack: if others had political motives, his were clearly personal. Aware of Richard's public declaration to remove those responsible for his brother's downfall, Hastings could not help but see his power and influence vanishing under Richard's protectorship, now set to be extended formally by Parliament. Buckingham had ostentatiously cornered the position of right-hand man, being heaped with honours and offices, while Hastings was merely re-appointed to the Mint, affording no place at Court. This was a major setback in a status-driven world where preferment depended on royal access. It must have dawned painfully on the older man that, far from being drawn into the elite circle of the protector, he had been identified among the corrupting influences Richard was determined to eradicate.

Hastings's second reason for dismay was that the report of the precontract, which would have reached him as soon as it reached Richard, was being taken very seriously. It threatened the bastardization and disinheritance of Edward IV's children, with the crown devolving elsewhere (the principal candidates being Richard of Gloucester and Clarence's eight-year-old son Edward, Earl of Warwick). After so many years building close ties with the Prince of Wales, such an eventuality would eliminate Hastings's hopes of pre-eminence in the service of Edward IV's successor, a second mortal blow to his expectations.

I believe there was a clincher in the humiliation that now faced Hastings. With the investigation of the precontract he could well expect to face some unpleasant questioning as to his knowledge of Edward IV's liaisons with the young women who entered into secret marriages with him. If suspicion emerged that he connived at the Woodville marriage in full knowledge of the Talbot marriage, he could expect to pay the time-honoured penalty of disgrace and punishment as the royal adviser whose influence led to the downfall of his master's heirs. Richard had already made it clear what he thought of those who encouraged his brother's grosser predilections.

The question then arises: what might Hastings gain as a result of his defection? Simply that if Richard were eliminated, the *status quo ante* would be restored. Admittedly the balance of power would revert to the Woodvilles, but necessity made them bedfellows. Rather the devil you know than the devil you don't. The Woodvilles had the boy-king's favour; they had his siblings in sanctuary and they still had plenty of funds and status and influence. Given their urgent need for support, he could look forward to rich rewards in the offing.

From the Woodville point of view this was an acceptable bargain. Even before the precontract emerged, it had become clear that for the boy to rest securely on the throne he needed more power behind him than could be raised by his mother's family. Now, if he should be declared illegitimate, only a power base of massive proportions could retrieve the situation. Hastings was one of the few magnates who commanded sufficient wealth, position and military might to provide this.

If Hastings struck immediately, Richard's and Buckingham's puny contingent would be overwhelmed easily. As for Bishop

Stillington, they would expect little difficulty in silencing him under suitable pressure (or simply clapping him in prison, as Edward IV had done). Without his testimony the precontract could be hushed up once more, or a procession of other witnesses coerced into refuting his assertions.

All this would be possible once they reversed the embarrassing position of weakness in which they presently found themselves. The catalyst that brought Hastings on board was undoubtedly the threat to his prospects, and theirs, contained in the precontract revelation.

In Hastings's eyes, a *rapprochement* between himself and Elizabeth Woodville would present no difficulty. After all, his quarrel over the years had not centred on her, but first on Rivers and more recently on Dorset. If he allied himself with Edward V and his mother, he would still be the senior partner; lesser members of the family would fall into line.

Of course he could never afford to be seen personally visiting Elizabeth in sanctuary, and the same applied to any agent of his household, so negotiations would have been carried out through third parties. This would explain why Mancini drew attention to the fact that Hastings was one of a small group of council members, which included the Bishop of Ely (John Morton) and the Archbishop of York (Thomas Rotherham), who met together in each other's homes – intimating that a conspiracy was being hatched. Two grey-haired clerics were otherwise unlikely associates for the carousing, wenching Captain of Calais. It is scarcely surprising that these dissenting councillors were also present at the Tower, though they may never have expected Hastings to resort to an armed attack.

Six people were certainly arrested, and a seventh is mentioned: a person who was so wily as to have kept his nose clean in the course of many previous double-dealings, and whose loyalty generally depended on where the best profit lay. This was Thomas, Lord Stanley, Hastings's brother-in-law and the current husband of Lady Margaret Beaufort, Henry Tudor's mother.

We know from her later activities that Lady Margaret was adept at insinuating her agents wheresoever she chose, and at this point in her political career she would have been at her most apparently innocuous. Thus she might well have been the conduit for the conspirators to deal with the dowager queen.

Margaret's household included several useful people who later played a leading part in the secret preparations that led to her son's invasion of England. One was her receiver-general, Reginald Bray, who would become one of the Tudor king's most prominent councillors; Bray was a close relative of Hastings's wife, Catherine. There was also Lady Margaret's personal physician, Dr Lewis of Caerleon, who by happy coincidence doubled as Elizabeth's personal physician.

Although Mancini and Crowland do not include Lord Stanley as one of those arrested, there are other sources that do,[1] including Thomas More. On this occasion, one is tempted to believe More owing to the likely eyewitness source of his story, namely Bishop John Morton (see below). If so, Stanley's arrest seems to have been seen immediately as a mistake, which reinforces the idea that it was the involvement of his wife's agents that cast suspicion on him. Stanley himself usually avoided personal involvement until he knew which was the winning side. No censure seems to have been levelled at Lady Margaret, confirming that Richard constantly made the mistake of underestimating her.

His treatment of the remaining conspirators was typically restrained: they were held pending further information-gathering, then in due course released. Lord Stanley was not only quickly liberated but generously compensated. Rotherham was allowed to return to his diocese and Morton, who was placed in the custody of the Duke of Buckingham, later decided his own fate (and revealed his true allegiance) by fleeing to support the Tudor party.

Hastings was not attainted: his family estates went to his widow and children. This suggests a trial and sentencing for treason under the Law of Arms in the summary Court of the Constable of England, with Richard presiding in his office as High Constable.[2] Rebellion by Hastings, captain of the only standing armed force in the realm, was too dangerous to be tolerated. Afterwards Richard behaved generously to his family, rewarding his brother for past services and absolving his widow of her late husband's offences, promising to protect and defend her. He even laid the late king's old friend to rest beside Edward IV at Windsor. Such kindnesses scarcely support the claim that Richard's aim was to terrorize and intimidate.

Crowland categorizes Hastings's execution as part of a plan to eliminate support for Edward V. Mancini gives more detail. The plotters were accused of preparing an ambush, they 'had come with concealed weapons so that they could be the first to unleash a violent attack' – a treasonous offence against the office of Protector of the Realm, although Mancini says it was a 'false name of treason'. The tenor of Mancini's report attributes it to Richard's 'mad lust to rule', and he asserts that it sent townsmen into a panic which could be calmed only when he sent a herald 'to proclaim that a trap had been detected in the fortress and the author of the plot, Hastings, had paid the penalty'. Mancini goes on to add one of his insights into the minds of Londoners, saying that 'many uttered the real truth, namely that it was a pretence by the duke so as to evade the odium of such a crime'.

We need to beware of these supposed motivations touted by Mancini, who does not reveal the identities of the 'many' who somehow know the 'real truth'. It must be remembered that throughout his narrative the Italian has committed himself to the assumption – incapable of proof, of course – that from the moment of Edward IV's death Richard is utterly bent on seizing power. We see this in the opening words of his first chapter where Richard is actuated by 'ambition and lust to rule'. Later, we hear that after Richard took custody of the king at Stony Stratford 'an ill rumour was being circulated that he had brought his nephew not under his care but into his power, with the aim that the realm should be subjected to himself'.

In another example: 'Thenceforward he sought in all things to win the good will of the people hoping that, if by their favour he could be pronounced the sole head of government, he might easily then obtain supreme power even against their wishes.' Then, on being appointed protector by the council, 'he directed his attention to removing or at least impeding everything that could stand in the way of his seizing supreme power'.

Most balanced commentators nowadays – even those critical of Richard – accept that such an assessment is extreme and unlikely; but Mancini has decided his stance, and the thrust of his report is geared to corroborating it.

We have Thomas More to thank for an even more dramatic scenario, copied by Shakespeare, which has rightly lost ground in recent years. More has Hastings being sounded out by proxy but refusing to support a naked grab for power on Richard's part. It's a good story, but clearly sheer invention, perhaps based on a popular rumour that Mancini also appears to have heard, although in Mancini's version Hastings and his co-conspirators are sounded out by Buckingham, the very man they most resent! In reality, the protector would be foolish indeed to send personal messages around town revealing dangerous ambitions for the throne to people whose support was questionable. Especially while Elizabeth still held the heir presumptive in her power.

More gives the go-between role to the Northamptonshire lawyer William Catesby, making the hindsight-driven mistake of assuming that Catesby was already the intimate adviser to Richard he later became. In fact, although an established employee of Hastings, Catesby in May/June 1483 was very much a newcomer to the protector's service. The idea that Richard would send an untried functionary to discuss a topic of such sensitivity is almost as laughable as the idea that Hastings would unburden himself of such a dangerously negative response to that same functionary.

It is widely acknowledged that Thomas More's viewpoint was to some extent influenced by what he learned as an adolescent in the household of John Morton – Edward IV's Bishop of Ely and Henry VII's Lord Chancellor. Further, thanks to the work of Dr Arthur Kincaid, who published the authentic 1619 text of Sir George Buc's *History of King Richard the Third* in 1979, it has become an accepted argument that More, as Buc asserted, based his *Richard III* on a manuscript written by John Morton which came into his possession; and that Morton's manuscript was also seen by Buc's contemporary Sir William Cornwallis, who found it so tendentious that it prompted him to write his *Encomium of Richard III*.

At one time there was a theory attributing the actual composition of More's *Richard III* to Morton himself, but scholars have debunked that idea. Nevertheless, the existence of the Morton tract was recorded by Buc and several major literary and antiquarian figures around the late sixteenth and early seventeenth centuries (see Appendix for detailed discussion of these arguments).

The likelihood is that when Morton's tract reached Thomas More, it reinforced the picture of the protector that was imprinted on his mind during his years in the establishment of Richard's long-standing antagonist. More's *Richard III* seems to have started out as a polemic based on this manuscript – dramatic, vivid, but not necessarily true.

Given that Morton was setting down his version of events for others to read, he would understandably take pains to justify his own treachery, and that of Rotherham and Hastings, by the attribution of righteous motives. Thus the plotters must somehow gain incontrovertible knowledge that Richard was scheming for the crown, hence the device of the go-between who carries messages that incriminate the protector out of his own mouth. By characterizing Richard as the offending party, the Hastings-Morton-Rotherham plot is neatly transformed into an attempt to resist a *coup d'état*. Richard's exposure of their treason then becomes a cynical propaganda exercise on his part, even though, having been legally confirmed as protector, he was entitled to their implicit allegiance.

When Richard's actions are examined carefully, they suggest far more a sudden response to threat than a calculated move in a diabolical game of chess. It was surely a spontaneous act – and potentially a foolhardy one – to sentence the popular Lord Hastings to summary execution, thereby setting London in a turmoil.

Furthermore, although it has become customary to remember only the arrests of Hastings, Morton, Rotherham and Stanley, we should bear in mind that others were arrested with them. Unlike the ringleaders, these were not the kind of people whose removal might be necessary to clear the way to the throne. They included Hastings's legal associate John Forster, and Edward IV's secretary Oliver King and mistress Elizabeth Lambert. Their very involvement lends credibility to the picture of a swift reaction to a genuine danger. Elizabeth, or 'Jane Shore' as she is commonly known, owes her prominence in history to Thomas More. In reality, she was probably included in the round-up in hope that she could shed light on the whereabouts of her current lover, Thomas of Dorset.

We also have some independent items of evidence which seem to support Richard's claim that Hastings was engaged in treasonous activity. First there is Mancini who, in a report to his French masters (who would immediately grasp its significance), names Hastings, Morton and Rotherham as meeting privately. So those arrested had already formed a recognizable group. They were not random targets of terrorism.

Next, there is a fragment in a miscellany of records dating from the early 1500s, collectively known as MS2 M6, which has been analysed by Professor Richard Firth Green.[3] It has been suggested that the original may have been written by 1487 and later copied (see Appendix). This fragment provides a categorical statement by a local observer that Hastings was executed for plotting Richard's death: 'And in the mene tyme ther was dyvers imagenyd the deyth of the duke of Gloceter, and hit was asspiyd [discovered] and the Lord Hastinges was takyn in the Towur and byhedyd forthwith, the xiii day of June Anno 1483.'

The register of St Albans Abbey also records that Hastings's fate 'was deserved, as it is said.'[4]

Finally, there is an even more vivid report that may refer to these events. This is found in the collection of written material left to posterity by the London wool merchant George Cely, where several panicky remarks have been noted hastily on the reverse of a document which itself seems to date from late 1481 or early 1482. The dating of the memorandum is disputed, as is understandable from the mish-mash of speculation it contains, but given its reference to the troubles of the chamberlain and the Bishop of Ely, it is difficult to avoid the conclusion that it was written as the dramatic events of mid June unfolded:

> There is great rumour [i.e. uproar] in the realm. The Scots has done great in England. Chamberlain is deceased in trouble. The chancellor is disproved and not content. The Bishop of Ely is dead. If the king, God save his life, were dec[eas]ed; [if] the Duke of Gloucester were in any peril; if my lord prince, [which] God defend, were troubled; if my lord of Northumberland were dead or greatly troubled; if my lord Howard were slain.
>
>   De Monsieur Saint Johns.

Perhaps evidence will one day come to light to clarify the date of this note, but at present Alison Hanham, like C.A.J. Armstrong, takes it to refer to the execution of Hastings. She identifies 'Monsieur Saint Johns' as very likely the Celys' patron Sir John Weston, Prior of the Order of St John in England, a member of

Edward IV's council and probably of Edward V's also.[5] If such wild tales were circulating even among the well-informed, this would confirm Mancini's report of uproar in the capital, but there is no suggestion here of evil machinations on the part of the protector. On the contrary, he is listed as one of those in peril.

Dr Hanham continues:

> What is clear is that [these rumours] implicated Hastings and his friends in a widespread and dangerous conspiracy ... The suggestion would seem to be that the conspiracy which Richard had foreseen on 10 June had now come to a head. Whether it ever had more than imaginary existence is another, insoluble question.

Later she draws further inferences: 'There is some slight evidence – in the Cely note – that rumour after Hastings's death did suggest that an attempt had been made to rescue Edward and his brother, and even that the young king had been killed in the course of the enterprise.' This is perhaps reading too much into the actual memorandum, but it fits well with Vergil's report and with Lord Hastings's career as a military leader.

Even the anti-Richard Victorian James Gairdner concludes, 'It must not ... be too readily presumed that there was no foundation at all for Richard's charge of conspiracy against the queen and her relations.'

Evidently Richard felt that, with his decisive action on 13 June, he had nipped a dangerous plot in the bud. This is apparent because, despite Sir Richard Ratcliffe spurring his way to York at breakneck speed to raise forces, those forces did not arrive in London until after the beginning of July. The reason can only be that soon afterwards word followed to indicate haste was no longer required.

The true nature of Hastings's motives may prove to be a secret he took to the grave. Although it continues to exercise commentators, more perplexing is Richard's hasty and uncharacteristic action in summarily executing him, apparently without trial. However, having only a small personal force at his disposal, and given the delay until troops from the north were expected, Richard would have had to reckon without military back-up in dealing with an imminent insurrection. He could not safely assume that clapping Hastings in custody would ensure he stayed there, or prevent his supporters from continuing whatever actions had been set in motion. The threat could be reliably scotched by only one route: eliminating its chief instigator.

In fact, we do have proof that this strategy had its desired effect. As Simon Stallworth confirms in his postscript to a letter dated 21 June, within a week Hastings's men had gone straight over to the Duke of Buckingham.[6]

There could be another potential reason for that merciless execution if Richard had obtained proof of Hastings being implicated in Edward IV's assassination. Admittedly no evidence whatsoever can be advanced to support this theory; it is no more than a hypothesis, and a speculative one at that. But if it were true, it might account for the strange absence of reward to Hastings when Richard took power. And it suggests a combination of cause and effect that might explain the protector's swift and terrible retribution.

This was, after all, the age that gave birth to the statecraft of which Machiavelli wrote. Hastings is on record as a clever operator, and is known to have received pensions from the rulers of Burgundy and France. He was quite capable of carrying out intrigues under an outer show. And if Richard of Gloucester was responsible for separating a fair number of English nobles from their heads, it had been an integral part of his job as Constable of England since the age of seventeen. There were many without office or authority – Warwick the Kingmaker, for one – who meted out death for motives of vindictiveness or personal gain, and whose victims history forgets while remembering the singular death of William, Lord Hastings.

★ ★ ★

The incident is recounted in several sources, but the chroniclers were not there and could do no more than relate what they were told. We have no record by an avowed eyewitness. What we do have, however, in the polemical exercise written by Thomas More, is a reflection of an account by someone who was very much present at the time: John Morton, one of the conspirators and later Henry VII's right-hand man. Shakespeare's memorable scene, with Richard thrusting a withered arm in Hastings's face and accusing all and sundry of witchcraft, is of course derived from More and has no factual basis. Stories of Richard as a deformed one-armed hunchback are disproved by his well-attested prowess in battle, and no one who is known to have seen him ever mentioned deformity or disability.

The reader is invited to consider whether the entire scene in the Tower, with the Bishop of Ely innocently sending for strawberries and the protector suddenly transformed into a raving despot, might not have been one of Morton's favourite after-dinner anecdotes. Over the years one can imagine the bare bones of the tale becoming festooned with ever more colourful trimmings: the witchcraft, the withered arm, the victimization of Elizabeth Lambert ('Mistress Shore'). Mancini, Crowland, Fabyan and *The Great Chronicle* make no mention of witchcraft accusations, but under More's busy pen all of this is concocted into a scene combining high melodrama with buffoonery, and as Alison Hanham confirms, none of it need be taken seriously.

For example, More – or Morton – has Richard vow to Hastings, 'I will not to dinner till I see thy head off!' As Hanham points out, 'Historically, there is just one thing wrong with this nasty addition to the story. Richard had eaten dinner some three hours before. Hastings was executed about noon, and the councillors must have dined about 9 a.m. in accordance with custom at the time.'[7] Indeed, *The Great Chronicle* has Richard and Hastings actually dining together before the meeting. A small example of the fiction that runs through all of More's narrative.

The dramatized story of the arrests also found its way to the ears of Polydore Vergil who included it, in less extravagant form, in his own texts. Maybe it came to him independently from members of Morton's household. Historians, however, believe that Vergil and More cross-pollinated each other's work. They mixed in the same circles, and probably shared sources. Although he eschewed More's dramatic excesses, it would be rash indeed, where tales of Richard are concerned, to take Vergil at face value unless independently corroborated.

There is no doubt as to the date of the next significant event that month. It was on Monday 16 June that the dowager queen agreed to allow Edward V's younger brother, the nine-year-old

Richard, Duke of York, to quit sanctuary and join the king. The council had unanimously decided that Edward should process to his coronation at Westminster in traditional manner, starting out from the royal apartments at the Tower of London, the premier royal palace of England. They then concluded that his brother must join him in order to play his proper part in the ceremony. As Ross comments: 'It was clearly unsuitable to stage the coronation of Edward V while his younger brother, and heir apparent [*sic*], was so blatantly withheld from public view.'[8]

Although still obdurate as to her own occupation of sanctuary, Elizabeth handed over the young Duke of York to a deputation led by Cardinal Thomas Bourchier, Archbishop of Canterbury. Richard, having just foiled the Hastings plot, took the precaution of sending a force of arms with the cardinal.

Mancini describes the scene, giving plenty of circumstantial detail:

Therefore with the consent of the Council he blockaded the sanctuary with soldiers. When the queen saw herself blockaded and preparations made for force, she surrendered the boy, trusting the word of the cardinal of Canterbury that the boy should be restored after the coronation: indeed the cardinal, suspecting no treachery, had so persuaded the queen in the interests of resisting both a violation of the sanctuary and equally of assuaging, by compliance, the grim determination of the duke.

We can safely dismiss Mancini's flourish that a violation of sanctuary was contemplated. It is impossible to envisage any good purpose being served by such an outrage at so delicate a juncture. No other source suggests as much, yet the scene is widely described in a variety of reports. On a purely practical level, Richard was not yet supported by the presence, or the threat, of those northern forces. With unease already stirring at Hastings's execution, he would have been risking an all-out riot which such scant troops as he had at his disposal in London would have been unable to control. What good would that have done?

Here one must seriously question Charles Ross's assertion that 'it is scarcely possible to doubt' that Richard was prepared to force the sanctuary.[9] For this, Ross cites two supposed precedents, both conspicuously unrelated to the present circumstances. First, the occasion when Richard's father, as protector during Henry VI's insanity, broke into Westminster sanctuary in 1454. His purpose was to seize the Duke of Exeter, who had been rampaging up and down the country at the head of a band of armed rebels, laying claim to the king's Duchy of Lancaster and demanding to rule England. It was a violation of sanctuary, certainly, but Exeter's behaviour was egregious and the dignity of the crown was at stake (incidentally, Exeter came to no harm as a result).

As his second precedent, Ross cites the actions of Edward IV in seizing the leaders of the Lancastrian army who ran from the battle of Tewkesbury in 1471 to seek shelter in the abbey. Although Professor Ross states that Edward 'forced the sanctuary', he must have known the abbey's franchise for the protection of traitors was disputed. Further, this was an instance of hot pursuit in the wake of a savage battle; to claim that Richard was guided by it as a precedent for hauling the queen dowager and her (mostly female) children out of sanctuary, only a few weeks after the death of her husband, is an assault on common sense unworthy of this otherwise rational academic.

More apposite for comparison are Richard's own actions on a later occasion, as king, in the aftermath of the rebellion of October 1483. With rebels being tracked down everywhere and brought to judgement, it happened that Bishop Lionel Woodville and others took sanctuary at Beaulieu Abbey in Hampshire. Richard believed that the Marquess of Dorset, a prime mover in the uprising, might also be sheltering there. Nevertheless, the action he took was not to extract these condemned reprobates by force in the manner suggested above by Ross. Instead he ordered the abbot to come to Westminster to provide proof of the abbey's rights, which he clearly did, because Woodville remained there unmolested. So much for Richard's record of violating sanctuary.

The Crowland chronicler gives an even more dramatic account than Mancini of the confrontation of 16 June, stating that Richard and Buckingham:

> came by boat to Westminster with a great crowd with swords and clubs, and compelled the Lord Cardinal of Canterbury to enter the sanctuary, with many others, to call upon the queen, in her

kindness, to allow her son Richard … to leave and come to the Tower for the comfort of his brother the king. She willingly agreed to the proposal and sent out the boy.

Regrettably, the Crowland chronicler's partisanship intrudes. Historians have noted that his intimacy with proceedings of the council and around the Court becomes noticeably more shaky after Richard takes over the reins of power. Here he says the cardinal was 'compelled', yet Mancini's version is that the decision to cordon off Westminster Abbey was one made in council, of which Thomas Bourchier was a leading member. Nor could compulsion have been involved in Bourchier's personal guarantee (reported by Mancini) for the boy's safety – which we can probably believe since it is also mentioned by Fabyan (see below).

Viewed objectively, this blockade to contain the comings and goings that attended Elizabeth Woodville's baleful presence at Westminster, all too close to the centres of power, was a necessary move after the turbulent events of the previous week. Moreover, it may be that the Hastings conspiracy encompassed not only snatching the king, but also taking Edward IV's other children from sanctuary and secreting them until they might be useful. Reports of plans to do precisely this are given in Crowland. As we shall see, even the council's ring of steel did not prevent the queen dowager from continuing to intrigue and plot.

It is perhaps worth looking at Polydore Vergil's account of the episode, since even this official Tudor history recognizes that Richard's primary intention all along was to induce Elizabeth, as well as her children, to leave sanctuary and return to Court: 'to perswade the quene with many fayre wordes and perswations that she wold returne with hir children into the palace, unto whom they gave both pryvate and publyke assurance'. It was only when she refused that 'fynally they demanded to be delyveryd to them hir soon Richard onely, which they obtaynyd hardly after many fayre promises'.

As mentioned previously, this deputation was not the first that had tried to prevail upon her to cease her inappropriate use of sanctuary: a committee had been negotiating with her at least as long ago as the third week of May. No one has suggested that the purpose of those negotiations was to get hold of Edward V's younger brother.

Robert Fabyan, in *The New Cronycles of England and France*, writes that there were 'at Westminster great plenty of armed men' as a natural consequence of the troubled state of the metropolis. This, however, is not linked to 'the deliverance of the Duke of York'; he mentions only the princely reception given to the royal child on his emergence from sanctuary. He also tells how Cardinal Bourchier gave his pledge for the young duke's safety, and confirms Richard's offer that if the queen dowager would voluntarily emerge from sanctuary, her sons would not be separated from her.

Yet still Elizabeth insisted on remaining. Obviously her behaviour amounted to a continued silent accusation against the new government, a slur which was keenly felt and which the council wished to extinguish.

We need shed no tears, by the way, over the prospect of her enduring a spartan existence at the Abbey of Westminster. It is an easy mistake to imagine the poor queen-mother shivering in a monkish cell with her babes huddled around her, but the image bears little relation to the truth of the times. On the occasion of a religious order hosting eminent persons, quite commonly the abbot or other high-ranking officer would go so far as to give up his own private accommodation to make them comfortable. And Elizabeth certainly had the means to pay for her comforts. She is said by Thomas More to have been housed in the lodgings of the abbot (John Esteney), which authorities believe was probably the case: there would be plenty of space for the dowager queen, her family and her retinue of servants in the very large Abbot's House complex, probably the Cheyneygates mansion. We may safely assume that all was ordered for her convenience during her stay, and she could draw on her previous experience in 1470 to ensure suitable provisions and luxuries were regularly delivered by the tradesmen of London.

Westminster offered an ideal headquarters from which to operate without constraint. Indeed, it suited her so well that she elected to remain there, 'willingly' handing over nine-year-old Richard to join twelve-year-old Edward, both recently bereft of their father, and now separated from their mother too.

How strange it seems to abandon her children in this way, especially if the protector had shown himself to be such an impulsive murderer only three days previously. Richard of York was Elizabeth's trump card, and her knowledge that Gloucester needed the boy would have given her all the leverage she needed to negotiate a triumphant emergence from sanctuary, to be honourably lodged together with her children. That she preferred to relinquish the child and remain sequestered speaks volumes.

If violence was threatened – or perceived to be threatened – as some claim, why did she not call their bluff and challenge them to remove the boy forcibly, thereby ensuring Richard's reputation would be tarnished? What did she have to lose? Yet no force proved necessary to make up Elizabeth's mind.

Evidently she recognized reality for what it was: her London-based ringleaders had been neutralized, Richard had carried the entire matter off without a hitch and the council was behind him to a man. Clearly he was not considered to pose any threat to either of her sons, or she would have put up some resistance.

Let us be clear, once and for all, that the decision to take sanctuary and remain there was purely that of the dowager queen and her relatives. Although historians of the stature of Charles Ross have fallen into the trap of speaking of plans to 'rescue' Elizabeth and/or her daughters, this is plainly a misconception; she could have emerged at any time she wished. The necessity to blockade the abbey arose from a combination of the vulnerability of the princesses, who might be snatched and used by rebels, coupled with the subversive activities Elizabeth was carrying on inside, which will become evident in later chapters.

That Elizabeth released the boy from her control surely argues that she was not unduly dismayed at Hastings's fate. She had gambled all on the conspiracy and now realized the game was up. The plot had been exploded, and the conspirators summarily dealt with in a way that did not greatly shock her.

If now the mailed fist was revealed in the protector's dealings with the queen dowager, it was because her intransigence placed him in an impossible position. Young King Edward V himself, thanks to family allegiance, would almost certainly have adopted a similarly hostile stance. Thus even an extended protectorship would provide no guarantee of Richard's personal safety. Now, as he came to realize, in the interests of self-preservation he must aim directly for the throne. It is my suggestion that the fateful decision had been forming in Richard's mind ever since his discovery of the conspiracy on 10 June, which prompted his appeals for troops. It was, I believe, cemented when the plot was found to run as high as Hastings.

All this time it seems that Richard's actions were generally perceived as appropriate. Michael Hicks observes: 'Hastings's death did not stir fears amongst the political leadership that Richard aimed for the throne, but, if anything, served to reinforce fears of the queen and the Wydevilles and to strengthen trust in Richard.'[10] (Professor Hicks favours an antique spelling of the name generally written nowadays as Woodville.)

Despite this, Hicks's thesis is that Richard was aiming for the throne from 'at least' April, and that he duped the foremost political minds of the realm. But an alternative theory is much more credible: that he was simply taking such steps as occasion demanded, and the notion of seeking the crown, now forming in his mind, was dictated by unfolding events.

His most pressing problem was the imminent date of Edward V's coronation, which had been announced for 22 June, with Parliament fixed for three days later, on 25 June. So his first move toward the throne was to postpone these events. A new date on 9 November seems to have been favoured. It must have become obvious that the ceremony simply could not go ahead while the problem of the precontract remained unresolved. News as explosive as this could never be kept secret, and if the boy ascended the throne he would be engulfed in conflict. The bad old days of Henry VI would once again rack the land, with even more cause for dynastic strife.

To pre-empt both coronation and Parliament, a few writs of *supersedeas* were actually issued: evidence of just two survives in local civic records, indicating that they were probably sent around 16–17 June. But their issuance was cancelled as soon as it began, even though there would still have been time for recipients within a few days' ride to receive and act on them; which strongly suggests their discontinuance was on the orders of the protector. This meant, as Richard knew and intended, that London would soon be filled with representatives of the lords and commons who would scrutinize his every move.

While the impediment to Edward V lay in the charge of illegitimacy, underlying the entire situation was the need for a competent pair of hands to maintain the peace and security of the kingdom. Richard needed to be seen as the legitimate successor on all counts. Had he feared serious opposition, he would surely have made efforts to send out writs cancelling Parliament with the fastest couriers to every destination that could be reached in time. There were many good roads from London which would afford speedy travel in the month of June. The conclusion is unavoidable that he felt the disposition of the crown was of paramount concern to those expected representatives of the realm, and that if his aim was to assume it himself, he must win their support.

Gaining control of young Richard of York, as well as Edward V, was an integral part of the process; otherwise there would have been two separate focal points around which acts of resistance could revolve. An additional necessary precaution was to send for another of his nephews, Clarence's son, young Edward Plantagenet, Earl of Warwick, whose wardship and marriage were in the hands of the Marquess of Dorset, now absconded. The little earl was to be brought with all haste to reside in the comfortable family household of his aunt, Richard's wife, Anne Neville.

Edward of Warwick had received his earldom from his mother's side of the family, as his father's attainder in 1478 prohibited him from inheriting anything from Clarence. But for this, he would have been the leading heir to the throne after Edward IV's two sons by Elizabeth Woodville. True, Clarence's sentence did not specifically mention debarring his son from the succession, but attainder extinguished the right to transmit any entitlements by descent. An enactment by Parliament might reverse the attainder, and when the lords and commons discussed the succession Warwick's claim would be properly taken into account. Nevertheless, compared to an unblemished adult heir, eight-year-old Warwick was scarcely a more serious proposition than twelve-year-old Edward V; any move to legitimate either would be mired in controversy and dissent. Nor is there a record of any party actually promoting Warwick's candidacy.

It was certainly prudent for the protector to secure the person of this little boy. Being even younger than the sons of Edward IV, and with none of their precocious upbringing, he would be considerably more vulnerable as a pawn in the game of power.

Since young Warwick was a putative rival for the throne, many writers have tried to characterize Richard's treatment of him as incarceration, probably because of Armstrong's translation of Mancini: '[He] commanded that the lad should be kept in confinement in the household of his wife … For he feared that if the entire progeny of King Edward became extinct, yet this child … would still embarrass him.' What Mancini's Latin actually says is that the lad should be 'placed in his wife's keeping' (with no suggestion of confinement). On the contrary, the boy was knighted in September, and seems to have lived out Richard's reign as a member of the royal household at Sandal Castle, centre of his council in the north, where records refer to lavish accommodations for a number of high-born children.

By contrast, little Edward of Warwick's fortunes changed drastically as soon as Henry Tudor ascended the throne: for at least twelve of the next fourteen years, as he grew from boy to man, he was held prisoner until Henry eventually found a suitable excuse to have him executed.

★ ★ ★

With the king and his brother established together in the royal apartments of the Tower on Monday 16 June, the rest of the week is undocumented by any chronicler. It was, however, a momentous week for Richard of Gloucester, when far-reaching decisions had to be made.

While realizing he must supplant his nephews on the throne, his lifelong loyalty to his brother would have made this a difficult conclusion. On the other hand, it was certainly made easier by the fact that the Woodvilles had proved implacable in their enmity. With the positions of the two parties now irretrievably polarized, time had run out for the three hostages.

Little is known about the circumstances surrounding their execution, but there is one near-contemporaneous report that has the Earl of Northumberland carrying out both trial and execution at Pontefract Castle on 25 June. Unfortunately the writer is none other than the unreliable John Rous. But his account gains credibility from its wealth of circumstantial detail, not only quoting the whole of a sad little lament written by Rivers while in captivity, but also mentioning the hair shirt he was found to be wearing next to his skin.

Northumberland was the obvious person to carry out such a task: he was at the time acting as Richard's lieutenant in the northern regions, gathering troops to be brought to London. The two were obviously in constant contact concerning the muster, but the relevant correspondence has not survived and neither has the warrant to indict the hostages; but any such warrant from the Lord Protector and Constable of England would have commanded immediate action. It was probably sent in the early part of the week, as two of the three accused needed to be brought for trial from different places of detention (Middleham and Sheriff Hutton).

Some commentators have protested that no trial ever took place, but if this were the case, why risk transporting them to Pontefract at all, when they could have been safely despatched where they were? Either way, there was little doubt about the outcome. Along with Hastings, they made up a grand total of four deaths at Richard's command since he had assumed the protectorship. A modest tally for one who has been described as murdering his way to the throne.

It is, by the way, pointless being squeamish 500 years later about the ruthlessness with which enemy leaders were executed in the fifteenth century. Certainly Earl Rivers himself was philosophical enough about the matter to name Richard as supervisor of the will he made two days before his death. Such was the high price of defeat.

There remained several Woodvilles who failed to learn from the fate of their kinsmen. Sir Edward was scheming with his new friend Henry Tudor across the Channel, and the Marquess of Dorset was fomenting unrest at home. They would be major players in the rebellion that would take place that autumn. Even the dowager queen's brother Lionel, Bishop of Salisbury, who had emerged from sanctuary in late June and ingratiated himself with Richard, would resume his plotting a couple of months later. Thus, there was still reason to beware Woodville antagonism. In the case of Dorset the most Richard could do to clip his wings was to seize his estates, as he did those of Rivers. After these actions, the die was cast. Only the power and status of sovereignty would give Richard the protection he needed against factions who were committed to his overthrow.

6

'This Eleccion of us the Thre Estates'

Between 16 and 26 June we are without word from our Crowland chronicler, so we continue with Domenico Mancini's narrative which moves on to the events of Sunday 22 June. It was on this date that Dr Ralph Shaw preached a sermon at St Paul's Cross, London's recognized podium for public declarations, explaining Edward V's illegitimacy to the populace and pointing out that the protector was now the only legal heir to the throne.

On the following days, between Monday 23 and Wednesday 25 June, the Duke of Buckingham is said by various chroniclers to have given orations on the same topic to the mayor, aldermen and justices of London at the Guildhall, and to other assemblies.

The *Great Chronicle of London*, which is reasonably accurate when recording author Robert Fabyan's eyewitness testimony, confirms Buckingham's Guildhall speech 'upon the Tuesday next ensuing'. Although most of the Tudor writers piously relate that Buckingham's speechifying met with scepticism, it is interesting that Fabyan, who could well have been among those present, differs by reporting that the mayor and civic dignitaries were actually convinced by his arguments.

Curiously, not one of our principal commentators – neither Mancini nor Crowland nor Vergil (nor even More) – saw fit to record the most significant event of that particular week, which was an assembly of the representatives who had been summoned for the post-coronation Parliament. If the assembly met as normal at Westminster Palace, perhaps ordinary citizens were unaware of it. However, there is no excuse for its omission from accounts that represent themselves as giving a true report of events, Crowland in particular.

Not all parliamentary representatives were present, since a few received writs of cancellation. However, it was evidently not far short of a full complement of the three estates. J.C. Wedgwood's register volume of the *History of Parliament* gives a figure of 32 lords temporal, 66 knights and 30 'others elected' (commons). Plus there were in office at the time approximately 44 lords spiritual who, according to report, were 'well nigh all' represented. Undoubtedly a total of over 150.

The assembly almost certainly met on 25 June, the day for which Parliament had been officially called. Thus we have first Dr Shaw's Sunday oration, then Buckingham's speech at the Guildhall on Tuesday, then the quasi-parliament on Wednesday when the constitutional crisis was debated and a decision made that the crown be offered to the protector.

A deputation from this assembly, led by Buckingham, made its way the following day, Thursday 26 June, to Baynard's Castle, the London home of Richard's mother, Cecily, Duchess of York. Although Richard was staying at his own town house, Crosby Place, he was using his mother's home as a base throughout these events and appears to have enjoyed her ongoing support. The deputation was joined there by dignitaries from the city comprising the mayor, aldermen and chief commoners, and in their name Richard of Gloucester was offered a parchment roll setting out their formal petition to him to take the crown.

In Vergil and More the dating of these events is unreliable, which again reminds us that neither spent any great amount of time with his nose buried in historical records. Vergil actually claimed to have searched unsuccessfully for pre-1500 written annals, which reinforces suspicion that upon the Tudor accession a wholesale destruction of inconvenient documents took place. Later commentators even accused poor Polydore of perpetrating the destruction himself.

C.A.J. Armstrong, who produced the first edition of Mancini's manuscript in 1936, made some unfortunate translations, among them asserting that Richard 'secretly' sent Buckingham to the lords to discuss the disposition of the crown. Mancini's *actual* words indicate he stayed apart and left it to Buckingham to argue the case.

The Crowland chronicler makes no bones about his disapproval of these developments, reporting: 'The pretext of this intrusion and for taking possession in this way was ... by means of a supplication contained in a certain parchment roll'. There is not a word about the deliberations of the parliamentary assembly which had sat to consider this weighty matter, and whose decision to confer the succession on Richard made the 'intrusion' a remarkably democratic process.

As the nineteenth-century historian James Gairdner admitted:

> in point of form, one might almost look upon it as a constitutional election. Indeed, it was rather a declaration of inherent right to the crown, first by the council of the realm, then by the city, and afterwards by Parliament – proceedings much more regular and punctilious than had been observed in the case of Edward IV.[1]

Gairdner's views were echoed by the historian Malcolm Laing: 'Instead of a violent usurpation we discover an accession, irregular according to modern usage, but established without violence on a legal title.'[2]

As for those of the population whose understanding depended on sermons or word of mouth, it is abundantly clear, from the many garbled reports, that the momentous topics under discussion – precontract, bigamy and bastardy – were so complex, or so poorly set forth, or both, that different listeners came away with vastly different impressions. These impressions were then passed on to our various chroniclers, and the result was a jumble of conflicting accounts. The principal elements that made their way into the more important narratives are as follows (and are not mutually exclusive):

- According to Mancini, preachers claimed that Edward IV was a bastard (having been 'conceived in adultery' he was 'wholly unlike' the late Duke of York). If Edward was not a legitimate king, neither could his progeny be. Mancini says this was proclaimed by 'preachers of the divine word ... in their sermons to the public'. He does not give names or dates.
- Polydore Vergil has a similar version of Dr Shaw's sermon accompanied by a politically-correct denial that King Edward's children were ever called bastards.

- *The Great Chronicle of London* has it all ways, with Shaw preaching 'that the children of King Edward were not rightful inheritors of the crown, and that King Edward was not the legitimate son of the Duke of York'.
- Mancini then switches to an account of the Duke of Buckingham arguing that at the time Edward married Elizabeth Woodville, Warwick the Kingmaker had already precontracted him to another wife 'by proxy, as they say, over the Channel'. Richard, recusing himself, sent Buckingham to present this unlikely story to the peers summoned for Parliament. This presumably refers to the well-known fact of the Earl of Warwick's negotiations for the hand of Bona of Savoy, which were in full swing at the time of Edward's Woodville marriage.
- Mancini also attributed the following statement to Buckingham in his discussions with the peers: 'Elizabeth herself had been wed to another husband, and Edward had taken possession of her rather than married her. As a result all their progeny were unworthy of the realm.'
- In *The Chronicles of London*/Vitellius A XVI, and in the *New Cronycles of England and France* by Fabyan, who could have heard the sermon for himself, Dr Shaw declares that the children of Edward IV are not legitimate or rightful inheritors of the crown (without elaboration as to reason, and without alleging Edward IV's illegitimacy).
- In the *Crowland Chronicle*, Edward was precontracted to Lady Eleanor Talbot before he married Elizabeth, and his sons were consequently illegitimate. This, says the chronicler, is the 'colour' or 'excuse' for offering the crown to Gloucester, 'put forward by means of a supplication in a certain parchment roll'. He is not interested in sermons or public orations, but goes directly and correctly to the legal evidence of the written petition which was framed by 'the lords and commonalty of the kingdom' (a nod to the parliamentary assembly) who besought Richard 'to assume his lawful rights'. We will examine this petition later, since it encompassed other topics in addition to the matter of the precontract. Suffice to note that this chronicler, the one contemporaneous writer who seems to have known English law, made reference to no other argument or pretext (such as illegitimacy on the part of

Edward IV). Philippe de Commynes agrees with this version of what was proclaimed.

As is evident from the above, Mancini's coverage of this episode is all over the place. Hence, we must conclude that he attended none of these gatherings. Even had he been present, his lack of English would have forced him to rely on translations by others, which may be why he made rather a mare's nest of what the speakers were supposed to have said. This again confirms that he had no access to Richard's party. Quite probably his informants took pains to keep him ignorant of the real grounds for Richard's entitlement.

Edward IV's supposed illegitimacy is another example of the kind of gossipy story that appealed to Domenico Mancini. This was an allegation which arose repeatedly during Edward's reign, the earliest supposed occurrence being cited by Mancini himself in one of the more colourful anecdotes he picked up during his visit. His story goes that when Edward was found to have married Elizabeth, 'a lady of humble origin', his mother the Duchess of York 'fell into such a fit of madness that she offered to submit to a public enquiry, asserting that Edward had not been conceived from her husband the Duke of York but was begotten in adultery, therefore was by no means worthy of the eminence of kingship'.

There was then prevalent in England, as Mancini's early editor Armstrong explains (his endnote 12), a xenophobia so irrational that 'a member of the royal house born abroad was liable to be called a changeling or a bastard by his enemies'. Edward IV was susceptible to this accusation since he had been born at Rouen. Armstrong suggests that Warwick the Kingmaker also employed the same imputation to discredit Edward in 1469, intending to declare him a bastard and replace him with Clarence.

It was a calumny well known to foreign sources, including Philippe de Commynes who recorded that when Edward fell out with Charles, Duke of Burgundy, the latter insultingly took to calling him the son of an archer named 'Blayborgne'!

On this topic Michael K. Jones claimed the bastardy story was true, with Edward's conception having occurred when the Duke of York was separated from his wife by a campaign at Pontoise; this was even made into a 2004 TV documentary fronted by Tony Robinson. Unfortunately the Rouen records were misread in this instance, and an article by the historian Dr Livia Visser-Fuchs has now indicated that York was in Rouen with his duchess at least between 1 and 10 August 1441, within the estimated time-frame for his son's conception.[3]

In later Tudor writing it was said that Richard slandered his mother by declaring that the late king was born of an adulterous liaison. An example occurs in Polydore Vergil:

> ther ys a common report that king Edwards chyldren wer in [Shaw's] sermon caulyd basterdes, and not king Edward, which is voyd of all truthe; for Cecyly king Edwards mother, as ys before sayd, being falsely accusyd of adultery, complanyd afterward in sundry places to right many noble men, wherof soome yeat lyve, of that great inury which hir soon Richard had doon hir.

But Vergil's assertion is not only at odds with Mancini, it also contradicts the fact that the illegitimacy of Edward's children was recorded by the lords and commons in their parchment roll. Did Vergil so disdain the truth that he was prepared to publish a lie so as not to offend his patron King Henry, whose queen was one of those proclaimed bastards? Very likely the sources Vergil consulted knew better than to disclose the true facts.

It must be evident from the extracts mentioned above that very few people, other than those representatives gathered for Parliament who framed the petition, had any clear understanding of the legal case for setting aside Edward V and preferring Richard. Undoubtedly the niceties of canon law, precontract and clandestinity must have gone wholly over the heads of most listeners. Even people who were in London at the time came away with confused ideas of what was said. Consequently it was easy for Vergil's informants to blacken Richard's name in retrospect with the additional calumny that he called his mother an adulteress (presumably they were unaware he was staying under her roof at the time).

Nevertheless the idea of Edward IV's bastardy had clearly gained a foothold in popular legend, as had the story that his mother swore to it. In 1535 Thomas Cromwell, Henry VIII's personal secretary, said that at the time Richard seized the throne Cecily actually gave a formal statement, before witnesses, affirming that Edward IV was a bastard.[4] This interesting suggestion of a 'formal statement' immediately invites comparison with Mancini's story of the duchess's 'offer to submit to a public enquiry' in connection with the same assertion. It also calls to mind a tale told in similar terms by Thomas More about an 'examination solemnly taken' by Cecily when, furious on learning that Edward had married beneath him, she is alleged to have made another derogatory statement about her son. All three stories sound remarkably like different versions of an urban myth centred on Cecily's displeasure at Edward's marriage to Elizabeth in 1464, stoked up by his opponents in later years.

Returning to the events and public pronouncements of 22–25 June, it seems not unreasonable to conclude, after examining all the flim-flam given out by the chroniclers, that neither Dr Shaw nor the Duke of Buckingham ever seriously claimed that Edward himself was a bastard: only his children were declared illegitimate, on the grounds of the king's precontract.

It is easy enough to visualize the shocked reaction of anyone learning the news for the first time that King Edward had compromised his children's succession. Thus it may well be that, hearing the terms 'illegitimate' and 'bastard', those who were present failed to understand that it was Edward's offspring who were being so categorized. They had repeatedly heard rumours about the king's own illegitimacy over the past fifteen years or so, and in the general confusion their minds probably leapt to the conclusion that this hoary old tale was being dredged up again.

Mancini's 1936 editor John Armstrong tried to explain away some of his misunderstanding: 'The fact that Mancini does not report [the precontract with Eleanor Talbot] may indicate that by the time he left England no official charge to invalidate Edward IV's marriage had been formulated.' This is actually not so. We know that the petition urging Richard to take the throne, presented to him by Buckingham on behalf of the quasi-parliament, clearly cited the precontract with Lady Eleanor; and the Crowland chronicler informs us that the petition had been prepared in advance. Is it not a more straightforward conclusion that Mancini simply got his precontracts mixed up? He had been told that Buckingham mentioned a precontract, and from his international background he knew approaches had been made for Edward to marry a wife on the continent of Europe, so he conflated the two.

There is a pivotal point to remember here. In fifteenth-century England the gentry and merchant classes had begun to influence political outcomes, especially in times of turbulence. Certainly the citizens of London had a will of their own and could make or break an attempted takeover. It might have been with mixed feelings that the quasi-parliament decided to set aside Edward IV's sons, but London's city fathers were intimately involved with the decision, and they had already indicated a willingness to accept Richard's pre-eminence in the new régime. Rosemary Horrox, in an article outlining Richard's relations with London, points out: 'Londoners certainly did not want to see a slide into civil war, which reinforced their pragmatism by inclining them to back whoever looked strong enough to preserve the *status quo*.'[5]

Most members of the lords and commons would have shared that view, and would have known that the Woodvilles had already attempted to whip up armed resistance. Thus, given the alternatives, placing Richard in control of the realm evidently seemed the most desirable option. Presented with the will of this assembled body, Richard's accession to the throne was duly legitimized.

But there were others whose opinion was never canvassed: the many strata of Court servants and royal office-holders who were vital to the administration of government, performing such duties as law enforcement, land management or revenue collection. These were persons of note and influence in their communities. They, and the circles in which they mixed, were the people whom, crucially, Richard failed to reach with his arguments that made good sense only to the sophisticated ears of the parliamentary assembly. Where the ruling classes recognized a matter of peril to the realm, many men of lesser rank saw only an interruption in the dynastic succession to which they had committed themselves, and regarded it as a career threat.

★ ★ ★

The petition presented to Richard was later incorporated into an Act of Parliament to confirm his right to the throne. This act, usually called *Titulus Regius*, is known to have quoted the petition verbatim, so we have a clear record of the contents of the original parchment roll.

Nevertheless it has been contended (inevitably) that the same text did not appear in both documents. This suggestion has been comprehensively refuted by Dr Anne Sutton, who points out that in the words of the act itself, 'it is precisely stated that it contains a text of the 1483 petition'. She cites corroboration in Richard's letter to Lord Mountjoy at Calais on 28 June 1483, which 'says clearly that a copy of the petition to Richard to take the throne is annexed to the covering letter in order that all the details and reasons may be known to the citizens of Calais'. It should also be noted that, far from claiming appointment by Parliament (as some commentators insinuate), Richard's letter correctly speaks of 'a bille of peticione whiche the lordes spirituelx & temporelx and the commons of this land solemplye porrected unto the kinges highnes at London the xxvi day of Juyne'. At the same time emissaries were sent to the royal houses of Europe announcing England's new monarch and detailing the circumstances of his accession. Having done all this, Dr Sutton continues, it would obviously have been unacceptable, indeed foolhardy, to formulate an 'improved' version to put before Parliament several months later.[6]

In the knowledge, therefore, that we have the full text, it is worth examining the grounds upon which Richard's title was set out. Briefly summarized they were as follows: Edward IV's precontract with Lady Eleanor Talbot rendered his marriage to Elizabeth Woodville bigamous; his bigamous marriage was clandestine and suspect and rendered its offspring illegitimate; the Duke of Clarence's attainder debarred his issue from the succession; and Richard of Gloucester was the sole 'uncorrupted' descendant of Richard, Duke of York.

Phrased in the elaborate and fulsome prose of mediæval officialese, the petition (obviously drawn up by lawyers) starts by invoking every possible objection against the previous régime. Missing no opportunity to use ten words where one will do, it opens with a preamble extolling the golden days of yore when kings followed the advice and counsel of persons who were wise and God-fearing. In contrast to this, 'afterward, whan that such as had the rule and governaunce of this Land, delityng in adulation and flattery, and lede by sensuality and concupiscence, followed

the counsaill of personnes insolent, vicious, and of inordinate
avarice', England's prosperity declined, the laws of God and man
were confounded, and the realm was likely to fall into misery and
desolation unless a speedy remedy was found.

Specific allegations follow: 'Over this, amonges other things,
more specially wee consider' how it was that 'after the ungracious
pretensed Marriage' of Edward IV and Elizabeth, 'the ordre of all
poletique Rule was perverted', and laws and customs were broken,
so that 'this Land was ruled by selfewill and pleasure, feare and
drede ... whereof ensued many inconvenients and mischiefs' (e.g.
murders, extortions and oppressions), 'soo that no Man was sure
of his Lif, Land ne Lyvelode, ne of his Wif, Doughter ne Servaunt,
every good Maiden and Woman [was] standing in drede to be
ravished and defouled'.

Doubtless Harry of Buckingham had a hand in piling on the
grievances, remembering how he had been kept at Court tied to
the queen's skirts while she enjoyed the income from his estates;
and how, contrary to the distinguished match which should have
befitted his royal lineage, he had been forced to marry one of
Elizabeth's nondescript sisters. (He soon had the satisfaction of a
small act of personal revenge: at Richard's coronation ten days
later, the despised Duchess of Buckingham was conspicuous by
her absence.)

Though Richard was undoubtedly a party to the whole thing,
the framing of the argument from start to finish is assuredly the
work of that legal brain which belonged to Edward's former
chancellor, Bishop Stillington. Indeed, it was later recognized as
such (see Postscript, p. 320).

Stillington probably had at least four days in which to formulate
his arguments, so the drafting was not a hurried affair. Having
been clapped in the Tower himself only five years previously,
he was, like Buckingham, no stranger to the oppressions of
Edward IV. For a mediæval lawyer, the concern was to cover
every possible nuance and make everything as watertight as
possible (as it is today), employing a style that can scarcely be
matched for florid grandiloquence. Nevertheless, even Charles
Ross, while protesting that it was a 'gross misrepresentation' as
a general comment on Edward's government, acknowledges:
'There was just enough plausibility in the charges of sensuality at
court, Woodville greed and the difficulty of obtaining impartial

justice in Edward IV's time to make it worth attempting to grind some political capital from them.'[7]

In this overheated style the petition laments the way Edward's rule deteriorated after his 'pretensed marriage' to Elizabeth, characterized by Hanham as 'the kind of thing standard in the conventional process of deposition, which meant showing that the reigning monarch was incompetent by reason of his persistent reliance on evil counsellors'.[8]

There then follows a list of four separate objections to the Woodville marriage, ascending in importance to culminate with the precontract with Lady Eleanor Talbot.

The first is that the marriage was made 'of grete presumption, without the knowyng and assent of the Lords of this Lond'. This is more a complaint than an objection, since there was no formal requirement for prior assent. Nevertheless their approval was evidently felt to be one of those customs which had been 'broken, subverted and contempned' in Edward's day.

The second is that the marriage was made 'by Sorcerie and Wichecrafte, committed by the said Elizabeth, and her Moder Jaquett Duchesse of Bedford, as the comon opinion of the people and the publique voice and fame is thorough all this Land; and hereafter, if and as the caas shall require shall bee proved sufficiently in tyme and place convenient'. The witchcraft charge was a serious one, but nowhere near as deadly as such accusations came to be in the centuries that followed. Because this calls for detailed analysis, it will be fully discussed in chapter 7; meanwhile let us continue with the third objection.

This says the 'pretensed Mariage was made privaly and secretely, without Edition of Banns, in a private Chamber, an prophane place, and not openly in the face of the Church, aftre the Lawe of Godds Churche, bot contrarie thereunto and the laudable Custome of the Church of Englond'. There was a good reason for publishing banns and marrying publicly: so that a marriage should not later be voidable owing to a pre-existing impediment that never came to light. Probably this was why Edward IV was so attracted by the idea of clandestinity, in case he should find it convenient to repudiate the marriage later. Evidently he failed to take into account that his children were also left vulnerable, not merely the wife whom he felt thus able to take 'on approval'.

It was necessary to record the secrecy of the marriage to Elizabeth (now plain 'Elizabeth Grey') in conjunction with the last and most important objection, which cited the impediment of the precontract with Lady Eleanor. Thus the fourth objection reads as follows:

> at the tyme of contract of the same pretensed Mariage, and bifore and long tyme after, the seid King Edward was and stode maryed and trouth plight to oone Dame Elianor Butteler, Doughter of the old Earl of Shrewesbury, with whom the same King Edward had made a precontracte of Matrimonie, longe tyyme bifore he made the said pretensed Mariage with the said Elizabeth Grey, in maner and fourme abovesaid.

It therefore follows:

> that the said King Edward duryng his lif, and the seid Elizabeth, lived together sinfully and dampnably in adultery, against the Lawe of God and of his Church. ... Also it appeareth evidently and followeth, that all th'Issue and Children of the seid King Edward, been Bastards, and unable to inherite or to clayme any thing by Inheritance, by the Lawe and Custome of Englond.

It is significant that an offer of future proof was made in support of the witchcraft accusation, but not in support of the precontract. This is a clear indication that evidence of the latter had already been presented, as was well known to Bishop Stillington who would have been rigorously questioned by Richard and his advisers in the first instance, by the Great Council which met on 9 June, and by yesterday's quasi-parliament.

The petition then makes it clear there is no question of the succession passing to young Edward of Warwick because his father, the Duke of Clarence, was convicted of high treason and attainted by Act of Parliament: 'by reason wherof, all the Issue of the said George [of Clarence], was and is dishabled and barred of all Right and Clayme ... to the Crown and Dignite Roiall of this Reame'.

There follow several effusive paragraphs containing compliments, entreaties to accept the crown and avowals of Richard's right to succeed. On the latter point, although no specific slur is cast on the late king's legitimacy, nevertheless it is confirmed that

Richard is 'undoubted Son and Heire of Richard late Duke of Yorke', and 'born withyn this Lande', from which circumstance is derived more certitude of his birth and descent.

> And herupon we humbly desire, pray, and require youre seid Noble Grace, that, accordyng to this Eleccion of us the Thre Estates of this Lande, as by youre true Enherritaunce, Ye will accepte and take upon You the said Crown and Royall Dignite … as to You of Right bilongyng, as wele by Enherritaunce as by lawfull Eleccion.

The age-old question that must now be faced is to what extent people generally credited the precontract allegation.

What about our chronicler of Crowland Abbey? The writer had access to inside information, and was certainly not backward in giving his readers the benefit of his opinions. He evidently had accurate knowledge of the contents of the petition. But although he dismissively characterizes the illegitimation of Edward IV's sons as 'the colour for this act of usurpation', and goes on to describe the offer of the crown to Richard as 'seditious and disgraceful', we do not find in Crowland a specific rejection, let alone refutation, of the precontract's existence – only the use to which it was put. He is far more concerned about who was responsible for getting up the petition (professional curiosity perhaps?).

It will also be remembered that the Crowland chronicler was quick to complain that Elizabeth Woodville's dignity was not preserved. Had he considered the story about Lady Eleanor a fabrication, one would expect him to leap to defend the dignity of both ladies. Of this, however, he utters not a word. Apparently his only reservations about the precontract lie in the matter of a lay court (Parliament) presuming to reach conclusions on matters of marriage validity, which were properly the province of his colleagues in the ecclesiastical courts. So in summary, his view was that the precontract allegation had not been properly adjudicated.

However, as commented by C.S.L. Davies, 'the unilateral invalidation of Edward's marriage by a secular institution seems not to have generated formal ecclesiastical protest either in Rome or in England'.[9]

The only other fifteenth-century chronicler who refers to the precontract is Philippe de Commynes. Doubtless he pumped his sources for all they were worth in order to give his employer, Louis XI, plenty of ammunition in his conflict with England. Yet, writing with hindsight after Richard's name had long since been blackened, he reported the precontract as a simple matter of fact. He evidently found it believable. And so, conspicuously, did the English lords and commons gathered in that quasi-parliament on 25 June 1483, who were confident enough to accept it when Bishop Stillington was on hand to be examined and probed on the subject.

A significant consideration is the deafening silence of the Woodvilles in response to all this. As the injured parties, Elizabeth and/or persons acting on behalf of her children were free to raise strenuous objections and demand that the case be tried before a formal ecclesiastical court, where they could challenge the authorities who argued their illegitimacy. Her brother, the Bishop of Salisbury, could advise her in this, and depositions could be made if she still refused to emerge from sanctuary. The lack of any Woodville challenge to the precontract points to a tacit admission that they could offer no objection to it.

Indeed, according to Mancini, Queen Elizabeth was alleged to have got rid of Clarence precisely because of her sensitivity to charges that she was not 'the legitimate wife of the king'.

Perhaps the strongest validation of the precontract lies in the steps later taken by Henry VII to cover it up. Henry's supporters, after he seized the crown, were vociferous in demanding a marriage with Edward IV's eldest daughter, Elizabeth of York, to prop up his feeble claim to the throne. So he could not afford to let *Titulus Regius* remain on the statute books with its declaration that his proposed wife was the offspring of a bigamous liaison. Yet instead of publicly repudiating the declaration, or giving Elizabeth and her family the opportunity to challenge it in court, Henry merely ordered that *Titulus Regius* be repealed and every copy destroyed.

Some years later, before Thomas More started working on his *History of King Richard the Third*, Henry VII's Cardinal Archbishop John Morton had written his tract hostile to Richard III which cleverly muddied the waters on behalf of the Tudor régime. Morton evidently produced a number of elaborate fictions that were believed and retold by More: (a) that the precontracted bride named as an impediment to Edward IV's marriage was a well-known mistress of his named Elizabeth Lucy, (b) that Edward's mother attempted to *prevent* the Woodville marriage by citing the Lucy precontract and (c) that it was only after Elizabeth Lucy herself repudiated the allegation in an official enquiry that Edward was free to marry his queen – 'with great feast and honourable solemnity' says the disinformed More, unaware of the shamefaced secrecy that actually surrounded the marriage.

This story is so irrational that it seems unlikely it was invented by Morton (we know Morton's tract contained the Lucy story because it was repeated by Cornwallis, see Appendix). Possibly Morton had to do his best with propaganda given out earlier by someone of less intelligence. The wily cardinal would surely have had more sense than to cast in the role of Edward's precontracted wife a mistress who was probably the mother of at least one of his bastard children. Once she was implicated, another layer of invention became necessary so as to remove the absurd possibility that an earlier bastard by her might now be regarded as ostensible heir to the throne. Hence Morton had to come up with the alleged inquisition (for which no evidence exists), in which she denied the precontract.

Since the initial publication of this book, new research into this 'Elizabeth Lucy' has cast doubt on the pedigree suggested by John Ashdown-Hill which echoed the general belief that her maiden name was Wayte, mother of Edward IV's bastard son Arthur Wayte.[10] 'Elizabeth Lucy' was probably Margaret Lucy, widow of Sir William Lucy of Dallington. No Lucy connection with the Wayte family has been found, and Arthur's mother was more likely a much later mistress.[11]

Now, we have already noted that the story believed by Henry VII's favoured historian, Polydore Vergil, was that the only impediment brought against Edward V was that his father was illegitimate. Why did Thomas More, writing at the same time, come up with a contradictory story (and a dangerous one) of an alleged precontract, full of names and circumstances known to no one else? More was a clever man with a trained legal mind, and must have felt that, however extraordinary, the information in his possession was above suspicion. Yet it was false.

Clearly the Lucy fabrication was designed to discredit both Richard III and the precontract itself, by parodying elements of the true case to the point of ridicule. The Tudor camp thought they were safe making up such a story because they believed all documentation had been destroyed, and Stillington silenced, when Henry VII seized the throne. Two things, however, they could not know. Not only were the facts of the precontract recorded by the Crowland chronicler, but also a copy of *Titulus Regius* in the Rolls of Parliament miraculously escaped destruction. The Parliament Rolls became available for inspection only in the 1580s, too late for More to have had access to them, but they were seen by members of the antiquarian movement of the day. Buc was the first to use *Titulus Regius* and the *Crowland Chronicle* as source material, revealing the true circumstances which rendered Edward IV's heirs illegitimate. Otherwise historians would never have challenged the Tudor lies immortalized by Thomas More.

★ ★ ★

Given the documentary evidence cited above, it is unwise to dismiss the precontract complacently as a mere ruse. Today's commentators are inclined to take it more seriously, and there are three sound reasons for doing so: the endorsement by Parliament, the rank and status of the lady in the case and the eminence of the Bishop of Bath and Wells who asserted it to be true.

As for Lady Eleanor Talbot, daughter of the Earl of Shrewsbury and sister of the Duchess of Norfolk, she was a scion of one of the most famed and distinguished families of the English nobility. They far outranked Edward's Woodville wife. Moreover Eleanor's connections extended deep into the powerful Neville clan whose chief was Warwick the Kingmaker. This was not the kind of personage about whom scurrilous claims were lightly concocted.

Robert Stillington, as Bishop of Bath and Wells, was a figure of even greater distinction. In the English Church at coronations, since at least the fourteenth century, the monarch has been flanked on right and left by the Bishops of Durham and of Bath and Wells. He was also a leading statesman in his own right having been appointed, *inter alia*, Edward IV's Lord Chancellor, and remaining his chief minister during that king's reign from June 1467 until June 1473 when he retired for health reasons. Thereafter he was called again to serve his king in January 1479, when he was appointed alongside the Earl of Essex, Earl Rivers and Bishop Morton to negotiate an extension of the Treaty of Picquigny with France.

Any suggestion that Stillington merely sought revenge on Edward may be quickly discounted: we know his imprisonment in 1478 to have been brief – a month at the outside – and he was pardoned on payment of a fine which he could well afford. He had been fully reinstated in Edward's favour by the time he was appointed to the Picquigny negotiations. He would have been foolish indeed to carry a grudge to the extent of jeopardizing his entire future by manufacturing a concatenation which, if false, could be repudiated in a trice by Lady Eleanor's powerful relatives.

The noted American attorney Bertram Fields, in his book *Royal Blood*, devotes almost an entire chapter to examining the likelihood of whether it was Stillington or Richard (or both) who came up with the precontract, or whether Stillington might have made it up for his own reasons. Fields's forensic skills are formidable, and he clearly shows that Stillington was a man of upright character, a most unlikely candidate to have fabricated a falsehood (or permitted his name to be attached to one), and that he gained no reward for coming forward. Indeed, his only recompense was that of being persecuted at the end of his life by Henry Tudor, who realized, in Fields's words, 'the bishop's testimony might be difficult to disprove'.[12]

For nearly 150 years the truth remained concealed, and even in the 1600s it was only a small circle of antiquaries who found out how facts had been twisted. In the ensuing centuries, the exposure of Tudor misrepresentation has still been insufficient to pry opinion away from the jaundiced sentiments of the Crowland chronicler.

Our current view of history would be markedly different if the monks of Crowland had instead invited Bishop Stillington to write his recollections in the abbey's chronicle.

7

Witchcraft and Sorcery

Although modern-day commentators pay scant attention to the accusations of witchcraft that were set out in *Titulus Regius*, these would certainly have struck a resonant chord with the people of England at a time when the existence and practice of magic were widely acknowledged.

In the fifteenth century the ancient arts of magic flourished throughout Europe, whether 'innocent' activities of divination, healing, beneficial charms, etc; or the 'legitimate sciences' of natural or intellectual magic – such as astronomy/astrology, astral magic, alchemy and books of secrets – derived in great part from Arabic learning and occult sciences. Or, indeed, the 'black arts' of witchcraft, sorcery, necromancy and conjuration.

In fact, the distinctions between the categories were frequently blurred: our friend Angelo Cato, Archbishop of Vienne (who commissioned reports from Mancini and Philippe de Commynes), was an astrologer of note who was credited with foretelling a number of important events, presumably based on divination and casting horoscopes. His skills were valued by the French royal family along with those of a fellow astrologer, Symon de Phares, who confirmed Cato's powers of prediction. Phares enjoyed the protection of Charles VIII despite arousing the envy of enemies who managed to have him condemned for practising the black arts.

At a humbler level, particularly among the rural communities where people lived amid poverty and insecurity, magical protection was sought against such disasters as adverse weather, crop failures, sterility, illness and premature death. Long-established folk beliefs encompassed healing and herb-lore, protective charms, and rites to summon up rain or to find lost and stolen goods.

For its own part, the Catholic Church subscribed to the idea of supernatural powers both for good and for evil. It was concerned in its rituals with promoting fertility, well-being and health. A substantial crossover occurred between religion and magic, with magical practitioners using Christian formulae and prayers, as well as objects and substances which had been blessed by the clergy.

This was a period when Christianity required unquestioning belief in miraculous entities and events, with the penalty of eternal damnation for those who entertained doubts. Surrounded by innumerable invisible spirits, both good and bad, who watched and interfered with their lives, it is not surprising that individuals attempted to harness the powers of such spirits to better their own daily existence.

Then of course there were many traditional activities that meant no harm and were merely intended to help one's neighbour, such as administering herbal nostrums to aid a sick cow; a few words of a traditional healing spell might also be muttered for good measure.

Crossing over to raise malignant spirits (the devil or demons) was a logical progression for those of ambitious or malicious intent. It would seem to offer a source of supernatural power in competition with the power available to Christians through miracles, divine intercession and the expensive range of pardons, indulgences and similar devices by which it was possible to purchase the favours of the Almighty. 'Assistance by the devil,' in the words of Henry Kelly, 'did not necessarily involve the idea of a pact with the devil or of worshipping the devil. Devil worship was a patristic concept that was revived on the Continent in the Middle Ages, but it only rarely enters the accounts of English witchcraft.'[1]

The attitude of the Church was that magical powers were a delusion and a deception. In England, it was not until the sixteenth century that the idea of the 'witch-cult' took root, when witchcraft, sorcery and magic were officially castigated as heresy with punishments to suit. Until then, witchcraft (a peculiarly English term) 'was almost never', according to Kelly, 'formally associated with heresy'. Sorcery, incantations and other superstitions were forbidden by the first commandment, whereas heresy was forbidden by the second. Another distinction lay in the area of jurisdiction: heresy was one of the major issues which pertained to bishops alone, while witchcraft was a minor item that fell within the jurisdiction of lesser officials.

Prior to the famed sixteenth-century witch mania, the crime of witchcraft in England was serious enough, but it was a crime among others. In continental Europe, by contrast, sorcery was routinely identified with heresy, and torture and burning were commonplace.

In English statutes dated 1401 and 1414, the penalty for a relapsing or non-abjuring heretic was to be burned. 'Before that time, burning was commonly used as a means of capital punishment only for women convicted of high treason'[2] (for which men were hanged and quartered or beheaded). Burning had previously been available as a penalty for both heresy and witchcraft, but its use had not been widespread. For example, a writ dated 1406 against witchcraft in Lincoln required those convicted merely to be imprisoned until they reformed. Essentially, unless the practice of witchcraft involved treason or homicide, penalties in England stopped a long way short of capital punishment.

No matter what tenets the reader may hold, there are millions in the world today who believe in magic and witchcraft. Cases heard at the Old Bailey as recently as 2005 and 2012 concerned children tormented for being witches. And witchcraft can have powerful effects on believers.

Whatever the goal, it was and still is possible to engage the services of individuals skilled in such arts. Control of the weather is a common example: many people attributed the freak weather during the battles of Towton and Barnet to witchcraft. In 1493 one Elena Dalok told the Commissary of London that 'if she bids the rain to rain, it rains at her command'. As late as 1814 Sir Walter Scott bought a wind in Stromness from Bessie Millie, and recorded the transaction in his diary.[3]

Divination was another popular form of magical art, whether to foretell the future or to detect the whereabouts of people and objects. In 1467 William Byg (or Lech), accused of sorcery in the Archbishop of York's court, confessed that he had for several years discovered thieves and found stolen goods by means of crystal-gazing.[4]

If such lowly practitioners of magic seem a far cry from royal circles, consider William the Conqueror who travelled with his own astrologer and was reported in the chronicles of Crowland to have employed a witch in his campaign against Hereward the Wake.

Henry V brought a celebrated case against his stepmother, Joan of Navarre, for attempting to murder him by magic. Her confessor, a friar named John Randolf, acknowledged that he had taken part with her in 'sorcery and necromancy', and it was his statement which seems to have been the main prop of the king's case. Queen Joan was committed to Leeds Castle in Sir John Pelham's charge, and her property was taken from her (a few weeks before he died, Henry directed that her dower be restored). As for John Randolf, he must surely have expected death – the obvious sentence for treason – but he was merely imprisoned during the king's pleasure. In 1429 he was murdered by a mad priest.[5]

Not long afterwards there occurred the case of Eleanor Cobham, the wife of Humphrey, Duke of Gloucester, protector during Henry VI's minority. The duchess had failed to produce a child since her marriage and, in 1441, attempted to procure the desired result by magic with the assistance of two priests, Roger Bolingbroke and Thomas Southwell. Also involved was the Witch of Eye, a woman living in the manor of Eye-next-Westminster named Margery Jourdemayne, who had been arrested for sorcery in 1430 and kept in custody, but later released on her husband's bond.

Unfortunately Eleanor allowed her association with magic to be carried too far, and landed in treasonable territory. She was already said to have gone to Jourdemayne in 1428, obtaining magical charms and potions which helped her induce Gloucester to marry her. Now, in 1441, the duchess prevailed upon Jourdemayne, Bolingbroke and Southwell to assist her in bearing a child. In Fabyan's *New Cronycles* a waxen image was said to have been involved, which she declared in court was employed for fertility purposes but which the prosecution alleged was a representation of the young Henry VI and designed to bring about his death.

Image-magic is one of the best-known techniques of causing harm to one's victim, and is practised in many countries of the world to this day (a Gloucestershire museum until recently contained an exhibit of an effigy of a WAAF officer from the Second World War, dressed in uniform, with a long pin driven through one of its eyes).[6]

The fate of the accused was sealed when Bolingbroke confessed he had, at the duchess's request, used magic to divine her future. He admitted he had 'presumed too far in his cunning', but claimed nothing treasonable was intended: the duchess had merely wanted to know her future and to what rank she would rise.

This was an area fraught with danger. The court construed that enquiring whether her husband might succeed King Henry was tantamount to divining the length of the king's life, something Bolingbroke should have known was forbidden: 'according to the determination of Holy Church and the teaching of divers doctors it was forbidden to any liege of the king to make such calculations about kings and princes without their consent'.[7]

Bolingbroke was certainly a practising magician: at his execution he was made to stand on the scaffold in his conjuror's robes with his instruments, images and other curious objects displayed around him. Among these was a painted chair with swords at each of the four corners, from the points of which hung copper images.

Thomas Southwell died in prison, and Margery Jourdemayne was burned at Smithfield. In the sources she was not directly associated with the treason charges, nor was she accused of heresy, so her punishment was particularly severe. However, it was stated in the *English Chronicle* that this was 'also for cause of relapse', and Professor Kelly suggests perhaps her second conviction for witchcraft drew the death penalty for recidivism, as with a second conviction for heresy. Even more likely is the possibility that, since the Duchess of Gloucester was let off lightly (her civil prosecution was evidently abandoned), Margery bore the brunt of the punishment. The duchess, after abjuring, was sentenced to do public penance on three separate occasions in London, walking barefoot and bareheaded through the streets and carrying a heavy candle which she laid on the altars of three prescribed churches. She spent the rest of her life in prison.

Significantly, Eleanor's marriage to the Duke of Gloucester was annulled in consequence of her use of witchcraft to ensnare his affections. Canon law was explicit that a marriage was valid only if both partners entered into it willingly, and coercion by means of witchcraft (or drugs, potions, etc.) removed the free will of the bewitched party.

This was precisely the impediment cited against Edward IV's marriage to Elizabeth Woodville in the petition drawn up in 1483 and later enshrined in *Titulus Regius*; more than likely it was intended to invoke the precedent of the Eleanor Cobham annulment.

The petition also harked back to an earlier accusation of witchcraft against Elizabeth's mother, Jacquetta de Luxembourg, Duchess of Bedford. During the Warwick-inspired rising against Edward IV in 1469, Warwick's prosperous adherent Thomas Wake, Sheriff of Northampton,

> was bold enough during 'the late trouble and riottous season' to cause Jacquetta ... to 'be brought in a comune noyse and disclaundre of Wichecraft and Sorcerie' by producing before divers lords at Warwick, during the king's visit, an image of lead, broken in the middle and made fast with a wire, saying that it was made by the duchess to use with the said 'Wichcraft and Sorsory'. He also claimed that two others existed, one for the king, the other for the queen. Mortified, the duchess accused Wake of spreading stories throughout the realm of her witchcraft and sorcery.[8]

Although the exact purpose of the witchcraft was not specified, it seems certain that the charges by Warwick's party – currently holding Edward IV in captivity – were an early attempt to invalidate Edward's marriage by formalizing the many rumours that accused Jacquetta of using magic to secure his astonishing liaison with her daughter.

Wake called upon John Daunger, a parish clerk, to bear witness to the dolls representing Edward and Elizabeth. The hearing, however, did not take place until January 1470 when times had changed and Edward was free again. Daunger refused to give the desired evidence, which was well advised since the case was heard by the king himself. Not surprisingly, Jacquetta was cleared.[9]

By the time of the 1483 petition and subsequent Act of Parliament, the charge had widened to include Elizabeth in the alleged witchcraft, 'as the common opinion of the people and the public voice and fame is through all this land'. This common knowledge probably harked back to Jacquetta's sorcery charges which were sensational enough to be remembered still.

★ ★ ★

The circumstances of Edward's second marriage on 1 May 1464 are known to us principally from Fabyan's *New Cronycles*, where it is described as a secret ceremony at which were present a priest, his assistant, Jacquetta and two gentlewomen to witness the contract. The union was then immediately consummated. The date of 1 May seems beyond dispute; although the year is mistaken for 1463, the day is confirmed in the chronicle known as *Hearne's Fragment* (probably the fragmentary memoir of Thomas Howard, Duke of Norfolk),[10] and the same day is given in the Gregory continuation, pseudo-Warkworth and other London chronicles.[11]

The question inevitably arises, did Edward IV visit Grafton on 30 April/1 May 1464 (the spring festivals of Roodmas and Beltane in England, and Walpurgisnacht in Germany) with the full intention of wedding Elizabeth Woodville? Or did he go there expecting the pleasures of the marriage-bed without the liabilities? And was he fed a potent cocktail of aphrodisiacs and love-charms and intoxicating potions to confound his senses and induce him to answer 'Yes' when asked, 'Do you intend to marry this woman?'? If the latter was the case, Edward must have awakened with a rather urgent need to investigate whether he could extricate himself from the new marriage without revealing his previous one with Lady Eleanor Talbot. Could this be the reason he deferred acknowledging it for four whole months?

As W.E. Hampton summarizes:

It is clearly apparent that the young king, one of our history's notable voluptuaries, on a date of obvious significance, and in circumstances and company which were, to put it mildly, dubious, entered into a form of marriage which may well have been precisely what *Titulus Regius* claims, a marriage made by 'sorcerie and wichecrafte, committed by the said Elizabeth and her moder'.[12]

Dabbling in the occult was apparently a popular pastime with the rich and high-born. No retinue, it seems, was complete without its astrologer or necromancer, and the freakish weather of Edward IV's battles of Towton and Barnet was supposed to have been invoked by a certain Friar Bungay.

From the Crowland chronicler we know that George, Duke of Clarence had in his household a man, Thomas Burdett, who was in league with 'Master John Stacey, called the Astronomer though he had rather been a great necromancer'. These two were convicted and executed as the authors of a plot, uncovered in 1477, to procure the king's death by necromancy. Clarence is unlikely to have been innocent of these goings-on, and indeed the magical arts seemed to dominate his thoughts in the last years of his life. By way of retaliation, he employed servants to give public entertainments in which they insinuated that the king used sorcery. Similarly he claimed Queen Elizabeth Woodville had caused his wife's death by the same means. Even so, Edward forbore to take action against his brother, possibly because allegations of witchcraft against Elizabeth were nothing new.

When the king did eventually arraign the duke for treason in 1478, he was charged with spreading the word 'that the king our sovereign lord wrought by nigromancy and used craft to poison his subjects', and 'that the king intended to consume him [Clarence] in like wise as a candle consumeth in burning'. We have already noted that, according to the Crowland continuation, Clarence ostentatiously refused food and drink whenever he visited the king, as if in fear of poison.

To complete the list, we have Harry, Duke of Buckingham, who had among his supporters a certain Thomas Nandyke. Professor Kelly observes that in Nandyke's attainder for rebellion he is described as 'Thomas Nandyk, late of Cambridge, nigromancer', the black art being given prosaically as his profession. Because Nandyke studied medicine it has been suggested he should properly be described as a physician; however, the two arts were certainly not mutually exclusive. He was described in the same way in Henry VII's first Parliament.[13]

So sorcery was not far removed from the highest in the land, nor was it yet categorized in England as heresy, nor viewed with the abhorrence it later acquired. But leading the King of England into a love-trap was certainly playing with fire.

Why did Edward not repudiate the marriage on the grounds of being seduced by witchcraft? There are any number of answers to this, the most obvious being that it was, otherwise, a valid marriage in front of witnesses at which a member of the clergy had officiated. He would need strong evidence to make his accusations stick in the sober context of an ecclesiastical court. Edward was twenty-two years old, with a history of womanizing, and had occupied the throne for just three years. Did he dare take the chance of laying himself open to calumny and ridicule, demeaning the dignity of the crown, and with the chance that the marriage might be ruled valid anyway? Such a circumstance would doom him to endure a tainted queen, with the legitimacy of her offspring jeopardized in the eyes of his people.

Moreover, if a court were convened to deliberate on the matter, would it not open up the perfect opportunity for Lady Eleanor Talbot's claim to be advanced – if not by herself, perhaps by some member of her family? Edward must have had good reason for keeping the marriage secret from May to September 1464.

★ ★ ★

In considering the events of June 1483, it will be remembered that Richard's letter seeking armed support from the north accused Elizabeth Woodville and her supporters not only of attempting his death but also forecasting it (see p. 92). 'There was no more damning accusation than treason, except perhaps sorcery', writes Michael Hicks, completely misunderstanding the relative positions of treason and divination in fifteenth-century law. Richard's primary concern, now that these threats were out in the open, was for arms to defend himself. Hicks, however, seizes on the phrase 'as it is now openly knowen': [14]

It implies the existence of other propaganda now irretrievably lost. Again the source is Richard himself. Should not we perhaps take more seriously the claim of the Tudor chroniclers that Richard also charged her and Hastings with causing his physical deformity by sorcery?

A few things need to be said about these comments by Professor Hicks, author of several books that advocate the traditional view condemning Richard as scheming to become king even before Edward IV's death ('the case for the prosecution' in his *Richard III*, which he modestly advocates as 'the best account of the usurpation').

With the myth of the withered arm and hunchbacked body now dispelled by Richard's own mortal remains, hopefully Hicks will no longer publish such absurdities as suggesting we take more seriously those allegations made by that well known 'Tudor chronicler', Thomas More, i.e., that the deformed creature so ill-favoured of limbs, with his congenitally shrivelled 'withered arm and small', should invent a bogus charge of bewitching him rather than the straightforward charge of treason for which they were actually arrested, according to the contemporaneous reporter Mancini. Even the historian Charles Ross asserts that this is More embroidering fancifully using inventions and dramatic embellishments. Sadly such measured views have never suited Michael Hicks, whose stock in trade is ringing denunciations untroubled by the rigours of careful research: 'serial incestor' is another of his inapt pronouncements on Richard, discussed on p. 294.

As to the central charge of Elizabeth and her adherents forecasting Richard's destruction, Rosemary Horrox comments: 'it would hardly be surprising if they had been hopefully dabbling in witchcraft'.[15] Even so, the prevailing attitude at the time would have regarded this as purely a matter of treason, which must be remembered when writers make the anachronistic claim that such charges were designed to stir up hysteria.

If witchcraft was 'damnable', the sexual immorality of the late king and his cronies was even more so in the eyes of the orthodox. The difference between the two charges lay in the fact that lechery was a matter for the Church, whereas witchcraft employed to the detriment of the crown was a lay crime. Lechery (whether lust, or fornication, or adultery) was in religious terms a mortal sin which entailed the total loss of grace. In the Middle Ages, lechery, murder and apostasy were the three most heinous of such sins. Since the sinner's immortal soul was at stake, it was a far more serious matter than the delusions of witchcraft.

Returning to the subject of Richard's withered arm, let us deal with the episode of the arrest of Hastings. It is notable that only the Tudor writers have Richard accusing Elizabeth Woodville of bewitching him and causing his arm to wither away, since neither Mancini nor Crowland mentions anything of the sort.

We have Thomas More to thank for Shakespeare's famous scene where the protector, complaining of bewitchment, crassly displays to members of the council an arm that has been withered since birth.

Polydore Vergil, though aware of the story, offers a more restrained version:

> for the speace of a few days by past nether nyght nor day can I rest, drynk, nor eat, wherfor my blood by lyttle and lyttle decreaseth, my force fayleth, my breath shorteneth, and all the partes of my body do above measure, as you se (and with that he shewyd them his arme), faule away; which mischief veryly procedeth in me from that sorceres Elyzabeth the quene, who with hir witchcraft hath so enchantyd me that by the anoyance thereof I am dissolvyd.

This occurs in the very earliest layer of Vergil's manuscript, so we may safely conclude that it was a story he shared with Thomas More. Hence no corroboration is provided by the fact that both mention it.

More, however, had little need of prompting since he was thoroughly familiar with the reminiscences of John Morton, who as Bishop of Ely was present at the scene. Whether picked up while in Morton's household, or via the lost Morton tract, he could not fail to have imbibed the Morton-Tudor version of events, no doubt copiously embroidered in the retelling. Typically for such men who have risen by their wits, Morton cannot resist crafting a leading role for himself where in reality he was only a bit-part player. Hence the inconsequential dialogue with Richard requesting strawberries from his garden.

Vergil has no truck with such irrelevances. Presumably he had little choice but to include the story as related to him, since it was doubtless a favourite anecdote trotted out to illustrate the protector's ruthlessness. Indeed, without it there was little else the Tudors could cite to back up their allegations of tyranny and bloodlust.

But despite having heard the current tales, Vergil seems to have reserved judgement as to whether Richard truly brandished before the council an arm which had been withered all his life, or which was even visibly wasted. Vergil's description of Richard, relying on third-party information, exhibits none of More's venom: 'lyttle of stature,' he writes, 'deformyd of body, thone showlder being higher than thother'. He must have struggled with the historical truth that Richard of Gloucester had been Edward IV's foremost military general and led his troops repeatedly in hand-to-hand fighting. It was well attested that in Richard's last mounted charge he was able single-handedly to kill Henry Tudor's standard bearer and unhorse his bodyguard, Sir John Cheyney, described as a man of outstanding strength and fortitude. Vergil himself reports Richard as fighting 'manfully in the thickkest presse of his enemyes' at Bosworth Field.

There is nothing in Vergil, either, of the supposed witchcraft allegations against Edward IV's mistress, Elizabeth Lambert ('Jane Shore'). If More had heard of them we must suppose Vergil had too; but Vergil was a man of the cloth and did not share More's special interest in Edward IV's bed-hopping concubine, an interest that runs to several pages. Thomas More writes as if he had seen her in extremity as a very old woman but, remarkably, does not mention seeking word from her as to the many mysteries on which she might have shed light. Being a mere woman – and a fallen woman at that – her role for him is purely as an object to moralize upon.

From what we learn she was mistress not only to Edward but later to his step-son Thomas, Marquess of Dorset. She was arrested after the Hastings plot was exploded, and eventually required to do penance carrying a taper through the streets of London. This penance was a generic kind of punishment: it could apply to sins such as adultery and fornication (which she could scarcely deny), or equally to the crime of plotting against the protector (for which, if so, it was a remarkably light sentence). It might also have been applicable to witchcraft, though there is no record that she was ever tried or convicted of this. Quite possibly the nature of the penance gave rise to such assumptions.

She also seems to have been suspiciously close to the old warhorse Lord Hastings, for the report in the *Great Chronicle* states that she was 'called to a reckoning for part of [the lord chamberlain's] goods and other things ... all her moveables were attached by the Sheriffs of London, and she lastly as a common harlot put to open penance, for the life that [she] led with the said Lord Hastings and other great estates'. If correct, this is a clear refutation of More's other allegation that Richard plundered her of her possessions. The chronicle plainly says her goods were seized in order to return certain of them to Hastings's widow.

In summary, More's claims in relation to Elizabeth Lambert are clearly very questionable, with no other source mentioning any witchcraft charge against her; let us put it down to dramatic licence.

What is tremendously significant is that no *contemporaneous* source mentions any witchcraft allegation against anyone that day. Mancini paints a dramatic scene with the protector crying out that an ambush has been prepared for him, but relates not a word of accusation against the queen or the mistress.

The Crowland chronicler merely notes cryptically that 'Lord Hastings was beheaded'. By contrast, he has waxed eloquent enough regarding discussions at previous council meetings, even to the extent of quoting several of them verbatim. Yet of this most momentous occasion he tells us nothing.

It is insufficient to claim that, not being present, he had no knowledge of the incident. This does not deter him elsewhere. If we scan his accounts of events such as the confrontations at Northampton and Stony Stratford, we see they contain no lack of detail (and dialogue) despite the obvious fact that he could not have been there. We even have a report of Richard's supposed dreams on the eve of Bosworth. If our chronicler was able to put together that kind of information, he was certainly better able than Mancini to discover what transpired on 13 June at the Tower of London.

Why, then, did he let it pass without comment? Probably he had no justification to offer for the actions of his paragon,

Elizabeth Woodville, when her treasonous scheming with Hastings came to light. Until now he had characterized her as purely benevolent and innocent. Had Richard truly accused her of blighting him with witchcraft, it is inconceivable that the chronicler would not have leapt to her defence. Indeed, any such accusation would have provided a welcome distraction, enabling him to fulminate against such scurrilous vilification while allowing him to pass over the more uncomfortable implications of her criminal activities.

What really happened is not difficult to visualize. We may easily imagine Richard, having discovered a treasonous plot, inveighing against 'that Woodville witch', and likely dredging up all those past suspicions of spell-casting and divination. In his rage he probably expatiated on what would seem like a new bewitchment: that of Hastings, who only recently appeared to display enmity towards her family, but had now been magically induced to join their intrigues. Faced with such betrayal, who would not suspect witchery? The pantomime of the withered arm is merely another of those Tudor red herrings thrown in later, just like the substitution of 'Elizabeth Lucy' for Lady Eleanor: a fiction designed to discredit the truth simply because the fiction is so ludicrous.

Alison Hanham reads it as dreamed up (like the Lucy story) by More alone, which would seem perverse on the part of a man usually considered upright and impartial. But Hanham does not subscribe to the thesis that there was a tract written by the political schemer Morton which set out the Tudor stall so as to discredit the preceding régime. She believes that both the 'arm withered since birth', and in all probability the entire witchcraft recital, are More's personal dramatic creations. 'More in fact probably invents the whole charge, and then says it is a lie of Richard's.'[16]

Whoever was responsible, the effect was calculated. More, and indeed any writer of the Tudor period, would expect to engender a special *frisson* of horror by dwelling on anything to do with witchcraft, as by then the sixteenth-century witch mania had truly begun to take hold in England.

The origins of this extraordinary hysteria may be traced directly to a member of the Inquisition, the Dominican friar Heinrich Kraemer, who in 1486 wrote *Malleus Maleficarum* or *Witches' Hammer* (note the feminine gender), a work that became the handbook of witch-hunters throughout Christendom.

The entire climate surrounding witchcraft changed radically in the wake of this publication; especially after a reprint implied papal approval by quoting a Bull, issued by Pope Innocent VIII in 1484, which had supported the activities of Kraemer and his partner Johann Sprenger in rooting out heresy. The name of Sprenger has been associated with *Malleus* ever since.

In reality, the obsession with witches was a phenomenon that had developed almost exclusively in continental Europe. Before the sixteenth century, 'In England, where the Inquisition never gained a foothold, and where the use of torture was illegal except in very special cases, the concept of a malignant and dangerous witch-cult, dedicated to the worship of the Devil and the performance of every sort of evil, was very slow to take root.'[17]

Although *Malleus* did not go unchallenged, it subverted the established doctrine that Satan could produce only illusions: its claim was that demonic entities actually did interact with humans. It propounded at great length the depravity of witches, and set out the legal procedures for witch trials. Now under the banner of heresy, and within the purview of the Inquisition, official Church policy towards witchcraft underwent an ominous change, with torture sanctioned even in England as a means of securing confessions.

So by the time of Vergil and More, witchcraft had taken on the loathsome mantle of heresy and consorting with the devil, with terrifying results for anyone accused of it. Naturally this colours their writing.

It is therefore instructive to reflect that Richard III, despite being assumed guilty of many crimes, was never accused outright of practising the black arts. This did not prevent myth-making about his physiognomy which was clearly intended to show that he was marked by evil. John Ashdown-Hill writes that 'a physical deformity could be both the punishment for, and the unmistakable sign of a twisted and evil mind'.[18] In witchcraft beliefs, it could also be the visible sign of a pact with the devil.

Hence, Richard was endowed by Tudor writers with several signs of monstrousness, starting with John Rous's description 'retained in his mother's womb for two years ... emerging with teeth and hair to his shoulders'.[19]

Rous also reported that in adulthood those shoulders were not level – a common enough occurrence, but represented by his detractors as a hunched back. More's jeering term 'crook-back' (taken up enthusiastically by Shakespeare along with the 'withered arm' and a hobbling leg of his own invention) is not visible in the 1510 Paston family portrait shown on the cover of this book; it is seen only in later portraits, starting with the one in the Royal Collection (logically enough), dated *c.*1515–20, in which the addition of a raised right shoulder has been revealed under X-ray.

The unreliability of such stories is evidenced in inconsistencies between writers, where the one cannot agree with the other which shoulder was higher, and a withered arm bewitched in Vergil is congenital in More. Of course the symbology of depicting a villain as monstrous runs contrary to modern sensibilities. But 'to the sixteenth-century mind,' says John Ashdown-Hill, 'it was largely irrelevant whether or not accounts of Richard's deformity were objectively true. What mattered was that they represented a perceived psychological truth.'

8

Dynastic
Manoeuvrings

History tells us a great deal about mediæval kings and princes, but not much about their advisers and supporters. Relatively little is known about Harry Stafford, Duke of Buckingham, and his ambitions and motivations remain a mystery.

Although we have no record of any previous relationship, we must assume Gloucester and Buckingham knew each other to some degree. They were about the same age, both habitués of the Yorkist Court, and after the death of Clarence the two senior royal dukes of England. There, however, the resemblance ended. Buckingham had grown up as a pawn in the hands of Edward IV and his queen, and without ever receiving the kind of public office that befitted his eminent rank. His family, for example, had hereditarily held the office of High Constable of England, a role denied him by Edward.

Since Buckingham seems to have been energetic and articulate, Edward must have had a reason for blocking his progress. We have to assume the answer lies in Domenico Mancini's report that he detested the queen's kin, having been forced to marry her sister whose humble origins he scorned.

It is worth spending a moment to review Buckingham's exalted bloodline, since such matters were of paramount importance in the fifteenth century, when families and their lawyers would spend happy hours poring over pedigrees and charts of inheritance.

Humphrey Stafford, first Duke of Buckingham (Harry's grandfather), had been a wise and noble councillor to Henry VI, with a reputation for integrity that was unique in those times of aggressive self-interest. The Harry Stafford who shot to fame in 1483 was the second duke, having succeeded when he was about five years old upon his grandfather's death in 1460 – the title skipped a generation when Harry's father died of the plague (as C.A.J. Armstrong ascertained) in 1458. As the senior descendant of Thomas of Woodstock, Duke of Gloucester, youngest son of Edward III (see Table 4), he headed one of the longest-established and wealthiest English magnate families.

Buckingham's mother, Margaret, was also descended from Edward III: she was a daughter of Edmund Beaufort, Duke of Somerset, whose father was the eldest child of John of Gaunt's adultery. All of Gaunt's illegitimate offspring were eventually legitimated, but as we have seen in chapter 3, when Henry IV became king he barred the Beaufort line from succession to the crown.

Harry Stafford's mother was not, in any case, the senior female of the legitimated Beaufort line: that position belonged to her wealthy and much-married kinswoman Lady Margaret Beaufort, mother of the exiled Henry Tudor.

Buckingham's standing was such that Warwick the Kingmaker would have considered him an excellent match for one of his daughters, Isabel or Anne; but Edward IV had neatly pre-empted any such alliance by purchasing Buckingham's wardship for his sister Anne. Soon after his marriage to Elizabeth the boy was bestowed on the Woodville clan as husband for the queen's younger sister Catherine. Young Harry's mortification must have festered for years. Subsequently he lived at Court as a member of the queen's household, being honoured solely as a Knight of the Garter and Knight of the Bath.

Buckingham evidently harboured ambitions commensurate with his rank and status. Acutely conscious of his royal line, in 1474 he obtained 'a heraldic decree allowing him to display the arms of Edward III's youngest son, Thomas of Woodstock, Duke of Gloucester, "a coate neire to the king and of his royall bloude"'. Significantly, when he adopted the royal arms, he did not quarter them with those of Stafford. Edward IV was reportedly furious; nevertheless he acted as godfather to Harry's son, named Edward in his honour. Yet he still prevented Buckingham from wielding influence even in his own territorial heartland of Wales, where lay his great marcher lordship of Brecon. Instead the area was carved out as the main sphere of influence for the Prince of Wales, with a council controlled by the Woodvilles on which there was, conspicuously, no place for Buckingham.

In the spring of 1483, from a position of relative obscurity, Harry of Buckingham suddenly emerged as a central figure in events of the highest national importance. Self-appointed supporter of the protector, he appears to have been constantly at Richard's elbow for nearly three months; so much so that the Crowland chronicler referred to them ('the two dukes') as jointly instigating all that ensued. Perhaps they enjoyed cutting a dash as the two leading magnates in the land: young, fashionable and closely tied by blood, with many interests and ambitions in common. Perhaps both of them had found, for the first time, a friend and confidant of similar age and rank.

As Buckingham's career took off he received a string of high offices, effectively making him the supreme power in Wales. Having taken a leading role in the arrest and execution of Hastings, he received most of that lord's offices after his death, adding the command of Hastings's midlands power base to his already overwhelming control in the south-west, Wales and Welsh Marches. We hear from Edward Hall that he progressed splendidly about the city at the head of a large entourage, and from John Rous that he boasted his livery was worn by as many men as had worn the badge of Warwick.

Appointed Great Chamberlain of England, he played a central role at Richard's magnificent coronation on 6 July. On 15 July, he was given his family's traditional office of High Constable. But the most valuable boon granted him was the second moiety of the vast Bohun inheritance, which he claimed from Richard by right of being the heir after the death of Henry VI. This he was granted provisionally – needing only the confirmation of Parliament – as soon as Richard was able to convey it to him, by a signet letter on 13 July. This was followed by a signed warrant dated 27 August.

After all these demonstrations of friendship and esteem from his sovereign, it is hard to believe that by mid-September Buckingham had turned his back on Richard and led a rebellion against him.

* * *

Before this turn of events, with the coronation approaching, at last the long-awaited force from the north arrived and encamped outside the city. Armstrong, in his notes to Mancini's text, estimates it was unlikely that they arrived before 1 July. Alison Hanham plumps for 3 July.

As to its numbers, there were conjectures as wildly high as 20,000 circulating in June, and Crowland refers to 'armed men in frightening and unheard-of numbers' being sent for. However, when the army did arrive Mancini estimated its size at 6,000, the *Great Chronicle* at between 4,000 and 5,000, and Fabyan and the *Chronicles of London*/Vitellius at no more than 4,000. The hastily-summoned northerners soon became an object of mirth as the citizens caught sight of their rusty gear and makeshift harness. Immediately after the coronation, having assisted in policing the capital, they were sent home with thanks and rewards.

Jeremy Potter has admirably summed up the exaggerated claims that Richard had used these men to cow the whole of London. Potter is citing James Gairdner's *Richard III* in the following extract, but Gairdner's views are echoed by many authoritative voices who similarly declare that the only reason Richard met with support was because people were thoroughly terrorized.

> The executions of Hastings in London and of Rivers and two others in Yorkshire, taken together with Richard's summons of troops from the north to secure his position in the capital, are said to constitute a 'reign of terror'. 'For with us,' wrote Simon Stallworth in London to Sir William Stonor in Oxfordshire on 21 June, 'there is much trouble, and every man doubts the other'. This is evidence of uncertainty and apprehension, but the high colour of some of Gairdner's authorities seems to have been infectious. Mancini estimated that Richard and Buckingham entered London with no more than 500 retainers between them, and the armed northeners, estimated by Fabyan at 4,000, did not reach the capital until the beginning of July and went home immediately after the coronation on the sixth, noted for nothing except the contempt of Londoners at their antiquated equipment and rusty armour. This would seem to constitute the least bloody and terrifying reign of terror in history.[1]

Domenico Mancini, writing to please his French patrons, attributes the petitioning of Richard to the fear of those northern troops which had not, at the time, even left Yorkshire:

> ... warned by the example of Hastings, and aware of the alliance between the two dukes whose power it would be difficult and dangerous to resist *in view of their numerous forces, the lords felt as if cornered and powerless in their hands.* So they looked to their own safety and resolved upon declaring Richard their king ... [the emphasis is mine].

Michael Hicks makes the same mistake, suggesting the quasi-parliament in June was 'perhaps overawed by the northern army encamped at Finsbury Fields.'[2]

To restore some balance, we must remember that this was the heyday of what has come to be called 'bastard feudalism', when every wealthy lord and local magnate worth his salt maintained a force of armed retainers. Moreover, we know from Mancini that each lord had arrived in London 'with the retinue that his dignity and rank warranted', and that these numbers of armed retainers so frightened the citizens that Richard asked the lords to remove the majority of them from the capital. 'They complied with his counsels,' says Mancini; yet in times of such uncertainty, is it likely these magnates were foolish enough to denude themselves of armed support? Rather than disbanding their retainers, they doubtless found them billets outside the city. Looking at facts realistically, just how overawed were they by a northern contingent of unknown size which was well over a week's march away?

At any rate, all remained peaceable in London. The coronation was a most splendid occasion, exceeding all previous coronations in the numbers of peers of the realm attending. Ricardians note that this alone might lead one to assume that Richard enjoyed considerable support. Anti-Richards naturally insist any show of approval was due to intimidation. The reader must judge which is more likely. Certainly Richard's support by the city fathers of London never wavered.

Both Lord Stanley and his wife, Lady Margaret Beaufort, played prominent roles at the ceremony, and Richard prudently commanded Stanley to accompany him on his coronation progress. This tour of the realm took several months, wending its way westward towards Gloucester and Tewkesbury, then northward to its farthest destination of York, and ultimately back through central England to Leicester and Oxford in October.

In Richard's absence there occurred at least one attempt to remove the deposed Edward V and his brother from the Tower of London, and ideas were also conceived to remove their sisters from sanctuary and spirit them overseas. The Crowland chronicler confirms this information, but his account of events between July and September, though important as a time-frame, is telescoped into few words with scant detail.

More useful is the evidence of a signet letter from Richard written at Minster Lovell on 29 July, which cryptically gives instructions to Russell, his chancellor, to arrange for the full force of law to be applied to 'certaine personnes' who 'of late had taken upon them the fact of an enterprise' (i.e. would have attempted to undertake a plot or dangerous scheme, had they not been prevented) and are presently 'attached and in ward' (i.e. in prison). It has been ventured that the plot refers to the murder of Richard's two nephews, but this can instantly be ruled out: had the culprits been so promptly apprehended and convicted, it would have scotched all later rumours as to the fate of the boys.

The more natural reading is that the letter refers to proceedings against the instigators of a failed conspiracy to abduct them. This is supported by other convincing evidence of an unsuccessful plot at about this time, recounted by the Elizabethan antiquary John Stow:

> After this were taken for rebels against the king, Robert Russe sergeant of London, William Davy pardoner of Hounslow, John Smith groom of King Edward's stirrup, and Stephen Ireland wardrober of the Tower, with many others, that they should have sent writings into the parts of Brittany to the Earls of Richmond and of Pembroke and the other lords; and how they were purposed to have set fire to divers parts of London, which fire whilst men had been staunching, they would have stolen out of the Tower the Prince Edward and his brother Richard of York.[3]

Stow says they were tried at Westminster, condemned to death, publicly beheaded at Tower Hill, and their heads exhibited on London Bridge.

This account receives corroboration in a report by Thomas Basin, Bishop of Lisieux, cited by Michael Hicks, who recounts 'a plot by fifty Londoners on the princes' behalf which failed to attract support and led to the execution of four of them. Brief though his account is, it is strictly contemporary – probably written by the very beginning of 1484 – and prompts us to give greater credence to Stow's version than would otherwise be the case'.[4]

Hicks has found no other mention of this crime and the consequent executions: no indictments survive, and no records of convictions and executions appear in the King's Bench Controlment Rolls. 'The story could nevertheless be true,' he concedes. 'They could have been summarily tried before the court of the Constable: we do not have his records, do not know indeed whether he kept any, and cannot therefore speculate whether Stow's evidence accords with such a source'.

Looking again at Richard's letter of 29 July, it is striking that he is at pains to conceal names and details, even when writing to his chancellor who knew all about it. Obviously it had been decided, in the interests of public order, to keep the whole thing quiet (after all, the plot had been frustrated) and thus the use of the Constable's powers makes sense. This summary court, which had responsibility for trying treasonable offences, could be convened on an *ad hoc* basis and the culprits quickly and quietly despatched.

As we know, the High Constable now was none other than Harry, Duke of Buckingham. Had he been involved it might suggest that he was still in the London area in early August, despite Vergil's statement that he was with the king at Gloucester (whence the royal progress departed on 2 August). But evidence indicates that the matter was probably handled by Richard's recently created Earl Marshal, John Howard, Duke of Norfolk: the Earl Marshal was empowered, like the Constable, to try cases of treason. Entries in Norfolk's household books show that he left Richard's progress and returned urgently to London, making a number of arrests en route at Bray. On arrival he set preparations in train for some considerable business to take place at Crosby Place, Richard's London mansion. They included laying down quantities of straw, obviously indicating an assembly, and paying for nails to construct a 'sege' (a chair or throne). This could very well have been for Howard to preside over a session of the Constable's Court.[5]

We can usually be confident in the word of antiquaries such as John Stow, a member of the erudite 'College or Society of Antiquaries' founded in 1586, which inaugurated strict standards of research and objective analysis. It would be surprising if Stow made significant errors of fact, or took his notes from a less than wholly reliable source (which in this case we are led to believe was the original record of the indictment).

Nevertheless, Professor Hicks has challenged one aspect of the indictment, being the statement that Russe and company were charged, as part of their intrigue, with writing to 'the Earls of Richmond and of Pembroke and the other lords' in Brittany, the earliest known indication of Tudor involvement in treasonable designs. Hicks objects on the grounds that it does not work chronologically. 'Is this likely to have featured in any trial record in July,' he asks, 'given that communication with [the Tudors] abroad was not yet treasonable? ... Stow mentions them communicating with the two Tudor earls "and the other lords". What other lords? Surely there were only "other lords" after Buckingham's Rebellion caused many other gentry to join the Tudors in Brittany in the winter of 1483?'

Based on this reference to 'other lords in Brittany', Hicks postulates that the plot happened after October 1483. But this cannot be so: as we are told in Crowland, by the time of the October rebellion Edward V and his brother were presumed dead by the rebels. Yet Stow and Basin clearly state that the attempt was mounted to remove them from the Tower of London. Indeed, the conspirator Stephen Ireland was an officer of the wardrobe who worked at the Tower and was obviously in a position to know that his associates were not wasting their time trying to remove a pair of dead or missing children.

On examination, the caveat regarding treasonable correspondence is not difficult to resolve: though it might not have been treasonous *per se* to correspond with the Tudors in July, it certainly was if that correspondence concerned taking Edward V from the Tower.

As to 'other lords' being in Brittany at this date, it is unknown whether Stow was quoting or paraphrasing, and he might have used the word 'lords' as a generic term for unnamed high-ranking personages whom he did not actually know to be members of the nobility. One such was the ex-queen's exalted brother, Sir Edward Woodville, who had already fled to Brittany in early May bringing with him two ships and large amounts of treasure. Woodville family members enjoyed courtesy titles such as, for example, that of 'Lord Grey' which was given to Elizabeth's son Sir Richard Grey. Exactly who sailed as Woodville's cohorts and commanded his ships is not known, but he was certainly accompanied by what was described as a retinue, and one of its leading members, Robert Ratclyff, an associate of Earl Rivers, was prominent enough to be denounced by name as an enemy of the State. I suggest we need not fret too much about these 'other lords'.

To digress for a moment, Sir Edward Woodville's activities in Brittany are interesting to consider. Richard III found them of sufficient concern to name Woodville as one of the principal matters to be raised with the Duke of Brittany in negotiations with his personal agent, Dr Thomas Hutton, within days of his coronation. By contrast, the Tudors were not even mentioned in Hutton's written instructions.

As a man with his sights set on a military career, Sir Edward presumably did not spend his sojourn in idleness; logic suggests he would use his time recruiting the Tudors (as he thought) to the Woodville cause of restoring Edward V. His party was desperate for support after Hastings was eliminated, so in secret correspondence with his relatives in sanctuary and elsewhere, Woodville doubtless hatched plans to offer suitable inducements. We cannot doubt that Edward's ill-gotten treasure would constitute a great attraction, hence Tudor involvement in Stow's plot is perfectly feasible.

Lady Margaret Beaufort, communicating simultaneously with the Tudor camp, would have advised her son to demand a high price for his supposed allegiance to the Woodville cause. Nothing less than the hand of Edward IV's eldest daughter, young Elizabeth of York, would suffice (or, if she should die, her next sister).

Elizabeth Woodville, for her part, would consider it a fair bargain provided the betrothal was contingent upon her son being restored to the throne. Indeed, she would not have been surprised at the demand – it was a prize on which Lady Margaret had long set her sights.

Margaret had only recently enjoyed political influence under the Edwardian régime since marrying her fourth husband, Thomas Lord Stanley, in 1472. A great and politically dangerous magnate, Stanley had risen to a position of prominence under Edward despite equivocal loyalties in the turbulent days of the Yorks' power struggles, when he and his family had pursued a policy of hedging their bets. Through his new wife Stanley now made valuable territorial gains, and through her new husband Margaret enjoyed enhanced influence at court, including a certain intimacy with the Woodvilles: in 1480 she was permitted the honour of carrying Queen Elizabeth's new daughter, Bridget, at the official celebrations of her birth.

Profoundly ambitious for her exiled son, it was in an attempt to claw a way for him into the bosom of the royal family that she essayed negotiations from an early date for Henry to marry a daughter of Edward IV. This comes to light in sworn depositions by Lord Stanley and others in 1486, which are worth examining since historians have been quick to read into them rather more interest on the part of Edward IV than necessarily existed.

These sworn statements were recorded on behalf of Pope Innocent VIII in 1486 in connection with the dispensation sought by Henry for his marriage to Elizabeth of York, which was otherwise prohibited by their close family relationship. Various witnesses stated what they knew of the kinship between the proposed marriage partners, and how they had come by their knowledge. A number of people came forward, including Thomas Stanley (by now Earl of Derby) and the Earl of Nottingham. In reality the witnesses merely said that in the past they had heard certain named people mention the degree of kinship existing between Henry and Elizabeth; no context was given, and nobody claimed to have heard it in connection with plans for any marriage. Stanley and Nottingham added that Edward IV and Margaret had 'held themselves to be kinsmen' – but again, despite the obvious insinuation, no specific claim was made that marriage was under discussion at the time.

We get a clue as to the dates when such remarks had been heard, since two or three witnesses recalled Warwick the Kingmaker and his brother George, Archbishop of York, being party to them. We know George fell from favour in 1467 and rebelled in 1469, and Warwick was never again intimate with the king after his own role in the same rebellion. In 1469 Edward IV's three little princesses were aged about three, two and one respectively, hence marriage was a far distant proposition: so far distant for discussions to be safe *vis-à-vis* a possible arrangement for Margaret Beaufort's son, on a strictly hypothetical basis. No need for a particular girl to be specified, far less promised. Indeed, Edward might have had one of his bastard daughters in mind.

Elizabeth of York, as Edward's first-born, was most unlikely to have been a candidate in view of her significance. Certainly by January 1470 she was betrothed to her second cousin George Neville, Duke of Bedford; subsequently her availability can be ruled out from the year 1475, when she was contracted in marriage to the dauphin of France. Edward's second daughter, Mary, seems to have been kept out of the marriage market from the latter date owing to her position as 'first reserve' for the dauphin (Mary died in 1482). His third daughter, Cecily, was destined for a Scottish marriage from 1474 until at least 1478. No love-matches, we note, for Edward's children.

Prior to these arrangements, there was nothing to stop the king humouring Margaret by talking in a general way about his young female offspring, which was quite probably all he did. Of course, in the papal depositions of 1486 the only sister mentioned was Elizabeth of York because it was for her marriage to Henry VII that the dispensation was sought. If the impression was given that it was a marriage favoured all along by Edward IV, so much the better for public relations.

Given the above position, we can safely rule out the suggestion by Griffiths and Thomas that Edward was thought to have dangled such a marriage in front of Henry around November 1476 in the hope of luring him back to England: 'Francis II [of Brittany] commended Henry Tudor to King Edward, apparently believing that he would treat the young man honourably and marry him to his own daughter, Elizabeth of York.'[6]

Even more recently, Margaret Beaufort had tried in 1482 to arrange a deal for Edward and Henry to be reconciled, in an attempt to clear the way for her son to reclaim a family inheritance that now sat invitingly on the horizon. There is no record of any marriage discussions at that date, and it was not until December of that year that Elizabeth of York became free after her betrothal to the dauphin was repudiated by Louis XI of France. Tudor, meanwhile, preferred to remain in exile, unwilling to trust Edward sufficiently to take advantage of any opening Margaret might have devised.

The chronicler Edward Hall adds that marriage approaches on behalf of Henry were also made to Richard of Gloucester in June 1483, for which the Duke of Buckingham acted as a go-between. This is unsubstantiated, and seems rather doubtful since at this time Elizabeth Woodville still held all her daughters out of reach in sanctuary. If such discussions did take place, one wonders whether Margaret's primary motivation might not have been to test the waters with a view to building a closer political relationship with the protector via her newly powerful kinsman, Harry of Buckingham. If so, she perhaps noted that malleable streak in Buckingham's nature which she would later be able to exploit.

* * *

Meanwhile we have not quite finished our examination of Stow's plot and its aftermath. Given that it was a failed enterprise, and that the records of the time do not help us, we are left to draw our own conclusions as regards the public executions. Louise Gill confirms the fact that the four were executed, but adds no further elucidation. It could well be that the executions were not carried out in public after all, which may explain why these commoners were, unusually, beheaded rather than hanged and disembowelled for the edification of the masses. The official sentence of public execution with heads displayed, as recorded by Stow, might have been changed later to a private affair in the interests of discretion.

Rosemary Horrox, who managed to identify one of the accused, John Smith, also pointed out that John Welles was carrying on subversive activities which led to his being declared a rebel on 13 August. Details of the Welles case are provided by Gill: 'Another plot in early August focused on Margaret Beaufort's half-brother, John Welles, who organized a conspiracy at the Beaufort manor of Maxey in Northamptonshire. On discovery, he forfeited his lands on 13 August and joined

Henry Tudor in Brittany.' This was long before the October uprising known as Buckingham's Rebellion, so what was Welles conspiring to do at the beginning of August (or late July)? As Dr Horrox observes, 'He is known to have been in rebellion sufficiently early for his initial aim to have been the restoration of Edward V.'[7]

We cannot guess at Welles's motives, but there seems little doubt that he was enlisted by his half-sister. Just as Gill believes Margaret Beaufort was up to her ears in the attempt reported by Stow, so her biographers, Jones and Underwood, affirm it was 'almost certainly at Margaret's prompting' that Welles became involved. Rosemary Horrox adds, 'Lady Margaret presumably hoped that a grateful Edward V would restore her son to political life and to the earldom of Richmond.'[8]

Knowing Margaret Beaufort's steely ambition for her son, it is hard to believe she merely hoped for preferment. The only possible conclusion is that some kind of deal was being hatched with the Woodvilles. King Richard might have had his doubts about Thomas Stanley, but it was Stanley's wife who proved to be the arch-schemer of the two.

Such was Richard's reaction to the Welles conspiracy that immediately upon its discovery, on 9 August, he started stockpiling weapons. Preliminary orders sent from Warwick Castle to his servant Nicholas Spicer were followed by more orders issued at Leicester on 17 August, for Spicer to 'cause 20,000 Welsh bills to be purveyed and made in all haste possible, with the power and authority to take in the king's name, wherever should seem most expedient, as many smiths as he considered necessary to accomplish this'.[9]

We receive confirmation of two important facts from these plots: first, the boys were still lodged in the Tower at least until late July, thanks to the inside knowledge of the wardrober. Second, they had not, by 13 August, unaccountably disappeared or been found dead: this is evident from the fact that Welles, having been declared a rebel on 13 August, walked free within a week and endured no worse fate than having his lands seized. This would have been inconceivable had anything sinister befallen the boys.

By the same token, had they been killed by Richard he could not afford to pass up this golden opportunity of pinning the crime on a ready-made scapegoat, one who had been apprehended in the very act of scheming to get his hands on them. He merely had to accuse and convict Welles and the matter was closed.

So, for those die-hards who really believe the 'princes' were murdered in the Tower of London, the deed had to take place after 13 August 1483. Despite this, the list of chroniclers who recorded talk of their deaths at an earlier date is very long indeed, and is headed by Domenico Mancini.

We need not, by the way, suppose that the Welles-Beaufort conspiracy was aimed at removing the princesses rather than their brothers, even though this idea might suggest itself in light of the special value they now held as a reward for Tudor-Beaufort support. True, there were whisperings of plots to spirit the girls overseas, which led the king to place an armed guard around Westminster Abbey. But Elizabeth Woodville knew full well that her strength now lay in her absolute personal control of her daughters. The reason is simple: she and Margaret Beaufort had not by this time concluded any formal marriage agreement (as confirmed by our main source, Polydore Vergil). It would have been far too risky to jeopardize the honour and safety of the young princesses – especially Elizabeth and Cecily, who were of primary interest to Tudor – when they represented the very crux of ongoing negotiations. To the ex-queen they offered the means of bringing rich and powerful forces to the cause of restoring Edward V, while to Margaret Beaufort they represented the key to her son's glorious destiny.

For the betrothal negotiations and their effect on Henry Tudor's plans we must try to make sense of Vergil who, although he had access to Tudor informants, including Lady Margaret herself, was often given a massaged account of events. Here Vergil offers two separate versions of how the marriage idea was conceived. Vergil's first version appears on pp. 194–5 and starts with Buckingham excusing himself from Richard's progress when they reached Gloucester (2 August). On arrival at Brecon he is described as suggesting a plan to his prisoner, John Morton, Bishop of Ely, to marry Henry Tudor to a female heir of Edward IV, in support of which Buckingham is to rebel against Richard III. That this idea was Buckingham's is less than credible; but we can learn much from the logistics.

Historians (e.g. Hampton and Gill) appear to agree that Buckingham made his way to Brecon via south or south-east Wales, presumably in order to visit his Stafford estates on the way; the earliest date for which we have evidence that he was in Brecon is 23 August when an order passed under his personal signet.[10] Let us assume this detour lasted a week or so, giving us an arrival date at Brecon of, say, 9–10 August.

A series of conversations follow during which Buckingham persuades Bishop Morton of his plan; this must take us to a date a few days later, say, conservatively, 12 August. Next, Vergil tells us that Morton – who evidently has a long-standing association with Margaret Beaufort – procures the countess's servant Reginald Bray as a messenger, presumably by sending word to her in London that he needs a confidential go-between (this must consume another eight or ten days before Bray can reach Brecon, say around 21 August). Bray subsequently returns to Lady Margaret and reports the outcome of the Buckingham-Morton intrigue (another five or six days for the turnaround and the journey back to London, taking us to 26–27 August).

In Vergil's second version of the story (p. 195) he tells us that Margaret has earlier and independently secured Elizabeth Woodville's agreement to the identical marriage plan: 'Now before the duke all in a rage had begun to be alyenate in mynde from king Richard, the same very time a plot of new conspiracy was layd at London betwixt Elyzabeth the quene, wyfe to king Edward, and Margaret mother to erle Henry.' So in this version the marriage idea was first hatched by the two mothers in London. This chimes exactly with Edward Woodville discussing it as part of an attempt to enlist Tudor-Beaufort aid in restoring Edward V.

The idea of the marriage was never, in my view, conceived by Buckingham, and doubts on this likelihood are also expressed by Griffiths and Thomas.[11] Neither does the Crowland chronicler support this notion: he writes that the duke, while in Brecon, repented his part in previous events and proclaimed that he would become captain-in-chief of the rebellion which had been set afoot to right the wrongs of supplanting Edward IV's sons; and that later, after rumours said those sons were dead, the rebels supported the prospect of a Tudor married to a daughter of York. No suggestion that Buckingham ever promoted the marriage himself. Indeed, the true motivation for his *volte face* is still not known; it is possible (see chapter 11) that he had his own sights on the crown.

Regarding this much-discussed marriage proposition, which Elizabeth Woodville knew perfectly well was long desired by Margaret Beaufort, it has been my suggestion that it was the price for the Tudor party's help in reinstating Edward V. Elizabeth would not have been willing to commit any daughter to a contract of marriage without cast-iron guarantees. Most likely, therefore, these discussions were protracted and complex with both sides jockeying for the best deal they could get. Probably those Beaufort-backed attempts at removing Edward V and his brother from the Tower constituted demonstrations of good faith demanded by the ex-queen before she was prepared to negotiate seriously. What other incentive would induce Margaret to become involved with highly treasonous activities which furthered her precious Henry's career not one whit?

After some weeks of discussions, by our putative date of 26–27 August Margaret and Elizabeth had so recently reached agreeable terms that (as Vergil tells us) Margaret had not yet sent the good news to her son in Brittany by means of her intended messenger, the priest Christopher Urswick. When she heard from Brecon that Buckingham had been induced to join the rebellion to unseat Richard III, we are told she now decided to send a different messenger, Hugh Conway, accompanied by (significantly) large amounts of cash.

This was the moment at which the Tudors started to see their schemes bear fruit. They now had a plan they could take to their host Francis II, Duke of Brittany: a Tudor-Woodville alliance, a royal betrothal in prospect, a couple of ships and funds to pay for more, and Buckingham leading an army the size of which he was boasting rivalled that of the late Earl of Warwick. They would, of course, claim that it was all to restore Edward V.

Certainly John Morton was clever enough to foresee that the idea of the betrothal could be used to Henry Tudor's advantage without the inconvenience of the Woodville restoration. Elizabeth Woodville would remain on side as long as she thought they were working on behalf of her son, and anyway she and her daughters were closeted in sanctuary and unable to follow the twists and turns of events except at a distance. Much could be

claimed on Henry Tudor's behalf without the ex-queen's side of
the story ever coming to light.

Margaret's message to her son must have impressed Francis of
Brittany, whose expressions of friendship towards Richard III
were soon given the lie by his agreement with the Tudor-
Woodville camp to supply cash, ships, provisions and fighting
men for an invasion of England to coincide with the planned
rebellion. The accounts of Francis's receiver-general show that a
flotilla was being assembled during the first weeks of September,[12]
which Polydore Vergil tells us comprised fifteen vessels and 5,000
Breton soldiers. This was in preparation long before the rumour
of Edward V's death was spread, so Francis clearly thought he
was supporting his restoration, as evidently did the Woodvilles.
Corroboration can be seen in Sir Edward Woodville's personal act
of gratitude in 1488 when, without Tudor approval, he headed an
expedition to try to save Brittany from conquest by France.

The clincher for Francis's support was surely the arrival of
Hugh Conway bearing not only money but, importantly, the news
that they had a new ally in Buckingham. Meanwhile, the latter
had left Brecon in response to letters from Richard III requiring
him to head a commission of oyer and terminer (*ad hoc* assizes)
in London and the Home Counties. Ironically, the letters were
issued on 28 August, the day after the king had signed the final
warrant allowing the ungrateful duke to enter upon his coveted
Bohun inheritance. Since the commission required him to look
into the very same rebellious elements which John Morton had
encouraged him to join, it was a simple matter for Buckingham
to make contact with the ringleaders and assure them that his
magnificent army was at their disposal. Soon he was taking his
place as the leader of the planned insurrection.

★ ★ ★

To return to the betrothal of Henry Tudor and Elizabeth of York,
we must bear in mind when reading Vergil's account of Margaret
Beaufort's role in the summer of 1483 that it is calculated to make
her seem the chief instigator of England's salvation. Understandably
both Henry and his mother (and Morton in his lost manuscript)

would wish to foster the impression that they were the heroes of their own legend, with Buckingham and Elizabeth Woodville eager supporters of their great and splendid destiny.

Thus they would have us believe (Vergil p. 195) that it was 'after the slaughter of king Edwardes children was knowen' that the glorious notion came to Margaret to unite the 'bloode of king Henry the Sixth and of king Edward', an idea which she conceived only then and quite independently. The whole of the next page is taken up by Margaret's secret stratagems in cooking up the marriage deal with Elizabeth, using their mutual physician, Dr Lewis of Caerleon, as chief negotiator. It is only after this that Margaret supposedly hears about Buckingham suggesting precisely the same idea.

This scenario is close enough to the truth to have been believed by many historians. However, the devil is in the detail, and as usual it is chronology that lets Vergil down. He has confidently told us the exact time-frame within which Richard arranged for his nephews to be killed, allegedly sending instructions during August which were not obeyed until he despatched Sir James Tyrell from York in September to see the job done. He then assures us that 'within a few days after [Richard] permyttyd the rumor of ther death to go abrode'.

Yet Margaret's hopes for a marriage were kindled, he says, only *after* the slaughter of the boys 'was knowen' (*recte* mid-September), which was *before* Buckingham began 'to be alyenate in mynde from king Richard' (*recte* mid-August).

Fortunately the Crowland chronicler precisely pinpointed the sequence of events for us, stating first that there were rebels, second that Buckingham volunteered to lead them, and third that rumours of the boys' death began to circulate, which had the effect of bringing about a change in the rebels' leadership. This time-frame is examined in detail in chapter 11.

Richard, of course, never started the rumour that they were dead. Had he wanted to put this news in the public domain, he had only to announce that they had succumbed to some illness or mishap, and exhibit their bodies reverently at St Paul's as his brother had done with that of Henry VI, another deposed monarch whose death is assumed to have been by judicial murder.

Vergil was evidently given an account that purposely confused the order of events, since this achieved several useful objects.

First, all record of public support for reinstating Edward V is obliterated (there is not one word of it in Vergil), and likewise Margaret Beaufort's part in attempts to abduct him from the Tower. Second, Margaret is credited with initiating the idea of uniting Tudor with York, but only after Edward V and his brother are decently dead. Third, Buckingham is characterized as supporting Henry Tudor as king from the outset.

Naturally the Tudors would not wish to tarnish their legend by admitting the entire marriage deal was intended to dupe the Woodvilles, or that the brothers, had they survived the process of 'liberation' from the Tower, would soon have found themselves removed by a new rival for the throne. One cannot help calling to mind Sir George Buc's cryptic comment in his *History of King Richard the Third*: 'I have read in an old manuscript book it was held for certain that Dr Morton and a certain countess, conspiring the deaths of the sons of King Edward and some other, resolved that these treacheries should be executed by poison and by sorcery.' Buc later reveals whom he has in mind as 'some other' when he speaks of foul play in the question of Edward IV's death, 'and that may be understood to be either poison or sorcery. Who were the dealers in these arts I have showed before.'[13]

On this occasion, Buc tantalizingly fails to identify his source. Perhaps the fragment remained in his memory from years before he became actively interested in Morton's calumnies and Richard III's defence. It is primarily useful for revealing that not everybody was taken in by Margaret Beaufort's assiduously cultivated reputation for piety. Indeed, her dealings with her employees and retainers clearly reveal those traits of flinty meanness and materialism with which her son also was endowed.

The rumour that Edward IV's sons had been killed, which was spread in September, was a ploy that bears the hallmarks of a mind as devious as that of Bishop Morton. He would have started it while the betrothal terms were under discussion but not yet signed, thereby lending a veneer of truth to the announcement which would soon be made that Elizabeth of York was now promised in marriage to Henry Tudor. The rumour neatly pulled the rug from under Elizabeth Woodville's feet, keeping her occupied frantically trying to establish what had happened to her sons while smoothly setting up Tudor as a York-friendly candidate for the throne in right of his proposed marriage.

9

The Disappearance of the Princes

The disappearance of the 'princes in the Tower' is one of history's most famous vanishings.[1] To investigate their disappearance, certain essential facts need first to be established. Fortunately we are able to cite records of when and where the princes were last seen.

We have noted that as a result of the conspiracy for which Lord Hastings was executed, it was necessary to tighten security around the deposed Edward V and his brother Richard of York, currently residing in the Tower of London.

The Great Chronicle of London tells us they were initially 'well entreatid wythyn the kyngys lodgyng', but after the Hastings plot they were 'holdyn more strygth'. Later we hear that during the mayoral year of Edmund Shaw, who left office on 28 October 1483, 'The childyr of kyng Edward were seen shotyng & playyng In the Garden of the Towyr by sundry tymys.'

Perhaps because of this, tradition has held that the boys were lodged in the Garden Tower – a tradition reinforced by the appellation 'Bloody' Tower which it later acquired thanks to the unpleasant activities of the Tudors.

The Garden Tower was, anyway, an unlikely choice, situated as it was in an area of constant traffic. A more appropriate location would have been the Lanthorn Tower, where recent monarchs had installed up-to-date royal apartments. Located farther east along the inner curtain wall (and easily visible from the Thames, see Tower survey, Plate 18), it also had a secluded garden area nearby.

After the Hastings plot a necessary precaution had been to vet their personal attendants; those removed were soon replaced by new servants, of whom we have evidence, but these were necessarily fewer in number and carefully screened. Mancini writes that the last of Edward's former attendants to leave was his physician, Argentine. Then he relates that the princes were 'conducted back into the more inward apartments of the Tower itself, and day by day came to be observed more rarely through the lattices and windows, up to the point that they ceased to be visible'. So when and where did Argentine last see them? We find an interesting clue in Mancini's phrase 'conducted back into the more inward apartments of the Tower itself', a description implying a familiarity with the geography of the place that would be unlikely in a foreigner. The 'Tower itself' with its 'more inward apartments' almost certainly indicates the White Tower, the ancient keep that was the earliest part of the castle structure built in the eleventh century. Mancini the outsider could know nothing about the location of apartments and window structures in this enormous keep, or about the frequency with which the boys were to be seen, unless told by someone like Argentine who was visiting them.

Mancini apparently met Argentine between July and December 1483, which is when he probably obtained material from the doctor about Edward's appearance, accomplishments, state of mind and location when last seen. Had Argentine known anything about the fate of the princes, we may be sure he would have related it with equal alacrity.

We can rest assured that information derived from Argentine was rock solid. Unfortunately his reminiscences suffer from lack of detail, condensing a gradual unfolding of events into too narrow a time frame. For example, the account that the princes were 'conducted back into the more inward apartments ... day by day came to be observed more rarely ... ceased to be visible' follows immediately upon the report of their attendants being replaced. Yet we know these replacements happened in mid-June, whereas Argentine himself was still in service when the princes were transferred to those inner apartments he described. Obviously a period of time had elapsed, confirmed by the phrases 'day by day' and 'up to the point that ...'; therefore it may well have been the plot to remove the princes, as reported by Stow, probably around the second to third week of July, that prompted their change of location.

Not surprisingly, any opportunities to glimpse them from the outside would soon decrease as the extent of the unrest was uncovered, which suggests that Argentine probably last saw them in late July or early August when the John Welles conspiracy was discovered.

We have another item of documentary evidence which supports this timeline. On 18 July 1483, a warrant appears in the records in Harleian Manuscript 433 authorizing payment of wages to seventeen named men for their services to Edward IV and to 'Edward Bastard late called king Edward the Vth'.[2] The payments have been taken to suggest that Edward V was still alive in mid-July. Since Argentine was the last to be dismissed, he presumably continued attending to the boys after that.

So we may perhaps piece together this sequence of events. First, the princes were lodged in the Lanthorn Tower. Second, their attendants began to be replaced. Third, a number of servants remained to look after them until mid-July at least, with Argentine retained later. Fourth, probably after the discovery of plots, they were transferred to more secure apartments inside the White Tower and those pleasant playtimes in the garden came to an end. Fifth, probably pursuant to the Welles conspiracy, from early August they were kept out of sight and under constant surveillance.

We first hear of concerns for Edward V's future from Mancini. Even before his departure from England around the time of the coronation (6 July) he records hearing 'a suspicion that he had been taken by death' (a more accurate translation of *sublatum*). Such fears were understandable given the known fate of Richard II and Henry VI, both deposed in recent times.

Though prone to judgements about inner thoughts and motivations, Mancini was a conscientious reporter and clearly made exhaustive yet fruitless enquiries: 'Whether, however, he has been taken by death, and by what manner of death, so far I have not at all ascertained.' This switch from historical reporting to a present-tense comment indicates that Mancini has been actively pursuing the mystery right up to the date of making his report in December 1483.

Since many of his conclusions are based on hearsay, Mancini introduces colourful details to reinforce his case. One such is an emotional quotation from Edward V's physician, Dr John Argentine, afterwards physician to Arthur, son of Henry VII. He is said to have declared that 'like a victim prepared for sacrifice … [Edward] reckoned that his death was imminent'.

It is certainly possible that Edward, now installed in royal apartments in a vast, unfamiliar castle, and with many of his attendants removed, might have feared for his future in such uncertain times; his anxiety would not have been assuaged by his mother's insistence on remaining in sanctuary as if under threat. He might, understandably, have been undergoing a bout of depression. Or perhaps he was simply frustrated and infuriated by having power so rudely snatched away, and was indulging in the dramatics of a typical twelve-year-old.

It has been suggested that the boy was suffering from some form of physical ill health. But if so, since Mancini had personally interviewed his physician, why did he not include specific information about Edward's health in his report to his political masters? Even if couched in generalized terms, Argentine would surely have afforded Mancini some clue if his charge was ailing.

Instead, our reporter concentrates on the drama of the nameless fate awaiting the young Edward, but somewhat over-eggs his pudding by describing how he has seen 'several men break out in tears and lamentation when mention was made of him after he was removed from men's sight'. A French or Italian reader might believe him, but anyone familiar with the English temperament will be sceptical. Such outbursts (except by professional clergy) were unlikely on the part of the everyday London public, of whom few outside those with Court and government connections could have clapped eyes on the boy before his arrival in May. Any tearful men observed by Mancini were perhaps not entirely sober.

As an accomplished writer, Domenico Mancini was as fond of a good anecdote as anyone: witness his story of Edward IV's wooing of Elizabeth Woodville with a dagger at her throat. He was aware that the report he was writing for Archbishop Cato would be circulated in high places, and was obviously out to provide not just information but an entertaining read. We must not begrudge Mancini his flourishes, but we need not accept them as wholly reliable.

Mancini provides no further evidence, but in the *Crowland Chronicle* we have the last reliable sighting of the princes. Having outlined Richard's post-coronation progress from London, the chronicler records his arrival in York in September and the lavish ceremonies which accompanied the investiture of his son Edward as Prince of Wales.

'In the meantime and while these things were happening,' he continues, 'the two sons of King Edward remained in the Tower of London with a specially appointed guard,' a fact which he was likely to be in a position to know from personal observation.

The Crowland chronicler's words are not chosen by accident, and the translation into English is exact; he was very probably a doctor of law and also a government administrator, so he knew to use words accurately. *Interim et dum haec agerentur* is not a vague remark such as 'Meanwhile', which could have been rendered simply by *Interim*. Instead, he writes 'while these things were happening', specifically referring to the things just described (i.e. the ceremonies in York). We know the king spent three weeks there, with the investiture taking place on 8 September, so this is a clear indication that at least on this last-mentioned date the chronicler knew the princes were still resident in the Tower.

We also have confirmation in two sources that September was the month in which the rumour arose that they were dead. From Polydore Vergil we hear, as in Crowland, that they were alive in the Tower when Richard reached York. The story he heard was that Richard sent Tyrell from York to murder them, then within a few days 'permyttyd the rumor of ther death to go abrode'. Vergil's concord with the Crowland chronicler suggests that people who had a close interest in the whereabouts of the princes (and the means to find out) remembered their disappearance occurring after the lavish investiture celebrations.

The Crowland chronicler, a southerner who was close to events around the capital, expresses no belief in their murder, but agrees that a rumour of their death was spread in September (see chapter 11). Logically, therefore, this was when they disappeared.

$$\star\ \star\ \star$$

With their freedom curtailed and movements restricted, these were self-evidently unacceptable conditions in which to confine two young boys. Richard III, far away on his progress around his realm, was faced with making a decision about what to do with them. Moreover, whatever was done must be done in secret.

Sending them to one of his estates was too obvious, these would be the first places to which hostile spies would be sent. His northern castle of Sheriff Hutton would otherwise have been an appealing choice, especially as several children are documented as residing there. But during the long journey northwards, which would take the best part of a week, their travelling party would be too conspicuous and too vulnerable. They would need overnight lodgings, supplies of horses, and litters, carriages or other special conveyances for the boys, at least for the younger one. Anywhere less distant would be ruled out in light of the attempts on the Tower: only a truly inaccessible location would deter repeat performances.

There was, however, a bold if risky alternative. Richard might have been prompted to this by recollection of a scheme thought up by his late brother George, Duke of Clarence, in 1477 at the height of his headstrong agitation against Edward IV. One of the charges brought against Clarence in his treason trial was that he had conspired to send his infant son over the sea, to Ireland or to Flanders, evidently as a potential rallying point for opposition against the king.

To convey the princes overseas was an attractive ploy, and not difficult to achieve. The Low Countries were nearby, easy to reach, and had long enjoyed exchanges of trade, population and influence with England. Nor was it an unusual step: Richard and his brother George had been sent, as little princes themselves, into the care of the Duke of Burgundy in Flanders while their elder brother fought for the English throne in 1461. Richard would retain further fond memories of the Low Countries as a safe haven during his exile in 1470 with the newly deposed Edward.

A foreign destination was also mooted in 1483 for the daughters of Edward IV. According to the Crowland chronicler, disaffected parties wanted them to 'leave Westminster in disguise and go overseas' so that, in default of the princes, they should remain available to breed further heirs.

Since the thought of hiding-places abroad occurred so readily within the Yorkist polity, it is rather surprising that modern authorities give the idea such short shrift.

Map: The Low Countries *c.*1483

Richard would have no qualms about entrusting the princes to their powerful aunt across the Channel, namely his devoted sister Margaret of York, Dowager Duchess of Burgundy. She would have the means and the contacts to sequester the boys safely, sufficiently out of the way to avoid attracting attention, while her maternal instincts would ensure their well-being remained a priority.

This was an important matter that Richard could not have failed to consider in advance. More than likely he would have despatched secret letters to Margaret as long ago as the month of June, when his plans for seizing the crown were cemented. He would need, in any case, to apprise her of events, and this would be the right moment to elicit her promise of help in case the princes – or his own son – should need a refuge. Armed in advance with the assurance of her support, it would be a relatively simple matter to arrange their secret passage by sea: Richard owned ships, as did his reliable lieutenant, the Duke of Norfolk.

An ideal route out of London was offered by the River Thames. It could be accessed directly from the Tower, whose constable (Sir Robert Brackenbury, another trusted supporter) could arrange for them to slip away swiftly and quietly by boat. No more than a handful of attendants needed to be aware of their impending departure. If a few others learned that a small party was leaving by the water gate at dead of night, this still revealed nothing of their destination. It would be a routine departure, probably not unexpected, and the servants who came to clean the empty apartments next morning would simply learn that the princes went away the previous night.

The only problem with such a plan, as Richard would have known, was that the moment they left the Tower there would be suspicion as to what had happened to them. Doubtless he was aware that already there were whispers as to their demise, past or future, which would only grow stronger if they were spirited away secretly. He would not be able to produce the boys to refute such whispering, and the only comfort he could take would be that he and his God knew the truth of the matter. Lesser men have carried greater secrets to the grave.

Certain it is that the boys disappeared. Whatever happened to them, Richard's fatal mistake lay in failing to realize that their disappearance would be used by the Morton-Beaufort-Tudor axis as an opportunity to manoeuvre the unlikely Henry Tudor to centre stage as a challenger for the throne. Regrettably, Richard appears not to have taken sufficient regard of this threat. Thus he would not have foreseen that removing them from view, even if done for the most benign of reasons, would play right into the hands of his opponents.

As to the believability of the plan to hide them overseas, we have only to look at other children, post-1485, put forward as pretenders who were supposed to have been concealed beyond the sea. Among them was the pretender supported in 1486 by Francis Lovell and the Stafford brothers, later by the Earl of Lincoln. The *official* story went that this boy, whom Henry VII was forced to face at Stoke Field, was masquerading as the young Earl of Warwick, and his whereabouts were variously given as the Channel Isles, Ireland and the Low Countries.

Another such case was 'Perkin Warbeck', as the pretender came to be known who surfaced in the early 1490s claiming to be Richard of York, younger son of Edward IV and widely accepted as such by large numbers of people all over mainland Europe and the British Isles. To explain his emergence from the Low Countries, Henry VII had to concoct a story that he was the son of a boatman from Tournai. The *Great Chronicle* during the mayoral year 1492–93 reported talk that Margaret of York was (or had been) 'keeping' the Duke of York. Many people, including Henry VII, believed he had been concealed and trained by her.

Were there sea crossings by the princes, and did one or both survive in hiding? For safety they would need to be separated and kept unaware of the other's movements. Personal danger to the boys would have escalated exponentially after Henry VII seized the throne, by which time the elder boy would have reached his majority and started making his own decisions. For the younger boy, however, the need for false identities and changes of location would be paramount. Such possibilities were mere conjecture when I first wrote of them in 2008: but now see Chapter 15. It has been said their total concealment was impossible; but given the difficulties of Henry VII, with all his resources, in trying to conjure up a satisfactory explanation for 'Perkin', it seems hiding a child under a false identity was not such a problem after all. It is at least as feasible as those lurid tales of murder in the Tower.

★ ★ ★

Common gossip, of course, thrives on lurid tales, which is the principal reason why the murder rumour, once set in motion, caught the public imagination: we have only to look at the conspiracy theories that surround high-profile events today. And of course rumour was used effectively, in the fifteenth century, as a potent weapon and political tool.

But let us examine how far this particular rumour was actually credited. Many traditionalists think the boys were murdered by their uncle because it was the general belief of people at the time. But was that what people generally believed? Anthony Pollard, author of a popular book which accuses Richard of the murder, quotes briefly from several reports to support this theory.[3] Though admitting they are based on no more than 'hearsay, gossip and rumour', nevertheless he dignifies them with the collective description, 'an impressive array of evidence ... which points to the boys meeting their deaths at Richard's hands in 1483'.

Professor Pollard is careful to comment that 'none of it proves his guilt', but then quickly despatches all other possibilities. The evidence against the Duke of Buckingham, he concludes, 'is not strong enough to support the hypothesis ... that he murdered the princes without the king's authority'. Other suggested culprits are dismissed because 'they beg the question of access to the Tower without Richard's knowledge and overlook the fact that Richard was responsible for the safekeeping of his nephews. If not a murderer, then he would still stand guilty of criminal negligence'. We will return later to Buckingham and the question of access.

There is a world of difference, of course, between the intent that lies behind Pollard's idea of murder, and the lack of intent behind an inadvertent failure to prevent some action by a malignant third party. Richard III has not been vilified for 500 years on grounds of being a negligent custodian.

Thus, while Pollard purports to sift objectively through the evidence, we find he actually starts with the preconception that the princes cannot have died otherwise than in the Tower of London during Richard's reign, and therefore the king must be to blame.

The case against Henry Tudor falls down, in Pollard's view, because 'any such case has to rest on the assumption that the princes were still alive when he came to the throne'. This is rejected without examination because it does not fit the preconception. While willing to believe that Richard engaged agents to murder the boys, he will not entertain the thought that agents might have done the same on behalf of some other interested party. If a murder did take place – and there is no proof that it did – the prime suspect in a modern investigation would be the person who derived most benefit from it: namely Henry Tudor, whose mother (aided by a network of highly efficient agents) was in London at the time, diligently arranging means for her son to seize the throne.

Pollard, however, claims that 'any argument based on [Henry's] motive has to recognise that Richard III before him had *exactly the same reason* for getting rid of them' (my emphasis). Most readers familiar with the matter will recognize no such thing. In Richard's case, he had been chosen as king while the boys were still alive, on the grounds of their illegitimacy: ascending the throne did not require getting rid of them. Whereas for Henry Tudor to become king, they had to be dead. Attorney Bertram Fields concludes that Henry's motive for killing them was 'considerably stronger than Richard's' and he adds, 'unlike Richard, he had no ties of blood or loyalty that would make him hesitate before committing such a crime'.[4]

When Pollard eventually comes to examine the possibility that 'at least one of the boys survived even beyond Henry's accession', he limits this to two specific theories. First, that 'Perkin Warbeck may truly have been Richard of York', which he discounts without explanation: 'there can be little doubt, however, that Warbeck was an imposter'. Second, that 'Richard of York survived to reappear in Sir Thomas More's household', an ingenious and unsubstantiated notion based on clues in a painting. Beyond these possibilities he does not venture.

Having set up and demolished his two Aunt Sallies, Professor Pollard proceeds as if all arguments for the boys' survival have been refuted. No mention, for example, of the proposition that Richard of York lived on to become 'Richard of Eastwell'[5] and no admission that, if they did survive, we may simply have no evidence of their later lives. His dismissal of 'Perkin', in particular, is unsatisfactory and ignores the fact that the pretender's true identity had never yet been convincingly established.

To reinforce the preconception that the princes died during Richard's reign, Pollard even cites certain Latin translations which are contested by scholars. 'When contemporaries,' he states, 'who were not absolutely certain of the manner of the young king's death, wrote that [Richard] had "destroyed" or "suppressed" him, they wrote with finely judged ambiguity.'

Yet the fact that our two main chroniclers chose words other than 'kill' and 'murder' does not in the least demonstrate ambiguity, nor had they anything to fear from being explicit. Rather, it indicates that they intended a precise meaning, as the reader will be able to judge below.

Unfortunately Professor Pollard conflates two conclusions, neither of which withstands close scrutiny: 'Equally important as the probable guilt of Richard III is the certainty that, well before his downfall two years later, he was generally believed to have killed the children.'

Richard died in mid-1485. Let us look at all the known pre-1486 sources (Pollard's and others) to test his certainty that there was a general belief before this date that Richard killed his nephews.

- Looking at Domenico Mancini, writing in 1483, the first of our two controversial Latin translations occurs in the 1936 edition by C.A.J. Armstrong, the only translation in print until that in 2021 by the present author. Jeremy Potter (in 1983) explained it clearly: 'Referring to Richard and the protectorship, Mancini writes *qui paulo post, Eduardi liberis oppressis, regnum sibi vindicavit*: literally, "who shortly afterwards, when Edward's children had been set aside, claimed the throne for himself". *Oppressis* carries the meaning of "suppression", being overthrown or subdued. Armstrong opts for the strongest sense – destruction – and rejigs the sentence so that Richard is the destroyer, an accusation specifically not made by Mancini.'

    Armstrong's translation reads, 'who shortly after destroyed Edward's children and then claimed for himself the throne'.[6] (Another example of Armstrong's judgemental translations occurs in the title he gives to Mancini's report, see Appendix.) Should there remain any doubt as to what Mancini meant, remember that despite hearing apprehension for the young king's life, in concluding his report six months later he confessed he had still not been able to discover whether anything untoward had happened to Edward V. Thus nowhere does Mancini support Pollard's claim.

- Probably the earliest useful civic record has recently been discovered by John Ashdown-Hill in the Colchester Oath Book, which names *inter alia* the borough's bailiffs whose tenure ran annually from Michaelmas Day. Hence the entry for 1482–3, citing the regnal years of Edward IV, Edward V and Richard III, can be dated on or after 29 September 1483. The reference for Edward IV is *nuper Regis anglie, iam defuncti* (lately king, now deceased). Yet for Edward V we have merely *Edwardi quinti nuper filii domini Edwardi quarti* (lately son of Lord Edward IV) without, significantly, the word *defuncti*. The adverb *nuper* (lately) could signify that Edward V was recently deceased, although one Latin scholar's reading is that it may simply refer to his being a son whose father had died. Thus it is not certain whether the clerk believed he was living or dead. No mention of murder or murderer here.[7]

- The *Kalendar* of Robert Ricart, Recorder of Bristol, states that 'And this yere the two sonnes of King E. were put to scylence in the Towre of London' (presumably 'put to death').[8] 'This yere' was a mayoral year (Sept. 1483–Sept. 1484) and the brief comment takes the form of a marginal note; so although it appears alongside that year, it was written in as an addendum after the official entry for 1483–84 had been completed. Unfortunately the date of writing is unknown. It may be the first statement in an English source that they were killed, though it does not suggest who killed them.

- Looking farther afield,[9] the Danziger Caspar Weinreich noted in his chronicle for 1483 that 'later this summer Richard, the king's brother, had himself put in power and crowned in England and he had his brother's children killed'. This is the first recorded accusation against Richard, and it is written by a foreigner who does not say whether this is a widespread belief in England.[10]

- Our last pre-1485 item is another foreign source which dates from January 1484. The chancellor of France, Guillaume de Rochefort, in a speech to the States-General, reported scathingly that Edward IV's sons were murdered and the crown of England given to their murderer (reversing events as they are usually alleged). There was a tradition in fifteenth-century French attitudes which praised their own loyalty to their kings in contrast to the regicidal proclivities of the English. Thus we must bear in mind that politics lay behind the chancellor's message: France had just acquired its own child-king, and it made good sense to smear the barbaric English for deposing theirs. Armstrong's claim that the chancellor's murder story came from Mancini cannot be sustained, as Mancini recorded *having failed to discover* what fate befell Edward V. Probably it came from English rebels fleeing to France following their defeated rebellion at the end of 1483.[11]

• Let us now stretch Pollard's time frame and go forward into 1485–6, allowing us to include the *Crowland Chronicle* on the grounds that it records recollections from the period in question. Yet despite having had perhaps two years since their disappearance to mull over and modify his thoughts, the chronicler does not report that the boys were killed. All we are told is that 'a rumour arose' that they had died 'by some unknown manner of violent destruction'. As Professor Ross comments, 'Although he was probably in a position to know about the fate of the princes, he states no clear opinion thereon.'[12]

Later in his narrative, the chronicler comments that 'the cause' (not the death) of King Edward's sons was avenged in the battle of Bosworth. He then appends twenty lines of doggerel by an unnamed poet about England's three King Richards. In this verse we encounter our second argument about Latin translations. The words *nisi fratris opprimeret proles* were translated in the old 1893 edition as 'must destroy his brother's progeny'; but the more recent edition used here, by Pronay and Cox, gives 'suppressed his brother's progeny', which accords with the comments of Jeremy Potter:[13] '*opprimere* (to suppress) is as likely to mean "put down the cause of" as "kill"; and the princes were certainly destroyed politically and as royal persons by the loss of their inheritance'. The exact position is explained by Armstrong: 'the two sons of Edward IV were *legally* dead in the sense of being incapacitated from holding any honours from the crown downward, but this need not imply that either of them was then *physically* dead'.[14] As Potter summarizes, 'If this [verse] is to be interpreted as the chronicler's sole record of a sensational murder committed by the Richard he so detested, it is strangely oblique.' In fact the writer confirms by omission that he knows as little as everyone else.

So Professor Pollard's 'impressive array of evidence' indicating general belief that Richard murdered the princes comes down to precisely nothing by way of contemporaneous English records, although we can find a couple of statements by foreigners recounting scandals which they affected to believe. We have stretched the professor's time frame, and even included evidence of which he was unaware, but still I suggest he has not proved his case.

If a more positive rebuttal is sought, surely the strongest counter-evidence is the complete lack of any reaction on the part of Richard himself. Although absent from London, he could not fail to have been informed if widespread accusations were flying around. Compare this with his instant public denial in early 1485 when there arose a very specific – yet less damaging – rumour accusing him of seeking an unpopular marriage. In 1483 he issued no such denial about the deaths of the princes, though it would have been an easy matter either to parade the children if they were at hand, or issue a public statement if they were not.

An argument often repeated, and none the less true for that, is that if Richard eliminated the boys in order to secure the throne, his only way of ensuring the security he craved lay in proving they were dead by displaying their bodies in the time-honoured manner, having had them killed by poisoning, suffocation or the like so as to leave no visible trace. Otherwise he deprived himself of his most effective weapon against insurrections such as the one that duly arose to restore the deposed (and undead) Edward V.

This illustrates the essential weakness of the case for Richard's ordering their murder, since exhibiting their bodies would have to be the automatic and necessary sequel: what security did he gain by killing them *and keeping it secret*? Moreover it would be the height of folly to kill the boys, who were safely under his control, only to make automatic heirs of their sisters, who were beyond it. Richard was well aware of the potential danger posed by the princesses in the Westminster sanctuary, with people already intriguing to remove them overseas: witness the guard he placed around the premises. But this did not give him power to control them any more than it prevented Thomas of Dorset from slipping out.

The only reason so far offered for such foolishness as murdering the boys and keeping it secret has been 'to keep Henry Tudor guessing'. But this is to give Tudor credit for a prominence in Richard's thinking that he did not enjoy. As we shall see, Richard (to his cost) never considered Henry a serious contender for his crown until November of 1484. It would have been unthinkable to play such a high-risk game merely to confuse someone who was little more than a distant annoyance.

Richard's silence could reasonably be adduced to indicate his innocence, but instead it has been taken to prove his guilt. Nor were his accusers in any position to know what really happened – quite the opposite, in fact. Commentators during and after Henry VII's reign wrote down recollections and opinions in hindsight, but this hindsight was heavily influenced: from the moment Henry took the throne it became an article of faith that the previous monarch was a tyrant and a murderer. Those who rushed to be first to voice this accusation did so knowing it would gain the favour of the new king: compare early poems by the Welsh bard Dafydd Llwyd (1485/6) and the Italian Court poet Pietro Carmeliano (1486). Thus the tone of approval for such calumnies was set by the Tudor Court itself.

In the same category are reminiscences by John Rous, the priest who, along with Carmeliano, praised Richard during his lifetime and vilified him after his death. Nor are the English civic chronicles free from bias; they were also written in Tudor times, when the 'crimes' of Richard III were accepted as fact. Yet despite such orthodoxy, they are not all of one accord: *The New Cronycles of England and France*, *The Great Chronicle of London*, and the chronicle known as BL MS Cotton Vitellius A XVI are all judged to share a common source, yet only the earliest of them, Vitellius, alleges in plain language that Richard put the princes to death. The others merely report rumours to that effect without repeating the certainty of the first.

What about the October rebellion – wasn't that aimed at avenging their murder? Not according to the Crowland chronicler, who tells us that the uprising was already in motion, with the aim of restoring Edward V, before any rumours of their death were circulated. Up to that point the chronicler has the boys residing in the Tower, with people forming assemblies 'in order to release them from such captivity'. This is the nearest we have to a contemporaneous account; it offers a scenario where those already plotting Edward's restoration hear the rumours, believe them, and are led to alter their plans (see chapter 11).

In previous editions of this book, based on what we knew then, I observed 'we cannot be sure of the truth, and honesty demands we admit as much'. The mere fact that certain sources spoke of rumours that the princes met a mysterious end, or were killed, proves nothing except that such stories were circulated. It cannot be known to what extent they were believed in Richard's reign, unless by people already up in rebellion. But we do know they were widely believed in later years, having been encouraged and repeated in print under the Tudors. In chapter 15 we will at last see documentary evidence for the princes' survival that we can set against the absence of evidence for their death.

* * *

It has been the scrupulous aim of this book to avoid citing as evidence the highly-coloured narrative of Thomas More. However, we cannot leave the subject of the alleged murder of the princes without referring to the best-known story of all: the dramatic tale of their death peddled by More and seized upon by Shakespeare. This is based on More's unsubstantiated story of an eve-of-execution 'confession' on the part of Sir James Tyrell, Richard III's Master of the Henchmen, who allegedly had the children suffocated in the Tower of London on the king's orders. This supposed confession not only named Tyrell's two confederates in the crime, but claimed that one of them, having admitted his guilt, was still walking free and unmolested. Neither was ever pursued.

Every aspect of the story points to its being an obvious fiction. In 1502, when Tyrell was executed, the alleged confession was never recorded or publicized. No announcement or speech was made from the scaffold, as would normally be expected, and when he was attainted two years later, nothing was mentioned of his confessed regicide. Nor was any requiem mass conducted for the two princes, as required most straitly on behalf of their souls now they were 'known' to be deceased. (A Mass Book in Salisbury Cathedral contains anniversary details of sovereigns for the purpose of celebrating masses for their souls: no provision is made for Edward V or Richard III.)[15]

We can thank More, writing in the 1510s and 1520s, for the confession story, although Francis Bacon, a century later, attributed it to Henry VII ('as the king gave out'). It was obviously designed to bury the princes for all time, in reaction to the pretenders who plagued Henry's reign, with Tyrell a convenient scapegoat thanks to his close connections with Richard. This is evident from its timing: Henry VII was sick and unpopular, and the heir apparent, Arthur, had died a mere month before Tyrell's execution. Thus, the future of the Tudor line hinged on their sole surviving male heir, Henry, Duke of York (later Henry VIII). In order to affiance him to Arthur's widow, Catherine of Aragon, it was necessary urgently to convince her father, Ferdinand, that the boy was heir to a throne that was not under threat from the two missing Yorkist princes whose alleged murder was by no means universally believed.

Such a confession as Tyrell's ought to have been sensational stuff, yet Henry's own historian, Polydore Vergil, who seems to have made some effort to sift information, gave it no house-room. Although naming the killer as Tyrell, he plainly states that nobody knew how the children were 'executed'. Better still, Henry VII's official biographer, Bernard André, did not credit the confession either. He related that the boys were put to the sword; a far cry from being secretly suffocated. Robert Fabyan, author of the *New Cronycles of England and France*, lived and wrote at this precise time (1502), yet although he expressly mentions Tyrell's imprisonment and execution, he says nothing about the dramatic confession.

If it sounds extraordinary that Thomas More, the upright London under-sheriff – with access, one would think, to legal archives – should relate such a cock-and-bull story, let us not forget that his *Richard III* was never written as historical fact, nor did he entitle it *History*, nor intend it for publication. No fewer than five different versions have come down to us, and who knows how many others he started and destroyed? Despite its outstanding literary and dramatic merit, the work lay unfinished for fifteen to twenty years. So if it was not the quality of the writing that dissatisfied the author, most likely it was the quality of the information on which it was based. Having spent years working with source material that he felt was above reproach, one may imagine his dilemma if he later uncovered serious discrepancies.

This would account for many glaring errors remaining in the text that could have been rectified in a trice. It would also account for occasions where an apparently solid fact is later undermined by an alternative or contradiction. This is even evidenced in his account of the murder of the princes, where he tells us Tyrell's confession was 'very truth and well known'. Despite this well known truth, however, he admits that there are some who are disinclined to believe it: their 'death and final misfortune,' he says, 'has nevertheless so far come in question that some remain yet in doubt whether they were in [Richard's] days destroyed or no'.

Despite this equivocation, it is primarily from More's murder tale that the centuries-old belief in Richard's guilt derives. More's readers have not thought to question the preposterous claim that the bodies were immediately buried *at the foot* of a staircase within the Tower (note that the location is not 'within' or 'behind' a staircase). For this to happen the garrison, staff and other residents of the Tower – numbering probably 600 to 1,000 – would need to have been deaf to an inordinate amount of digging and gouging of well-compacted flooring at dead of night. Indeed, these hundreds of people had to be so ignorant of anything untoward happening that not one of them later retailed the thrilling story of a mysteriously empty bedchamber subsequent to sounds and signs of nocturnal excavation. And what about the boys' clothing, playthings, books and other valuables, some of them doubtless costly and adorned with gems? Were chests full of such possessions also buried? Of course not: if the killings had taken place as More describes, there would have been loose ends everywhere for people to notice, remember and speculate about.

That no witness ever mentioned such occurrences is evident, because for decades the fate of the princes was mentioned only in terms of mystery and guesswork. Had the boys really been despatched in this way, untold numbers of people, including those who constituted the immense daily supply chain that kept the Tower serviced and provisioned, would have eagerly spread the news of what they had seen and heard, together with dates, locations and precise times of day.

Yet when Henry Tudor took the throne as Henry VII a mere two years later, he was conspicuously unable to produce a soul who could provide confirmation of their fate; nor did he ever bring any specific charge against Richard III.

Another aspect that exposes the fiction of More's tale is his usual penchant for circumstantial detail, with Tyrell being given the dread task pursuant to a page recommending him while Richard is 'sitting on the stool'. Historians have meekly accepted this as fact, but how could More have known such intimate details? Who could have known the nature of the very private occasion on which Tyrell was supposedly suggested? From More's vague description of how he 'heard' the story, his informant clearly was not the page. It overstretches credulity to suppose that such irrelevant information was included in Tyrell's alleged eve-of-execution confession. The conclusion is that this sardonic touch was a product of More's own dramatic muse.

It is difficult not to suspect that Henry's circle, noting how successful had been the ploy of composing a confession which the wretched 'Perkin Warbeck' was made to sign, decided to use the same device to deter further pretenders once and for all.

Thomas More's murder story is discounted by more and more commentators nowadays, and some are even prepared to doubt whether a murder ever took place. Yet there still remains an urn in Westminster Abbey containing bones which are believed to prove the gospel according to More. The contents of this urn are discussed in chapter 10.

* * *

We have noted that even More added the caveat that some people remained in doubt whether the princes were killed at all, and indeed it is instructive to reflect on the striking number of suggestions that one or both might have survived.

The earliest is a comment, apparently written during Richard's reign, by the Silesian Niclas von Popplau whose meeting with Richard is described in chapter 1. Niclas refused to believe the princes were dead: 'Many people say – and I agree with them – that they are still alive and kept in a very dark cellar.'

Next, in 1496, there is an intriguing reference to the younger prince being alive in or after 1484. Ferdinand and Isabella of Spain claimed in a letter that Rui de Sousa, as Portuguese ambassador in England, 'knew the Duke of York very well, and has seen him there. Two years later he saw this other person ['Perkin Warbeck'] in Portugal.' Barrie Williams argues it is unlikely that de Sousa saw 'Perkin' in Portugal before 1486, the earliest date postulated for the pretender's arrival there (later dates are more usually given). Williams traces a number of possible occasions around 1484 when de Sousa is known to have been in attendance in England and might have seen the young duke alive.[16]

Moving on to around 1500, the French observer Jean Molinet covered all eventualities. In his *Chroniques* he opined that the princes were possibly smothered, or starved, or suffocated. Elsewhere, however, he was quoted as believing that only one prince died, while the other was merely 'a prisoner' (*esclaves*).[17]

At about the same time the Dutch writer of the *Divisie Chronicle*, a chronicle of Holland, Zeeland and Friesland written in about 1500, implicated the Duke of Buckingham in the killing of the princes, but added 'some say' that, after murdering one of them, Buckingham spared the other 'and had him secretly abducted out of the country'.[18]

In 1503 Bernard André described how the matter of the 'dire death' of the princes had flared up anew, and (though obediently disbelieving them) dilated on the credibility of both pretenders.[19]

Then in the printed texts of Polydore Vergil's history dating from 1534 onwards (as opposed to his manuscript of 1512–13, which was subject to government scrutiny), Vergil admits that 'a report prevailed among the common people that the sons of Edward the king had migrated to some part of the earth in secret, and there were still surviving'.[20]

Another such reference is found in Sir George Buc's *History of King Richard the Third* (1619), which Arthur Kincaid produced in a new edition in 2023. Buc was a man of scholarly attainment and acumen which he put to use in the pursuit of his hobby, antiquarian research.[21] Kincaid ascribes to him a standard of accuracy which was, for the time, outstandingly responsible: 'Even more than his increasingly conscientious contemporaries, he was careful about his documentation … [and was] one of a group of enthusiastic scholars who sought to systematise as well as to collect sources for historical research.'

Sir George nailed his colours firmly to the mast of 'Perkin' as the younger prince. He is to be counted as yet another of those who believed the brothers had been sent by their uncle to safety in Flanders. Some reports, he says, told how they 'embarked in a ship at Tower wharf, and that they were conveyed from hence into the seas, and so cast into the deeps and drowned. But some others say that they were not drowned, but were set safe on shore beyond the seas'. There had been, according to Buc, 'English noblemen and gentlemen which were privy to the conveyance of the Prince Richard ... and who knew where he lurked or lay close'.[22]

To end this selection of nonconformist opinions, we have rumours even among Tudor supporters that the boys survived. Prompted by André's biography of Henry VII, Francis Bacon, in his history of that king's reign published in 1622, related the story that the pretender later known as 'Lambert Simnel' initially claimed to be Richard of York [*sic*]. At that time (about 1486–7), Bacon says, there were 'secret rumours and whisperings – which afterwards gathered strength and turned to great troubles – that the two young sons of King Edward the fourth, or one of them, which were said to be destroyed in the Tower, were not indeed murdered but conveyed secretly away, and were yet living'. A few pages later he reiterates that in the second year of Henry's reign 'it was still whispered every where that at least one of the children of Edward IV was living'. Noting Henry's insistence that his claim to the throne must reside in himself, not his wife, Bacon also let slip another such heretical opinion: that Henry's reason for this was the possible survival of one or both brothers.[23]

Indeed, there were and are a great many people who have argued that Richard did not kill the boys but had them 'conveyed secretly away'. One of the most persuasive arguments is plain common sense.

Here is a man who prior to 1483 had no inkling that the throne might fall into his grasp. He had made the best of being a younger brother by carving himself a hard-won position in the north. He enjoyed a high reputation as a military campaigner, and a higher one as a fair and just administrator; indeed his concern for justice and law had been an overriding theme in his life. He was not a pampered princeling brought up in the hothouse climate of a royal Court, but a man who had lived with adversity, mixed with the common people and experienced life at its most raw. He had adjudicated in criminal cases, and seen for himself the revulsion of the community when a man sinks to committing an act of cold-blooded brutality.

Why, then, at the most vulnerable point in his tenure of the throne, when he had everything to prove and everything to lose, would he take the egregious risk of having the princes murdered?

England's parliamentary representatives had proclaimed him as king, at the same time accepting that, in law, the princes were as ineligible to succeed as was the son of the attainted Clarence. He had been triumphantly crowned. Wouldn't killing the princes constitute tacit admission that his supposedly legal entitlement to the throne was a tissue of lies? The critical post-coronation period must now be dedicated to winning over the populace: the whole fabric of society rested on respect for the king and confidence in the king's justice.

Claims are sometimes made that the boys, once declared illegitimate, posed no threat to Richard; but the position was not so simple. They presented all too easy a focus for disaffection and any number of future risings could be expected to use their name as long as they remained in London. For that reason he needed to remove them and keep them away from men's eyes. Not a difficult proposition when you had extensive connections and a circle of faithful and trusted retainers.

Yet the idea that they were spirited away alive seems difficult, for some reason, for many people to countenance. A discreet departure of the princes, together with their attendants and belongings, would not have raised an eyebrow and was doubtless what their attendants were expecting sooner or later. When stories of murder started circulating, perhaps one or two who would have seen the small party leave by the water gate might have spoken up and said so; but what chance of credence did their humdrum story stand in the face of rumour-mongers crying foul play? They had no proof, they had probably forgotten the date, and they had no idea where the party was headed. It would merely have been part of a normal day – no sensational disappearance, and no need for secrecy save on the part of those few charged with taking the princes to a destination they were sworn not to divulge.

Perhaps it is relevant here to note that the forms and faces of Edward and Richard were not widely known. Most citizens, if they had seen them once, would not have seen them twice. Only those in exalted circles would know even Edward V well enough to recognize him. So secrecy of movement would not be difficult.

Of course we have no proof that the princes were spirited over the sea. But there exists documentary evidence of comings and goings across the Channel in 1484–5 which could be indicative of clandestine activities: for example, a covert mission which Sir James Tyrell carried out for Richard III, of which a record exists in the king's warrant for payment sent to the collectors of customs at the port of Sandwich in January 1485. This warrant provides for the reimbursement of certain monies advanced by 'the Mayor, &c, of Dover … for defraying the passage, &c, of Sir James Tyrell, the king's councillor and knight of his body, who was of late sent over the sea, into the parties of Flanders, for divers matters concerning greatly our weal'.[24]

In January 1485, Tyrell was appointed commander of the castle at Guisnes, part of the Calais outpost and an important conduit point for travellers heading for destinations on the continent of Europe. Simultaneously he received a vast, unexplained payment of £3,000. So vast, it might aptly be called a king's ransom.[25]

Attention is called to several of Tyrell's activities by Audrey Williamson, who uncovered a Tyrell family tradition 'that the princes and their mother Elizabeth Woodville lived in [the Tyrell residence, Gipping Hall] by permission of the uncle'.[26] If this carries any basis in fact (and oral history is not always to be dismissed), it could point to the hall, conveniently situated in Suffolk, being used secretly as a halfway house for the princes prior to their conveyance elsewhere; and since it is not claimed that mother and sons lived there *at the same time*, it might even refer to the hall's later use in some similar capacity by the mother on her emergence from sanctuary in 1484.

Henry VII's treatment of Sir James Tyrell suggests that the spurious confession was not pinned on a random candidate. Initially penalized as an adherent of Richard III, he was later taken into Henry's personal service, pardoned twice within the space of a month, then set up permanently in Guisnes in 1487. Yet in 1502, so determined was Henry to execute Tyrell for treason that he had him treacherously seized after giving him a formal promise of safe conduct. Throughout his reign, Henry seems to have been ignorant of the fate of his brothers-in-law and anxious to find out more. Fifteen years spent cultivating Tyrell suggests he suspected the latter of involvement not in their murder but in their concealment; and when the desired information was not forthcoming, Tyrell was recast in the role of scapegoat.

There are two more cryptic entries in Harleian Manuscript 433, both relating in some way to the Duchess of Burgundy. The first is a grant for Sir Philip Goguet, her chaplain, and 'three persons with him given at Nottingham the 23 day of April 1484'. The second and most intriguing refers to Clement Goguet, probably a relative of Sir Philip, who 'hath a like letter to pass and repass to my Lady Burgundy with a servant with him and two horses without any search etc. Given at Westminster the 6th day of December 1484'. 'Without any search' sets one wondering what clandestine messages Richard III and his sister might have been exchanging.[27]

Even with the most strenuous efforts at secrecy, it is always possible that apparently mundane records may contain clues that slip through the net; and who knows what more is waiting to be uncovered?

We also have another significant name to add to the tally of Richard's well-rewarded representatives commissioned to perform unspecified services – men of substance, not mere minions or nameless agents. This was the adventurous Sir Edward Brampton, a converted Portuguese Jew who rose to be an intimate of Edward IV and became the first Jew ever knighted.

Under Richard's protectorate he wrested the fleet from the clutches of Sir Edward Woodville in May 1483, and received valuable rewards in return. Then, in 1484, Brampton was mysteriously allocated £100 a year from the customs for a period of twenty years, in consideration of undisclosed services 'to be rendered by him according to certain indentures' as from Easter the following year (1485).[28] If anyone could be trusted with the daring and dangerous task of seeing to the safety of the princes, there was no better choice than Brampton. As if to round off his involvement in this web of intrigue, he was soon intimately involved in the earliest known appearance of the pretender 'Perkin Warbeck', who surfaced within a couple of years in Portugal in the household of Brampton's second wife.

⋆ ⋆ ⋆

Inextricably bound up with the mysteriously vanished princes are the pretenders who disturbed the reign of Henry VII. Without getting involved in questions of their authenticity, it is nevertheless impressive how widespread was the belief that one or other of the princes had returned to claim his rightful inheritance, to the extent that men were prepared to fight and die for them.

As to 'Lambert Simnel', Henry VII was responsible for all the obfuscation around this pretender's identity and the claims he was posing as young Edward, Earl of Warwick, son of the executed Duke of Clarence. It was certainly the case that the youngster who was crowned King Edward in Dublin cathedral in May 1487 was widely held to be Clarence's son. But this was very likely an identity-concealing ploy on Henry's part to throw people off the scent. He had good reason to insist on publicly identifying this lad as a spurious Earl of Warwick, knowing he could produce the original at any time he wished. But the supporters of this young King Edward made no such claim, and the lad himself was found convincing by all who put him to the test.

Among modern-day theories there are some that the crowned boy was actually Edward V and that he was killed in the uprising.[29] According to this view the 'Lambert Simnel' ostensibly captured by Henry VII was an impostor set up to replicate and discredit the deceased Edward. This would not be difficult, especially if the chosen boy were some by-blow of a loyal retainer promised advancement in return for the subterfuge. Which might explain why the young captive was one of a tiny minority of Henry's enemies who were not eventually liquidated; indeed, he rose in Henry's household from kitchen-boy to the substantial rank of royal falconer.

Margaret of York certainly endorsed the Dublin pretender, providing him with a force of 2,000 mercenaries in the employ of Burgundy under the command of the Earl of Lincoln. Most surprising of all, suspicion also fell on Elizabeth Woodville as secretly supporting him (see Postscript).

After the battle of Stoke in 1487, when the Earl of Lincoln died and 'Lambert Simnel' ended up in captivity, Margaret became a proponent of the subsequent pretender, 'Perkin Warbeck'. Another of his staunch supporters was Maximilian, King of the Romans and later Emperor. So was James IV of Scotland, who gave him the hand in marriage of a near kinswoman, the celebrated beauty Lady Katherine Gordon.

Even more remarkably, Vergil reported that Sir William Stanley – brother of Thomas, and saviour of Henry Tudor at Bosworth – was beheaded by Henry in 1495 on a charge of treason for declaring that if 'Perkin Warbeck' were indeed the son of Edward IV, he would never bear arms against him.

There are many aspects of 'Perkin Warbeck' – or 'Piers Osbeck' as Henry Tudor later liked to call him – that are difficult to reconcile with imposture. Among them are his evident dignity, royal comportment and 'princely countenance' (as remarked in *Hall's Chronicle*) which allowed him to be accepted in royal circles throughout Europe; and his ability to inspire thousands to risk all in order to place him on the throne of England. His biographer Ann Wroe says his English was so good that Henry's historians had to go to great lengths to account for it, Bernard André even claiming, for Henry's private reading, that he had been brought up in England and had lived at Edward's Court. Vergil believed the boy already knew English, and remarked on his 'natural acuity and elegance'.

By way of surviving documents there are few we can be sure were penned by the pretender, least of all the pre-prepared 'confession' that he signed under duress. There is no mention of Richard III in anything authentic that survives, although plenty of Tudor writers put reported speech into his mouth.

In manuscript copies of his proclamation of 1496 he does not suggest attempts to murder him, or mention Richard III at all (unlike the embellished version by Francis Bacon), but says 'wee in oure tender age escaped by godes might out of the tower of London and were secretlie conveyed over the sea into other divers countries there remayninge certaine years as unknowne.'[30]

Sir George Buc (pp. 142–3) had no doubts in the matter:

> it hath been made plain enough that the younger son of King Edward was conveyed into a foreign land by sea, and that foreign country was Flanders, as all the stories testify … And he was still, and a long time, kept close. And there may the more credit be

given to that report of these matters because it agreeth well with that which was made thereof by Duke Richard, or Perkin Warbeck himself (for so he was now called or nicknamed).

Buc says the boy was placed in the care of Margaret of York who gave him 'all princely and virtuous education in Tournay, in Antwerp, and after in the court of the Duke of Burgundy ... because he was not yet of years and of strength and of knowledge ripe enough to undertake the enterprise for the recovery or gaining of a kingdom'.

As regards the fate of young Edward V, Buc surmised that he did not survive to accompany his brother across the Channel:

> some write that they were both secretly taken out of the Tower and both set afloat in a ship and conveyed together over the seas. But because I find no mention of the being of the elder brother in Flanders, but very frequent mention of the younger brother's being there and of his other adventures and travails, I will let the elder brother, Edward, rest, and speak of his brother's transportation and the rest of his actions and life.

Buc offers no evidence to explain his theory that Edward died of natural causes; he is, however, certainly correct in saying that by the time 'Perkin Warbeck' appeared claiming to be Richard in 1491, the elder prince was no longer spoken of.

Inevitably 'Perkin' became a pawn in the game of international politics, but to dismiss his claimed identity on such grounds alone will not suffice. There can be little doubt that James IV of Scotland genuinely believed him to be the younger prince, and never withdrew his support. Maximilian also continued trying to secure his release even after he had been sent to the Tower. Margaret of York was of course his leading supporter, and although she was undoubtedly anxious to cause as much trouble as possible for Henry Tudor, one needs to consider carefully whether, had her plans proved successful, she would truly have been prepared to see an impostor on the English throne begetting bogus descendants of her own noble house of York.

It is in this Burgundian connection that most clues seem to lie. In Margaret's household accounts there is a curious reference to a gift of wine to the 'sone van Claretie uit Ingelant' (son of

Clarence from England) in 1487.[31] This coincides with a time at which rumour placed little Edward of Warwick in Flanders. Or we may take another view and postulate that George of Clarence, like his brothers, fathered bastards: this 'son' could well have been one of them. Alas for poor Warwick, although he was initially kept a short time in ward by Margaret Beaufort, he spent all of his remaining years in captivity until the Tudor king finally trumped up a charge of treason and had him executed in 1499.

Interestingly, Ann Wroe speaks of discovering the presence in Margaret of York's household of a boy who came into her life in 1478, a year after the death of her husband, the Duke of Burgundy. He was at the time aged about five, the same age as Richard of York, and she paid for his keep and instruction for seven years.

Margaret had failed to bear her husband a child, and it was not long after her brother Clarence was executed that this little boy, known as Jehan le Sage ('good little John'), started appearing regularly in the accounts for her palace at Binche, south of Brussels, where he was educated by a priest. 'Although she helped other children,' Dr Wroe observes, '... Jehan was the only one whose upbringing and teaching she personally supervised. Yet this was done at a distance and out of the public eye, a long way from Brussels or Malines, with Margaret often absent, and with the priest officially in charge of him.'[32]

Ann Wroe has amassed a fair amount of evidence about young Jehan's upbringing, including the fact that considerable sums of money were spent on him, and he seems to have been clothed as 'a little nobleman'. His priest-instructor also came from a noble family.

Reading of this cosseted little boy, cared for as Margaret's child, one cannot help recalling the 1486 rumours that Clarence's son had surfaced in Flanders. Perhaps there is also a connection with the gift of wine for the 'sone van Claretie' (the year again being 1486, by which date apparently Jehan was no longer residing at Binche). Plus, of course, one immediately associates 1486–87 with the appearance in Portugal of 'Perkin', who would claim to be Richard of York. In later years, Margaret named Jehan's room 'Richard's room'.

Dr Wroe suggests the possibility that Jehan was a love-child of Edward IV, sent out to comfort a childless sister. If Jehan and 'Perkin' were one and the same, this would account for the striking resemblance to Edward. But a close resemblance could also exist between Edward and a love-child of Clarence, said to have been Margaret's favourite brother. Either way, if this was the only realistic hope of ousting the hated Tudor, she might very well prefer to see a royal bastard on the throne of England.

* * *

We cannot leave the mystery of the princes without referring to a prevalent school of thought that suggests they were killed, with or without Richard's knowledge and consent, by Harry, Duke of Buckingham. It is certainly possible to imagine Buckingham engineering their deaths for his own private reasons, notwithstanding Anthony Pollard's contention that any such murder must be Richard's fault anyway (the 'criminal negligence' argument). After all, he did have full access to the Tower – as Constable of England he could enter and leave and command obedience in the name of the sovereign – and he did potentially have motive. Maybe he saw the princes as impediments to his own personal ambition. Or had he been persuaded to eliminate them in support of the Morton-Beaufort plan to set the crown on Henry Tudor? The reader may smile at the idea of Buckingham scheming to put Tudor on the throne, but it is the very tale put forward in all seriousness by Polydore Vergil.

It has been argued that Buckingham might have thought he was performing an essential service for Richard III which that king could not bring himself to undertake. In this connection there is a theory that the duke acted unilaterally to murder the princes in expectation of Richard's gratitude, only to meet with rejection and banishment. This, however, is plainly contradicted by surviving warrants showing that Buckingham was still receiving substantial favours from a trusting Richard as late as mid-September, long after their last meeting.

A number of early sources suggest Buckingham's involvement in murdering the princes:

- A fragment of manuscript in the College of Arms, dating from 1512–13 but possibly copied from originals that may have been written by 1487 (see Appendix), states that the boys were 'put to deyth in the Towur of London be the vise of the duke of Buckingham'. This could mean 'by his device' or 'on his advice', suggesting 'in compliance with his orders'.[33]

- A fragment of uncertain origin, completed early in the reign of Henry VII (perhaps about 1490), housed among the Ashmolean manuscripts in the Bodleian Library in Oxford, records that Richard took Buckingham's advice before killing the princes: 'Richard (first taking counsel with the Duke of Buckingham, as said) removed them from the light of this world.'[34]

- Another source was recently brought to notice by António S. Marques: the little-known notes of Álvaro Lopes de Chaves, secretary to kings Afonso V and John II of Portugal, include a passage dated 1488 in which Richard is said to have given the Prince of Wales and Duke of York into the charge of the Duke of Buckingham, 'under whose custody the said Princes were starved to death'. Regrettably his subsequent comments do not inspire confidence, since the events described are placed hopelessly out of sequence: 'Gloucester ... wishing to clear himself of so ugly an event, beheaded the Duke of Buckingham and rose to kingship.'[35]

- Philippe de Commynes, writing between 1488 and 1504, gives three different versions of the deaths of the princes, in one of which he cites the Duke of Buckingham as their murderer: 'King Richard did not last long; nor did the Duke of Buckingham, who had put the two children to death.'[36]

- Jean Molinet had also heard this story, possibly from the same source as de Commynes, although he did not credit it: 'on the day that Edward's sons were assassinated, there came to the Tower of London the Duke of Buckingham, who was believed, mistakenly, to have murdered the children in order to forward his pretensions to the crown'.[37]

- The Dutch *Divisie Chronicle* suggests that the princes were either starved to death or possibly murdered by the Duke of Buckingham, although some reports said he killed only one boy and allowed the other to live.[38]

Whether acting for Richard or on his own account, the problem is that there are insurmountable conflicts of timing and opportunity where Buckingham's personal involvement is concerned. We know the princes were still residing in the Tower while Richard was in York in early September. But by August–September Buckingham had certainly left London, and thereafter was never realistically in sufficient proximity to organize a murder there.

Could anyone acting in the duke's absence make all the arrangements necessary to gain secret access to the boys? Especially since they were now, according to Crowland, protected by a 'specially appointed guard'? For an agent to get that far, he would undoubtedly require signed orders from the Constable himself. Would Buckingham take that risk and leave the entire enterprise, together with incriminating papers, in someone else's hands while he was hundreds of miles away? Surely it would have been vital for him at least to supervise how the task was carried out, and to remain close at hand if only to cover his tracks in case anything went wrong. Likewise, if Richard himself had authorized the murders, would he not have insisted on Buckingham personally overseeing the arrangements? Otherwise he would surely have given the task to someone else. This was a matter which could not be botched.

Let us review the duke's recorded movements after the month of July, as examined in chapter 8. If we accept Vergil's narrative, he was last in the company of the king at Gloucester on 2 August. After that he returned to his estates in South Wales, with evidence showing that he was still in Brecon on 23 August, enjoying the company of Bishop Morton. In early September he would have received Richard's orders sent on 28 August to hold commissions of oyer and terminer in the southern counties of England; by mid-September he was heading up a treasonous rebellion, from which we may safely deduce that he had long ceased to do Richard's bidding.

Therefore any murder by Buckingham must have been performed prior to 28 July to allow time for that final meeting on 2 August. Or, if Vergil was mistaken, perhaps Buckingham did not join Richard at Gloucester but remained in London to commit the dastardly deed before leaving for Brecon by, say, mid-August. Either way, these dates are irreconcilable with the heightening of security surrounding the princes after attempts had been made to abduct them, the latest being when John Welles was punished (but not accused of murder) around 13 August. Would this not have been the most unpropitious time to choose? In the wake of recently-foiled plots, would there not have been a loud hue and cry, with their guards exhorted to maintain extra vigilance?

Common sense suggests that the only successful way to make the princes disappear without anyone taking particular note would have been as part of some unremarkable, low-key procedure such as an ordinary transfer elsewhere. This, however, could never have been accomplished in the hothouse atmosphere following attempted abductions, with all tongues wagging merrily and all eyes turning curiously toward their apartments.

Another nail in the coffin of the Buckingham theory is that Richard himself never blamed Buckingham for the murders, even when he was executed for treason.

Finally, if confirmation for Buckingham's guilt is sought in the Tudor writers, it will be found lacking. In Thomas More and Polydore Vergil, the guilty party is Sir James Tyrell.

Intriguingly, Vergil says he knows of a 'common report' that Buckingham encouraged the king in his 'mischievous dedes' in hopes of taking his place once those deeds had caused the people to hate and overthrow Richard; but Vergil insists that this belief is mistaken.

So there is no support for the theory that Buckingham killed the princes, and indeed the only credible clues to their disappearance indicate that it happened long after Buckingham had ceased to have access to them.

Thus Buckingham is ruled out. And, despite Shakespeare and centuries of tradition, the idea that Richard III had the princes killed in the Tower of London, with nobody noticing, is as laughable as the idea that he killed them and kept it secret. The obvious conclusion, therefore, is that they 'disappeared' because they were simply moved elsewhere.

10

Bones of Contention

Despite the improbability of Sir James Tyrell's supposed confession, to this day there exist certain remains in Westminster Abbey which are said to prove its veracity.

In 1674, some workmen were removing a forebuilding and stairs adjoining the White Tower, the eleventh-century central keep of the Tower of London. In the course of digging down to the foundations they came across some bones at a depth of about 10ft. The bones were thrown on to a rubbish heap, where they lay until someone thought they might be of significance (having presumably realized they were human remains) and sent the labourers back to retrieve them.

This was in the reign of Charles II, and the king commissioned for them a white marble urn, suitably inscribed, on the supposition that these were the remains of the 'princes in the Tower', taking Thomas More as authority for their death and disposal. Four years later, in 1678, the urn was installed in the Henry VII Chapel of Westminster Abbey. These remains have rested there ever since, with nothing more conclusive to identify them than that they are the bones of some children, of unknown gender, found buried under a staircase next to the White Tower.

Such was the power of the legend that this was not the first time bones found thereabouts were immediately assumed to be those of Edward and Richard. A few decades earlier, in 1647, one John Webb reported their discovery in a walled-up room; but it was concluded – with what accuracy is unknown – that these children were no more than about eight years old, and consequently they

were too young. In 1619 Sir George Buc wrote of an earlier
skeleton, again hailed as one of the princes, eventually identified
as an escaped ape from the Tower menagerie. The accuracy of this
identification is also unknown.

A great many more bones were exposed when the Tower
moat was drained in the nineteenth century; and another child's
skeleton, found in 1977, was firmly dated to the late Iron Age,
reminding us that there has been a human presence upon the site
for more than 2,000 years. Any of these might also have been
touted as belonging to the princes had not the rather precipitate
identification been made in 1674.

The report twenty-seven years previously, describing walled-up
skeletons which had been discovered earlier in the century, is best
known from the handwritten note signed by John Webb written
in 1647 on the flyleaf of a book published in 1641 entitled *The
Historie of the Pitiful Life ... of Edward V*, which was one of the later
versions of More's *Richard III*.

> August ye 17th 1647. Mr Johnson a Counsellor sonne of Sr Robert
> Johnson affirmed to mee and others that when ye Lo: Grey of Wilton
> and Sr Walter Raleigh were prisoners in ye Tower, the wall of ye
> passage to ye King's Lodgings then sounding hollow was taken downe
> and at ye place marked A was found a little roome about 7 or 8 fo.
> square, wherein there stood a Table and uppon it ye bones of two
> Children supposed of 6 or 8 yeeres of Age which by ye aforesayd noble
> and all present were credibly beeleeved to bee ye Carcasses of Edward
> ye 5th and his brother the then Duke of Yorke. This gent was also an
> eyewitness at ye opening of it, with Mr Palmer and Mr Henry Cogan,
> officers of ye minte and others with whom having since discoursed
> hereof they affirmed ye same and yt they saw the Skeletons. Jo. Webb.[1]

So Webb evidently double-checked Johnson's story with some at
least of these latter witnesses. The period when Lord Grey and Sir
Walter were incarcerated simultaneously was between 1603 and 1614
in the reign of James I; Raleigh was eventually executed in 1618.

Another account, first published in 1680 by Louis Aubery du
Maurier, claimed that his father had been told by Maurice de
Nassau, Prince of Orange (1567–1625), of a similar discovery:

> in Queen Elizabeth's time, the Tower of London being full of
> Prisoners of State, on account of the frequent conspiracies against

her person, as they were troubled to find room for them all, they bethought themselves of opening a door of a chamber that had been walled up for a long time; and they found in this chamber upon a bed two little carcasses with halters around their necks. These were the skeletons of King Edward V and the Duke of York, his brother, whom their uncle Richard the cruel had strangled to get the crown ... But the prudent Princess, not willing to revive the memory of such an execrable deed, had the door walled up as before. However, I learned that this same door having been opened a short time ago, and the skeletons being found in the same place, the King of England out of compassion that these two princes were deprived of burial, or from other reasons that I am ignorant of, has resolved to erect a Mausoleum, and have them transported to Westminster Abbey where the tombs of the Kings are.[2]

Obviously we have to make appropriate allowances for the account attributed to Prince Maurice, not a native of England, and reported at third or fourth hand by du Maurier; thus the confusion with the bones of 1674 and their inurnment in Westminster Abbey is understandable. Although 'Queen Elizabeth's time' seems at variance with Webb's report, a shift of a few years later would place both events in the reign of James I, so the two accounts could be compatible. The earliest published report can be narrowed down to 1622 in the second edition of a book by Ralph Brooke, York Herald, referring to remains of two children found in the Tower: 'which place ... hath been mured up, and not known untill of late, when as their dead carcases were there found, under a heape of stones and rubbish.'[3] Otherwise the essence of the story chimes well with Webb. The desire for secrecy suggests that the chamber, although ostensibly resealed, might perhaps have been quietly revisited and the skeletons removed in order to avoid the embarrassment of a repeat discovery in some future reign.

At this point we should examine the precise layout of the Tower of London. I am indebted to Historic Royal Palaces, the Royal Armouries, Geoffrey Parnell, Edward Impey, Roland Harris, Jeremy Ashbee and Anna Keay for archaeological and historical information; the conclusions, however, are my own.

The model pictured in Plate 15 gives an idea of how the castle may have appeared in about the year 1100, with the entrance to the White Tower some 20ft up its south wall at the first floor level (for US readers, the second floor). For security reasons it was accessed solely by means of a removable staircase made of wood. Today the entrance is again reached by a similar timber staircase. The upper floor contained the king's great hall and chamber, together with the Chapel of St John the Evangelist at the south-east corner. The only stairs originally providing upward access were internally sited in the far north-east turret, diagonally opposite the entrance (another security measure).

In the survey dated 1597 (Plate 18), showing the much-enlarged castle grounds as they were in the reign of Elizabeth I, a defensible forebuilding is seen attached to the south wall of the keep at the south-west corner. Constructed from stone, probably in the twelfth century, it permitted permanent stone steps in place of the removable timber staircase leading to the previously exposed main entrance (see overleaf and Plate 16). Little is known of its arrangements other than whatever can be gleaned from early illustrations.

There is also another smaller doorway to the White Tower which features prominently in our discussions. It is situated at a height of 14ft in the next bay to the right of the main entrance. Results of the recent White Tower Recording and Research Project show that it was inserted some time after the late 1350s, in a location previously occupied by a basement window. This small doorway, penetrating the 13ft thick south wall, gave on to the ground floor and may have provided entry to the basement where provisions were stored. Probably also in the fourteenth century the stairs inside the doorway were extended upward in a spiral through the fabric of the wall to reach the western entrance to St John's Chapel at the upper residential level, thereby giving direct access to the chapel *from outside* for the first time. It was under the external stairs leading up to this doorway that the bones were found in 1674.

Visitors to the Tower today pass this small doorway as they climb the timber access staircase. Inside an old plaque is preserved which refers rather misleadingly to the finding of the bones of the 'princes in the Tower' (Plate 17).

There are two possible options for the arrangement of stairs that led up to the small doorway, and it is argued here that something resembling that illustrated in Plate 16 was probably built to replace the original twelfth-century stone access stairs which are believed to have ranged along the south elevation of the White Tower, as with the first timber staircase. This space

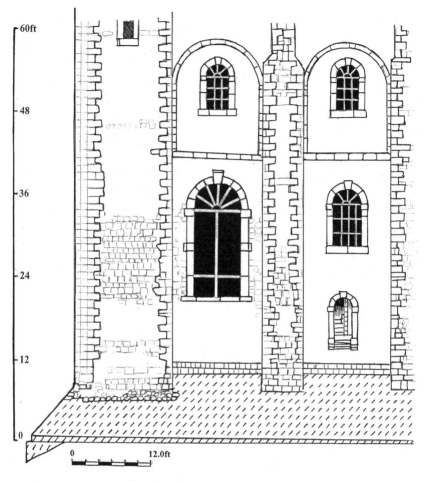

Detail, south elevation of the White Tower

east of the forebuilding saw many changes over the years which were incompatible with the original layout of stairs. Structures abutting the wall were added, removed and replaced, including living quarters for the Tower's constable. We have no record of these constructions, but when the Jewel House was built there at some time prior to 1508 (visible in Plate 18) it would certainly have entailed removal of any stairs occupying that space.

Plate 16 illustrates an arrangement of stairs that could have been built when the Jewel House was erected, or perhaps even earlier about the time the small doorway was opened up (around 1360) when there were no added structures to obscure the layout. It shows an exterior stone staircase rising from the south to a landing built level with the top of the plinth on which the forebuilding stands.

The White Tower also stands on a plinth, widely splayed, providing support for a construction whose walls are up to 15ft thick and 90ft tall. At the south-west corner this plinth reaches its maximum height of about 10ft, owing to the incline of the terrain falling away to the west and south-west. The forebuilding's plinth would have been about the same height, although not splayed to the same extent. A flight of about eighteen steps ascends to the landing, whereupon there is a choice of turning left to enter the forebuilding, or continuing up a few more steps to enter the small doorway.

From Elizabethan times onward, and especially during the Restoration, the Chapel of St John increasingly came to be employed as a repository for state records. Thus, although other entrances to the White Tower were opened up, the access stairs to the small doorway remained in constant use. Whatever the date of their construction, or that of other structures built around the same site, it seems inevitable that some such arrangement of stairs must have existed in the reign of Charles II. Sadly the only surviving copies of Elizabethan surveys fail to show it. They merely indicate the east wall of the forebuilding meeting the south wall of the White Tower at the beginning of the second bay. Seventeenth-century depictions are no more illuminating. It scarcely needs emphasizing that this entrance area must have been one of the busiest and most closely-guarded sites in the entire grounds. Not an ideal location for a secret interment of bodies.

* * *

Returning to Webb's 1647 report, a most intriguing part of his manuscript is the hand-drawn plan of the small, square structure within which the 'little roome' was located 'at ye place marked A'.

This was reproduced by Lawrence Tanner in a substantial article for *Archaeologia*, whose main thrust was to discuss the bones found in 1674. Tanner did us a great service by publishing Webb's plan, but he labelled it 'the king's lodgings', which is highly doubtful; Webb himself made it clear that the 'little roome' was discovered behind a wall of the *passage to* the king's lodgings.

The 'Stayres leading out of Cole Harbour' have misled other writers into assuming that the plan represents the forebuilding, which stood near the Cole Harbour Gate. However, unless the word 'gate' was used, the term Cole Harbour in Webb's day meant the general area of the Inmost Ward. Moreover, the forebuilding was an unlikely place to accommodate prisoners, occupying as it did an exterior location that would have seen large amounts of traffic.

There are other problems in matching the forebuilding to the plan drawn by Webb, not to mention the fact that he entirely omits a small tower or turret that existed at the south-east corner. The date of this turret is unknown. It is absent in a fifteenth-century illustration showing the forebuilding when Charles d'Orléans was a prisoner in the Tower of London, but a slender turret is clearly present in all copies of the well-known 1597 survey (see Plate 18). In mid seventeenth-century illustrations by Wenceslas Hollar, a larger structure (known as the 'brick tower') seems to have replaced it.

Webb has been identified by Helen Maurer in her very helpful two-part article in *The Ricardian,* where she describes him as apprenticed to the great Inigo Jones to study architecture.[4] As Jones's assistant and deputy, Webb undoubtedly knew the site well and could be relied upon to draw an accurate plan. So we can be confident he would not omit such a prominent feature.

As for the king's lodgings, preceding monarchs had adopted a variety of different residential quarters. In Tudor times, with the Tower of London favoured more as a prison than a residence, the lodgings eventually fell into disuse. By the reign of Charles II they had been converted to military stores. When Webb wrote his note, the royal apartments extended northwards from the Lanthorn Tower into a row of buildings stretching to the Wardrobe Tower at the eastern end of the White Tower's south façade, terminating to the right of the Jewel House (indicated as 'The Queen's Lodgings' in Plate 18).

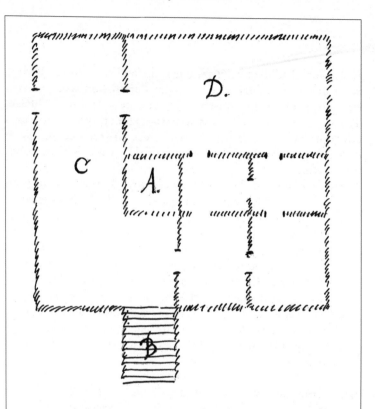

A. The 'little roome'.
B. The Stayres leading out of Cole Harbour to ye Kings Lodgings.
C. Passage to ye Kings Lodgings.
D. Ye Guard Chamber.

John Webb's plan

It is not possible to deduce what Webb meant by his 'Passage to ye Kings Lodgings', but according to his plan, the external entrance to this passage was reached via steps from the Inmost Ward. On entry, the only route on the plan that led to the king's lodgings was by *turning left*, which again rules out the forebuilding. It seems more likely that the area he sketched was located at that end of the lodgings nearest to the Lanthorn Tower, where the process of constructing new buildings had been started by Henry VII.

* * *

John Webb had died by 1674, when skeletal remains of children were discovered during some major demolition work carried out pursuant to the construction of a new Ordnance office. The forebuilding, the access stairways and all other structures contiguous to the White Tower were ordered to be taken down. It was during the last stages of this work that the bones were found.

Two accounts of the discovery are directly traceable to John Knight, Principal Surgeon to Charles II, one of which is signed by him. It reads as follows:

> Anno 1674. In digging down a pair of stone staires leading from the Kings Lodgings to the chappel in the white tower ther were found the bones of two striplings in (as it seemed) a wooden chest which upon the presumptions that they were the bones of this king and his brother Rich: D. of York, were by the command of K. Charles the 2nd put into a marble Urn and deposited amongst the R: Family in H: 7th Chappel in Westminster at my importunity. Jo. Knight.

The second account attributed to Knight appears in Francis Sandford's *Genealogical History of the Kings of England* (1677):

> Upon Friday the [17th] day of July. An. 1674 ... in order to the rebuilding of the several Offices in the Tower, and to clear the white Tower from all contiguous Buildings, digging down the Stairs which led from the King's Lodgings, to the Chappel in the said Tower, about ten foot in the ground, were found the Bones of two striplings in (as it seemed) a wooden Chest, which upon the survey were found proportionable to the ages of those two Brothers viz about thirteen and eleven years.

The report goes on to describe the bones being thrown on a rubbish heap and later retrieved. It is reproduced in full in the above-mentioned article in *Archaeologia*, which also quotes further accounts of the discovery, some more reliable than others. In the reliable category is an eyewitness account given by

John Gibbon, Bluemantle pursuivant of arms, in an autograph note which is now at the College of Arms:

> Die Veneris July 17 Anno 1674 in digging some fondacons in ye Tower, were discoverd ye bodies of Edw 5 and his Brother murdred 1483. I my selfe handled ye Bones Especially ye Kings Skull. ye other wch. was lesser was Broken in ye digging. Johan Gybbon, Blewmantle.

Christopher Wren, son of the famous Sir Christopher who was commissioned to design the urn that would hold the bones, wrote in his *Parentalia* (1750) that they were discovered 'about 10 feet deep in the ground ... as the workmen were taking away the stairs, which led from the royal lodgings into the Chapel of the White-tower'.

The Latin inscription on the urn also describes them as found 'deeply buried' under the rubble of the stairs that led up to the chapel, which confirms that the depth of the discovery was noteworthy, and that its location was where these specific stairs had lately been demolished.

Also reproduced in *Archaeologia* is an anonymous report of the discovery which mentions 'there were pieces of rag and velvet about them', from which some writers have inferred that these were royal remains. The account was originally found at some unspecified date 'on the margin of one of the pages of a curious MS on Heraldry', and Tanner suggests 'it is not improbable that the unknown writer of the note ... was Knight himself'. This, however, has been refuted by most authorities: nobody has been able to trace the manuscript containing the anonymous note, and it bears scant resemblance to any of Knight's authoritative accounts.

No textiles were found when the urn was opened in 1933, and velvet had been in use by royalty in England since at least around 1300, so its presence would scarcely have assisted in dating the remains. Other stories of 'two skeletons found face to face in a chest' are equally apocryphal.

Leaving aside such unreliable reports, let us return to what we know of the location of the bones in 1674. For this we must refer to the accounts by Knight and Wren, which unequivocally agree that they were discovered about 10ft under the ground. The well-informed Knight says the find was made 'in digging down a pair of stone staires leading from the Kings Lodgings to the chappel in the white tower', and Wren says 'as the workmen were taking away the stairs' which led from the royal lodgings to the chapel. Clearly they are describing the removal of the stairs leading to our small doorway.

Use of the chapel as a Record Office continued unabated throughout the reign of Charles II; therefore, after the demolition of 1674, alternative stairs were needed for transporting archives to and fro. A contract called for a new staircase of twenty-five steps rising from external ground level up to the small doorway.

Some details of the replacement stairway are given by Lawrence Tanner in *Archaeologia*. He quotes Lord de Ros, Lieutenant-Governor of the Tower from 1852, who wrote in 1866 to the effect that Charles II ordered a mulberry tree to be planted on the spot where the bones were found, but that another stairway was thoughtlessly built up against the wall which rapidly killed the tree. 'There was, however, in 1853 an old Warder who well recollected to have seen the stump still embedded in the landing of the stairs.'

From this we can discount, once and for all, the tradition upheld by the old plaque on the wall of the spiral staircase (Plate 17) indicating that it was under this *internal* staircase – hewn out of the 13ft-thick eleventh-century wall – that the bones were found in 1674.

Lawrence Tanner generated his own hypothetical plan of the forebuilding which is reproduced here.

Regrettably, Tanner's plan is way off the mark: he omits the turret in the south-east corner, and the indicated 'Scale of Feet' is hopelessly inaccurate, but if you substitute '40' for '20' you get something approaching reality. The plan also imagines the small doorway contained *within* the forebuilding walls, thus showing the immense size the forebuilding would be if this were the case. No depiction shows a forebuilding of such massive proportions.

We cannot leave the matter of the 1674 discovery without addressing certain doubts which have been expressed as to the 10ft depth of the bones. How seriously must we take this estimate, and why would the mere demolition of a stairway involve penetration to such a depth?

As to the estimate, while agreeing with Maurer's comment that the figure of 10ft should be understood as an approximation,

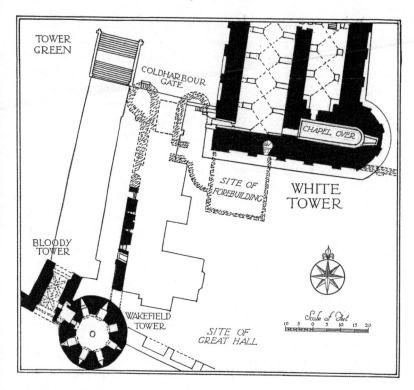

Lawrence Tanner's plan

I would nevertheless argue that it must be correct to within a foot or so. The artisans employed for this particular work would be men of experience who would have a clear idea of the depth at which they were excavating. They also remembered the discovery as interesting enough to mention later, which means they discussed it among themselves, something that would tend to crystallize their recollections. If reports by grander personages introduced any inaccuracies, one would at least expect the surprising figure of 'ten feet in the ground' to have been modified in the retelling, but the figure is constant whenever the depth is mentioned.

So why dig so deep? For an answer we must look at the site. The Tower of London was built on a gravel terrace on the flood plain of the then Thames watercourse. The natural terrain formed a slope that fell away from the east, where some useful foundations had been left by previous Roman structures. But these were not wholly sufficient and there was no natural rock base, the soil being Eocene London clay and gravel. So, as excavations beside the south and east walls have revealed, trench-poured foundations were used in building the White Tower: i.e. trenches were dug and hardcore rammed into them. Such trenches could be as deep as 15 to 20ft, extending at least 3ft beyond the splayed plinth to provide an adequate footing.[5]

We have noted that the slope of the land at the south-west corner required a plinth of 10ft, which is higher than at any other point. This area, then, had not previously been made level for habitation. It was a potentially vulnerable corner which needed reliable foundations as well as strong defences. So when the forebuilding was added to this same corner and tied to the south wall, the builders would have been careful to match their foundations to those of the keep. The same necessity applied to the construction of associated stone staircases.

Moving to the year 1674, we have work starting in March to remove these old structures. The master mason knows he will be contracted to build a replacement stairway, tied where it meets the south wall. Like his predecessors, to avoid subsidence he knows he must ensure its foundations lie at the right level. So he instructs his workmen to dig right down to the foundations of the demolished area. There is clear confirmation for this in the contemporaneous report by John Gibbon, Bluemantle pursuivant, who described the bones being found 'in digging some foundacons in ye Tower'. The date of mid-July fits exactly with excavating foundations, for the work had then reached its final phase: clearance was entirely finished by mid-August.

Given that we cannot fault authoritative reports by Knight and Wren of the bones being found 10ft in the ground while men were 'digging down' the stairs that led to the chapel, with Gibbon confirming they were digging foundations, it is surprising that opinions differ as to exactly where the discovery took place. Can this be because the eyewitness descriptions are impossible to reconcile with Thomas More?

Let us see how burying the bodies might have been accomplished by More's murderers. Looking at Plate 16, either we can choose to believe the bones were buried in the ground under the stairway itself, which seems to have been the consensus of opinion in 1674, or we may consider suggestions that they were buried more conveniently in the ground beside the stairs.

If buried *underneath* the stairway, the task entailed removing a substantial stone structure (a job which required several workmen in 1674) to access this curious choice of resting place, not to mention excavating down a further 10ft. This, together with the subsequent reconstruction of the demolished stairway, was an impossible feat to accomplish on one night in secret. Self-evidently we can dismiss that option.

Looking at the easier task of excavating a 10ft hole in the ground *beside* the stairway, it should be remembered that to reach such a depth would require a pit large enough for at least one man, preferably two, to jump inside and shovel soil from the bottom up to surface level. Once they were halfway down, the surface was at head height. Already they would have needed planks to shore up the sides and buckets to transport the soil; yet, not content with a burial depth that would have been considered prodigious by fifteenth-century standards, when graves were routinely a maximum of about 3ft deep, we must now believe they pressed on and dug down a further 5ft, with more shoring-up of walls, presumably using a pulley system to hoist the soil (or mud) to the surface – and to lower the chest, if chest there was – plus, of course, a 10ft ladder. This is beginning to look as ridiculous as the understair option.

In fact, the sheer depth alone would lead us to deduce that these bones never arrived at their resting place by being secretly buried in the 1480s, when the Tower was teeming with people and bristling with guards. The obvious deduction is that they were already there before structures were unknowingly built over them. They could have lain buried for 500 years, if not a thousand more than that.

Some writers, including Tanner, have suggested that the depth may be explained by surface deposit accumulating over bones buried in a shallower grave in the 1480s. We can thank Helen Maurer for debunking this possibility: 'a surface build-up of six or seven feet – probably the minimum one would have to assume – over the course of 190 years would have covered doors and windows in an area that was in daily use!'

My own enquiries of the authorities at Historic Royal Palaces reveal that the ground surface in the fifteenth century was about 2ft 3in higher than in the thirteenth century. If we extrapolate from this roughly one foot of deposit accumulation per century, it would take six centuries to build up 6ft: making the latest possible burial year 1066.

★ ★ ★

In terms of identifying the bones, let us first deal with the fact that they were of children. Superficially it may seem that two children being buried within the walls of a castle might be a rare occurrence. Yet the White Tower had stood for 600 years on top of a site where earlier fortifications had also existed, dating at least as far back as the Roman occupation. During all of these centuries it was customary for those who died in the fortress from violence or disease to be buried within its walls.

When the Tower was erected, as may be seen from the three-dimensional model, no permanent structure stood on the site later occupied by the forebuilding and stairway. Thus two deceased children might have lain buried there undisturbed for hundreds of years.

It must be remembered that nobody who has actually examined the remains has had access to any method of determining how ancient they are, least of all today's sophisticated radiocarbon dating techniques.

If we were to consider the bones as forensic evidence, we would also have to admit that their sojourn on a rubbish heap does not add to their credibility, and neither does the lack of certainty as to how safely they were guarded from 1674 until their inurnment in 1678. Apparently some of them during this period found their way into the possession of the Ashmolean Museum at Oxford, but were ultimately lost. Since many bones were missing and a variety of animal bones were present when the urn was opened in the twentieth century – fish, duck, chicken, rabbit, sheep, pig and ox – it seems possible that other collectors (or looters) had their pickings and left substitute material before the urn was sealed. None of this gives us tremendous confidence in the value of its contents as evidence.

It was in 1933 that Lawrence Tanner, Keeper of the Muniments at Westminster Abbey, came on the scene together with Professor William Wright, one of the foremost anatomists of his day, having obtained permission to examine the bones in an undisguised attempt to prove that they belonged to the 'princes in the Tower'. Aided by Dr George Northcroft, a renowned dental specialist, they published a report in 1934 in which they obviously believed they had proved their case. Essentially they concluded that the skeletons were of two boys with a family relationship, being of about the same ages in 1483 as Richard (who was ten on 17 August) and Edward (thirteen on 2 November). Their assessment, based primarily on dentition, put the younger child as 'about mid-way between nine and eleven', and the older child as 'somewhere between the ages of twelve and thirteen'. Alas, there was little foundation for such convenient conclusions.

Of course, once the bones had been disturbed in this way, the chances of any similar investigation in the future were stymied. Proposals for a new examination have been discussed, and – unsurprisingly – have been resisted by the authorities. So it is particularly galling that Messrs Tanner and Wright, well-intentioned though they were, carried out their task in such an unobjective manner, and with insufficient scientific resources at their disposal to be able to determine with any certainty the very facts they hoped to verify.

Their findings were discussed in February 1963 in a talk given by another anatomist, Dr Richard Lyne-Pirkis, who had made a close study of the report and photographic records of the 1933 team. He drew some interesting conclusions.

First, Tanner and Wright failed to seek evidence to determine the gender of the children. Progress has since been made in this area of study, but certainly in 1933 Professor Wright had no way of substantiating his early assumption, by the fifth paragraph of his anatomical report, that the deceased were males. (By the seventh paragraph he was naming them Edward and Richard.)

Second, Dr Lyne-Pirkis commented that examination of the bones of children has been shown to yield nothing better than approximate age. In a major study of bone development conducted at Western Reserve University, Ohio, tracking the development of about 1,000 babies from age zero to twenty, the results clearly showed a great deal of difference between the apparent age of a bone as seen on the X-ray plate and the real age: 'there was a big range of variation in the maturity of the bones'. In fact, after thousands of X-rays had been taken and compared, a child could 'easily be two years older or two years younger' than the age apparently shown on the X-ray.

There were other factors, he noted, including diet and health, which added further degrees of uncertainty. The mediæval diet, and especially the lack of vitamins A and D, would necessitate adding another one/one-and-a-half years to the estimated ages, and in the case of the older child, who suffered from a visible disease of the jaw, a further one/one-and-a-half years should probably be added to Professor Wright's estimate, which could mean that he was really 'between fourteen and sixteen'.

Although Wright placed his reliance on the teeth rather than the bones of the children, the Ohio survey also examined teeth and came up with results that showed equally wide variations from child to child. 'Their conclusion was that it was quite impossible to arrive at the age of a child from the time the teeth erupted, because there were such enormous variations even in normal children ... so it really knocks completely sideways anything definite that can be said about these bones.'

While speaking of diet and health, Dr Lyne-Pirkis made a significant observation: in the lower jaw of the older skull there were areas of diseased bone. This phenomenon had been described by Wright as follows:

> extensive disease affecting almost equally both sides of the lower jaw, originating in or around the molar teeth ... On the left side the disease had spread to such an extent that it had destroyed the inter-dental septum between the first and second molar teeth. The disease was of a chronic nature and could not fail to have affected his [sic] general health ... The gums of Edward [sic] in the lower molar region would be inflamed, swollen, and septic, and be no doubt associated with discomfort and irritability. ... [Another effect of the disease] must, I imagine, have entailed irregular movement of the temporo-mandibular joints.

In Lyne-Pirkis's opinion it was

probably the condition known as osteomyelitis or chronic inflammation of the bone, which was quite a common condition in those days; it's fairly rare now. It's a very slow, chronic disease; in those days there was no means of curing it so it just went on for years until either the body was able to defeat the infection and leave itself with a disorganized and rather odd-looking bone, in this case the jaw, or of course if the defences of the body weren't good enough it finished you off and you died.

For the purpose of calculation, Dr Lyne-Pirkis used an adjustment of one-and-a-half years for this skull: 'any chronic disease that goes on for years will always retard a child's growth, and it's very likely in fact that he [*sic*] was retarded by one or possibly two years as a result of this disease'.

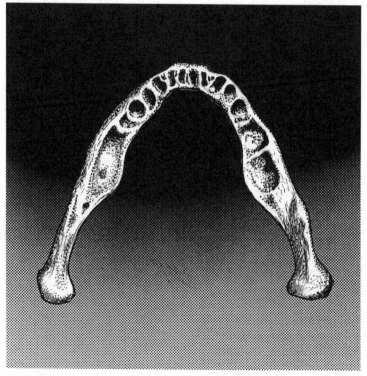

Lower jaw-bone of older skull in the urn

'Of course we don't know when it developed,' he continued, '... but it had obviously gone on long enough to produce a hard mass of bone that must have been there several years.' Showing the photographs to his audience, he indicated the evidence: 'Now you'll have to take my word for it, but in this area here which you'll see is fatter than this area over here, the bone is very dense and hard ... there was no sign of any sockets for teeth – you'll see it from the other side – there are these sockets going back here and they come down here and they stop here, and then they start again here.' (See illustration on p. 217.)

Clearly, therefore, the areas of diseased bone were visibly deformed and lacked teeth. In addition, the gums in these areas would have been 'inflamed, swollen and septic', making for a very painful mouth.

If the disease was indeed osteomyelitis, whoever owned this jawbone suffered for several years from a painful and noticeable disease. Osteomyelitis is inflammation of the bone and bone marrow by pus-forming bacteria, resulting in an enlarged mass of bone which the body develops to enclose and seal off the area affected (Lyne-Pirkis's 'disorganized and rather odd-looking bone').

This disease is an extremely important factor, and it is surprising that Dr Lyne-Pirkis seems to be the one and only expert, among all those who have offered opinions as to the ages of the skeletons, who reports taking into account a specified allowance for its effect on the owner's likely growth retardation.

Given the seriousness of the suggested disease and its equally serious implications, it seemed advisable to consult Dr William J. White, Curator of the Centre for Human Bioarchaeology at the Museum of London, not only an acknowledged authority on anatomy but the originator of a considerable amount of research on the identities of the skeletons in the urn. He was, *inter alia*, co-author with Peter Hammond of a definitive summary of the anatomical evidence relating to the bones.[6] Dr White commented that he was not confident of the diagnosis of osteomyelitis, and tended to the view that 'the published photograph and X-rays [by Tanner and Wright] are inadequate in themselves to render any diagnosis sound'.[7]

Nevertheless, several authorities have attempted a diagnosis. The leading dental expert Professor Martin Rushton says of the disease in the elder skull: 'The most probable cause of this would be chronic osteitis following abscesses on 6|6 resulting from dental caries.'[8] Also a chronic disease of the bone, osteitis would still have been debilitating and could have retarded a child's growth. Dr White commented that osteitis of the lower jaw 'would have been uncomfortable, even painful, but not necessarily have been life-threatening or producing a visible deformity'.

Osteomyelitis, however, is a different proposition: 'Osteomyelitis of the jaws is a serious and potentially lethal lesion because of its frequently-associated bacteremia and surely must have been associated with many deaths in antiquity.'[9] Dr White added that there would be 'a constant drooling and severe halitosis caused by the exhalation of the odour of infected pus'.

In summary, although we cannot reach a definite diagnosis based on the available photographs, it is clear that the owner of this skull suffered from a chronic and painful condition which had produced deformities in the jawbones. Whether osteitis or osteomyelitis, it must have been (at minimum) like a never-ending toothache. In a child of royal birth it would have demanded constant attention from physicians; and in an age when we can scarcely assume they knew the difference between the two conditions, or whether the one was an early stage of the other, it would surely have given rise to enormous concern. It would also have prevented normal eating, and would surely have required a special diet to avoid the pain of biting and chewing.

If it was indeed osteomyelitis – and Dr Lyne-Pirkis was confident he had detected it in the 'hard mass of bone that must have been there several years' – then it would have been impossible to disguise and would certainly have been widely noted in the heir to the throne. Being quite a common condition, and associated with 'many deaths in antiquity', it would have been realized that a person with this disease might never recover; again a matter that cannot fail to have caused comment had the Prince of Wales been so afflicted.

Other opinions have been offered, one by A.S. Hargreaves and R.I. MacLeod, specialists in dental/oral medicine, who suspect that the skull may show evidence of histiocytosis X. This is a group of disorders of which the version favoured in their view is eosinophilic granuloma of bone. Should this be the case, it would still be a disease which, untreated with today's techniques, 'unless it burns itself out can be a progressively destructive condition which may prove fatal' ... 'even if Edward [*sic*] had been crowned, he might not have survived beyond 5 years'. However, 'the disease cannot be confirmed conclusively in the absence of soft tissue histological examination'.[10]

In previous chapters we have examined the only existing report of Edward V's health and state of mind, by Domenico Mancini, and concluded that Mancini would almost certainly have learned of any illness from the boy's doctor, Argentine, who would surely have protested Richard's cruel treatment of a boy who was sick and in constant pain from his mouth disorder. Yet neither Mancini nor any other chronicler has anything to say about any detectable, disfiguring or even possibly fatal disease afflicting the young Edward. Had he suffered from even the less severe osteitis, his mouth would have caused him constant misery for years, with abscesses on both sides of his lower jaw resulting in inflammation and loss of teeth.

Mancini gives the most reliable personal description we have of Edward V, and in the opinion of Edward's biographer, Michael Hicks, might even have met him: 'He had such dignity in his whole person and in his countenance such charm that, however much they might feast their eyes, he never surfeited the gaze of observers.'

The French chronicler Jean Molinet, who served in Burgundy, describes young Edward as 'unsophisticated and very melancholy, aware only of the ill-will of his uncle'.[11] While his brother Richard was 'merry and frolicsome', Edward is said to have believed that both of them were marked for death. It has been suggested that Molinet could also have got his information from Argentine, but still there is no mention of a sick little boy suffering from a sore mouth and in want of the care of his faithful physician.

An important commentator in this debate is Sir George Buc, who thought Edward might have died in childhood of natural causes: 'for he was weak and very sickly, as also was his brother'. He theorizes that Edward died while still residing in the Tower. 'But wheresoever he died, I verily think that he died of a natural sickness and of infirmity.'[12] Unfortunately Buc supplies no evidence to support his theory save that Edward's siblings did not live to make old bones: 'their sisters also were but of a weak constitution, as their short lives showed'.

It is true that Edward IV's children by Elizabeth Woodville did not live beyond their thirties, but Buc's theory is refuted by their half-brother, the bastard Arthur (Wayte) Plantagenet, later Lord Lisle, who must have been about sixty when he died in 1542.

Despite exhaustive researches, it has not been possible to corroborate Buc's suggestion of a sickly Edward V. Even Mancini's statement, 'he reckoned that his death was imminent', is highly ambiguous.

Michael Hicks, who presumably has examined all known descriptions and likenesses, describes Edward V as 'a very good-looking boy', and observes that on arrival in London he was 'lodged in the Bishop of London's palace, a relatively public venue in the City, where he was visible, accessible, but also secure'.[13]

Subsequently Edward moved to the royal apartments in the Tower of London, a densely populated area with a permanent garrison and multitudes of workers. He would have been personally attended and his quarters and activities serviced and observed by large numbers, possibly running into hundreds of curious onlookers.

As the Prince of Wales, he had previously maintained a substantial household at Ludlow where he headed a very active council, again serviced by large numbers of workers, with a physician and surgeon among his personal attendants as well as any number of clerics, priests, confessors and the like.

It is therefore significant that we are left with not the slightest hint that he might have suffered from a painful and noticeable disease.

Further, young Edward was not kept from public view. Looking at his tenth year onwards, he was seen at Shrewsbury in 1480; at Greenwich with the king in July that year; with the king again during February 1481 and also in May when his father took him to Sandwich for a royal inspection of the fleet, afterwards proceeding to Canterbury where they visited the cathedral. They were seen together again in August and in the winter of 1481–82. Young Edward was also at Bewdley in Worcestershire in 1482; and he resided at Court with his parents for the Christmas festivities of 1481 and 1482.[14]

It seems he was also present at the parliamentary session which commenced in January 1483, and of course he paraded through the streets of London with Gloucester and Buckingham in May that same year. These are merely occasions of which records exist and there must have been dozens more. Still nobody reported anything amiss.

One would imagine that such an affliction of the heir apparent would also play an important part in how the two boys were raised. Yet no provision seems to have been made for the younger boy to receive appropriate training in kingly responsibility; he remained at his mother's side even after the appointment of his council in 1477. In 1483, approaching the age of ten, he had not yet been given his own household, nor had the alternative course been followed of placing him under the tutelage of a suitable nobleman to learn the arts of arms and chivalry.

The reason for this lack of concern over Edward's health seems obvious: quite simply, the diseased jawbone did not belong to him.

How disappointing, therefore, that the only modern biographer of Edward V, Professor Michael Hicks, confines himself to just two brief references to the bones.[15] His stance as to their identity, even then, is equivocal. Having wagged a metaphorical finger at 'those who do not wish to believe' in the face of 'the best medical opinion of the day', the professor thereafter tells us that he himself has yet to be convinced: 'If the bones were those of the princes, it remains to be demonstrated' and later, 'The evidence, however, is far from conclusive.' Sitting squarely on the fence, he opines: 'If they are the right bodies, modern anatomical skills ought to locate their deaths within or beyond the reign – where it already appears certain that they belong.' A safe assertion if ever there was one!

It is particularly revealing that Hicks omits any mention of the condition of the jaw of the elder skull, thus failing to investigate the conspicuous disease from which the young Edward, on the evidence of the bones, is claimed to have suffered. Can it be that Professor Hicks is as sceptical about the bones as are the revisionists he so disdains?

* * *

Numerous commentators have since discussed the conclusions of Tanner and Wright, and many have found fault with their 'pre-judged and over-simplistic approach,' as Dr White observed, with no attempt made 'to perform an exhaustive determination of the

Minimum Number of Individuals (MNI) as would be done by modern forensic specialists'. He pointed to certain inconsistencies in lengths of bones attributed to the younger child, with the lengths of arm bones being more consistent with the dental age quoted for the skull, as opposed to the lengths of leg bones which were difficult to reconcile with this age. This, he concluded, could mean that the bones 'represent the co-mingled remains of more than two individuals'.[16]

Another observation in the same article indicated that, as a result of recent research in osteology by Scheuer and Black, the age of the older child can now be revised to conclude that this individual died 'certainly under 15 but probably *under 12* years of age'.

Tanner and Wright not only exhibited an unwarranted certainty as to the ages of the children, but made assumptions of a family relationship between them. These were based primarily on two phenomena: first, that they both allegedly showed signs of congenitally missing teeth (hypodontia), and second, that both allegedly had large and similarly shaped Wormian bones (small extra bone structures evident in the skull). The hypodontia was addressed by M. A. Rushton in his article mentioned above. He reported that Lady Anne Mowbray, a cousin of the princes (and wife of the younger), had hypodontia that was genuinely rare, such anomalous dentition being usually a hereditary trait. But in the jaws of the older skull in the urn (identified by Wright as the upper second premolars and lower third molars or wisdom teeth) the missing teeth are 'a more common deficiency'. Far from being anomalous, such missing teeth are scarcely unusual at all – 'the most common combination of missing teeth' – and are normally *excluded* in modern studies of hypodontia.[17]

To this must be added the fact that a third molar (wisdom tooth) which Professor Wright *presumed* was likewise missing in the younger skull belongs to 'the category of tooth most often missing congenitally'. Further, the same child's *actual* missing lower second deciduous premolar (milk tooth) can be easily accounted for by having been knocked out at an early age, which Wright admitted and Rushton confirmed as the most likely cause. So it is pointless comparing Richard III's teeth looking for anomalies when we know already there are no special anomalies in the dentition of these skulls. Authorities say that much more research would be required before any such congenital absence could be held to indicate close relationship.

To rub salt into the wound, it has been shown that girls are twice as likely to have teeth missing congenitally. And congenitally missing wisdom teeth are also more frequent in females. Thus, if conclusions are to be drawn from such general propensities, the older child should be assumed to be female.

As for the Wormian bones, it is now known that these are not necessarily indicators of close kinship and that their incidence varies with the population concerned. 'Wormian bones appear to have been far more common in ancient skeletons than in modern Europe (hence, probably, misleading Wright).'[18] They are estimated to be prevalent in some 50 per cent of skulls from the Middle Ages. Insufficient grounds, again, for assuming consanguinity.

★ ★ ★

Among writers who have seriously considered the identity of the bones, Paul Murray Kendall called in his own experts whose opinions he quoted.[19] These included Dr W.M. Krogman, a professor of physical anthropology, who opined that the children could have been the princes but found the ages were 'a little too precisely stated'. He felt the evidence of age to be derived from the bones was 'limited', and the dental evidence was the most sound.

Dr Arthur Lewis, an orthodontist, seemed less confident, describing the terminology of the dentition as set forth in the article as 'not altogether clear'. He offered conclusions only for the older skull, which he took to be anywhere from eleven to thirteen years, but most probably about eleven-and-a-half.

Professor Bertram S. Kraus, another anthropologist, agreed that the dentition terminology (presumably that of Dr Northcroft) was 'questionable'. Kraus felt the conclusion that the skeletons were male was unsubstantiated. His opinion was that the older child was 'not over nine years of age'.

This can scarcely be regarded as resounding support for the 1933 findings. Nevertheless, Kendall commented that 'the dental evidence, according to authoritative opinion, is, in certain respects, beyond dispute'.[20] This is surprising in the light of the comments of his own experts, especially considering he also consulted Dr Lyne-Pirkis who presumably told him of the results of the Ohio survey. Kendall did not, unfortunately, tell us in what respects the dental evidence was beyond dispute, nor whose authoritative opinion said so. But then Kendall's biography, despite its superlative literary merits, takes Thomas More as a valid source. As does that of Charles Ross.

Ross spends a page and a half on the bones.[21] He quotes Kendall and also the historian A.R. Myers, who enlisted the opinion of R.G. Harrison, an anatomist, for a substantial 1954 article. Harrison gave guarded support to the Wright report: 'In spite of some difficulties in the evidence which he does not discuss, [Wright] appears to be correct in his conclusion that the bones were consistent with the sizes and ages of the two princes in 1483.'[22] The question of gender is not mentioned, nor how Professor Wright could have formed a reliable opinion as to the 'sizes' of the princes.

Moving away from comments dating from the 1950s, Ross, writing in 1980–81, then reveals that he has consulted three experts of his own from the University of Bristol. Dr Juliet Rogers, who had made a special study of ancient bones, sensibly expressed reservations: the sex of the bones could not be determined, nor their antiquity except that they were pre-1674.

Dr J.H. Musgrave of the Anatomy Department, by contrast with Professor Kraus, was entirely happy with Wright's 'assessment of the age of Edward V [*sic*] from the state of development of his axis'. Musgrave continues: 'The skeletal – as opposed to dental – remains of Richard Duke of York [*sic*] are perhaps less informative. But the dental evidence is strong.' One cannot help but be uncomfortable with Dr Musgrave's happy assumption of the gender, antiquity and indeed precise identity of the remains, which suggests a less than objective starting point.

Ross's third expert is Professor E.W. Bradford, Professor of Dental Surgery. His assessment of the ages comes within the range of twelve for the older child and seven to eleven-and-a-half for the younger. He adds that 'not very much credence can be attached to evidence of consanguinity'.

In his summing up, Ross admits that the medical evidence is 'not conclusive'. Yet he is happy to conclude that 'on balance, it suggests that the bones ... might well have been those of the princes, and it certainly does not rule out the possibility or even probability that they were'. Neither, it must be said, does it rule out the possibility that the remains were of two girls, the younger aged between about seven and eleven-and-a-half, and the older not over nine, or perhaps eleven-and-a-half, or perhaps twelve or thirteen, or even between fourteen and sixteen.

In February 1984, when London Weekend Television staged a televised *Trial of Richard III*, a single witness was called for a cursory discussion of the evidence of the 1674 bones. This was Dr Jean Ross, a Senior Lecturer in Anatomy at the Charing Cross Hospital, London. Dr Ross was given a copy of the report and photographs produced by Tanner and Wright, and also a copy of the 1965 report on the dentition of Anne Mowbray, Duchess of Norfolk, by Martin Rushton.

In her evidence she supported Wright in that the ages of the bones at the time of death were consistent with twelve and ten years. She added that it was 'impossible at that age' to tell what sex they were. Later she stated her opinion that on the basis of the development of the axis, the older child would have been about eight – on the basis of the sacrum 'perhaps nine' – and that it was not unusual in bone development to have a two or three year difference depending on environmental factors. The teeth and jaw were a better criterion and showed that the same child was 'at least twelve years old and certainly not more than fourteen'. Speaking of the younger child, 'He [*sic*] was at least nine and not more than ten.' She admitted that there was 'a head-on contradiction' between the evidence of age derived from the axis and that derived from the teeth.

Gender was not discussed in relation to teeth until Dr Ross was asked a question by the programme's trial judge, Lord Elwyn-Jones. In reply she acknowledged that the development of teeth in a female child was perhaps six months in advance of that in a male. From this, and from the fact that she consistently referred to the individuals as 'boys', and at one time spoke of 'Edward' by name, we may assume that Dr Ross's evidence was based on estimates for male children only.

She also postulated some evidence of blood relationship based on Wright's claims that their missing teeth were 'unusual'. This directly contradicted Martin Rushton, the eminent odontologist who refuted this claim (see above) saying that those supposedly 'unusual' missing teeth were actually *commonly absent*. He clearly had far greater experience in the area of hypodontia, and his conclusions offered *no basis* for assuming consanguinity between the skulls. Subsequent authorities have agreed that hypodontia remains largely unexplored as an indicator of close family relationships.

Dr Ross considered the Wormian bones to be 'unusual too' and could 'possibly' indicate a blood relationship between the two children. Again this contradicted research by specialists (cited above) of which she was presumably unaware. Such research would be known to anatomists who studied ancient bones; but Dr Ross was being asked to give opinions outside her area of expertise.

* * *

From the foregoing gamut of expert opinion, the most obvious conclusion to draw is that there seem to be so many variables, depending on diverse areas of specialty, that agreement can be found only within the very broadest of parameters. Estimates of age are necessarily affected not only by the state of health, diet, environment and gender, but also (significantly) by whether you are looking at bones or teeth. In either case, as shown from the Ohio experiments with thousands of records, there is always room for a tolerance of four years, two years either side of any estimated age. Moreover, it seems you need to know about oddities that crop up in ancient communities, like the incidence of Wormian bones, plus you need to distinguish which is an anomalous missing tooth and which a perfectly normal accidental loss.

Based on the teeth – obviously the most reliable indicator – it is evident that the broad spectrum of possible ages for the remains in the urn certainly encompasses the ages of the princes as they were in 1483–84. More valuable would have been accurate evidence for the difference in age between the two skulls, but on this the experts are, as usual, unable to agree.

There are claims in some quarters that recently devised methods of calculating ages of ancient remains can be applied

with confidence to the bones because they have been shown
to work when applied to Lady Anne Mowbray's skeleton. The
research of Theya Molleson has been cited in this connection.[23]
But Miss Molleson opines that 'the age at death of a juvenile
is best deduced from a study of the teeth'. Using evidence of
dentition she offers two alternative methods of scoring age:
according to the method advocated by Demirjian, Goldstein
and Tanner, which scores Anne at a median age of 8.45 years,
the older skull in the urn would be 12.8 to 16.2 years (Molleson
plumps for a roughly median age of 14.3); and the younger skull
between 8.5 and 10.7 (median age 9.6).

Using another method (Moorrees, Fanning and Hunt), which
scores Anne at a median 7.1, we have the older skull assessed at
10.6 to 12.7 years (median age 11.6); and the younger skull at 6.3
to 9.3 (median age 7.8). 'It is possible,' Molleson notes, 'for the
older child to have been fifteen years and seven or eight months
at death.' She later adds, unsurprisingly, 'It is important that the
appropriate ageing charts are selected.'

Too old to fit Edward V according to Demirjian *et al*? Never
mind, try Moorrees *et al*. Too young now? Let's see if we get a
better result using bone lengths (despite Molleson's own assertion
that teeth are a better indicator). Here she tries four different
systems of age assessment. Three of the four systems assess the
older child at twelve to fourteen years, and the younger child at
ten to fourteen years.

The fourth system (Maresh) is particularly interesting. Based
on bone lengths, it produces raw figures of, respectively, ten to
twelve years for the older child and eight to ten for the younger.
However, we learn that Molleson has applied *a corrective factor
of 2.5–3.5 years* to the Maresh figures to compensate for the
assumption that children of the past were this amount behind
modern children in their skeletal growth. Her adjusted figures
emerge as 13.5 to 14.5 (older) and 11.5 to 12.5 (younger). But this
is a conservative adjustment: the actual spread could be as wide as
12.5 to 15.5 (older) and 10.5 to 13.5 (younger).

To the onlooker it certainly seems amazing that, after all this
careful measuring of bones down to the last half-millimetre, we
find the resultant figures subject to a subsequent adjustment of up
to three-and-a-half years! This blunt instrument approach surely
cannot be regarded as producing a scientifically accurate indication

of age. Moreover, we are not told whether any comparable adjustment for skeletal growth has been applied to the other three bone measurement systems.

Importantly, nowhere in her article does Miss Molleson mention the disease evident in the skull of the older child. Recalling that Dr Lyne-Pirkis estimates this child could be 'retarded by one or possibly two years as a result', evidently we should add a further blunt-instrument correction to the age range for the older skull: 12.5 to 15.5 years now becomes a range of 13.5 to 17.5. How can we safely deduce the age of either child from such massively varying parameters?

Theya Molleson, however, having happily plotted her findings on a chart, asserts 'if one wishes to propose that they died or were killed at the same time, the most likely period that is compatible with the dental and skeletal age for both skeletons would be some time in the year 1484'. This will certainly disappoint those who claim that the bones in the urn prove the truth of the Thomas More story.

To disappoint them further, they should note that Molleson arrives at this date purely because she has taken a particular view as to the reason for the wide discrepancy between the dental age and skeletal age of the younger child. 'Either he [*sic*] was tall for his age or dentally retarded,' we are told. Predictably she takes the former view, pointing out that a tall child is more likely to have a tall parent, and Edward IV was over 6ft tall. But what if we prefer the explanation that he was dentally retarded? Now, according to her chart, the most likely compatible period turns out to sit squarely in the year 1485.

If the reader has now heard enough of supposedly scientific computations of age, let us examine the topic of hypodontia. Molleson quotes from A.H. Brook's findings in 1984 that the prevalence of missing permanent teeth in a British sample is 3.1 per cent in boys and 5.7 per cent in girls, with virtually no observed difference in the frequency of this phenomenon between mediæval and modern population samples. This would reinforce the likelihood (mentioned above) that the older skull was female, with odds of nearly two-to-one in favour.

Claims of hypodontia have been much vaunted to prove consanguinity of the 1674 skulls, but in this respect Molleson observes only that both upper second premolars are missing in the older child: these she adduces to suggest consanguinity with Lady Anne Mowbray, not between our two skulls in the urn.

To substantiate this suggestion she quotes more findings of Brook, to the effect that there is a considerable inherited component in the causes of hypodontia, with a 30 per cent incidence of first-degree relatives likely to share the phenomenon with an individual who has one to five teeth missing. Incidence among the first-degree relatives of someone like Lady Anne, who had six such missing teeth, might rise to 47 per cent. However, these findings do not help us in regard to the mysterious skulls, since Anne was related to the princes only in the third and fourth degrees.

Nor do we know from which line of her descent the hypodontia emanated: was it from her father's Mowbray ancestors, her mother's Talbot ancestors or from one of her many other ancestral lines?

As John Ashdown-Hill relates in the course of interesting research into the identity of remains which may possibly be those of Lady Eleanor Talbot (Edward IV's first known wife), the dentition of the remains in question reveals the absence of the left upper second premolar, almost certainly missing congenitally. Although not an unusual deficiency, this form of hypodontia is not so common as that of missing wisdom teeth. Since Lady Eleanor was Lady Anne's aunt, it is possible to infer from this that the remains under research may indeed be those of Lady Eleanor. Certainly this inference holds at least as much water as the supposed consanguinity between Lady Anne and the older skull in the urn.[24]

For supporters of the latter consanguinity, any evidence that traces Anne's hypodontia through the Talbot line is likely to be uncomfortable news. As John Ashdown-Hill explains, the 'really close relationship' between Lady Anne and her young husband Richard was their common Neville descent. 'If those who have claimed that Anne Mowbray's congenitally missing teeth prove that she was related to [the skulls of 1674] are correct, Anne's dental anomaly must almost certainly have descended to her via her Neville ancestry.' The young couple's closest common ancestor in the Talbot line was extremely remote, going as far back as King Edward I.

To add yet another interesting dimension, 'there is some further evidence,' Ashdown-Hill continues, 'that the absence of teeth was, in fact, a Talbot trait'. He cites the record that on the death of John Talbot, first Earl of Shrewsbury (Lady Eleanor's father and Lady Anne's grandfather), 'it was by his missing left molar that his disfigured body was identified'. Whether the tooth was missing congenitally we cannot know. 'Nevertheless, it is certainly a very interesting coincidence that the tooth in question was a left molar.'

In the argument over consanguinity, another point was raised by Theya Molleson quoting Professor Roger Warwick that the metacarpal (palm) bone in both thumbs of Anne Mowbray exhibited a rare anomaly, and that the first metatarsals (equivalent bones in the sole) of the older child as illustrated by Tanner and Wright also appeared to exhibit a similar anomaly. This might seem to suggest evidence of a family relationship, but again there are experts who disagree. As Dr White pointed out: 'Quite apart from the fact that one is dealing with two entirely different categories of bone, Miss Molleson seemed utterly unaware of the contradictory data presented in a letter printed in the *London Archaeologist* … [in which] Drs Juliet Rogers and Tony Waldron pointed out that a clinical radiological study had demonstrated that 80 per cent of modern children aged between 4 and 8 years' already showed the phenomenon mentioned, and that it was certainly not such a rare abnormality in the past as Professor Warwick had presumed.

Moving on to determining gender, Molleson's article mentions interesting work based on differing developmental rates of teeth:

> In a girl the canine tooth erupts *shortly after* the roots of the lateral incisor and first molar are completed. In a boy eruption of the canine takes place *a year after* the completion of the root of the lateral incisor. The canine of the mandible of the younger child is not ready to erupt, although the incisor and first molar roots are complete. This suggests that it might be a male.

When it comes to the older child, alas, dentition alone is not sufficient. Once again in her search for support Molleson introduces the imponderables of estimates based on bones. Her conclusion, 'probably an adolescent boy', offers no conclusive proof that it might not be an adolescent girl.

Furthermore, as we seem to see so often, her scientific method of sexing teeth is contradicted by another scientific method, quoted by Hammond and White, which determines sex by differences in the sizes of crowns, the most useful for this purpose being a lower permanent canine tooth. This particular tooth was present (unerupted) in the younger skull, and if Dr Northcroft's published X-ray is to scale it was less than 7mm in diameter, producing the possibility that the child was female. Moreover, Hammond and White challenge Molleson's conclusion in the case of the younger child that, had it been a girl, the lower canine should have erupted: 'The latter is a conclusion by default, and is less tenable because it arose after an age calculation that presumed the remains were male. If the same calculations were made assuming female gender the anomaly disappears.'[25]

★ ★ ★

Most advocates who nowadays believe the bones are or could be the princes have the grace not to rely entirely on 'scientific' evidence, which is vague at best and conflicting at worst. Generally they fall back upon the argument that the circumstances of their discovery are 'too great a coincidence' when compared with the burial place related by Thomas More.

However, we have already noted that More's prose drama contained a great deal of colourful detail which we are not necessarily meant to take as fact. As to the specific burial place described in More's story, evidently it seems only to be remembered that the murderers *initially* hid the bodies at the foot of a stairway ('at the stayre foote, metely depe in the grounde under a great heape of stones'). The proponents of the bones conveniently ignore his extra flourishes, to the effect that King Richard *subsequently had them disinterred* by a priest and buried somewhere more appropriate (or, in another version, thrown into the Thames) – if, of course, they were killed at all, notes the careful Master More. Thus, the bones were discovered precisely where More said they weren't.

At the risk of giving More's literary flights of fancy more credibility than they merit, perhaps we should also examine the questions raised by his story of Sir James Tyrell's mysterious 'confession', wherein it was observed that one of the murderers, Dighton, remained alive and unpunished. Buc asserts that Henry Tudor searched unsuccessfully for the bodies when he assumed power in 1485. Did he not then search again in 1502 when he supposedly had Tyrell's description, and Dighton's word, to indicate precisely where to look?

If the argument is that all searches were unavailing because the mysterious priest had removed the bodies, what then is the explanation for where the bones were found in 1674? Did this priest (who had to be alone for his secret to die with him) exhume the decomposing bodies from one understair resting place and heroically reinter them 10ft below another? Obviously Thomas More was not versed in the realities of manual labour, since a conservative estimate for a lone person to perform such a task amounts to two entire days without sleep and without rebuilding either staircase.

One final comment needs to be made before we leave the subject of More's story, which is that his collation of disinformation, gossip and hearsay represents only one man's gleanings from countless suppositions, and is best known purely because it was adopted by Shakespeare.

As Hammond and White appositely observe, Professor Wright's report reveals an acquaintance with every detail of More's tale, inextricably linking date of death and presumed identity of the bones in a circular fashion. 'What conclusions might have been reached,' they ask, 'had the argument been from Molinet or even the *Great Chronicle* as the source?'

11

The October
Rebellion

We saw in chapter 8 that Richard III ordered stocks of weapons in early August 1483 on the heels of attempts to abduct the princes from the Tower.

When eventually he had need to use these weapons, it would be to resist the astonishing rebellion of his former close friend, Harry of Buckingham. As confirmed by Rosemary Horrox, Richard so little suspected Buckingham in August that, pursuant to the Welles-Beaufort plot, he sent orders to the duke, his 'dearest kinsman', to hold commissions of oyer and terminer to enquire into treason all over the southern counties.[1] (Horrox argues, from these and other events in August, that the October rebellion was in preparation from this month at least.) Indeed, as late as 16 September the king was despatching writs directing receivers in north and south Wales to pay their accounts to Buckingham.[2] Clearly Richard was taken utterly by surprise, and one can well imagine why he wrote of Buckingham as 'the most untrue creature living' in a bitter personal postscript to his chancellor John Russell.[3]

The uprising had germinated independently of Buckingham, with a series of loosely connected stirrings aimed at restoring Edward V. When it came to a head in October, as we shall see later, it was swiftly quelled. Though the consequences would be far-reaching, it provided neither Buckingham nor Henry Tudor the glorious role each envisaged for himself.

What is more fascinating is the question of Buckingham's reason for joining such a revolt against his king and benefactor.

Nothing specific is suggested in Crowland, and his motivations as offered by Vergil are muddled and misleading. Among them is the tale that he was refused the Bohun inheritance: patently untrue, but sufficiently widely circulated to sound suspiciously like Tudor propaganda. Vergil seems wholly credible when he reports that Buckingham's plans for rebellion were abetted by Bishop John Morton, who still languished in the duke's custody following the Hastings plot.

If we look at Thomas More – while exercising the usual caution – we see, after a catalogue of Buckingham's possible woes (some people say this, others say that), Bishop Morton is credited with persuading him to revolt. But More goes further: he specifies that the duke was led by Morton to aspire to the crown. The one version of More that takes us right into the supposed Morton-Buckingham conversation (Grafton's *Chronicle of John Hardyng*, 1543) stops tantalizingly after Morton's opening salvos. Here the bishop, having privately noted Buckingham's envy of Richard, decides to capitalize on it by venturing to wish the new king had been blessed with 'such other virtues meet for the rule of a realm as our Lord has planted in the person of your Grace.' At this point More's narrative suddenly ends, and what follows in Grafton is a crib from Vergil.

We know, of course, that More frequently indulged in dramatic invention: this conversation could simply be another of his flights of fancy. On the other hand, if his writings about Richard are taken as directly based on Morton, it seems unlikely that, making allowances for embellishments, More would invent a scenario that directly conflicted with his source. Morton's role as set out in his own tract is corroborated by Sir William Cornwallis, who wrote his *Encomium of Richard III* in the early 1600s with knowledge of Morton's text which he, too, had almost certainly read: 'the prisoner corrupted the gaoler,' he says. Unfortunately he tells us nothing about the bishop's arguments and little about the duke's motivations, save that the latter, whom he describes as ambitious, grew discontent, 'not thinking himself sufficiently regarded, nor rewarded'. Evidently Morton, 'the Corrupt Chronicler' as Cornwallis characterizes him, was happy to crow about his manipulation of the gullible Buckingham; but Cornwallis's *Encomium*, the earliest extant version of which is a mere sixteen folio pages, goes into few details beyond his main theme of refuting certain specific calumnies spread by the Cardinal Archbishop about Richard III.[4]

Sir George Buc, though aware of the contents of Morton's tract, has nothing new to add. He closely follows Thomas More's account (and its derivatives), mentioning Buckingham's ambitions for the throne. 'But he was not resolutely determined to make his claim to the crown,' says Buc, '... until he was earnestly incited and animated and persuaded thereunto by the factious and seditious clerk, Dr Morton, Bishop of Ely'.[5]

So the consensus seems to be that Buckingham was lured to revolt by Morton, who perhaps incited him to aim for the throne.

Similarly open to question is Buckingham's relationship with the Tudor-Beaufort party. As we have seen in chapter 8, Vergil, informed by Tudor sources, and committed to the myth that Henry Tudor was the saviour of England, writes that Buckingham conceived a desire that Elizabeth of York should be married to Henry Tudor, so that the blood of Edward IV should be united with that of Henry VI. (To be precise, the 'blood of Henry VI' was actually that of his French mother and her Welsh retainer.) Thomas More is more credible in claiming this plan was devised by Morton.

Since Buckingham had little to gain from the arrangement and everything to lose, the only possible explanation is divine intervention; which is, of course, the theme of Vergil's entire tale of England's salvation thanks to the Tudor dynasty. Buckingham in Vergil's story is a true penitent whose one desire is to relinquish his exalted position in favour of serving a new King Henry. Thus the turncoat is recast in the useful guise of chief evangelist of the Tudor-York settlement.

Discounting this miraculous wish, what was the real reason why Buckingham supported the aspirations of Henry Tudor? Or did he? Aside from More, we have only two sources for this assumption, the first being Vergil's report of private conversations between Buckingham and Morton at Brecon.

Our second source is the report of 'writings and messages' sent by Buckingham on and about 24 September 1483, to which the Act of Attainder refers in the Parliament of 1484:

And also the said duke on the 24th September by his several writings and messages by him sent, procured and moved

Henry calling himself Earl of Richmond and Jasper late Earl of Pembroke being there in Brittany, great enemies of our said sovereign lord, to make a great navy and bring with them an army from Brittany.

Note that Parliament did not recognize Tudor as Earl of Richmond.

We do not, alas, have these actual writings and messages to refer to, but their absence has not prevented a surprising number of historians and commentators from assuming their contents. Audrey Williamson, for example, confidently states that 'on 24 September a letter written by the Duke of Buckingham to Henry Tudor on the proposed invasion … gave the "liberation" of the princes … as one aim'.[6]

Louise Gill, on the other hand, believes that Buckingham 'wrote to Henry Tudor informing him of the rising and asking for his cooperation'. It is unlikely that Buckingham informed Tudor of the rising at this late date, when we know the Duke of Brittany's invasion flotilla was already being fitted out. By now a substantial amount of preparation was under way on both sides of the Channel. The fact that the cautious Tudors were ready to sail in October speaks volumes for their forward planning.

Griffiths and Thomas, writing about the Tudor camp, take up almost an entire paragraph on what Buckingham supposedly wrote to Henry. They, too, declare that the duke informed him when the rebellion would commence and 'invited him to join in'; 'he made no pretence of acknowledging Henry as the next king of England,' they add, 'or of welcoming his marriage to Elizabeth of York'.[7]

Yet the Crowland chronicler claimed Buckingham's messages urged Tudor to take Elizabeth to wife and, with her, 'possession of the whole kingdom'.

The fact is, whatever our pet theory, we cannot know precisely what the letters said; we know only that Buckingham 'procured and moved' the exiles to invade England. As for his underlying motive, it is indeed possible that, duped by Morton, he believed the Tudors would support him as a challenger for the throne in return for suitable rewards. He was, after all, their clear superior in legitimate bloodline, rank, wealth and military might. Morton was certainly devious enough to feed Buckingham such a line, intimations of which are found in writers familiar with his lost tract. Buckingham might never have regarded Henry Tudor as a potential king at all.

But whereas Morton evidently felt the duke would be a useful lieutenant, would it not be dangerous to allow him to entertain such grandiose delusions? After all, once at the head of a major rebellion, he might at the first sign of success see fit to proclaim himself England's next monarch – effectively sidelining Henry Tudor who might still be sitting in Brittany awaiting favourable winds.

There is an alternative scenario, which Buc postulates:

> Morton had destined [the kingdom] to another, whom he loved much better ... But this prelate, to draw the duke on the faster into his net and to make him apt to rebel, first he persuaded earnestly the duke to claim his title to the crown. ... The ambitious and silly duke bit at this cunning, deceitful bait and swallowed it.[8]

By feeding him this heady poison, Morton's strategy was to get Buckingham entirely committed to the rebellion, so that when Tudor made his bid there could be no turning back for the duke. Margaret Beaufort's biographers, Jones and Underwood, suggest she was behind the plan: 'Serious consideration must be given to the possibility that Margaret duped Buckingham, encouraging him to claim the throne himself.'[9]

On this basis we may conjecture that, once Buckingham was up to his neck in treason, Morton would find the right moment to drop his bombshell: news had arrived that the princes were dead, which had caused consternation among the rebel leaders. These men, Morton would explain regretfully, had found themselves urgently in need of a replacement candidate for the throne and had not realized that Buckingham might be prepared to undertake such a role. Thinking only of Edward IV's line, they had determined that someone must claim the crown in right of the elder daughter; and Henry Tudor, the Beaufort heir, had stepped forward.

★ ★ ★

Perhaps this accurately reflects the way Morton worked on Buckingham's mind to induce him to risk everything in rebellion, or perhaps it is mere supposition. We do not, to this day, know the truth of the matter.

But there can be only a limited number of explanations. Was he desirous of the crown? Did disappointed expectations play a part? Or even a deeply-held devotion to the cause of the Lancastrians (or Beauforts or Tudors)?

It is hard to conceive of any expectations on the part of Buckingham that were not fulfilled to overflowing. Richard III had given him everything he wanted: office, power, and the enormous Bohun inheritance. What unfulfilled desires remained?

Equally difficult to believe is that Buckingham nurtured any deep political allegiances. From what little we know, he seems to have been shallow, volatile, a grasping overlord, and above all proudly aware of his royal bloodline. His mother was a Beaufort, his father a Stafford, but he boldly took the arms of his Plantagenet antecedent, Thomas of Woodstock, without any quartering. As for any attachment to the dynasty of Lancaster, there is no sign of this in Buckingham's career. In any case, the Lancaster title had fallen into abeyance in England after the old king's death; it certainly did not reside in the Beaufort line, even if some of them portrayed themselves as custodians of the cause.

Mancini attributes to Buckingham some waspish remarks about women involving themselves in men's business, and in 1483 the chief standard-bearer for the Beauforts was not a man but his mother's kinswoman, Margaret Beaufort. Even her loyalties were equivocal. In 1471, when Margaret had been married to Buckingham's uncle, neither she nor her husband had responded to calls from her Beaufort kin to support Henry VI. Indeed, her Stafford husband had died from wounds sustained fighting *against* him. She herself in recent years had become close to Edward IV's queen. Would the proud duke have placed his life in peril for a faction, whether supposedly Lancastrian or supposedly Beaufort, represented by this woman of unproven allegiance, whose main hope was an unknown young exile of dubious patrilineage without title or estates? The idea does not chime well with what we know of Buckingham's sense of status and self-regard.

So we return to the possibility that he really did desire the throne for himself. At first glance such aspirations are difficult to credit given the number of heirs whose superior claim placed them before him in the line of succession. But a closer look reveals that he would have had reason for optimism.

Being descended from Thomas of Woodstock, Edward III's youngest son, Buckingham was superseded by heirs whose descent came from three senior sons of the old king after the eldest son's line had died out. In 1483, the superior line of succession was the present house of York as descended from Edward III's second surviving son Lionel, Duke of Clarence, through the Mortimer line (Edward IV's siblings, and their offspring, followed by the Bourchier offspring of Edward IV's aunt Isabel – see Table 3 below).

Following in the Mortimer line were the heirs of Lionel's granddaughter Elizabeth Mortimer, who married Henry 'Hotspur' Percy (see Table 4 for these and other family lines described hereunder).

John of Gaunt was the second of those sons of Edward III whose heirs still lived, so the descendants of his legitimately-born daughters came next. Principal among these in 1483 were members of the Portuguese, Burgundian and Spanish ruling families.

Third came the old house of York as founded by Edmund of Langley, from whose granddaughter Isabel descended two family lines as a result of her marriages to the earls of Worcester and Warwick. Only then came the heirs of Thomas of Woodstock, Buckingham's great-great-grandfather.

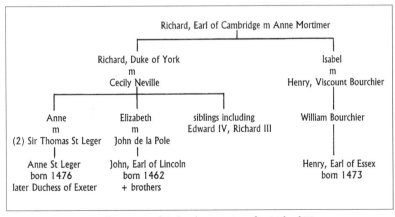

Table 3: House of York – the succession after Richard III

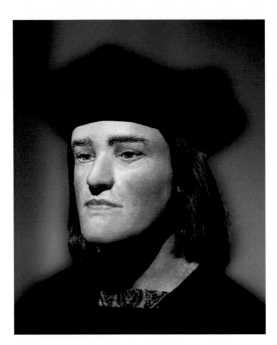

1. Richard III facial reconstruction by Professor Caroline Wilkinson, commissioned by the Richard III Society, February 2013. (Colin G. Brooks)

2. Edward IV. Panel portrait, painted soon after 1510. (© Society of Antiquaries of London)

3. Queen Elizabeth Woodville. Panel portrait, early seventeenth-century copy of a contemporary likeness, The Deanery, Ripon Cathedral.

4. Middleham Castle, Richard's principal residence in North Yorkshire. Reconstruction of its possible appearance in the 1480s, based on a Terry Ball/ English Heritage painting.

5. Baynard's Castle, London residence of Richard's mother Cecily, Duchess of York. 1930s reconstruction model by J.B. Thorp of its appearance in 1550, as exhibited by the London Museum at Kensington Palace.

6. Interior of Crosby Hall, the great hall of Crosby Place which was built by Sir John Crosby and leased to Richard as his London residence. Engraving from C.W. Goss, *Crosby Hall*.

Exterior of Crosby Hall in the 1840s. Crosby Place fell into disrepair but the surviving hall was removed from Bishopsgate to Chelsea in 1908–10.

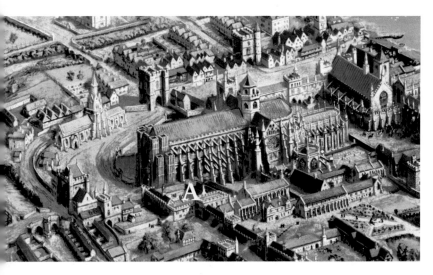

Abbey and Palace of Westminster in 1537. Reconstruction by Drake Brookshaw after A.E. Henderson. **A:** the Abbot's House complex where Elizabeth Woodville took sanctuary in 1483. (TopFoto/Woodmansterne)

9. Richard III and Queen Anne Neville. Victorian stained glass by Paul Woodroffe, 1937, Cardiff Castle.

10. Richard's signet letter of 29 July 1483 ordering trial of conspirators. (The National Archives, Chancery, Warrants for the Great Seal, series I, C 81/1392, no. 1)

11. Richard's signet letter of 12 October 1483 calling for the Great Seal (Plate 26) as rebellion broke out. A postscript in his own hand describes Buckingham as 'the most untrue creature living'.

12. Parliament Roll documenting the Act of January 1484 that defined Richard III's title to the throne, widely known as *Titulus Regius*. (The National Archives, Parliament Roll, 1 Richard III, C 65/114)

13. The urn placed in Westminster Abbey by Charles II containing the skeletal remains of children presumed on dubious grounds to be Edward V and his brother Richard, Duke of York.

14. 'Perkin Warbeck'. Drawing, probably by the herald Jacques le Boucq, in a volume compiled in the 1560s comprising copies of various portraits. This one is subtitled 'Pierre Varbeck … taken to be Richard Duke of York'. (Visages d'Antan, Le Recueil d'Arras – éditions du Gui 2007)

15. The Tower of London: model formerly exhibited at the Museum of London showing the Norman castle as it may have appeared in the early twelfth century. (Museum of London)

16. Forebuilding to the White Tower, Tower of London. Artist's impression illustrating possible arrangement of stairs built *c.*1360 or later. The staircase demolished in 1674 may have appeared something like this. (Anthony Pritchard)

7. The White Tower's small doorway with plaque reading:

THE TRADITION of the TOWER has ALWAYS POINTED at THIS as the STAIR UNDER WHICH the BONES of DWARD the 5th and his BROTHER WERE FOUND in HARLES the 2nd's TIME and from WHENCE THEY WERE EMOVED to WESTMINSTER ABBEY.

(Photograph Jane Spooner)

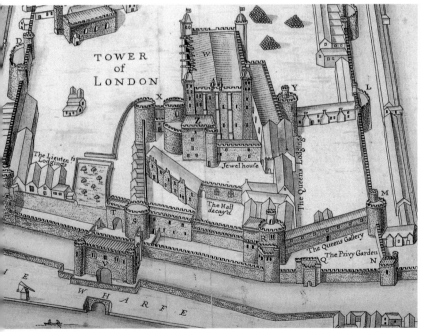

. The Tower of London. Detail from a 1741 watercolour copy of the 1597 survey y Haiward and Gascoyne. R: Lanthorn Tower. T: Garden Tower. W: White ower. X: Cole Harbour Gate. Z: Forebuilding.

ELIZABETHA · VXOR
HENRICI · VII ·

19. Elizabeth of York, eldest daughter of Edward IV and Elizabeth Woodville, later queen to Henry VII. Panel portrait, late sixteenth-century copy of original *c*.1500. (National Portrait Gallery, London)

20. Manuel I of Portugal, formerly Duke of Beja, who was to have been husband to Elizabeth of York. Statue by Nicolau Chanterêne *c*.1517, Mosteiro dos Jerónimos, Belém. (Photograph Luís Pavão/Instituto de Gestão do Património Arquitectónico e Arqueológico, I.P., Lisbon)

21. Joana of Portugal, who as second queen to Richard III would have united the legitimate heirs of York and Lancaster. Late fifteenth-century panel portrait attributed to Nuño Gonçalves. (Museu de Aveiro/Divisão de Documentação Fotográfica, Instituto dos Museus e da Conservação, Lisbon)

22. The Bosworth Crucifix, fifteenth-century bronze gilt, recovered *c.*1778 at the site then associated with the Bosworth battlefield. It was apparently mounted on a staff and is consistent with the kind of processional crucifix that Richard III's royal chaplains would have taken to Bosworth. (© Society of Antiquaries of London)

23. Richard III falls at Bosworth. Detail from the 1954 Shakespeare Window by Christopher Webb, Southwark Cathedral.

24. Richard III as warrior king. Statue by James Butler RA, erected in Castle Gardens, Leicester, by the Richard III Society in 1980 (now relocated beside the cathedral).

25. Richard III armed and mounted, wearing a battle-crown. Equestrian model by Roy Gregory, a variant of that displayed at Bosworth Battlefield Centre.

26. The Great Seal of Richard III, held by the Lord Chancellor of England. The Great Seal alone truly authenticated documents of highest importance issued by the king, who might take it into his own hands at times of national emergency (see Plate 11)

27. Richard III's full achievement of arms. (Andrew Stewart Jamieson www.andrewstewartjamieson.co.uk)

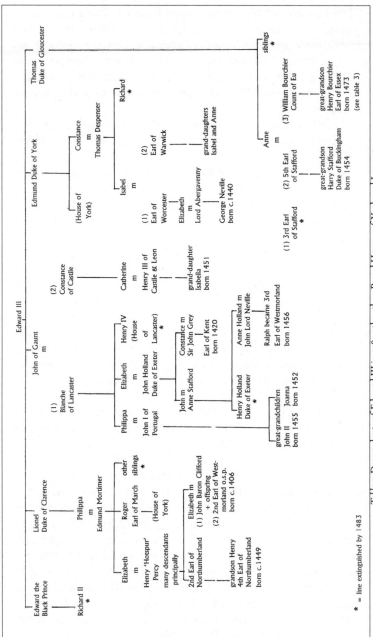

Table 4: Descendants of Edward III in 1483 other than Royal Houses of York and Lancaster

* = line extinguished by 1483

The Beauforts have been omitted from the foregoing, being debarred from the succession. Should the prohibition be reversed one day, their line would logically appear somewhere among John of Gaunt's heirs; however any such reversal, had it been enacted, would certainly have contained exact stipulations as to their place in line to the throne. That, after all, would have been the purpose of the proceedings.

There being no such reversal, and no shortage of *bona fide* candidates ahead of them, we may safely dismiss the Beauforts from the succession.

Let us return to Harry of Buckingham's motivations, and view the succession through his eyes. It must now be admitted that only a limited number of those heirs described above might realistically challenge him for the crown if he successfully dethroned Richard in October 1483.

It would be safe to rule out any resistance forming around a child in preference to himself, and indeed around any female. Whereas such candidates would enjoy rights of succession in peacetime, it was a vastly different matter when it came to a clash of arms. So the children of Clarence could be discounted, and the ten-year-old Bourchier boy, and the seven-year-old daughter from the king's eldest sister Anne's marriage to Thomas St Leger (already in his keeping and probably destined for his son). The nearest in succession to Richard III was John de la Pole, Earl of Lincoln, the son of Richard's next senior sister Elizabeth, a promising young man of around twenty. But John was unswervingly loyal to his king, and his brothers too junior to be contenders. They would all stand or fall by Richard's fortunes.

A different proposition was Henry Percy, 4th Earl of Northumberland, heir to Elizabeth Mortimer by her marriage to Henry Hotspur. As head of the principal magnate family of the north, Percy had worked in uneasy partnership with Richard while the latter was viceroy in that area. Buckingham might have been unsure of Percy's aspirations, but one thing he knew for sure: to the extent that Richard III was hated and mistrusted in the south for his northern connections, the same applied with a vengeance to the Percy family. Were the earl to make a bid for the throne after Richard III's overthrow, he was unlikely to attract more popular support than Buckingham.

Elizabeth's daughter married twice, producing heirs by her first husband, Lord Clifford, but the Cliffords had been effectively sidelined by savage reprisals following the battle of Towton. Her second husband, the Earl of Westmorland, could be ruled out as he was in his late seventies.

As for the descendants of John of Gaunt's daughters: the heir of Philippa, his senior daughter by Blanche of Lancaster, was presently ruling Portugal as John II. Blanche's other daughter, Elizabeth, had married into the Holland family, Dukes of Exeter, whose direct male line was extinct by 1483. Elizabeth's heir via her daughter Constance was the Earl of Kent, now in his sixties, who had no great wealth, ambition or influence; and her granddaughter's son was the young Westmorland heir, a supporter of Richard III.

Gaunt's only daughter by Constance of Castile was Catherine, who had married into the house of Castile and Leon and produced an heir, Isabella, whose marriage in 1469 to Ferdinand of Aragon had famously united Spain. Any scion of a distant foreign house trying to claim the throne would lack credibility with the English, and would face an uphill struggle when there were already senior domestic candidates. In any case, Buckingham could reasonably expect that his coup, if successful, would be accomplished before the news ever reached such distant lands.

We are thus left with the heirs of Constance, daughter of Edward III's fourth surviving son Edmund of Langley, Duke of York. Constance had married Thomas Despenser, Earl of Gloucester, and her daughter Isabel was married successively to the Earl of Worcester and the Earl of Warwick. Isabel's only Warwick heirs in 1483 were Richard III's wife and son, plus the two children of Clarence's wife Isabel, now orphans aged under ten. Her only Worcester heir was George Neville, son of Lord Abergavenny, born in 1440. Though a substantial landowner and parliamentary representative, George at the age of forty-three had a lifetime's experience of coming off second best in inheritance tussles with the all-powerful house of Warwick, and had exhibited no military tendencies or political distinction. He scarcely cut a figure on the national stage when compared to Harry of Buckingham, the premier royal duke of the kingdom.

All in all, Buckingham might well consider that a surprise bid for the throne would stand an excellent chance of success with little fear of challenge from other contenders.

★ ★ ★

In chapter 9 we have noted – and disposed of – suggestions that the reason Buckingham became alienated from his sovereign was because he supposedly murdered the princes without Richard's approval.

Another suggestion sometimes advanced is that Buckingham rebelled in revulsion because Richard killed his own nephews. This is a fanciful idea that never arises in the primary sources. In the *Crowland Chronicle* Buckingham is merely 'repentant of what had been done'. Nor does it occur in Polydore Vergil, although it can be found in the later Tudor chroniclers and myth-makers who built upon each other's tall tales. More – and, we may therefore assume, Morton – never spoke of the two matters in the same context. Not even Rous made any such association.

Our sole authoritative source for the exact sequence of events is in Crowland, where the relevant passage reads as follows:

> When at last the people round about the city of London and in Kent, Essex, Sussex, Hampshire, Dorset, Devon, Somerset, Wiltshire and Berkshire and also in some other southern counties of the kingdom, just referred to, began considering vengeance, public proclamation having been made that Henry, duke of Buckingham, then living at Brecknock in Wales, being repentant of what had been done would be captain-in-chief in this affair, a rumour arose that King Edward's sons, by some unknown manner of violent destruction, had met their fate. For this reason, all those who had begun this agitation, realising that if they could not find someone new at their head for their conquest it would soon be all over with them, remembered Henry, earl of Richmond, who had already spent many years in exile in Brittany. A message was sent to him by the duke of Buckingham on the advice of the lord [bishop] of Ely, his prisoner at Brecknock, inviting him to hasten into the kingdom of England as fast as he could reach the shore to take Elizabeth, the dead king's elder daughter, to wife and with her, at the same time, possession of the whole kingdom.

Those who remember their Latin will recognize the typically densely-packed sentences with multiple sub-clauses which require to be unpacked and translated in proper order. The Crowland chronicler, as is widely assumed, was a man who earned his living by the pen and knew the weight and significance of the written word. Hence we must not rearrange his various phrases, although we can certainly simplify them thus:

> When people in certain locations started considering vengeance, with Buckingham having been proclaimed leader in the affair, a rumour arose that the princes had been mysteriously killed. The rebels realized they could not succeed without a new leader, and they remembered Henry Tudor. Morton advised Buckingham to send a message hastening Henry to invade, marry Elizabeth and seize the kingdom.

It is interesting to note that the author of this part of the chronicle knew all about how John Morton was prompting Buckingham's hand. How, one wonders, did he know this, or know what the message said? A careful reading of this section shows that our friend is suspiciously well-informed about what was going on behind the scenes in the rebel camp.

Since so little evidence survives indicating what happened in the run-up to the October rebellion, it may be helpful to expend a little effort working out the timing of the principal events. First, according to Crowland, the rebellion was clearly under way – with Buckingham having assumed its leadership – before it was rumoured that the boys had died. Logically this has to point to the rumours being spread in mid-September, since Buckingham probably did not enter rebel territory (the south and south-west) until he set forth from Brecon to hold Richard's commissions of oyer and terminer in the early days of that month. He would have been kept busy during the first two weeks of September, establishing his unlikely new credentials as a rebel and calling on men to support him, before he could confidently announce himself as their overall leader.

We know Richard III had an efficient network of spies that uncovered the details of the rebellion, yet he was still unaware of Buckingham's involvement as late as 16 September, so the duke could not have been proclaimed leader more than a few days before that date, say 10–12 September at the very earliest. Then came the body-blow of the rumour that Edward V was dead, which forced the rebels to revise their strategy and adopt Henry Tudor. Note that no chronicler even hints at any proclamation regarding Tudor's role in all this: he knew better than to reveal his true motives.

That the rumour started circulating in mid-September fits with the Crowland chronicler's knowledge that the boys were still in the Tower while the Prince of Wales's investiture was taking place on the 8th; the same timeline is given in Vergil. This timing also chimes with the recollection of the Recorder of Bristol that the rumour started in the mayoral year which began on 15 September.

Evidently the rebels made the switch to Henry Tudor with remarkable speed – helped, no doubt, by the fact that they now had a command structure under Buckingham which provided a direct conduit for Bishop Morton and his manoeuvrings. Evidence shows that Richard learned there was fresh insurrection afoot during the third week of September, with conspiracies involving Bishop Lionel Woodville and Robert Morton, nephew of Bishop John Morton (though it should not be assumed that Tudor's role had been divulged). On 22 September Richard dismissed Robert Morton from his office as Master of the Rolls, and on the following day confiscated Lionel Woodville's worldly goods.[10] Suspicion was presumably cast on Buckingham because Woodville was working from Thornbury in Gloucestershire, the duke's principal seat, which explains why Buckingham's letters were intercepted.

We may reasonably assume that by the time Robert and Lionel had incriminated themselves, the rebels were back in full swing. Presumably there had been a temporary hiatus of a few days during which, first, the news of the alleged death of the princes was digested and, second, Tudor's candidacy was mooted and agreed.

The speed with which Henry's agents in England were able to convince the rebels, within a matter of days, that Tudor would marry Elizabeth of York, further endorses the contention that such a marriage was already in negotiation with the Woodvilles as the price for Tudor support.

★ ★ ★

The onrush of events favourable to the Tudor-Morton-Beaufort cause in the summer of 1483 gives rise to the suspicion that their machinations behind the scenes have been carefully camouflaged in Tudor 'histories'. Consider the following: even as late as mid-July Richard III, when briefing his envoy, assumes that the principal threat from Brittany emanates from Edward Woodville, not Henry Tudor. By August at least two plots have been formulated, the first involving correspondence with the Tudor camp in Brittany, the second involving Margaret Beaufort's half-brother John Welles. That same month Bishop Morton, Margaret's close adviser, sends her word that he has persuaded the Duke of Buckingham to join the insurgency; the rebels, who surely should never have trusted him, immediately make him their leader.

Margaret meanwhile conducts the Woodville marriage negotiations, and whips together large amounts of cash which she sends over to her son. Duke Francis now starts outfitting a flotilla of ships on behalf of the English rebels. And all this activity occurs before any rumour that the princes have been done away with.

If all this effort was bent towards the restoration of Edward V, how extraordinary of the Tudor-Morton-Beaufort axis to risk literally everything when they could have followed the classic Stanley strategy of remaining on the sidelines and ingratiating themselves with the winners. Could the inducement have been the chance of a marriage into the royal family? But this would have been perfectly possible under Richard III, who might not have been willing to hand over the eldest girl, but would probably have been happy to secure Tudor's allegiance in return for the hand of, say, Cecily, or even his own illegitimate daughter Katherine.

As soon as you realize that it had to be Elizabeth's hand, and why, it then becomes obvious why Tudor was prepared to throw his hat in the ring. Does any reader seriously believe he would have taken to sea had there not been a greater prize at stake than the rather wan hope of putting Edward V back on the throne?

It is surely understandable that a certain view is held by some people to the effect that Morton and Beaufort were planning all along for the princes to be eliminated and Tudor set up in their place. This plan became workable as soon as Margaret Beaufort found Elizabeth Woodville amenable to a marriage contract. No matter what caveats were placed on the deal by Elizabeth (i.e. support for Edward V) these would immediately fall away if the boys were presumed dead. At that point Henry Tudor would be able to emerge as, ostensibly, the Woodvilles' principal champion. The marriage was a trump card that Buckingham, whatever his pretensions, could not match.

It is not beyond the bounds of possibility that once this contract was tied up, the Morton-Beaufort conspirators employed agents to monitor the movements of the princes closely and set up an assassination the minute they were transferred from the Tower. It needed only a servant open to bribery, or a moment's loose talk, and the ambush was easily set. What their guards would be on the look-out for was an abduction, of course, which entailed serious logistics: an assault by several armed men, executed with care so the princes were not harmed, with horses and conveyances standing by to whisk the boys and their abductors away. By contrast, an assassination was a mere hit and run operation, easy to perform by two or three marksmen skilled with bow or throwing-knife, who would then melt into the night. If the little party was in the process of departing by the water-gate, it would present a conveniently slow-moving target.

It should be realized that whoever circulated the rumour of their death required one basic thing to occur for the rumour not to be exploded: the boys needed to disappear. Either they had to be removed secretly elsewhere in response to mounting rebellion, or they had to be killed. A combination of the two would be ideal.

The suggestion that they were disposed of 'in the black deeps' was a popular one, and appeared both in More and in Rastell's *The Pastime of People*, published in 1529, where the boys were murdered in any of several different ways and their bodies thrown overboard after being put on a ship for Flanders. (Once again we have that Flanders connection which modern historians find so hard to swallow.)

However, since it is not the purpose of this book to exonerate Richard by accusing others based on an equal absence of proof, I will leave this theory as one which readers may choose to reflect upon privately.

There is a significant point here which must be emphasized. In Richard's proclamation of 23 October naming the ringleaders of the rebellion, Henry Tudor's name does not appear. The Act of Attainder, framed in January 1484, refers to Henry Tudor as merely 'the king's great traitor and rebel' and 'great enemy'. It contains no charge of aspiring to the throne of England. The first such accusation appears nearly a year later, in Richard's proclamation on 7 December 1484, prompted by Tudor's own widely-circulated letters claiming that the throne of England was rightfully his. Until that time his only public claim had been through his projected wife.

With Buckingham's messages having been intercepted and minutely analysed, one would assume that any word therein relating to Tudor as a pretender to the throne would have led to specific charges against him. Yet even where Buckingham's letters are cited in the Act, they are merely said to have been directed to 'Henry calling himself Earl of Richmond and Jasper late Earl of Pembroke being there in Brittany, great enemies of our said sovereign lord'. Perhaps we may deduce from this that Buckingham still clung to royal pretensions of his own, wording his letters carefully so as not to give any specific status to Tudor.

So, we may be forgiven for asking, was Richard, with his large and efficient network of spies, completely unaware of Henry Tudor's ambitions? Did he not hear reports, as we learn from Vergil, that Tudor was so bold as to gather his supporters in Rennes, on Christmas Day 1483, when he swore to marry Elizabeth of York and they paid homage to him as king?

Possibly Richard knew nothing of the sort. It is not mentioned in Crowland. Vergil, the originator of the story, makes it sound like a solemn public occasion, but it could well have been a clandestine meeting that was later magnified into grand proportions. Although in Edward Hall's *Union* (fo.xii^v) the oath is sworn in a cathedral, Vergil merely says *templum* (church), not *templum divi Petri* or *ecclesia cathedralis* as would be expected for the ancient cathedral of St Peter. Nor is Rennes cathedral mentioned in Breton sources, only Vannes, where the exiles are recorded as attending an oath-swearing ceremony in 1483; but this was a ceremony called by the Duke of Brittany, pledging to support Henry with ships for an expedition, and it took place well in advance of the October rebellion.[11]

Before October, Richard apparently regarded Tudor as beneath his notice; and if word subsequently reached him about the exile's lofty aspirations, it would have been after he had put down a sizeable rebellion in which Tudor's role was nothing if not ignominious. Evidently Richard's mistake all along was seriously to underestimate Henry Tudor. To which must be added underestimating his mother.

★ ★ ★

Let us return for a moment to examine the rumour of the princes' deaths, as there are several aspects of it that are interesting. First, it came at precisely the most apposite moment for Henry Tudor's career, elevating his status at a stroke from a remnant of an ousted régime to a candidate for the throne. Compare it to the story of the Eleanor Talbot precontract: cynics dismiss this as fabrication on grounds that it was altogether too convenient, yet they have no problem at all believing the equally convenient murder rumour.

Second, the rumour was amorphous, unspecific and anonymous. Looking at the Crowland report, the rumour merely suggested the boys had met their fate 'by some unknown manner of violent destruction'. By contrast, the truth of the precontract was attested by at least one person, Stillington, who undoubtedly was probed and cross-examined at length by who knows how many members of the June quasi-parliament before they were prepared to set down its implications in writing. Yet nobody ever came forward to place on record a public accusation that Richard III killed his nephews, despite the large number of Tower residents and workers who would have observed anything suspicious (and despite the number of *dramatis personae* directly involved in Thomas More's alleged plot which mentions no fewer than eight people by name or job description).

Significantly, the rumour was planted in the most fertile ground available in September 1483: among the already disaffected rebels. Such men were more than ready to believe the worst of the new king, whereas in the rest of England Richard had no difficulty rallying loyal supporters to his standard.

It has been suggested that the rumour was true because those very rebels, many of them royal administrators and members of Edward IV's household, were best able to check its veracity. Not so: they could not be in two places at once. In September, when the rumour broke, most of them were busy making plans with Buckingham while gathering forces in their home constituencies in the belief that Edward V was still in the Tower patiently waiting to be restored. Their personal knowledge of what was happening in London was probably out of date by weeks. To obtain news (other than what they were fed by Morton and Buckingham) they would need to send messengers or ride themselves to the capital, taking several days for the outward and return journeys, not to mention the time spent in London seeking information.

What information was to be found there? The Crowland chronicler, who is generally categorized as an insider, never once divulges any knowledge of what happened to Edward V and his brother: he merely cites the existence of a rumour. If this well-informed person could not ascertain any facts, why should we assume the rebels could do any better?

Perhaps the brothers had by now been quietly transferred to another location. If so, enquiries would merely reveal they were no longer resident in the Tower. No great uproar in the capital is recorded, no mobs of anxious citizens marching on the centres of government demanding to know their whereabouts. So although much has been made of the king's failure to produce and display his nephews in rebuttal, we have to ask ourselves what pressure there was for him to do so.

By the fifteenth century, rumour was an effective way of swaying popular opinion. Mancini quoted a rumour or 'suspicion', even before Richard's coronation, that Edward V might have come to an untimely end, and we have more instances of rumours arising during Richard's later reign. The rebels who gave credence to the rumour of the boys' death doubtless followed the same reasoning as our latter-day historians, who argue that Richard must have killed them because this was what usurpers always did.

The pressing business of the rebels was not to ride about the country seeking to verify the rumour, but to decide what to do in light of it. Were they to carry on as before, and if successful in deposing Richard find there was no Edward V to restore? That would leave them with the unlovely Duke of Buckingham as their candidate for the throne, whom they evidently rejected. Their acceptance of Henry Tudor's offer might well have been quite cynical, as a way of covering all eventualities, and not based on a belief that the brothers were dead at all. On the contrary, if the boys were found alive, a victorious rebellion could easily result in discarding Henry Tudor in favour of the true line of Edward IV. Their sister would certainly not marry him in order to help him depose her brothers.

As for Bishop Morton, whom we must list as our prime suspect as inventor of the rumour, he achieved his main purpose as long as he created an urgent need for an alternative candidate for the throne. This very urgency meant that his protégé, Henry Tudor, was transformed into a viable proposition because the notice was so short. This was quite a coup for the bishop.

No one could possibly deny that Morton had the kind of political savvy to use the power of rumour in furthering his objectives. Moreover, he was in the right place at the right time, pushing Buckingham to throw in his lot with the rebels, doubtless attending meetings, suggesting strategies, encouraging disaffection, tut-tutting sympathetically over slights and injustices. Who was more credible than a churchman, a former linch-pin of the royal council, if he was the one passing on the latest 'news' that had just reached him hot-foot from London?

★ ★ ★

The 1483 rebellion against Richard has been well researched, and despite its common name of 'Buckingham's Rebellion', its origins clearly had no connection with that duke. Charles Ross sums up its participants thus: 'most were loyal former servants of Edward IV, and amongst these some of the most influential had had close connections with his household.'[12] The names of the rebels eventually attainted 'show clearly that it was essentially a rising of the substantial gentry', and indeed it was supported by none of the nobility of England save the duke himself and, inevitably, the Marquess of Dorset. The most eminent of the remaining gentry was probably Sir Thomas St Leger, who had married Edward IV's sister, Anne, Duchess of Exeter. 'He had tied his fortunes to the Woodville group,' Ross explains, 'and especially to Dorset, whose son was now contracted in marriage to St Leger's daughter by Duchess Anne, so that together they might inherit the Exeter estates ... He had everything to lose if Richard remained on the throne.'[13] Edward IV had arranged this appropriation of the Exeter duchy and had it sanctioned by Parliament in order to enrich his step-son's family, although Ross describes it as essentially illegal.

Without going into massive detail, which the reader can readily find in specialist accounts, it is plain to see that the people who resented Richard III enough to rise against him were men who desperately wanted to reinstate Edward V because their careers had been predicated on the continuity of the Edwardian-Woodville régime. Rather like William, Lord Hastings.

Unfortunately for those who suppose that loyalty or commitment to the house of York was involved, or a sense of outrage that the laws of inheritance had been flouted, an assessment of the rebellion shows that this was not the case. Once they believed that Edward V and his brother had died, good Yorkist rebels ought properly to have turned their support, according to prevailing customs of heredity, to one of the next legitimate heirs male of the York line. The most senior of these were the Earl of Lincoln and his brothers, followed by ten-year-old Henry Bourchier, heir to the earldom of Essex. Indeed, since the rebels were obviously happy with the discredited child Edward V on the throne, and had so little regard for the forms of law that they were later prepared to impose a Henry Tudor on the nation, it would have been more appropriate, in terms of succession, to discount Clarence's attainder and make their primary candidate the young Earl of Warwick.

They chose none of these. The reason being, of course, that self-interest would not be served by any of them. The rebels sought restoration of the old order of things where they could be assured their profitable careers would continue. Buckingham was ready to promise to reinstate Edward V, and Tudor was ready to promise anything. This was enough for the rebels, and absolved them of the chore of considering the proper Yorkist heirs – or even the good of the realm – rather than their own personal gain.

Ross dismisses the idea that fear of loss of patronage lay at the root of the rebellion, and prefers 'the outrage and resentment felt by Edward [IV]'s loyal servants of Richard's treatment of his heirs'.[14] In the real world of 1483, such tender feelings on behalf of Edward's children seem a flimsy reason for risking everything – life, limb, land and livelihood. As concerns most of the rebels, we can surely discount emotional motivations among hard-headed men who had built careers on clawing their way to advancement in royal service, administration, the law and similar areas where they effectively wielded control over their fellows. Plus it must be remembered that the vast majority of the insurgent forces constituted these men's retainers, supporters and family members. Probably 90 per cent of those up in arms would not recognize Edward V if they fell over him.

If the massive degree of resentment asserted by Ross genuinely existed, it must have centred on an objection to the principle of the princes' inheritance being set aside. Among ordinary folk the laws of inheritance were sacrosanct, and not infrequently gave cause for violent altercation. Yet the succession to the crown, as we have observed, depended on considerations other than mere heredity and on many previous occasions in England a deceased or deposed king had been succeeded by a claimant other than his nearest blood descendant. As people well knew from the events of the not too distant past, acclamation and election – not to mention conquest – could play a decisive part, and so could a parliamentary ruling on an issue of legitimate claim, such as that of 1460. Indeed, these rebels knew exactly what they were doing by timing their uprising so as to prevent the upcoming sitting of Parliament scheduled for November 1483. They knew the grounds for Edward V's disinheritance had been examined and accepted by an overwhelming majority of parliamentary representatives the previous June, and they could expect a formal Parliament to endorse that decision: their overriding concern was to set aside not just Richard III, but the constitutional framework that had set him on the throne.

Moreover, as mentioned above, if their purpose was to rectify an irregular succession, the rebels chose a strange solution in the person of Henry Tudor. As Rosemary Horrox observes, Tudor was 'an implausible alternative candidate … [whose] own claims to the throne were virtually non-existent and it is clear that it was only his promise to marry Elizabeth of York which made him acceptable to so much Yorkist opinion'.[15]

The question that most commentators fail to probe is why Tudor's glib promise was so readily believed. It was a thin guarantee indeed, conveyed by proxy and containing nothing to prove that Elizabeth herself, and her mother, were agreeable to the marriage, or had not indeed arranged some prior betrothal to a more appropriate partner. No written evidence exists to confirm the alleged marriage contract, and serious doubt is cast on its existence by assumptions in 1485 that the supposedly 'betrothed' Elizabeth was meekly available to be incestuously married to her uncle (see chapter 13). Further, common sense rejects the idea of the canny ex-queen handing Tudor her greatest bargaining asset on the eve of his attempted seaborne invasion, when his fortunes were at their most precarious. As suggested in chapter 8, despite the fact that negotiations were probably in progress, she had no reason to conclude any marriage deal without cast-iron guarantees in return; and until it was rumoured her sons were dead she must have been demanding, just like the rebels, the reinstatement of Edward V. What would be her revised conditions after hearing the rumour? Indeed, in the unlikely event that she actually believed the boys were dead, why should she have any further interest in Henry Tudor's hand for her daughter unless the rest of him was already firmly seated on England's throne?

For the Tudor-Morton-Beaufort camp, however, such details could be brushed aside. They had been negotiating the betrothal while Elizabeth's brothers were alive, but it was even more valuable to them if the boys were now alleged to be dead. The mother, tucked away in sanctuary, was of no consequence once they had a juicy half-truth which they could dress up as fact.

If the rebels were so ready to believe what they were told about the betrothal, what did they actually know of Tudor himself? Had they so soon forgotten their own beloved Edward IV's marital shenanigans? What if Henry Tudor, despite his promises, turned out to be already betrothed elsewhere? Or secretly wedded to some seductive Breton widow with a large number of unmarried siblings? Again we come back to the obvious fact that any champion would do; the claim of righting some great wrong was nothing more than a smokescreen. The rebellion was motivated by sheer self-interest – 'rebellion in pursuit of personal aims' in Rosemary Horrox's phrase – and any cover story would suffice so long as it carried a veneer of justification. This adds yet more support to the conclusion that Henry Tudor was adopted by the rebels purely as a stopgap in case the rumour of the princes' death proved true. Their first concern was to restore Edward V, and if this became impossible they now had an alternative, but it is unlikely they regarded themselves as irrevocably committed to Tudor.

Dr Horrox comments on the difficulty of ascribing motives to the rebels, whether supposedly dynastic (Lancaster versus York) or on points of principle or outraged sensibility. Neither will do:

> The majority of the Yorkist establishment was prepared to serve Richard III, or at least to refrain from overt opposition. Unless one is to categorize such men as time-servers and the rebels as men of principle, other factors have to be taken into account. One of the most important was simply opportunity: men were drawn into rebellion because kinsmen and friends were involved, or because the district in which they lived was affected.

She gives examples of malcontents drawing in family members who otherwise had no particular quarrel with the régime.[16]

With the rebels up in arms, did ordinary people flock to their cause through concern about the fate of the princes? Jeremy Potter reflects on the general mood that probably prevailed:

> The cult of the Holy Innocents placed special emphasis on children as sacred trusts, treasures of God, but it is improbable that many men and women stood aghast at the possibility that the deposed boy king had been murdered. If there was anything to be gained from expressions of horror – as there was by supporters of the Tudor pretender – they would express it. But since the death of the princes was essential if their own candidate was to succeed, this is evidence of little more than hypocrisy ... What stirred the southern gentry in October 1483 was not an outburst of moral outrage but the justified belief that they were losing power and influence to intruding northerners.[17]

In an England of two nations, with the 'savage brutes' of the north representing a threat to the prosperous and civilized south, Richard carried the wrong associations. When he ascended the throne, even those few rewards and offices bestowed on some who had served him in his previous administration were resented. True, we know he left the membership of his brother's council and administration essentially unchanged, but these positions were occupied by the higher clergy and lofty nobility. By contrast, those who rebelled were holders of lower-ranking positions of service which were far more vulnerable: stewards, constables, bailiffs, customs officers and the like. The sad thing is that, whereas at first Richard's importation of northerners had been remarkably modest in scale, it was the rebels' own actions that ensured everything they feared would come true in a way that fulfilled their worst apprehensions.

Once the rebellion got under way in mid-October, its very limited extent became glaringly evident. It was confined to a strip of south-eastern, south-central and south-western counties, with Buckingham alone raising a force in an otherwise unengaged Wales. Did the rebels represent the nation? Emphatically not. When King Richard needed to rouse England in defence against them, there was no shortage of loyal forces who flocked to his standard. By the end of the month the rebellion was over.

Inclement weather had seen off the threat from Wales when a tremendous storm flooded the River Severn and prevented Buckingham and his forces from crossing into England. His contribution was desultory at best, since the Staffords were disliked as harsh and grinding landlords, and his recruits were reluctant and resentful. Many deserted, and a few engaged in their own private action by plundering his castle at Brecon. Despite his newly-acquired dominant lordship in the county of Hereford, and despite that county's long attachment to the Prince of Wales, he was unable to muster any support there.

Although the rebellion was afterwards officially recorded as dating from 18 October, Horrox argues persuasively that it was set in motion at different times in different places. Vergil says Henry Tudor's flotilla set sail from Brittany on 10 October, but Horrox and Gill adjudge this date too early. Griffiths and Thomas have Henry still at Paimpol in Brittany on 30 October. He, too, suffered from terrible weather and was unable to reach the English coast until the first week in November, after many of his ships had been forced to turn back. He eventually dropped anchor in Poole Bay, but finding the coast guarded by the king's forces he scuttled back to Brittany without setting foot on English soil.

A few days earlier the defeated Harry of Buckingham had similarly taken to his heels, seeking refuge at Wem in Shropshire with a servant, Ralph Bannaster. Bannaster elected to hand him over to the authorities in return for a handsome reward.

As befitted a traitor, Buckingham was summarily tried, convicted and condemned to death by his own Constable's Court, over which the newly appointed Vice-Constable, Sir Ralph Assheton, presided. He was beheaded in Salisbury marketplace on 2 November, 1483. Richard spared a thought for Buckingham's widow, Catherine Woodville, granting her an annuity and ensuring that Buckingham's debts were not visited upon her after his death.

The loss of patronage feared by the rebels now came horribly true. Although there were large numbers of pardons and only ten executions, most of the leading rebels who were able to escape abandoned their jobs and estates and took refuge across the Channel with the bedraggled Tudor party. The rest remained in England and many sought accommodation with the Ricardian régime. About a third of those attainted were eventually pardoned and retrieved all or part of their lands, but they would never be trusted or hold office again.

In the immediate aftermath of the unrest, an administrative vacuum now existed from south-east to south-west which had to be filled without delay. Here Richard miscalculated the effect of his actions: he imported for this purpose too many of his trusted adherents from the north.

In the process he inevitably overturned long-established, often delicately balanced relationships between families and spheres of influence. An accusation has been made that he also flouted the norms of law and customary practice under which the king might grant away lands of attainted rebels. 'It was usual,' wrote Charles Ross, 'for kings to appoint to offices ... on the estates of rebels as soon as they came into royal hands, but no previous monarch had ventured to dispose of *lands* before they had been declared forfeit to the crown by a formal parliamentary act of attainder.'

In the belief that Ross was correct, previous editions of this book followed his lead in condemning such grants as a blot on

Richard's record. However, I can now verify that the professor was in error. There were ample precedents set by kings like Henry IV after Shrewsbury, and Edward IV after Barnet and Tewkesbury, in granting lands away before attainders were enacted. This was under the sovereign's ancient treason prerogative of forfeiture of war, which applied to open rebellion under arms.[18]

Richard's underlying reasons were obvious, of course, given the urgent need to transplant men he could trust into areas which had become hotbeds of revolt. Unfortunately, few men of substance, however loyal, would be much inclined to abandon their northern bailiwicks in pursuit of middle-ranking jobs in hostile southern parts without some considerable incentive. The gift of land was not only a sweetener but also a necessary means of integrating outsiders into the infrastructure of local society where they were now expected to exert an influence. Without swift action there would have been a dangerous hiatus before the resumption of law, order and good administration, which it was the king's duty to provide for his subjects. Perhaps a modern solution might be the announcement of a state of emergency, when the normal civil protections are suspended in extreme circumstances.

From his perspective, doubtless in his view the rebels on whose estates he planted his northerners that December, having been leaders of the revolt, must shoulder due responsibility. They might not have belonged to the rarefied ranks of the nobility, but as landed gentry and holders of office from the crown they occupied the next important stratum of civil society, giving them considerable power over their lower-status followers. Such men could not expect to escape sanctions, unlike the huge numbers of nameless rank and file drafted into the conflict in their service, against whom no reprisals whatsoever would be taken.

Ross, despite knowing how some Woodvilles had themselves acquired holdings with dubious legality, warmed to his theme of Richard's supposedly illegal actions. Looking back to the early days of the protectorate he deplored the 'arbitrary appropriation' of their estates. Yet these were measures to quell opposition to the legally constituted government of the day, with Richard performing the same role of Protector and Defender of the Realm as his father before him in Henry VI's turbulent reign. The Woodvilles had been beaten at their own game; they had seized treasure, refused to return crown property. Confiscations could be reversed, but meanwhile they could scarcely be left in peaceful possession of those estates that provided the means to subvert and suborn treason. Without adequate funds the machinery of state could not operate, as Richard well knew from the amounts by which he had personally subsidized it. He probably viewed confiscation of their estates as a fair kind of justice whereby resources were clawed back to keep the exchequer solvent.

On one issue, however, the absence of reprisal was particularly significant: he never tried to accuse Buckingham of murdering the princes. This would seem patently necessary if they had been killed either by the duke or by Richard himself, and Buckingham would have been the ideal scapegoat.

Had the boys died at Richard's hands — as is traditionally assumed to have happened by October 1483 — such a ploy would have neatly accounted for their disappearance, cleared Richard of culpability and even provided a fig-leaf of justification for those men who preferred to defect to the winning side, allowing them to claim they had been duped. This would help to avoid the necessity of so many hated attainders and forfeitures. The fact that Richard failed to accuse Buckingham is therefore highly important.

Whenever this question is raised, which is rarely, the counter-argument is generally that he knew people would not have believed him. This is manifestly nonsense: Buckingham was such an obvious suspect that history has produced legions of commentators who continue to accuse him to this day. In 1483 few people had reason or evidence to question what they were told; they would have found it entirely plausible since Buckingham, the most powerful and ambitious subject in the land, had plainly been caught red-handed leading a rebellion. This incomprehensible set of circumstances merited an explanation and, frankly, one explanation was as likely as any other.

Unfortunately for Richard, he did not make use of Buckingham as a scapegoat, despite the obvious benefits offered by such a course of action. One can deduce only one good reason for this: no scapegoat was needed, because the sons of Edward IV were not dead.

12

Brave Hopes

Bishop Morton had expertly crafted his plan to use the October rebellion to place Henry Tudor on the throne. Doubtless he had also hedged his bets: with fingers in all pies, he would assuredly have reaped the same rewards had Richard III been overthrown in favour of either Edward V or Buckingham or Henry Tudor.

With Tudor his preferred candidate, and Buckingham his dupe, Morton sought to remove Edward V and his brother from the running by means of the unattributable murder rumour. Fanning the movement to restore them had already ensured they remained sequestered; as long as they were hidden from sight, and/or removed from England, Richard was unwittingly playing into the conspirators' hands. There were, of course, ways in which rumour could become fact.

For Henry's candidacy to be credible he needed to be represented as betrothed to Elizabeth of York. Luckily for him, the betrothal was accepted as readily as the murder rumour. Unluckily for him, the rebellion was a disaster. But it had the effect of swelling his band of malcontents and forced him to the fore as their leader.

By January 1484 their hopes were in disarray. The rebellion had been stamped out, Buckingham had paid the ultimate price and Tudor was holed up in Brittany. Bishop Morton, pursuing his own agenda, chose not to join him: instead he fled to Flanders (Flanders again!).

Now came Richard's opportunity to start moulding the governance of England so that his subjects could enjoy greater peace and security, with rights respected and the weak protected against the depredations of the mighty.

During his years in the north he had built up a reputation as a fair and rigorous administrator of the rule of law. It should also be clearly understood that his status in life placed him in the position of one who meted out justice, not one who was subjected to it at the hands of others. Richard had been Constable of England for fourteen years, and viceroy in the north for eight; many high offices had come his way, placing him at the head of structures where his word was law. From all we hear, he had a fine legal brain[1] and his judgements were respected.

It is entirely in character that on 26 June 1483, when he assumed the crown as Richard III, he made his first statement when seating himself in the king's marble chair at the Court of King's Bench at Westminster. This was the seat of the King as Justicer, and Richard had an important message to convey.

As reported in the *Great Chronicle of London* and Cotton Vitellius A XVI, he delivered a lecture to all his judges and legal officers, straitly charging them to 'justly and duly minister his law without delay and favour', and declaring that all men, of whatever degree, must be treated equally in the sight of the law.

Two weeks later, when the nobility were about to return to their estates after his coronation, he commanded them to ensure that 'no extortions were done to his subjects'. The point was reiterated a few months later in a proclamation to the people of Kent: 'The king's highness is fully determined to see due administration of justice throughout this his realm to be had, and to reform, punish and subdue all extortions and oppressions in the same.' All the 'grieved, oppressed or unlawfully wronged' should therefore make a bill of complaint to be heard by the king himself at his coming now into his county of Kent:

> For his grace is utterly determined all his true subjects shall live in rest and quiet and peaceably enjoy their lands, livelihoods and goods according to the laws of this his land which they be naturally born to inherit. And therefore the king chargeth and commandeth that no manner of man, of whatever condition or degree he be, rob, hurt or spoil any of his said subjects in their bodies or goods upon pain of death.[2]

If this seems to sit oddly with Richard's post-rebellion confiscations, it should be noted that the promise of rest and quiet applied specifically to 'true subjects'. Rebels, by definition, were none such. Yet even after their punishment, some one third received pardons; indeed the number and frequency of pardons given by Richard to his enemies are an aspect of his reign that even his detractors respect. The Victorian James Gairdner, no supporter of Richard III, commented that his acts of clemency towards his enemies 'were done graciously and in no grudging spirit. Whatever other evil there was in Richard, there was nothing mean or paltry'.

Another nineteenth-century historian, Sharon Turner, also conceded that Richard was a just and liberal ruler: 'Our ablest lawyers have acknowledged that his statutes were wise and useful ... he was too liberal to be personally rapacious. ... He emptied his exchequer by his bounties to men who were enabled by his own generosity more effectually to betray him.'[3]

Arthur Kincaid points to Richard's concern with the proper forms and precedents. Here he closely followed those set by his family, starting with the legal case for bastardization 'to maintain the Yorkist platform of legitimism by which his father had claimed the throne', and ending with the ratification of his title by Parliament. In fact the formalities of his accession

> closely followed his brother's precedent: ... (1) popular petition, (2) formal protest. (3) political sermon at Paul's Cross, (4) the people's assent to his accession, (5) the act of sitting in the King's Bench, (6) addressing the judges, and making a symbolic gesture of pardon, all followed Edward's pattern.[4]

To quote Dr Anne Sutton:

> Of Richard's education in the law nothing is known. ... With or without a period at an inn [of court] his own ducal council would have provided an early forcing school of experience for Richard. By the time he was king he would have been familiar with the complexities of the land law, the difficulties of securing title and the endless squabbles that might arise over an inheritance. His ducal council became a valuable source of arbitration in such matters.[5]

Nor was Richard's interest in the law confined only to practicalities. He showed himself equally interested in jurisprudence as concerned the proper interpretation of the law. Described in *The Road to Bosworth Field* is one of his most distinctive actions, which was to call together all his justices and pose them three questions concerning specific cases, two involving official malpractice. The entire report of the interrogation is there to read, with the king demonstrating particular concern about the processes of the law itself being subverted by officers of the court. In this detailed account Richard's sharp intelligence and questioning mind are evident. One cannot but be impressed by his final remark which was intended to summarize the unimpeachable standards he expected in his courts: 'And this is the King's will to wit, to say "by his justices" and "by his law" is to say one and the same thing.'[6]

Richard's commitment to the rule of law carried through into the legislation enacted by the only Parliament of his reign, which opened on 23 January 1484. Of first importance was the Act known as *Titulus Regius*, whereby his right to the throne was recognized by Parliament. This confirmed and restated the petition offered to him the previous June, discussed in chapter 6.

There is an interesting statement inserted in the 1484 Act after the end of the quoted petition. It refers to the fact that most people are not sufficiently learned in the laws and customs on which the king's title was based; therefore this Act was to be passed because:

> the Courte of Parliament is of such auctorite, and the people of this Lande of suche nature and disposition, as experience teacheth, that manifestacion and declaration of any trueth or right, made by the Thre Estates of this Reame assembled in Parliament, and by auctorite of the same, maketh, before all other thyngs, moost feith and certaynte; and, quietyng mens myndes, remoeveth the occasion of all doubts and seditious langage.

So Parliament roundly declared itself the final arbiter of 'any truth or right'.

Anne Sutton mentions criticism by the Crowland chronicler that the 1484 Parliament, 'that lay court', had not referred the king's title to proper Church jurisdiction, since it concerned a dispute over the validity of a marriage. She continues:

> but in view of the part Parliament had already played in disputes over the succession to the Crown in the fifteenth century, and was to play in 1484 and 1485, perhaps the chronicler was being not only accurate but a little old-fashioned and pedantic as well. Parliament's role was developing beyond his experience.[7]
>
> There has been little notice taken of the fact that the terms of the *Titulus Regius* were actually discussed ... it seems that there was at least some argument, though no doubt more on the line of questioning Parliament's authority to pronounce on the King's title, especially when it involved a matter for an ecclesiastical court, than as to whether the King had a title or not. ... Compliant though Parliament was in fact, in the words of the *Titulus Regius*, however, it played a magnificent part. A part not favoured, it seems, by the Croyland chronicler. Such play was made with Parliament's authority that the *Titulus Regius* has been extensively quoted as an example of the conclusion of a long development of ideas about the three estates and Parliament in fifteenth century England by Professor Chrimes.[8]

This places in its proper context the claim in Crowland that Parliament presumed to rule on the validity of the marriage only through intimidation and 'great fear'.

The fact is that in June 1483 Richard had submitted himself to the only representative body constitutionally able to reach decisions in matters of succession, i.e. those parliamentary representatives who had been called for a session of Parliament. Commentators who accuse Richard of usurpation are at pains to emphasize that this was an irregular course of action. This is not denied. It was an irregular situation. The question they are unable to answer is this: faced with the challenge to Edward V's title, what body was better qualified to decide the succession? This was not merely a legal or ecclesiastical matter, nor even a matter of inheritance, but a vital political decision affecting the security and integrity of the realm. Would they prefer that the monarch should be chosen, as in previous irregular accessions, by members of a select, self-appointed faction speaking only for its own narrow interests?

Another complaint by historians is that the petition was signed under duress. Yet we know from Mancini that the lords had brought so many armed retainers that they had to be asked to lodge their men outside the city. More convincing is the alternative argument that after thirty years of intermittent civil unrest, they simply acquiesced for the sake of peace and quiet. Would the realm suffer more turmoil under a child of questionable legitimacy controlled by the Woodvilles, or under an independent adult of upright reputation who had shown himself a capable ruler? Richard felt he knew the answer and, when faced with a crisis, had the courage to seize the reins. If history is unhappy that the lords and commons agreed with him, let us not forget that they had the option to disagree.

So far, given the circumstances, everything had been placed on as legal a footing as possible. Nevertheless, there remains a cavil to be noted here, which is summed up admirably by Professor Helmholz. To the modern mind, the bastardization of the children of Edward IV may be legal, but does not seem just. The problem is, as Helmholz points out, we regard illegitimacy in a different way from the mediæval view, which was more hard-headed about visiting the sins of the parents on the children. Mediæval canon law was willing to follow logical arguments to their ultimate conclusion, and often forced people to live with the unwelcome consequences of their domestic acts. Importantly, although canon law generally held that external proofs must determine a dispute, nevertheless it was sensitive to the intrinsic truth or rightness of a case even if this were difficult to prove in court, e.g. when one person only (in our case Stillington) could vouch for it. Hence, 'The ease with which the claims of Richard III's supporters have been rejected is more a product of modern habits of thought than it is the result of study of the law applicable at the time.'

In the same vein, Helmholz adds that there is 'something seemingly unfair about summarily depriving the defenders of [the bastardized children] of the chance to prove their legitimacy before a proper court. What is most suspect about the deprivation was the lack of a fair hearing.' He assumes Richard's supporters would have countered this argument by stressing the urgency of the situation: 'Affairs of state had to prevail.'[9]

This is a crucial point, and it applied to the entire sequence of policy directions which had to be followed as soon as the precontract became known. Ruthless decisions had to be taken debarring the child from the throne, not merely for 'affairs of state' but for urgent security reasons.

As to a fair hearing for Edward IV's dispossessed family, it is not true that they had no access to an ecclesiastical court. Elizabeth, safe at Westminster Abbey, was in an ideal position to appeal to Church authorities for the necessary hearing, and the onus was on her to do so.

Most people suppose she had heard of the challenge to her marriage by at least 9 June, when the meeting took place after which 'there wass none that spake with the Qwene'. From that moment until Richard was crowned the following month, she and her supporters (including her brother the Bishop of Salisbury) had time to consult any number of experts in canon law, demand a hearing, swear depositions and refute the allegations as vocally as they might. In fact they could still do so right up until Parliament passed *Titulus Regius*.

Had she attempted to do so, we should certainly have been informed by the Crowland chronicler, and indeed by Mancini who mingled in clerical circles. Yet our informants report not a word from the ex-queen in defence of her children.

The same applies to the charge of bewitching Edward IV into wedlock. We hear from Fabyan that apart from the happy couple and Jacquetta, there were some four witnesses to the clandestine ceremony. Fabyan may be right or wrong, but if the marriage was perfectly proper why did the Woodvilles not name those who were present and induce them to swear statements in their favour? Once again, we hear nothing but silence.

This silence remained unbroken for the rest of Elizabeth's life, even during the years after her daughter became Henry VII's queen. Equally, at no time did she ever publicly accuse Richard III of killing her sons. Interestingly, in view of their disappearance, neither is there any recorded comment by Thomas Bourchier, the Archbishop of Canterbury who gave his pledge for the safety of young Richard of York (Bourchier lived into Henry Tudor's reign and died in 1486).

Once *Titulus Regius* was passed, the law recognized only one of Edward IV's marriages: that to Lady Eleanor Talbot. One

may not like or agree with a legal decision, but one cannot alter
its existence. Thus, from January 1484 until Henry VII repealed
Titulus Regius, the Talbot marriage was legal and the Woodville
marriage was not.

* * *

Richard's Parliament, which concluded on 20 February, is
remembered for introducing a catalogue of citizens' rights and
protections which was unparalleled in living memory. Jeremy
Potter summarizes thus:

> There was a programme of law reform which included measures
> to correct injustice in the ownership and transfer of land, measures
> to safeguard the individual against abuses of the law in matters
> affecting juries and bail, measures to prevent the seizure of goods
> of those arrested but not yet found guilty, and the abolition of
> a much resented form of taxation known euphemistically as
> benevolences. Richard insisted on fair dealing in the law courts,
> which had been notoriously lacking during a period when the
> nobility flouted the law and took it forcibly into their own hands.
> His policy of protection of the weak against the strong would have
> made him unpopular among some of the nobility, but to ordinary
> people he may well have been Good King Dickon.

Approval from different sources is quoted for Richard's
programme of legislation.

In 1962 H.G. Hanbury, Vinerian Professor of English Law at
Oxford, judged that it gave much protection to the liberty of
the subject and the sanctity of his property and concluded that
Richard was 'a singularly thoughtful and enlightened legislator'.
In his *Lives of the Lord Chancellors of England* (1845) a nineteenth-
century Lord Chancellor and Lord Chief Justice, Lord Campbell,
declared: 'We have no difficulty in pronouncing Richard's
parliament the most meritorious national assembly for protecting
the liberty of the subject and putting down abuses in the

administration of justice that had sat in England since the reign of Henry III.'[10]

Alison Hanham disagrees that Richard deserves any personal credit for this legislation:

> As Gairdner said, 'The public Acts of this Parliament have always been noted as wise and beneficial', but how far the ordinary legislation of this (or any) parliament was initiated by the king in person is a debatable point. So much has been made of Richard's good government that it ought to be said that he was in no position to enact oppressive measures, even had he wished to do so.[11]

Further confirmation, presumably, that *Titulus Regius* could not have been forced upon Parliament.

She adds that the abolition of benevolences, the enforced gifts whereby Edward IV extorted huge amounts of money from the rich, was 'probably a concession to popular feeling' and that acts dealing with commerce were 'likely to have been inspired (as usual) by the merchant community'. (Unsurprisingly, benevolences in their original form were revived by Henry VII with the able assistance of his chancellor, John Morton.)

What Dr Hanham conspicuously fails to address in this summary are the measures introduced by Richard that did *not* benefit the lords and merchants, measures that gave new protections to the common man. This was not minor or insignificant legislation; indeed, it included laws that still protect ordinary people today, including historians. Richard's Parliament, for example, reformed the bail and jury systems, *inter alia* granting persons arrested on suspicion of felony the ability to enjoy bail and not to have their possessions seized.

Bertram Fields, himself a lawyer, offers a view on some of these enduring protections:

> Richard's Parliament ... passed considerable sound and beneficial legislation. One such act freed juries from intimidation and tampering. Another protected buyers of land from secret defects in title. Still another made bail available to persons accused of

crimes. ... For the first time, Parliament's acts were published in English, so they could be understood by at least that part of the population that was literate, rather than being confined to churchmen, educated nobles and the few others who could read Latin.[12]

Other benefits specifically aimed at the humbler classes were introduced outside of parliamentary legislation. One was the establishment of a formal arrangement similar to that originally inaugurated with his council in the north, whereby Richard made himself personally accessible to appeals on the part of those who had insufficient means to apply to the courts. This institution later developed into the Court of Requests, aiding poor litigants to gain access to the law.

Another involved taking action, in large areas across England, against the masses of private military retainers which had long been maintained by the ruling classes to enforce their will and greed not only against opponents of their own rank, but also against common people who were helpless to defend themselves.

'To the commons and the gentry,' Paul Murray Kendall wrote:

> [his] laws offered a prospect of fair dealing in the courts which they had not seen for decades; but they undoubtedly were one of the chief reasons why Richard did not retain the support of a number among the nobility and upper gentry. For these laws were aimed directly at curbing the practices by which this class had overawed and preyed upon its weaker neighbours throughout the past century. By striking at evils which were mainly the result of the system of livery and maintenance, Richard was serving justice at the risk – a risk he must have realized – of alienating the men whose military power he would need in the day of battle.[13]

It may be true that Richard was in no position to enact oppressive measures, but neither did he need strive officiously to protect the weak at the cost of antagonizing the mighty. Undoubtedly some still smarted under his reformist measures when the call came to support their king at Bosworth Field. In the words of Sharon Turner: 'In these public benefits of Richard we see the real cause of his unpopularity with the higher orders. He was becoming too good a king to suit their interests.'[14]

Charles Ross contends that Richard's legislation should be viewed in the context of his overall search for support. Yet the support of the common man earned him no votes, brought him no armies, supplied him no lucrative taxes. Why should he seek to protect the poor from the rich, the weak from the powerful, when the rich and powerful were the only constituency that mattered to the sovereign? Despite his long career as a just and able administrator, commentators like Ross and Hanham allow Richard no genuine desire to reform a system that he must have found, during his rule of the north, to be cruelly unfair and oppressive to the common population.

Though modern-day historians have taken a cynical view of Richard's lawmaking, it was certainly still earning approval some forty years later. In 1525, in the reign of Henry VIII when Cardinal Wolsey tried to wrest from the citizens a 'benevolence', the Mayor and Aldermen of London cited the good laws of Richard as king, prohibiting these enforced loans which were so unpopular in Edward IV's reign. 'Sir,' said the irate cardinal, 'I marvell that you speak of Richard the third, which was a usurper and a murtherer of his awne nephewes'; to which the civic dignitaries stoutly replied that whatever evil he might have done, 'yet in his tyme wer many good actes made'.[15]

It will readily be seen that the view historians take depends less on the enactments themselves and more on the imponderables of Richard's supposed underlying character and motivations. Few verdicts in recent years have been generous.

Among those who have expressed a positive verdict on Richard's rule is A.R. Myers, Professor of Mediæval History at the University of Liverpool: 'During his brief reign he displayed many qualities which, if he had come to the throne in a more acceptable way, might have helped him to a long and successful reign.' After citing numerous illustrations of Richard's good governance, Myers adds:

> What brought him to defeat and death at Bosworth Field was not the feeling of the nation at large but the desertion of a few great nobles and their forces ... As Bishop Stubbs rightly said, he owes 'the general condemnation, with which his life and reign have been visited, to the fact that he left none behind whose duty or whose care it was to attempt his vindication'.[16]

Professor Ross, whose biography of Richard III is still considered by many as definitive, sees the king's beneficial legislation as mere political expediency. Yet his support for the Church and institutions of scholarship and learning are seen as genuine, presumably because unworthy motives are difficult to identify in these fields. Lest we should for a moment admire the man, this is quickly countered: 'There is, however, in historical experience, no paradox between strongly-held religious beliefs and violence and dishonesty in political behaviour.'[17]

Ross's hostility resurfaces when he gives his opinion that Richard's public fulminations against immorality 'are far more suspect'. These include Mancini's report that Richard made clear his feelings about people surrounding the young Edward V who had led his father into a life of vice, and the handing over of Elizabeth Lambert to the City Fathers of London for their verdict on her harlotry, which according to Ross is 'public persecution'. The professor's partiality in the case of 'the delectable Mistress Shore' is clearly exposed by his decision to quote selectively from Richard's letter seeking to dissuade her would-be new husband, Thomas Lynom, from contracting such an unsuitable marriage: 'We for many causes wold be sory that hee soo shuld be disposed,' says Richard, rather mildly for one so bent on persecution. What Ross fails to quote is the second half of the letter where Richard gives express permission for the marriage to go ahead (and orders her release from prison) if Lynom is 'utter set for to marry her'. But this would not suit Ross's thesis that Richard's moral strictures were purely for the purpose of character-assassination.

Possibly the most measured of Ross's judgements of Richard are expressed in the following lines:

> In many respects, therefore, Richard appears as very much a conventional man for his age and station. He seems to have shared to the full a taste for luxury and display common to the kings and aristocracy of the Yorkist and early Tudor period in England; and we should not forget the supplementary side of the medal, which made such things possible, the acquisitiveness, the land-hunger, the disregard for the rights of others, where his brother Edward and his father-in-law Warwick the Kingmaker had given him a splendid lead.[18]

As a summary, this overlooks many things including the commitment to religion and scholarship which even Ross admits was probably genuine. It is not the purpose of this book to go into Richard's religious and educational endowments, his financing and patronage of great building works, his love of books and music or his 'conspicuous loyalty to his friends and followers' which Ross found one of his more attractive features. It would be foolish to claim Richard was without fault or led the life of a saint. But it is necessary, nonetheless, to restore some sense of balance when considering him as a king whose brief reign exhibits more in the way of good intentions than it does in the way of tyranny and duplicity.

★ ★ ★

If Richard had started the year with a triumph of enlightened legislation, he would continue it with a triumph of negotiation: by 1 March he succeeded in concluding a deal with Elizabeth Woodville which brought her and her daughters out of sanctuary.

Traditional historians propound a variety of theories to explain Elizabeth's remarkable *rapprochement* with the man they deem to be the murderer of her sons, usually under the mutually exclusive headings of 'weak, vacillating woman' or 'cold, pragmatic politician'. These theories need to be constructed because of the belief that Elizabeth 'was clearly implicated in the plan of autumn 1483 to place Henry Tudor on the throne', in the words of Ross who, swallowing the line peddled by Vergil, describes a 'scheme proposed by Buckingham and Queen Elizabeth Woodville that Richard should be replaced by Henry Tudor ... on condition that he married Elizabeth of York, now King Edward's rightful heir' [sic].[19]

This belief presupposes that the ex-queen had limply assumed her sons to be dead, and promptly signed away any chance of their restoration, by betrothing her daughter to the dangerously ambitious Tudor – and all within the space of a few days? It's surprising how little regard historians pay to chronology.

All we need do is calculate the date when the rumour of her sons' murder reached Elizabeth, and the date when Tudor announced his felicitous 'betrothal' to her daughter.

Our *terminus a quo* is 10 September. This is calculated allowing a minimal amount of time for Buckingham first to be persuaded by Morton in August to join the rebellion, and then to become its leader in September. Obviously, given his recent status as Richard's right-hand man, it was the duke who needed to make approaches to the rebels. Remember, there was no cohesion behind this rebellion, no single mastermind in overall charge. Even if Buckingham sent out messages as early as the last week of August, rebel leaders would need to exchange views before anyone agreed to meet the ruling High Constable of England. The centres of rebellion involved places as far apart as Exeter, Salisbury, Guildford and Gravesend. Agreement could not have been unanimous or immediate, there would have been resistance, disbelief, heated private meetings. Much of the communication would have been by courier, with each rider taking several days out and back. If Buckingham was accepted as leader by Monday 8 September, it would have been a miracle; Wednesday 10 September is barely probable.

Time ought now to be allowed for the preparing of Buckingham's proclamation, as cited in Crowland. His involvement could scarcely have been proclaimed earlier than 12 September, otherwise Richard would not still be authorizing payments to him on 16 September. Also, still following Crowland, we need to allow Buckingham a brief spell at the helm before word was spread that Edward IV's sons were dead. Nevertheless, in an effort to give the traditionalists every leeway, let us take the earliest possible date – 10 September – for the rumour to start circulating. As an even greater concession, let us assume Elizabeth Woodville heard it in sanctuary that very same day.

Our *terminus ad quem*, 20 September, has been calculated as the date by which the rebel leaders accepted Henry Tudor's undertaking to marry Elizabeth of York and become their replacement leader.

To reach this date we must work backwards from 22 September, when Robert Morton was punished for a resumption of plotting along with Lionel Woodville. As Rosemary Horrox asserts, 'the rebels had got into their stride again, with the intention of putting Henry Tudor on the throne'.[20] That being so, they must have accepted Tudor at least forty-eight hours earlier: this allows for illicit actions to take place on 20–21 September which are detected and reported, then punished on 22 September.

It should now be clear that the very earliest date on which the rumour of the princes' deaths could have been circulated was 10 September (more likely later), and the very latest date that Tudor's betrothal could have been announced was 20 September (more likely earlier). Who is now ready to believe that Elizabeth Woodville ferreted out incontrovertible proof of the death of her sons – both of them – and promptly concluded a dynastically crucial marriage contract between her daughter and Tudor, all in the space of ten days?

When the rumour reached her ears, Elizabeth had no reason to give it immediate credence. With plenty of resources at her disposal, even in sanctuary, she would have left no stone unturned in her efforts to discover the truth. Ross asserts that she would not have abandoned their cause unless she had 'excellent reasons to believe them already dead', which she was 'well able to find out'.

Such efforts would be neither quick nor easy. Precisely what kind of proof would satisfy a distraught mother anyway? Short of being confronted with the actual bodies, would she not hold out for weeks and months until all hope was gone? Even had Richard personally confessed to her face, would she not harbour a nagging suspicion (or desperate hope) that he was lying in order to pre-empt moves to restore them?

More importantly, if she had discovered proof of their death at Richard's hands, why did Henry Tudor never produce it, whether to bolster his case for overthrowing Richard or to dismiss the claims of pretenders during his reign? Would not Tudor, whose fortunes hinged entirely on the demise of the brothers, need – indeed demand – to know what proof she had of their fate? Yet he exhibited every sign of being totally ignorant on the subject. Even if you believe the supposed Tyrell confession recounted by Thomas More, this still leaves Henry in the dark for the previous nineteen years.

The fact is that there is not the slightest evidence for assuming that Elizabeth Woodville knew her sons to be dead, so she had no reason for precipitately signing away their birthright in favour of Tudor. The only deal that could ever interest Elizabeth was one where Henry Tudor earned his bride's hand by first reinstating Edward V as king. She was not so foolish as to give him her daughter to aid him in supplanting her sons. It was Tudor who needed the girl, not the other way around, and he would still need her whether the October rebellion succeeded or failed. He could try again some other year, but her sons could not. If she abandoned them now, their fate was sealed.

Thus the marriage contract, so readily believed, had to be a spurious claim on the part of the Tudor camp. Elizabeth Woodville never allied herself to Henry's plans to seize the throne. This conclusion is supported by the fact that, although Margaret Beaufort had the entirety of her estates confiscated by Parliament as a result of her scheming, Elizabeth Woodville was never named as a co-conspirator; her only loss was to be deprived of the dower lands given her by Edward IV, an obvious reflection of the invalidity of their marriage. Certainly she was agitating for the restoration of her son, but Richard expected no less. Actively to set up a new challenger for the crown and marry her daughter to him would have been a different proposition meriting condign punishment.

The conclusion is also supported by the mutual willingness of both the ex-queen and Richard to negotiate an agreement in February of 1484, by which time we may safely assume she had satisfied herself about the fate of her sons.

By the date of her emergence, Richard's tenure of the throne had begun to look impregnable. He had enjoyed a popular coronation, royal progress and investiture of his son as Prince of Wales. He had also crushed a rebellion and held a well-attended Parliament which consolidated his title to the crown. He was under no compulsion to offer terms to the recalcitrant widow: he could simply have left her in sanctuary until her funds ran out. She, on the other hand, had every reason to conclude, from Richard's rigorous but not vindictive treatment of the treacherous Margaret Beaufort, that she had less to fear from him than originally supposed. She would end up far less generously treated by Henry VII.

The elaborately sworn oath that Richard eventually took, publicly promising to protect Elizabeth and her daughters and to make suitable provision for their marriage, was an act of supreme magnanimity on his part. Yet Ross claims that it 'reeks of the queen-dowager's suspicion', and suggests that she dictated the terms of her emergence. He fails to tell us how she suddenly gained sufficient power to dictate terms to the king at the height of his success, or explain the precise nature of her suspicion.

From his standpoint it certainly cannot concern the fate of her sons, since he has assured us she already knew they were dead.

Does he think she suspected Richard would kill her daughters? That cannot be, for he had made no attempt to remove them from sanctuary. It could scarcely have escaped notice that the two eldest girls were of marriageable age, and as such, if their bastardy were overlooked, could represent a tantalizing figurehead for rebellion (as the Crowland chronicler observed). In any case, anyone willing to turn a blind eye to the bastardy of the girls would have no problem ignoring the attainder which debarred the young Edward Earl of Warwick, a male heir whose claim was otherwise more senior. Yet this vulnerable boy was never in danger until Henry VII incarcerated and executed him. At Richard's hands he resided with a group of high-born offspring in a royal northern household which historians locate at Sandal castle in 1484, although Vergil placed him at Sheriff Hutton where Tudor's men came to haul him away with other children in 1485.

The worst Elizabeth might fear was disparagement of her daughters by marriage, and Richard's integrity in that regard ultimately contributed to costing him his crown and his life.

In reality, when Elizabeth concluded her deal with Richard she was at her weakest. Those who had rebelled in favour of her sons were still licking their wounds, while Henry Tudor was concerned only with his barefaced bid for the throne. With relatives and supporters now fled overseas, and Margaret Beaufort confined and closely watched, who remained to advance her schemes and plots? If she had any fight left, her sole remaining power-play lay in keeping her girls out of Richard's hands. Nevertheless she happily handed over her entire family. In these proceedings, clearly the king was the master of the situation.

Yet Richard's impetus towards reconciliation is seldom acknowledged. He had been willing for the past year to swear just such an oath promising Elizabeth's safety if she emerged from sanctuary. On 23 May the City of London Corporation had minuted that a delegation of leading councillors read aloud the oath they were ready to swear if that was what it took to persuade her.[21]

Her emergence to rejoin her peers undoubtedly offered an important opportunity for a public tableau of reconciliation: we may imagine all the pageantry of the lords spiritual and temporal in stately procession, attended by the civic dignitaries of London in their robes and regalia, culminating in the set-piece of the chivalrous king and the dignified ex-queen exchanging solemn oaths over the Gospels of the Holy Evangelists. Its occurrence after the quelling of the rebellion, and the consequent rituals of punishment and pardon, added even greater significance to the ceremony, effectively drawing a line under the whole episode and signalling a renewed sense of concord between erstwhile foes.

Concerned as ever that all people should understand by what title he held the crown, Richard arranged for the London companies to attend him in April at Westminster, and later at St Mary Spittal, to hear it read to them.

Of the few Woodville supporters that remained at large, none was of greater importance now than Thomas Grey, Marquess of Dorset, who had taken refuge across the sea with the Tudors. Whether it was part of Richard's agreement with Elizabeth, or whether on her own initiative, she invited Dorset to return to the fold and – remarkably – he accepted the invitation. It is unknown whether the same offer was made to her three brothers, also in Brittany, but logic suggests it was. Slipping away from the Tudor camp could not have been an easy prospect and although Dorset made at least one attempt, he was caught and forced back. This occurred in the spring of 1485, shortly after he had sent his Portuguese agent, Roger Machado, on a visit to Flanders in January and early February. Did Machado uncover information in Flanders (perhaps about Edward IV's sons) that helped persuade Dorset to defect?

Around the same time Elizabeth's brother Richard received a pardon. He might have been successful in returning to England, but his activities and whereabouts during the rest of Richard's reign are uncertain.

Of the other brothers, Lionel having died some time in 1484, only the seafaring Sir Edward failed to return to the fold. Perhaps he calculated that absconding with ships and gold placed him too far beyond the pale. Yet his adherent Robert Ratclyff returned to serve Richard, and was rewarded in April 1485 'after services for the king which involved his being imprisoned abroad'.[22]

Quite likely the exiled Woodvilles by now would have been less than wholly trusting of their Tudor allies. They surely had been dumbfounded by the sudden *volte face* the previous September when the uprising they had engineered in favour of

Edward V turned into support for Henry Tudor. Doubtless they had secretly itched to verify the surprising news that Tudor had obtained the hand in marriage of Elizabeth of York. What must have worried them most was whether the rumours of the death of her brothers, so readily accepted by their co-conspirators, had any basis in fact. In the aftermath of the rebellion they would have found means of corresponding with Elizabeth Woodville in sanctuary, and in this way learned the truth of the matter. Perhaps this had a bearing on the alacrity of Dorset and Richard Woodville to join her in reconciling with Richard. So it is not only the ex-queen's behaviour, but also that of her two kinsmen, that must be squared somehow with the tradition that Richard murdered his nephews in the Tower.

* * *

Despite such auspicious beginnings, what followed made 1484 a year of desperate misfortune. Richard and Anne's only child, Edward, to whom the greatest in the land had sworn allegiance as heir, died suddenly at Middleham in the second half of April. Born probably in the summer of 1476, he could not have been eight years old. What made matters worse was that Richard and Anne were absent at the time, being resident at Nottingham, which suggests they knew nothing of any illness in their son. Both parents were agonized with grief, and the Crowland chronicler, who could have been an eyewitness, described them as 'almost out of their minds for a long time'. Local tradition records that Richard ever after called Nottingham castle his 'Castle of Care', in a probable reference to Langland's *Piers Plowman*:

> 'Tis the Castle of Care; whoso cometh therein
> May mourn that he born was, in body or soul.

Suddenly a king without a dynasty, Richard's security on the throne evaporated. What was worse, in all likelihood Queen Anne was herself delicate; by the following January she was described as seriously ill. Possibly her condition was exacerbated by the death of their son on whom all hopes had centred.

To resolve the problem of the succession, Richard was reported by the chronicler John Rous to have chosen as heir his nephew, Clarence's son Edward, Earl of Warwick, then aged nine: 'He was proclaimed heir apparent [*sic*] in the royal court, and in ceremonies at table and chamber he was served first after the king and queen. Later he was placed in custody and the Earl of Lincoln was preferred to him.'[23]

Warwick was actually placed in custody by Henry VII, not Richard III, and for this and many other reasons Rous invites little confidence in his jottings. Perhaps his claim for Warwick merely reflects his desire to give prominence to the family of his patrons. It was Richard's loyal nephew John, Earl of Lincoln, then in his early twenties, who constituted his next legitimate male heir. John was certainly destined by Richard for great things, being created King's Lieutenant in Ireland, a significant appointment within the York establishment, and a position held until recently by the Prince of Wales.

John was also made president of Richard's newly created Council of the North, a body that was essentially a continuation of his original ducal council, providing an enduring legacy for the governance of those troubled parts and lasting for over 150 years. Richard's good rule of the borders was remembered long after his day as an outstanding model of efficiency. Regrettably his creation of the council had the side-effect of alienating the powerful Earl of Northumberland, who felt his family's local feudal rights had been superseded. Northumberland's resentment went back many years to the days of Edward IV and he proved, to Richard's cost, to be one of those magnates who remained equivocal about the new régime.

On the diplomatic front, having concluded a three-year truce with Scotland, Richard was deep in dialogue with Francis II, Duke of Brittany, who had facilitated Henry Tudor's invasion and was still harbouring rebels. A complicated tussle for power was in progress which involved Burgundy and France, under its new king Charles VIII, as well as England and Brittany. Eventually Brittany's treasurer, Pierre Landais, took the initiative during the duke's illness and sought an accommodation with Richard, which included placing Tudor under strict surveillance if not actually in custody. It began to look as if he might be handed over to England.

There is an expression 'the luck of the devil', and Henry Tudor seemed amply supplied with it. Forewarned of this plan, he fled from Brittany in September 1484, only an hour's ride ahead of pursuers sent to detain him. Bishop John Morton, in Flanders, had learned of the negotiations from agents at Westminster and sent word to Tudor to seek asylum in France. The suggestion of engaging Charles VIII's support had already been secretly urged by William Collingbourne and John Turberville, who were executed for treason as a result. Collingbourne was famously responsible for the insolent rhyme about Richard and three of his advisers (William Catesby, Sir Richard Ratcliffe and Francis, Viscount Lovell): 'The Cat, the Rat and Lovell our Dog, Rule all England under an Hog.' (The dog and the boar were, respectively, the badges of Lovell and Richard III.)

Richard at this time probably still made the mistake of viewing Tudor as little more than an opportunist who had attempted to ride the coat-tails of the October rebellion, and been sent ignominiously scuttling with his tail between his legs. Figures like Henry were routinely used as pawns in the cut and thrust of international politics, and seldom rose to any significance. Indeed, Michael K. Jones is inclined to view his ultimate success, and even his later support by France, as a sheer accident of timing.[24]

An important indication of Richard's attitude is that he made no move to find a safe husband for Elizabeth of York. Not that he failed to consider the topic of marriage; he was busy enough finding good matches for his own illegitimate daughter, Katherine (whom he married to William Herbert, Earl of Huntingdon, in early 1484) and for Elizabeth's next sister, Cecily (who married Ralph, later Lord Scrope of Upsall, probably in the same year). Admittedly it would have been tricky to find the right match, in view of Elizabeth's elevated rank combined with her illegitimate status, but Richard was the king after all, and had enormous incentives to offer. Had it been a question of spiking a serious threat, one would think it would be worth any price. On the contrary, Richard Plantagenet, scion of kings, acted all along as if he felt Henry Tudor was simply beneath his notice.

★ ★ ★

In October Bishop Morton, aided by Lord Stanley, was again subverting the security of his home country; this time by suborning desertion by a group of English officers at Hammes castle, where a dangerous Lancastrian, the former Earl of Oxford, had been imprisoned by Edward IV. Ordered to transport the earl back to England, the group instead betook themselves to join the last dregs of Lancastrian sympathizers gathered around Henry Tudor.

Not only were Richard's efforts undermined at home: the Duke of Brittany kindly allowed the rest of Henry's followers to join him in France, and by mid-October they were ensconced at the French court. In November Tudor received 3,000 livres to help array his men, just one more instalment after long years of taking money from foreign powers (his uncle Jasper Tudor had been a pensioner of Louis XI since the 1460s).

During Henry's sojourn in Brittany, in 1481–2 Duke Francis had been spending the sum of 2,000 livres a year on Henry's household expenses, with 620 assigned for his own use. By October 1482 Henry's personal allowance had increased to a handsome 2,200 a year. For the flotilla of October 1483, Francis had handed over 13,000 livres for wages and provisions, plus a loan of 10,000 *écus d'or*. Later, in March 1484, he had laid out more wads of cash for another six ships and 890 men, although these preparations came to nothing. By June he was supporting Henry's entourage in Vannes to the tune of 3,100 livres, guaranteeing their credit in the city, and handing out cash to individuals including Dorset (400 a month) and Edward Woodville (100 a month). When the group eventually left for France, he gave them another 708 livres to see them on their way.

These are just a few of the sums mentioned by Griffiths and Thomas in their survey of Tudor activities.[25] Such largesse is not handed out without expectations, and Breton mischief-making was nothing when compared to the territorial ambitions of the French, who had effectively renewed hostilities with England after rescinding the Treaty of Picquigny in 1482. Although money was not thrown at the exiles with quite such abandon in France, nevertheless Charles VIII provided, among other loans, a massive 40,000 livres for their planned invasion, and Tudor was able to borrow yet more elsewhere. If there was any room for equivocation previously, there could now be no doubt that Henry Tudor, by throwing in his lot with England's ancient enemies, was no longer merely a malcontent exile but a traitor.

Griffiths and Thomas confirm that on 30 October 1483 he was signing himself 'Henry de Richemont'. Things were different the following year, when with even less legality he started using the signature 'Henricus Rex'. 'The flight to France and the quickening pace towards invasion produced a change of attitude and style. According to the Burgundian chronicler, Jean Molinet, he was now urged by the earl of Oxford and, from England, by Lord Stanley to use the title of king.'[26]

What ensued was an example of the kind of blatant deception Henry Tudor would later employ, on seizing the throne, to give his position a spurious legitimacy. Although he was doubtless egged on by Lancastrian partisans (and probably his mother), the true fact is that Tudor adopted the royal pose as part of the price he paid for French support. The ruling party in France, in the face of growing internal criticism of foreign policy, demanded that Henry portray himself as something of greater appeal to the French than an undistinguished rebel who had promised to marry an English princess whom their own dauphin had spurned. Michael K. Jones writes:

> In November 1484, the minority government of Charles VIII formally approved Henry's claim as king and promised its backing. Yet astonishingly his right to that position was deemed to be that he was a younger son of the murdered Lancastrian King Henry VI. ... They were also fully aware that Henry VI had no son other than his sole heir, cut down in the aftermath of the battle of Tewkesbury. Tudor was therefore being asked to play the part of a pretender.
>
> The cost of French support quickly became apparent. Tudor's next action was to circulate a letter for potential allies in England. In it, the normally cautious claimant took an unusual step, laying claim to the throne directly and asking for support for a planned invasion. ... It was not enough for the French régime to announce the arrival of a son of Henry VI. They wanted to show Henry Tudor, their adopted pretender, now acting the part. A

confident assertion of kingship was required. So Henry wrote as if he were already king of England, about to return to what was rightfully his.[27]

The letter, which was in the nature of a round robin, seems to date from November 1484. It ran as follows (note the royal signature):

> Right trusty, worshipful and honourable good friends, and our allies, I greet you well. Being given to understand your good devoir and entreaty to advance me to the furtherance of my rightful claim, due and lineal inheritance of that crown, and for the just depriving of that homicide and unnatural tyrant which now unjustly bears dominion over you, I give you to understand that no Christian heart can be more full of joy and gladness than the heart of me your poor exiled friend, who will, upon the instant of your sure advertising what power you will make ready and what captains and leaders you get to conduct, be prepared to pass over the sea with such force as my friends here are preparing for me. And if I have such good speed and success as I wish, according to your desire, I shall ever be most forward to remember and wholly to requite this your great and moving loving kindness in my just quarrel. Given under our signet. H.[28]

On 6 December Richard ordered the arrest and punishment of distributors of such letters. On 7 December he issued a proclamation against the Tudor party. This was his first recognition of Henry's challenge for the crown.[29] In it he named their leaders as Bishop Courtenay of Exeter, the Marquess of Dorset (who had not yet tried to defect), Jasper Tudor, the attainted Earl of Oxford and Sir Edward Woodville. It castigated them in regal fashion for choosing as their captain Henry Tudor, 'late calling himself Erle of Richemond', who had the temerity to take upon himself 'the name and title of Royalle estate of this Royaulme of England', to which he had 'noo manere interresse righte or coloure as every mane wele knowethe'.

Historians have described Richard's proclamations as 'propaganda' and 'character-assassination', and have derided his 'holier-than-thou' pronouncements as hypocrisy. Of course, proclamations were street advertisements aimed at people of all levels, from the sophisticated to the ignorant, and overblown language was standard. This one spoke of the named exiles as traitors, murderers, adulterers and extortioners, and in all conscience it is difficult to disagree with those characterizations.

For a start, they were self-evidently traitors to rebel against their anointed king. Both Jasper Tudor and the former Earl of Oxford had murders on their hands, having raised forces and arbitrarily put men to death without legal authority. Oxford was a Lancastrian rebel and military leader who had fought against Edward IV (and Richard) at Barnet; both brothers had lost valued friends in that battle. The crime of extortion could legitimately be levelled at Oxford, who had *inter alia* committed many acts of marine piracy in the summer of 1473, whence arose his incarceration at Hammes; and Edward Woodville had extorted (to our knowledge) £10,250 in English gold coin from a carrack in Southampton Water. No doubt Richard had had to deal with the furious claims of the deprived owner.

As to adulterers, the Marquess of Dorset had already been named as such in Richard's October 1483 proclamation against those rebels who gathered traitorously to breach the peace of the realm, destroy the king and his subjects and damnably to indulge in vices and sins. Among Dorset's extra-marital activities he was known to have shamelessly 'devoured, deflowered and defouled' sundry maids, widows and wives. Making allowances for alliteration, one cannot argue with these accusations: even Domenico Mancini knew that Edward IV and his Woodville cronies had seduced women both married and unmarried, noble and lowly, and that Dorset was one of the 'panders who aided and abetted his lustfulness'.

We have noted previously that in mediæval times the sins of lust and adultery were viewed with severity. The seriousness of Richard's more moral approach is reflected in actions such as the circular he wrote in March 1484, addressed to his bishops, demonstrating that in his role as king he was committed to his princely duty of encouraging virtuous living and seeking the reform of sinners. Perhaps his aim was to signal a deliberate break with the past.

Another important point raised by Richard in his 1484 proclamation was Henry Tudor's indebtedness to the King of France. Again it is impossible to fault the logic of his warning that France would demand concessions if Henry ever came to power, including the relinquishing of England's ancient claim to the crown of that country together with her claims to Normandy, Gascony, Guienne, Calais, Guisnes and Hammes. When the proclamation was repeated in June 1485, the duchies of Anjou and Maine were added to the list.

All these predictions would come to pass in the reigns of the Tudors – Henry VII, his son and his grandchildren – with the last territory lost being Calais under Queen Mary Tudor. Indeed, one of Henry's earliest actions as king would be to sign a truce with France, which he renewed while standing by as Brittany collapsed under French aggression. Though Sir Edward Woodville launched an expedition in aid of his old benefactor Duke Francis, Henry Tudor was quick to assure the French ambassador it was not authorized by him. Effectively, Francis had signed his duchy's death warrant by supporting Henry Tudor against Richard III. By the time Henry sent a token few thousand men in 1489, Sir Edward had been killed and Brittany had already capitulated. By way of thanks, France repaid its friend and protégé by promoting the pretender 'Perkin Warbeck' to challenge him.

* * *

In Richard's reissued proclamation on 23 June 1485 there were some notable changes, the first being that Dorset's name was deleted after his attempt to become reconciled. To emphasize Henry's lack of status, he was now pointedly identified as plain 'Henry Tydder, son of Edmond Tydder, son of Owen Tydder'. The text expounded on Henry's 'bastard blood bothe of ffather side and of mother side', correctly giving his mother's descent from the adultery of Katherine Swynford, née Roët. But it seemed to miss the mark by claiming that the paternal bastardy arose from Henry's grandfather, Owen Tudor. Perhaps it did; but the more obvious bastardy was that of his father, Edmund, who was born before the marriage of his parents had been regularized. This scathing dismissal of Tudor's lineage ended with the undeniable conclusion that as a consequence, no title could vest in him.

Other dire predictions followed, and were none the less true for being obvious: i.e. that Tudor had already carved up England's honours and high offices for his friends and supporters, and that he would subvert existing laws and introduce new ones. Richard could scarcely have realized how close he came once more to the truth when he spoke of murder, slaughter, robbery and disinheritance, all of which England would see aplenty under the heel of the Tudors.

Doubtless Henry's spurious claim to have a lineal right to the throne undermined his credentials with his Yorkist followers. Not only were they acutely aware of his suspect bloodline (they scarcely needed Richard III to tell them), but they would also detect in this unexpected claim 'the spectre,' as Michael K. Jones puts it, 'of the discredited Lancastrian dynasty'. This course of action, he adds, 'ran so contrary to his interests that it could only have been forced on him by the French'.

Moreover, once Henry Tudor proclaimed himself king in 1484 by right of lineage, he had no further interest in Elizabeth of York; which attitude is made abundantly clear by the absence of any reference whatsoever in this year's letter to last year's solemn promise to marry Edward IV's daughter and thus commingle the blood of two dynasties. It mattered little that all the daughters (and their mother) were presently in the control of Richard III: the overthrow of the king had always been a prerequisite for Tudor's plans. And in November 1484, Elizabeth at eighteen and Cecily at sixteen still remained enticingly unmarried.

Naturally Tudor's blatant imposture, and the cynical shifting of position it entailed, finds no place in the writings of his fan club of chroniclers and historians. Nonetheless, it might well have contributed to the reasons why Dorset and others sought to abandon Henry and reconcile with Richard.

Barbarians at the Gates

At the Christmas celebrations of 1484 it must have been obvious to both Richard and his queen that she was now in the grip of a terminal illness.

Many authorities tend to the view that she might have suffered from tuberculosis, a wasting disease of which the onset would have been noticed months earlier, and which also presented a danger of infection.

Nevertheless the expectations of the Court and its illustrious guests must be met during the calendar's foremost festival of good cheer. Richard also had to provide a suitable welcome to the daughters of his late brother, and Elizabeth of York in particular, at nearly nineteen years old, needed to feel she still had a place at Court. Possibly Queen Anne Neville thought to take her under her wing, for it was remarked that the two young women were presented with several items of clothing of similar colour and style.

This was too much for the waspish chronicler of Crowland who remarked, 'At this people began to talk, and the lords and prelates were horrified.' He had already deplored the Christmas dancing and festivity.[1]

Conspicuous display was a prerequisite among royalty and the high nobility, and was recognized as part of their role to impress and inspire awe. This applied equally to the preparation and consumption of food, to ownership of jewels, fine objects, birds of prey, hounds and horses, to largesse, charitable and religious outlay and to magnificent robes and liveries. Richard well understood the need for opulence, and at this time of straitened circumstances he even sold a few items to enable the holy festival to be celebrated in appropriate style.

It was a traditional feature of mediæval courtly circles, both in England and in other countries, that an entire household would be dressed up for certain feast days in exactly the same colours: massive amounts of similar cloth would be purchased and made up into garments for everyone. To take it a step further, on lengthy festivals such as Christmas the king and his male family members might dress all in one colour on certain predetermined days, and all in another colour on other days. Similarly, the queen and her female family members would complement the changes in the men's outfits by appearing in their own chosen colour.

Other Court frivolities often consisted of 'disguisings', and the Latin here (*vanisque mutatoriis vestium*) could mean that the similarity in clothing was intended playfully to confuse the identities of Anne and Elizabeth.

At Christmas the previous year the royal couple had run up a mercer's bill of some £1,200, so costly garments were nothing new at Richard's Court. Nor, indeed, at that of his late brother, whose avant-garde fashions at Christmas 1482 were manifestly admired by our chronicler of Crowland. But if Edward could do no wrong, Richard could do no right.

At Court, every detail of Elizabeth's appearance would have been picked over minutely: too much finery and she was being elevated above her station, too little and she was being disparaged. If the two young women found diversion from their respective cares by wearing similar garments and playing games of pretence, it seems churlish to look for sinister motives. But evidently there were those at Court who read a special meaning into the increased attention paid to Elizabeth. Royal attendants and courtiers were politicians to an even greater degree than they are today, and the politics of Richard's Court in December 1484 were dominated by the illness of the queen and the question of the succession. On such pivotal matters hung many people's future careers. Thus all aspects of behaviour in royal circles would be analysed remorselessly, conclusions would be drawn and portents assumed.

As the freezing days of January dragged on, Anne 'became seriously ill,' says Crowland, 'and her weakness was supposed to get ever worse as the king entirely shunned his wife's bed. It was his doctors' advice to do so, he declared.'[2] Crowland is here inviting us to share the view that Richard in this way deliberately attempted to hasten her death. But the bedroom activities of princes were public knowledge, and this king was supposedly the consummate dissembler. Even the most diehard anti-Richard can recognize how foolish it would have been for him to invite apprehension and rumour-mongering by such a withdrawal unless a genuine risk to his own health were involved.

Inevitably fears for the queen were manifold, and would be linked to any perceived signs of Elizabeth of York's elevation, so as Anne grew weaker the speculation grew stronger. The king must obviously seek a new wife. He was young and capable of fathering many heirs. Maybe he already had his eye on the young Elizabeth. And, into the bargain, wouldn't it conveniently prevent her from marrying the upstart Henry Tudor? The moment this happy combination of ideas took hold, a ready-made rumour was born: 'It became common gossip,' the Crowland chronicler gloats, 'that the king was bent on marrying Elizabeth at all costs.'

By contrast with his previous meticulous reporting, in this particular section the Crowland chronicler's chronology is all over the place, which gives us another clue as to his preoccupations: he has other interests in mind than relating a straightforward narrative.

Immediately beforehand he describes Richard's foreign policy success in forcing Scotland to sue for peace some months earlier; then he moves on to the Christmas festival at Westminster. Next the king showed himself at Epiphany (6 January) in a lavish crown-wearing ceremony, when he was dramatically given intelligence that his enemies would attempt an invasion that summer. Richard wished for no better news than this, the chronicler says, since he believed it would settle the matter once and for all; and immediately he began to raise finances to meet the invasion. Here the writer resumes his mantle of disapproval, alleging extortion of 'great sums of money from the coffers of persons of almost every rank in the kingdom, by prayers or threats, by fair means or foul'.[3] However, although Crowland would have us believe Richard resorted to those hated benevolences which he had himself outlawed, the records show that funds raised from merchants were not treated as gifts but as loans, for which he gave 'good and sufficient pledges'; for other monies raised he set specific dates for repayment.

And now the lamentations start:

> O Lord, why should we dwell longer on this, multiplying accounts of things unbefitting which were so numerous they can hardly be counted; it is not expedient that the minds of the faithless should be filled with such things – such evil examples. There are many other things besides, which are not written in this book and of which it is grievous to speak.

This discredits Richard while telling us precisely nothing, but we do know he is unhappy with the way the king went about filling his war-chest. Indeed, the very obfuscation of the language suggests the resentment of one who has found himself a reluctant contributor. He seems not to resent the invaders who have occasioned such contributions.

Next, suddenly, the chronicler leaves the events of January–February 1485 in order to go back and recount the immoderate gaiety of the Christmas festival, and Richard's intention to contract a marriage with Elizabeth of York 'at all costs'. Thus far he has not mentioned a word of the queen's ill health, so he introduces speculation as to how the king will accomplish this extraordinary marriage: 'either in expectation of the queen's death, or after divorce, for which he thought he had sufficient grounds. He could see no other way of confirming himself as king, nor of putting down the hopes of his rival.'[4]

'Shortly after this,' Crowland continues, as if completing Richard's train of thought, 'the queen became seriously ill.' And so on. This is a clear invitation to connect the dots and come up with the conclusion that Richard did away with his wife so that he could marry his niece.

However, let us deconstruct this passage. Cleverly, the writer starts narrating in retrospect – or, in modern terms, in flashback – which gives him the freedom to take liberties with the time frame. So he is able to emphasize Queen Anne's gaiety and omit all reference to her failing health until Richard has been rumoured to be desirous of her death. Immediately upon that thought, the queen is reported to be seriously ill and the king spurns her bed, claiming doctors' advice. '*Quid plura?*' he ends – 'Need I say more?' – an expression in oratory indicating that the speaker believes he has made his case. Clearly this sequence of events has not only been skewed, but skewed in order to prove a point.

It is possible that the chronicler genuinely believed Richard to be responsible for his wife's death, but he could not have known unless told by her physicians, and the context clearly indicates that he never spoke with them. So his manner of insinuating Richard's guilt is really quite egregious. Respectable modern authorities dismiss the slur, and believe Anne simply died of natural causes. Her death coincided with a great eclipse of the sun on 16 March 1485, and she lies to this day in Westminster Abbey.

In reality, Queen Anne Neville was the very last person Richard would want to harm, since a huge part of his carefully-built empire in the north hinged on his twelve-year marriage with her. Without going into tedious details about inheritances and estates, suffice it to say that much of Richard's status as lord of the north rested on his being seen as the successor to Anne's father, the famous and powerful Earl of Warwick. For their entire married life the couple occupied the place left vacant by Warwick's death, and although Richard was respected for his just and effective administration, when it came to feudal loyalty (which ran deep in those parts) the people's sense of duty to him arose principally through his connection with the earl.

As Richard watched Anne's illness and death, he undoubtedly knew it was a body-blow almost as great as the death of his son and heir. The idea that he would wilfully spurn her bed, spread stories of her death before it happened or even do away with her by poison – all of which were later claimed by the Tudor chroniclers – would be to cut off the main prop of his vital northern support.[5] Moreover, the very fact that these claims existed suggests that Richard embarked on such risky activities so ineptly that people saw through them right away. Whatever happened to the clever propagandist who took everyone in?

As regards the queen's health, doctors would have been called in immediately upon little Edward's death to examine the worrying matter of whether she would ever bear another child. The stars would have been consulted and horoscopes cast. In this way, if no other, the reality of her frail condition would have been known to the inner circle long before it reached the ears of the Crowland chronicler. Such matters could not have been kept confidential for long, and undoubtedly reports led to conjectures, which in turn led to malicious rumours.

It is easy to conclude that the problem of the succession, and the possibility of Richard's remarriage, must have been the dominating topics at every council meeting in the second half of 1484, and more than likely the candidacy of Elizabeth of York was put on the table. Such a marriage would have required papal dispensation but was not, like marriage between aunt and nephew, expressly forbidden. But although not unknown abroad, it would have been abhorred in England. This, indeed, is the salient point. Richard and his advisers would certainly have realized what revulsion such a marriage would engender, and how it would undo all their careful work to reconcile and consolidate his position.

A poignant event took place around now, when Richard, already beset by sorrow at the loss of his heir, realized that he would also soon be bereft of the support of his wife. With the anniversary or 'year-mind' of little Edward's death due within weeks, it was on 11 March, with Anne rapidly failing, that Richard appointed his only known remaining son, his bastard John of Gloucester, as Captain of Calais. His patent for this appointment, like that for Edward of Middleham as Prince of Wales, reflected no small amount of paternal pride in his 'dear bastard son, John of Gloucester, whose disposition and natural vigour, agility of body and inclination to all good customs, promises us by the grace of God great and certain hope of future service'.[6] John did not long survive the rule of Henry Tudor.

* * *

The Crowland chronicler's handling of events from now onwards becomes very suspect, with quantities of mud-slinging in the knowledge that some of it will stick. Consider his remark about the king believing he had grounds for divorce from Anne: this should have been an earth-shattering revelation, yet it is thrown away in a mere handful of words (in contrast to his expatiation on all those nameless horrors of which it was so grievous to speak that he could not bring himself to speak of them).

Did grounds for divorce (or annulment) exist? The idea has given rise to much speculation, especially as it even seemed to be anticipated in the Act of Parliament that facilitated their marriage settlement (see below). Anne was related to Richard by blood (consanguinity) and by marriage (affinity) within degrees prohibited by the Church, so a papal dispensation was required; was this overlooked? Apparently not, for a record of a dispensation in their names on grounds of affinity has now come to light in the Vatican, dated 22 April 1472.[7] This has assisted my research in identifying the probable date of their marriage as February-March 1473 and their son's birth as the summer of 1476.[8] Since their 1472 dispensation omits any mention of their well-known consanguinity, it seems likely that this impediment had been absolved at an earlier date.

The latter possibility has been expounded by Marie Barnfield in an article that elegantly clarifies the intricacies of canon law on marital impediments. Her suggestion is that the Earl of Warwick (the Kingmaker) could have secretly initiated the first dispensation while Richard was in his charge between about 1465 and 1468.[9]

It was reported that Warwick had conceived a plan for his two daughters, Isabel and Anne, to be married to Edward IV's two brothers, Clarence and Gloucester. This was vehemently opposed by Edward, yet Warwick went ahead and applied to Rome for Clarence and Isabel's dispensation, which was granted on 14 March 1468 (a copy survived into the seventeenth century). Hence a papal dispensation might well have been obtained for Gloucester and Anne at the same time. This would have been entirely legal. The Vatican archives have so far yielded no record of either, despite the former being known to exist.

This action would have disposed of any problems of consanguinity at an early date. It was only as a result of Anne's subsequent brief marriage to Henry VI's son Edward, Prince of Wales, that her affinity with Richard arose. Hence the need for a new dispensation limited to this one issue, duly granted in 1472.

Barnfield also explains that this was the only affinity they shared. Despite Michael Hicks's excited claim that Richard entered into an incestuous marriage and intended to become a 'serial incestor',[10] no affinity resulted from the union of two brothers with two sisters.

Regarding the Act of Parliament mentioned above, Marie Barnfield suggests an unrelated technicality in canon law. Richard famously sought Anne in 1472, eventually discovering her in hiding in the guise of a kitchen-maid. Clarence claimed the rights of guardian over Anne after her husband's death in the battle of Tewkesbury, and clearly regarded her disposal (and that of her fortune) as his to determine. When Richard found her, removed her to sanctuary and later married her, this could possibly have been categorized as 'abduction' by the Church.

Barnfield notes that in 1473, still attempting to wrest back the gains won by Richard through the marriage, Clarence did in fact charge that it was invalid because Richard forced Anne's consent. Hence the interesting clause in the ensuing Act of Parliament which spiked his guns by stipulating that even if the union itself should be annulled, Richard would keep a life interest in her estates.

The Crowland continuator mentions none of this, despite the chronicle having written of the brothers' dispute in its account of the 1470s; perhaps he remained silent because he knew the charge was open to question, especially as Anne was evidently a willing bride. Furthermore, in 1485, an annulment instigated by Richard on grounds of abduction or statutory rape seems remote in the extreme.

In another suspect claim, our chronicler of Crowland contradicts himself by asserting that Richard saw 'no other way' of confirming his crown and confounding his rival than by marrying his niece. Yet only a few lines earlier he has reported Richard's eager anticipation of his enemies' invasion, and his confidence that it will settle the matter once and for all. This scarcely chimes with his being so desperate that the incestuous marriage was his only solution, and that he was prepared to murder his wife to accomplish it.

Another important consideration must also be examined at this point: the status of Elizabeth herself. Although she now had a place at Court, the law of the land still held her as a bastard child of a bigamous marriage. A royal bastard, certainly, but of no dynastic significance under the current régime. For a marriage to Elizabeth to confer legitimacy on Richard required a prodigious contortion of logic achievable only by the kind of thinking that presumed to legitimate Henry Tudor by the same means.

On the contrary, in Richard's case it would send a clear message that he felt his own entitlement to be inadequate, while at the same time casting doubt on whether the bastardization of Edward IV's children had been valid. If Elizabeth were legitimated in the process, what status would it confer upon Edward V?

Here we come to another conspicuous fact that rules out her usefulness as a bride: with effect from the previous November, Henry Tudor was claiming the throne by lineal right. Elizabeth featured nowhere in his advertised plans. Though hindsight has taught us that the marriage touted in 1483 did eventually take place, and Tudor propaganda has encouraged the notion that the intent all along was to 'join the House of York with the House of Lancaster', the truth of the matter is that in Henry's current stratagems Elizabeth was an irrelevance. Bearing this in mind, and considering the odium Richard would have invited by a marriage to his bastard niece, the rumour that he planned to make her his wife can be seen for the trumpery it was. (Nevertheless, it so beguiled Jean Molinet that he told his readers that Elizabeth was made pregnant by Richard and had a child by him.)

To follow the Crowland narration to its conclusion, we soon see a subtle transmutation of rumour ('it became common gossip' that the king wanted to marry his niece) into fact: 'In the end the king's earnest intention of marrying his niece Elizabeth reached the ears of people who wanted no such thing'.

Before we move on to look at this opposition, there is an interesting circumstance to examine. In Polydore Vergil's account of the death of Richard's queen (which is notable for the strength of its language in condemning his dastardly wickedness for hastening her demise), we learn that Richard has lamented her childlessness to 'many noble men'. Chief among these, we are astonished to hear, is none other than Thomas Rotherham, the Archbishop of York whom he imprisoned in 1483 for plotting with Lord Hastings. Vergil says that Richard confided in the archbishop because he was a grave and good man. These pointers to Richard's urge for reconciliation are all too often overlooked. Unfortunately, if you open your heart to your enemy, you stand a good chance that your confidences will be used against you; and this, according to Vergil, is precisely what happened.

Rotherham immediately spread the whisper that the queen was not long for this world. His reward was to be appointed Henry Tudor's first chancellor.

On the grounds that the motivations of Elizabeth *mère* may be inferred from her past actions, a number of commentators suggest she connived at marrying her daughter to Richard. This is a perfectly reasonable hypothesis, although we need not go so far as to believe that Richard was persuaded by the idea. There is, however, a simple reason why I believe that Elizabeth Woodville neither promoted nor supported the marriage, but first let us look at a controversial piece of evidence which has long muddied the waters.

In his *History of King Richard III* Sir George Buc wrote that he had seen, in the collection of his patron, the Earl of Arundel, a letter written by Elizabeth of York to the Duke of Norfolk towards the end of February 1485 which, as read by Buc, seemed to ask Norfolk to help facilitate her union with the king, whom she described as 'her only joy and maker'.

It has, however, been suggested that it might have been misread and misconstrued, not because any historian has made an avoidable mistake, but on grounds put forward by Buc's editor, Arthur Kincaid, that Buc himself might have misunderstood its contents.

The difficulties presented by Buc's text are discussed elsewhere (see Appendix); suffice to say here that Dr Kincaid's edition was the first truly reliable work of scholarship which redeemed it from the disdain in which it had been held owing to shameful adulteration of the original text. Let us first look at the relevant passage as transcribed and punctuated by Kincaid in his 1979–82 editions, then consider his correspondence with Dr Alison Hanham in *The Ricardian* in 1987–88, after which he re-examined Buc's text and proposed a new reading in 2023:

> [the Lady Eli]zabeth, being very desirous to be married, and growing not only impatient of delays, but also suspicious of the [success], wrote a letter to Sir John Howard, Duke of Norfolk. ... First she thanked him for his many courtesies and friendly [offices, an]d then she prayed him as before to be a mediator for her in the cause of [the marriage] to the k[i]ng, who, as she wrote, was her only joy and maker in [this] world, and that she

was his in heart and in thoughts, in [body,] and in all. And then
she intimated that the better half of Fe[bruary] was past, and that
she feared the queen would nev[er die.] And all these be her own
words, written with her own hand, and this is the sum of [her]
letter, whereof I have seen the autograph ... etc.[11]

Alison Hanham highlighted the dilemma posed by this letter 'of
such startling import' – supposedly seen once but now apparently
lost – 'amazingly indiscreet and out of character, one would think,
with what is known of Elizabeth in later life'. But she was content
to assume that the letter had existed: 'I think we may take it that, as
A.N. Kincaid argued, Buc had seen and handled a letter like the one
he describes. He would never have risked destroying his credibility
by claiming that his patron owned a non-existent manuscript.'
She then postulated the explanation that Buc, in writing his book,
might have misinterpreted the contents of the letter he had seen
at some earlier date, and added his own gloss in the light of his
knowledge of Richard's alleged plans to marry Elizabeth of York.
In Hanham's view the original letter might never have referred to
marriage, since the only words mentioning the topic ('in the cause
of the marriage') were an authorial alteration added by Buc in the
process of revision. Without those words the letter would merely
request the Duke of Norfolk to mediate for her with the king, the
subject of such mediation not being indicated.[12]

Dr Hanham then dealt with what might be construed as
effusive expressions of devotion on Elizabeth's part by pointing
out that, in terms of her circumstances in early 1485, 'Richard was
indeed her best hope of worldly fortune ("her only joy and maker
in [this] world"), since he controlled the provision of a suitable
marriage. ... Describing someone as one's "only joy" carried no
necessary amatory connotations.' The phrases concerning her
wholehearted obedience to the king's wishes ('his in heart', etc.)
might well occur, she explained, in the valedictory clause of a
fifteenth-century letter.

As for the reference to the queen, this might have been a
postscript. 'And Elizabeth could have benefited from her death in
other ways than by marrying the widower. One possibility is that
lands would be released in order to furnish her marriage portion.'
Assuming the word 'die' was correctly remembered and recorded
by Buc, an alternative explanation may be that Elizabeth, having

been drawn to Anne in recent months, might have prayed for her early release from the torments of a protracted illness.

Dr Kincaid's response took on board much of what Alison Hanham suggested. But from the very position occupied by the letter within the text, which was in a lengthy section discussing Anne's death and Richard's alleged plans to remarry, he felt it was clear Buc always thought the letter supported the argument that any plan for their marriage met with general approval.[13]

However, after re-examining the passage in the manuscript, Kincaid offered what he felt might be a more informed conjecture as to what the original letter said, and how it could have been misinterpreted by Buc on a more subtle level: 'Elizabeth in her letter was referring to a hoped-for marriage,' he concluded, 'though not necessarily with the king.' A more modern punctuation, inserting commas before and after the words 'in the cause of the marriage', would suggest that Norfolk is being entreated to mediate with the king about an unidentified plan of marriage, such a plan being already understood between Elizabeth and the duke. In other words, Buc could have confused 'mediator to the king' with 'marriage to the king'. Some years later Kincaid returned to the letter when preparing his 2023 edition, and spent several entire days scrutinizing the author's many crossings-out and amendments. He also reproduced the letter itself as an illustration. His reading of what it might really have said now runs something as follows:

> Dear Norfolk, I place my trust in you above all because of my father's love for you, your very faithful service to him and to the king now reigning, and your love and service ever shown to King Edward's children. Thanking you for your many courtesies and friendly offices, I pray you now to be a mediator for me to the king in the cause of my marriage, who is my only joy and maker in this world. I am the king's true subject in heart, in thought, in body and in all, Elizabeth.
>
> P.S. The better part of February is past, and I fear the queen will never die.[14]

So our next question must be: was there a different possibility of marriage on the cards with which Elizabeth might have hoped Norfolk would help her?

There certainly was – for Elizabeth and for Richard. Between March and August 1485 negotiations took place for the king to marry Joana, sister of John II of Portugal. Descended directly from John of Gaunt and his first wife Blanche of Lancaster, Joanna and John were the great-grandchildren of Gaunt's eldest daughter, Philippa, queen to John I (see Table 4). Thus they were at this time the senior heirs to what remained of the house of Lancaster. By marrying Joana, Richard would have elegantly achieved the unity to which Henry Tudor pretended, without shedding a single drop of blood.

As Barrie Williams records:

> On 22 March 1485, only six days after the death of Queen Anne Neville, Richard sent Sir Edward Brampton to Portugal to open negotiations. ... Joanna was sufficiently senior among the descendants of Queen Philippa to offer some hope that, as Queen of England, traditional Lancastrian loyalties might become attached to her rather than to Henry Tudor. She was just eight months older than Richard. At thirty-three, she was above the age at which queens usually marry, though not too old for a king's second marriage. Nor was she too old to bear her first child. Brampton brought a double proposal to Portugal – for Richard to marry Joanna, and for Elizabeth of York to marry John II's cousin Manuel, Duke of Beja (later King Manuel I).[15]

Negotiations were brought to a climax in August 1485, Williams continues, when Joana, known as the Holy Princess for her piety, retired for a night of prayer and meditation.

> A dramatic dénouement followed. ... She had either a vision or a dream of a 'beautiful young man' who told her that Richard 'had gone from among the living'. Next morning, she gave her brother a firm answer: If Richard were still alive, she would go to England and marry him. If he were indeed dead, the King was not to press her again to marry. It is not necessary to believe in the supernatural to accept that Joanna might have had a premonitory dream of Richard's death. Within days of her decision, news of Bosworth reached Portugal.

Williams makes an important point when he emphasizes that for events during this period English history is too heavily dependent on Polydore Vergil.

> Whether [Vergil] knew of the negotiations is doubtful; if he did, he kept silence, realising perhaps that they undermined the picture he was trying to paint of Richard III. ... [A]lthough these negotiations extended over five months of a twenty-six month reign, they receive no mention in Paul Murray Kendall's biography. In Charles Ross's more recent work, Portugal is not even mentioned in the index despite a whole chapter devoted to Richard's foreign policy. This, surely, is carrying English insularity to absurd lengths.

Another pertinent observation is that the Portuguese marriage negotiations raise some serious questions over the interpretation of Richard III.

> The Portuguese were under considerable pressure in 1485; John II could be a ruthless monarch, a worthy contemporary of Ferdinand of Aragon. But it strains credulity that the King and his Council of State should have tried to coerce Joanna into marrying a blood-stained usurper; still less that she, albeit under pressure and conditionally, should have accepted him when she had already refused Maximilian of Austria and Charles, Duke of Orleans. It was not that the court in Portugal could have been unaware of events in England. Portuguese ambassadors were in England in the summer of 1484 when they renewed the Treaty of Windsor with Richard III.

Recalling that an envoy had been simultaneously sent to Spain where another possible marriage was discussed, for Richard and the Infanta Isabella, Barrie Williams pursues his argument:

> Whatever pressure was upon Portugal in 1485, no such constraint was on Spain. Yet apparently Ferdinand and Isabella were as willing that Richard should marry their eldest daughter as John II that he should marry his sister. The attitude of the Kings of Spain and Portugal is the best testimonial we have to Richard's character. It should carry far more weight than the gossip and

rumour circulating in England and France which has been unduly
regarded by historians.

It certainly seems bizarre that such quantities of ink have been spilt
over Richard's unsubstantiated desire to marry his bastard niece,
when documentary evidence exists to show that he was actually
negotiating with two leading foreign powers for royal matches
that (unlike the incestuous marriage) would have forged alliances
of significant benefit to England. Looking at the corollary, how
likely is it that Richard would have made approaches to Spain
and Portugal – who must have responded to quiet soundings, in
the sad knowledge of Anne's condition, long before the despatch
of official embassies – if both he and his niece were likely to be
withdrawn simultaneously and peremptorily from the marriage
market? We have already noted that Isabella of Spain informed
him in no uncertain terms that she still felt herself to have been
insulted by Edward IV when he married an English commoner
while expressing interest in her own hand in 1464.

To return to the letter seen by Buc, I published my theory in
the first edition of this book (2008) explaining Elizabeth's urging
of Howard to mediate with her uncle regarding her marriage
prospects. Now aged nineteen, she had passed the age at which
a girl expected to become a wife, and was undoubtedly bored
with the limited pastimes currently available to her. Assuming
that Richard had held many discussions with his council on
the problem of Anne's health, by February it must have been
ascertained that, if the worst happened, both Spain and Portugal
would welcome marriage approaches. Emissaries were thus
waiting to be sent immediately upon her death. It is more
than likely that the prospect of Manuel, a promising young
man aged sixteen, was discussed with Elizabeth at Court over
the Christmas holidays. Indeed overtures might already have
been received from the Portuguese side, and perhaps portraits
exchanged. It has been suggested that the near-contemporaneous
portrait of Richard III in the collection of the Society of
Antiquaries of London (see cover design) might have been taken
from a likeness prepared when the king became a widower and
re-entered the marriage stakes.

Unquestionably Elizabeth Woodville would have been
consulted closely about the match for her daughter which, bearing

in mind Richard's oath to her, could not have reached the stage of official negotiations if she had objected. This is the main reason why I doubt she simultaneously tried to marry the girl to Richard. Thus my reading is that Elizabeth of York's preoccupation, when writing to the Duke of Norfolk in February, was specifically to ask him to argue in favour of the Portuguese alliance, and dissuade Richard from the Spanish match which carried for her no prospect of a husband. It is a reading recently endorsed by Sir George Buc's editor, Dr Arthur Kincaid.[16]

* * *

From the *Crowland Chronicle* we get the next episode in the saga of Richard's supposed incestuous marriage:

> the king was forced to summon the council and exculpate himself by denying profusely that the idea had ever entered his head. But there were men present at that council meeting who well knew the contrary. In point of fact, those who were most strongly against this marriage were two men whose views even the king himself seldom dared oppose: that is, Sir Richard Ratcliff and William Catesby, esquire of the body. These told the king to his face that if he would not relinquish the project (and what is more, personally issue an authoritative denial before the mayor and people of London), the northerners on whom he most relied would rise in a body against him. They would accuse him of killing the queen – the daughter and heiress of the Earl of Warwick, through whom he had first won their regard – in order to indulge an incestuous lust for his brother's daughter, a thing abominable to God. For good measure they brought in more than a dozen doctors of theology, who stated that the pope could not grant a dispensation within this degree of consanguinity. ...
>
> And so, a little before Easter, in the great hall of St John's, and before the mayor and citizens of London, the king made a total repudiation of the whole scheme in a clear and loud voice. But more, people thought, at his advisers' desire than his own.[17]

Note that Ratcliffe and Catesby are not reported as accusing Richard of desiring or hastening the queen's death; they merely warn of people jumping to that conclusion. As for the 'dozen doctors', since a dispensation would have been possible, the Crowland chronicler's memory, to put it kindly, must have been playing tricks. Clearly they were consulted for other reasons (see below).

The entire scene, remember, is set in a meeting of the King's Council, on which, based on previous indications, the writer probably no longer served. He next hides behind hearsay: it was 'thought by many', he says, that Richard's advisers were motivated by fear of an avenging Elizabeth who, once queen, might descend on them for the deaths of her kinsmen Anthony Woodville and Richard Grey. Anyone seeking clues to underlying attitudes may find it particularly significant that no one thought to mention avenging the deaths of her two brothers of the full blood, who were far closer to her than her uncle and half-brother. The omission would seem to speak eloquently for their survival.

The whole matter of the uncle-niece marriage has so perplexed commentators that they are forced to reach for the most unlikely of explanations. One school of thought suggests Richard himself started the rumours in order to discomfit Henry Tudor. To take such an incredible gamble with his own honour and hers, he must have been in conspicuous fear of losing his crown to the pretender. But all the evidence points to the contrary.

Did he fear that Henry Tudor had a better claim to the throne? The idea is laughable, and Richard disposed of it effectively in his proclamations.

Did he fear Tudor would validate his candidacy by taking Elizabeth to wife? Hardly, since Tudor himself had rashly undermined this route by claiming lineal rights instead. Further, Richard now had all his brother's daughters within his power, and a superior marriage with Portugal on the horizon.

Lastly, did Richard fear joining battle with Henry? Not even the most diehard anti-Richard would question his high courage as a fighter and commander. The Crowland chronicler himself admitted he had welcomed the news of an imminent invasion.

The idea of the false rumour spread by Richard to discomfit Tudor fails entirely when we consider the chronology: the public denial was not made until 30 March 1485 whereas we know his emissary Brampton had already been sent to Portugal on 22 March. Any such approach must have been preceded by putting out feelers long before an official delegation was sent, and would have involved lengthy deliberations in council hammering out a foreign policy that evidently involved playing off Portugal against Spain, an extra dimension to the story with implications previously unnoticed by historians before my researches.[18] These marriage plans had clearly been conceived well in advance of Queen Anne's impending death.

The simple explanation is that the prospect of a marriage with his niece never existed. It was probably mentioned on a list of matrimonial avenues open to the king, and was seized upon by the gossips (like Rotherham) who hoped to smear Richard with rumours of lust and murder.

There remains the opposition of Richard's close advisers Ratcliffe and Catesby, who allegedly acted as though desperate to dissuade Richard from a plan already in motion. However, there is little in their reported actions that supports this angle: it is only the Crowland chronicler's gloss.

We have already seen him, within the space of a few lines, changing rumour into fact. Now his description of Richard's statement to the council is loaded to make him appear compelled to rescind a guilty scheme: 'the king was forced to summon the council and exculpate himself by denying profusely that the idea had ever entered his head'. He certainly conjures up a strange picture of the ruthless tyrant grovelling before his own council!

If we remove the prejudicial language and cynical commentary, we are left with something different: the king summoned his council and declared to them that, despite the rumours that were circulating, he had no thoughts of marrying his niece.

To continue with the paraphrase: Ratcliffe and Catesby, whose advice the king relied upon, were concerned to scotch any such perception in the minds of the people, and insisted to his face that a public denial was necessary because the rumours spoke not only of marriage with his niece but of the murder of his wife. They held the latter allegation to be more dangerous since his northern supporters might believe it and turn against him. To prove to the council that marriage with Elizabeth was a non-starter, they brought in doctors of theology to argue against it.

Comparison will show that this alternative is perfectly in tune with the proceedings reported rather more nastily by the chronicler.

The public denial on 30 March took place in the Hospital of St John in Clerkenwell where the Mayor and commons of London were enjoined to ensure that all who spread such sedition should be apprehended and punished. On 19 April Richard's friends in York received a letter informing them of the whispering campaign which the king had seen fit to repudiate, and charging them to take similar measures against the bearers of such false information.

What is most regrettable is that Richard failed to marry Elizabeth quickly to some loyal young man. He must have known she represented a desirable prize to any rebellious faction, yet he allowed a year to pass before settling on a suitable marriage proposition. Buc, among others, accused Richard of underrating his enemies through scorn and contempt, which is probably correct. If Richard's concern was to accord Elizabeth due honour and consideration as merited by her position, it is probable that such sensibility eventually cost him his throne. There is no knowing how far Henry Tudor's support would have persisted had he lost the prospect of a bride from the house of York.

Nevertheless those very rumours soon spread as far as the Tudor camp in France, where the rebels were obviously eager for all news coming from home. Margaret Beaufort, with a husband on Richard's council who knew about the approaches to Spain and Portugal, would not have conveyed misleading rumours to her son; correspondence was probably rare, as it would have been subject to interception. But doubtless many of Henry's co-exiles received versions of the story from their contacts, and hastened to warn him.

Knowing that Cecily, the second sister, was now safely married off, Vergil described Henry as 'pinched by the very stomach' at the thought of Elizabeth marrying Richard, and casting about for another potential wife (more proof, if any were needed, that neither party was bound by any supposed pre-existing betrothal). With the nobility in England still loyal to Richard, his available choices were so few that the best he could manage was an undistinguished sister of William Herbert, Earl of Huntingdon, to whose father Edward IV had granted the wardship of Tudor as a boy. In his childhood the young Henry had been destined as the husband of William's sister Maud, but she was married to the Earl of Northumberland.

Henry now sent messages to Northumberland to intercede on his behalf in an attempt to marry one or other of the remaining sisters, but the letters never reached their destination. Note that it was Tudor himself who initiated the approaches on this occasion, not his mother. This was probably the most foolish move of his entire career, and demonstrates how dependent he was on her more able mind allied with that of Morton. One is tempted to visualize them tearing into him when they heard he had been such an imbecile. On such slight mischances hang the fortunes of princes.

The confidence with which the rebel approached the earl reveals much about his relationship with Northumberland, who had always resented Richard for superseding his former pre-eminence in the north. Thus it is not entirely surprising that he was inactive on the side of his king at the battle of Bosworth.

* * *

The story of Henry Tudor's invasion, his landing in Wales, his march to Bosworth Field, and the betrayal of Richard III by a small group of faithless nobles, is recorded to England's shame in the annals of history.

Doubtless Richard contributed to his own defeat by engaging the enemy before his army was at full strength. Even so, his attempt to settle the matter in ancient chivalric style, hand to hand with the pretender, was close to success until forces at his flank cut him down within sight of his objective – and within sight of winning the day, for there is no question as to who would have emerged the victor had it come to mortal combat.

Those forces belonged to the traitor Sir William Stanley, brother of Thomas, Lord Stanley, who (true to form) had found an excuse not to be present. This point is disputed, but the evidence of his sworn deposition in 1486 clearly states that Thomas Stanley had known Henry Tudor only since two days later, 24 August 1485, although subsequent self-glorification gave him a spuriously prominent role at Bosworth.[19]

As Tudor marched through Wales and England, with his banner raised against his sovereign, his obvious and immediate course of action should have been to issue a proclamation listing Richard's heinous crimes. It speaks volumes that he did no such thing. Instead he sent personal messages to people who had pledged their support, with the imperious heading 'By the King', and referring to Richard III as a 'usurper' of his 'right'; but of any just grievance against the king who sat on England's throne there was no public cry. Nor was there any popular uprising in Wales to bring Welshmen flocking to his banner, though he was aided by some Welsh chieftains who were seduced by his adoption of the dragon of Cadwallader into believing that this half-English, quarter-French, quarter-Welsh stranger from France somehow represented the resurgence of their nation. Their leading chieftain, Rhys ap Thomas, was bribed with the promise of the lieutenantship of Wales and brought men who, together with other arrays gathered en route, swelled Tudor's numbers by perhaps 2,000 men to add to his 4,000 or more brought from France.

No peer of England openly deserted Richard to join Tudor; the invader was actively supported only by those who were already outlawed or enlisted to his cause. Those who abandoned Richard, like the Stanleys, kept their betrayal secret; as did the resentful Earl of Northumberland who failed to ensure that Richard's staunch city of York received his call to arms, and sat silent on the field rather than engage with the Stanley forces.

The battle itself has been re-enacted a million times in theory, in print and on the stage. Now, after several years of research, we have a revised battle site and new insights into aspects such as the use of artillery, plus the poignant discovery of a silver-gilt boar badge almost certainly owned by one of Richard's companions who rode with him in his last desperate mounted charge.

There are many oral traditions about those dramatic events, which have survived in the great families and equally in the humbler communities of England. One such tradition was described in *The Saturday Review* of 13 April 1968 after a meeting in New York City of the Richard III Society Inc, the US branch of the parent Richard III Society in Britain. At this meeting, a reminiscence was offered by Jean di Meglio, who was raised in a hamlet on the edge of that area traditionally known as the site of the battle. She recounted an enduring recollection that under 'King Dick' the country people of those parts had begun to recover from the years of civil strife, and looked forward to reaping the harvest of 1485 which stood tall in the surrounding fields. 'Only when I was nine years old and studying the Wars of the Roses in the village school did I find that he was actually King Richard III,' she explained.

> At the same time I also learned of Henry VII, who until then was known to me only as 'that 'Enry Tudor' who came over the Brockey Fields in August, ruining the ripening wheat, instead of marching his men up Barwell Lane as any decent man would have done. ... The bitterness of their disappointment when Henry Tudor destroyed the crops has lasted for five hundred years.

Tudor made precious little compensation for damage to irreplaceable harvests as his army marched through Wales and England. There are records of only two grants, dated 29 November and 7 December 1485.[20] The one compensates Merevale Abbey, which also sustained damage to the fabric of its buildings at the hands of his men; the other compensates the population of Atherstone and a handful of neighbouring villages. Elsewhere, it seems, people were left to go hungry.

At the end of the battle, with Richard dead and the Tudor forces victorious, there occurred a particularly distasteful desecration of the late king's body. Flung naked and despoiled across the back of a horse, a felon's halter about his neck, he was exhibited uncovered, without mark of dignity, for two days in the city of Leicester.

Though disrespect for the dead may seem insignificant in comparison with the litany of outrages and extortions that would flourish under Henry Tudor's rule, yet this one act seems to linger over the centuries as singularly memorable. People who probably could not name any of those whom the Tudor king judicially murdered are nevertheless repelled by this. Nor can it be claimed as an outrage unauthorized by Henry and perpetrated by his unruly troops, for this was a body that had clearly been identified as England's anointed king. No common soldier would dare to engineer this tableau of disparagement without express permission.

If Edward Hall's account is to be believed, somebody who knew what he was doing sought out one of Richard's heralds after the battle and forced him to ride the horse that carried the disparaged corpse:

> His bodye was naked and despoyled to the skyne, and nothynge left about hym not so muche as a clowte to couer hys pryue members, and was trussed behind a pursiuaunt of armes called blaunche senglier or whyte bore, lyke a hogge or a calfe, the hed and armes hangynge on the one syde of the horse, and the legges on the other syde, and all by spryncled with myre and bloude.[21]

In the age of chivalry, and in the very year when Caxton published Malory's *Morte d'Arthur* with its uplifting theme of knightly virtue and purity, England found itself under the heel of a king whose very first act was one of calculated barbarity.

By contrast, Richard III's end would prove to represent England's last personification of monarchy as the fount of high courage and chivalry: the last king leading his men shoulder to shoulder in battle, but more than that, attempting to curtail the bloodshed by settling the outcome in single combat.

★ ★ ★

Following the battle, Richard III's body was brought to Leicester where he was immediately exposed to public view for two or three days (probably at 'the Newarke', the College of the Annunciation of St Mary), so that all should know of his defeat and death. According to the priest John Rous, and as confirmed elsewhere, Richard was 'ultimately' (*finaliter*) buried by the Franciscans, known as the Greyfriars, in their church near the Guildhall. Rous added that his grave was situated in the choir, the area between the nave and the altar, as would be expected for a person of such rank. Vergil reported that his body was 'buryed two days after without any pompe or solemne funerall'.

For the next ten years Richard's burial place remained unmarked. But by 1495 the Tudor king evidently considered it appropriate to provide a tomb for his former sovereign, and steps were taken to commission a Nottingham alabasterman, Walter Hylton, to erect a monument 'in the Church of Friers'. A budget of £50 was allowed, but a dispute arose over the contract and it is unknown whether Hylton's £50 project was completed as planned. The sole record of payment dates from September 1495 when one James Keyley was paid £10 1s 'for King Richard tombe'. No detailed description of this tomb exists, but it was a 'fair monument' of 'mingled colour, marble' (for 'marble' read 'alabaster'), with a recumbent figure of Richard, the effigy probably provided by Keyley. A Latin inscription, phrased as if in Richard's voice, celebrated Henry's magnanimity in providing it and requested prayers for his soul (as later translated) 't'atone my crimes and ease my pains below'.

In 1538, during Henry VIII's dissolution of the religious houses, the Franciscan friars were expelled. Tombs in these neglected and roofless buildings, unless moved elsewhere by caring relatives, usually suffered ruin and eventually their superstructures disappeared. After standing for 43 years, Richard's memorial could well have disintegrated in this way.

In due course the friary site was acquired by the Herrick family. Robert Herrick, a former Mayor of Leicester, constructed a house and laid out a garden which is shown in old maps of the town. In this garden, in 1612, Sir Christopher Wren's father, who was then tutor to Herrick's nephew (the poet Robert Herrick), saw and recorded 'a handsome stone pillar, three foot high', inscribed with the words 'Here lies the Body of Richard III, some time King of England', which had been erected by Alderman Herrick to mark the location of Richard's resting place.[22]

At the same time there grew up dubious stories claiming his grave had been deliberately desecrated, tales that were unknown prior to the seventeenth century. Many Ricardians, including this author, saw no reason to doubt that Wren was an entirely reliable reporter, and that Herrick knew and accurately commemorated the site where Richard's body lay. When this book was published in 2008, my personal research over several years had led me to state (on p. 270) that Herrick's site 'would now probably lie beneath the private car park of the Department of Social Services', which proved exactly right. Philippa Langley and John Ashdown-Hill were independently researching this topic, and his and my work, as I later learnt when contacted by Philippa Langley, helped inspire her to conceive the pioneering Looking For Richard Project for which she deserves such credit – the mounting of historical research and an archaeological dig to find Richard's lost grave. Thanks to the spectacular success of her project, we can now confirm that Richard did indeed remain peacefully in place for 527 years.

From their earliest meetings Ashdown-Hill agreed with Langley's suggestion to investigate the north of the site, and by 2011 his research confirmed the likely position and layout of the Greyfriars Priory Church in this location. Here it was that Herrick laid out his garden, which suggested the area could have survived as that open site which we knew was subsequently covered in tarmac and was now in use as parking for council offices. They were proved right when the site was excavated in August 2012.

He also investigated the dubious tale reported by John Speed who claimed, after visiting and drawing a map of Leicester, that Richard's tomb had been 'pulled downe and utterly defaced'. Speed had failed to find it because he was actually looking in the wrong place, therefore it might have been for this reason that he chose to cite a local story that Richard's body 'was borne out of the City and contemptuously bestowed under the end of *Bow-Bridge*'. This being insufficiently grotesque, a new version then emerged that he had been thrown into the River Soar by a 'jeering mob'. An even sillier tale claimed that his coffin was used as a horse-trough.

In the mid-nineteenth century Mr Benjamin Broadbent came upon the scene. The founder of a firm of builders, he was proud of his town's association with King Richard, and regretted the lack of any tangible memorial in Leicester to commemorate him. Accordingly in 1856 he erected a large stone plaque close to Bow Bridge, which reads, 'Near this spot lie the remains of Richard III, the last of the Plantagenets, 1485.' Mr Broadbent admitted that it was based solely upon local tradition; so to set the record straight a new plaque was erected by the Richard III Society in 2005, unveiled by Mr Broadbent's descendant Christopher, stating that the legend of Richard's bones being thrown into the Soar was discredited. The good citizens of Leicester had no reason to do such a thing and the story is now proved fictitious, just like the hunched back and withered arm. Inevitably new fictions have arisen, e.g. that Richard was killed by a Welshman named 'William Gardner' – an unsubstantiated claim made in a rather inaccurate Gardiner family history, cited by Wikipedia and repeated in *The Times* and other media.[23]

The following items of information may assist readers to distinguish between fact and surmise. King Richard's burial was understandably modest and performed in haste, without a coffin. Lack of surviving evidence of a shroud does not mean that none was used. Similarly, there is no evidence that his hands were bound: this is purely a suggestion based on their position across his body.

This was not 'a pauper's grave': though small and shallow, it was possessed of a place of signal honour in the holy choir, home to only the most prestigious burials. Its size, inadequate in length, remains uncertain due to damage caused by later building work, which means that although his body was otherwise intact and fully articulated, the area occupied by his feet was lost. We are fortunate that this, and the damage caused by the osteologist during excavation, was the only harm done to his remains.

Regarding his battle injuries, the suggested 'arrowhead' proved to be merely a 2,000 year old nail lying in his grave. The idea of post-Bosworth 'humiliation injuries' is equally speculative and not scientifically established. All injuries found on his body could have been battlefield wounds, we have no way of knowing.

Snippets of information have gradually been fed to the media about his physique. His suggested height of 5ft 8½in is a hypothetical calculation based on the long bones of the legs; it represents the mid point between an estimation of 1.7073– 1.7727m (5ft 7in–5ft 9¾in). One's legs can of course be relatively long or relatively short. Richard's limbs have been described as quite slender (as in von Popplau's diary), and all appear completely straight and healthy with no withered arms. As to his spine, a brief article has now appeared in *The Lancet* with an online 3D video, well worth viewing, in which scoliosis expert Piers Mitchell speaks of 'a slight spinal configuration' rather than Leicester University's previous description 'severe scoliosis'.[24] No one recorded his uneven shoulders in his lifetime, or in early portraits, so we cannot know what difference this made to his perceived height. Portraits are the best indicator of his hair and eye colour.

14

Postscript

Henry VII's coronation took place on 30 October, an ill-attended event conspicuous in its contrast with that of Richard III. So insecure did he feel that he took the prudent step of recruiting a permanent personal bodyguard of yeomen.

In the self-justifying climate engendered by this 'mean and unfeeling tyrant', as Horace Walpole described him, the unprincipled disloyalty of some of Richard's nobles to their former king had to be explained away. To encourage the nobility to unseat a reigning monarch, no matter how allegedly tyrannous, was something Henry VII could not afford to do. Knowing that it was not by the love of the people that he would rule, he found a truly novel way to avoid setting an unwelcome precedent for betrayal.

His solution was to build an edifice of deceit based on the pretence, first unveiled the previous year, that he was the rightful king by lineal descent and Richard the usurper. Thus, in his Parliament of November 1485, he dated his attainders from 21 August, the day before Bosworth Field. So all who fought for their anointed king upon that day were automatically branded traitors. Richard himself, and twenty-eight of his principal adherents, were attainted of high treason.

The *Crowland Chronicle*, taken up at this point by a new writer, now strikes a note of strong disapproval of Henry's tactics (by contrast with our previous chronicler, who compared him with an angel sent from heaven). 'O God!' this narrator laments, 'what assurance will our kings have, henceforth, that on the day of battle they will not be deprived of the presence of their subjects who ... if the royal cause should happen to decline ... will lose life, goods and inheritance complete?'

Of primary importance was to manufacture a valid title to the throne of England. He knew precisely how spurious was his claim by lineal descent and consequently he tried to bolster it by any means available, including the re-enactment of the Beaufort legitimation of 1397 (not, of course, including the bar to the throne). Another ploy consisted of appointing commissioners who obligingly traced his descent back to the ancient Welsh princes; links with King Arthur were also suggested.

The new Crowland chronicler demonstrated a more independent spirit:

> In this Parliament the king's royal authority was confirmed as due to him not by one but by many titles so that he may be considered to rule rightfully over the English people not only by right of blood but of victory in battle and of conquest. There were those who, more wisely, thought that such words should rather have been kept silent than committed to proclamation, particularly because ... there was discussion about the marriage to the lady Elizabeth ... in whose person, it seemed to all, there could be found whatever appeared to be missing in the king's title elsewhere.

Modern historians are usually reluctant to discuss Henry's usurpation of the throne and disinheriting of valid heirs such as the Earl of Lincoln. Nevertheless, it is obvious that many of his contemporaries viewed his 'lineal right' as a figment of his imagination.

This is a topic on which Sir George Buc dilates at length, doubtless because of his fascination with genealogy. He points out that although Henry VI was pleased to call Henry Tudor 'nephew', their relationship was of the half-blood via that king's uterine step-brother: i.e. Henry was not true male issue of the house of Lancaster and Plantagenet, nor of the royal house of England. In fact, he never represented Lancaster (nor had any previous Beaufort ever presumed to) until he became king and awarded the title to himself by royal prerogative; only then could he declare that his marriage represented 'the union of York and Lancaster'. This was, according to Buc:

> very honourable and acceptable to the king, at the least in the beginning of his reign. But afterwards … he affected, and chiefly, so as it were, only the title of his sword. And he claimed the kingdom to be his by conquest and *de jure belli*. Because he would have this told, there were at his coronation proclamations made with these titles: *Henricus rex Angliae, jure divino, jure humano, et jure belli*, etc.
>
> But the noble barons liked not this title *de jure belli*, nor would they allow it. But the king maintained and avowed that he might justly assume and bear it, and as a title and style due to him as a conqueror, because he entered this land with hostile and foreign armies and fought for the crown and won it. To this, the barons answered roundly and soundly that he was beholding to them for his landing safely and for his victory, and that he could never have had that commodity of fair and prosperous descending upon the coasts of England, and much less to have marched into the land and to have struck so much as one stroke for the crown and conquest of this realm without their favour and permission.
>
> For it was clear that without the love and help of the English nobles and people he had no hope nor strength but in his French soldiers … that, if ever they had landed … should all have been cut into pieces and never more have seen the sun. And besides this, the King Richard and the barons and people would have conceived so mortal an hatred against the invader of this kingdom that they would never have left him nor the pursuit of him until they had seen or wrought the death and destruction of him as of a most notorious traitor.
>
> Wherefore the barons humbly prayed his grace … duly and justly to ascribe his good success and his achieving of the crown to their loyal forces and not to the French ragamuffins nor to his Welsh sword.

Unfortunately for their sensibilities, however, 'the king changed not his mind'.

In the same section, Buc describes the underhand way in which Henry arranged to apply a veneer of legitimacy to his assumed titles. The king wrote to Pope Innocent VIII (in 1486) regarding his dispensation to marry his kinswoman Elizabeth, but used the opportunity to have the pope, in his reply, 'make a rehearsal' of those titles he had awarded himself, as though they were 'due and proper to him before'. The pope, of course, had no power to confer any such titles, but Henry's ambassador had it 'chiefly in his instructions' to ensure that in the requested papal bull (which was issued on 27 March) he would be addressed by them. Thus you see, says Buc, 'how the king received of the Pope the confirmation of these two noble titles, *de domo Lancastriae* and *de jure belli*, unasked, as it seemeth'. Who, after all, would argue with the pope?[1]

An equally devious action was to have *Titulus Regius* repealed unread. The repeal cancelled the statute that officially bastardized his bride-to-be, without which she brought little lasting benefit to him as mother of his heirs. But it was a risky move, since by removing the official illegitimacy of Edward IV's offspring it opened the door for the absent Edward V to his former position as king, with Richard of York his heir. Thus it was important that the reading of the act must be suppressed, 'so that all thinges said and remembred in the said Bill and Acte thereof maie be for ever out of remembraunce and allso forgott'.

In Henry's repeal act of November 1485 the customary summary was not included. The record itself was to be removed from the Parliament roll and burnt. Astonishingly, it was further ordered that *on pain of imprisonment* every copy must be delivered to his chancellor for destruction before the following Easter. This was utterly unprecedented: it revealed much about his fear that the princes could return to unseat him, as well as illustrating his self-serving habit of rewriting history. Who can doubt that such a man would set out to blacken the reputation of a defeated opponent?

Some commentators have deduced from this that Henry knew the brothers were dead, but in reality it proves nothing of the sort. He clearly needed to behave as if they were, and had done so since the autumn of 1483. Later on, as Vergil reveals, during the 'Perkin' affair he instructed his envoys to state categorically that the boys had been murdered by their uncle Richard, and in 1495 he made an ill-advised attempt to pretend to Maximilian and Margaret of Burgundy that he could show them 'the chapel where Richard of York was buried'. He was lucky his bluff was not called. 'Molinet was taken in,' Ann Wroe observes, 'saying that the boys had been given "royal obsequies" after King

Richard's death, but few followed him. No funerals would have been held with more pomp and show than those of the princes if Henry had discovered them.'[2]

More to the point, proclaiming their death – and perhaps even exhibiting corpses (genuine or not) – would have removed any surviving hopes of setting up pretenders to challenge him. But Henry was noted for his obsessive piety: had he found the bodies it was his urgent Christian duty to hold masses[3] for the repose of their souls. It would be a mortal sin, of course, to order such masses on bogus grounds.

It seems clear that Henry was, quite simply, in the dark about Edward IV's sons. He was ignorant of their fate upon his arrival in Wales, and he was no better informed after seizing the crown and interrogating everyone who might have knowledge of them. His best hope of information surely lay with Elizabeth Woodville, who was re-established in royal circles and had no reason to conceal the death of her sons from Henry (though she had every reason to conceal their survival).

Further, this was her golden opportunity if she ever wished to proclaim publicly that her marriage to Edward IV was valid, her children legitimate and her sons murdered by Richard III. She said none of these things.

Henry needed those boys dead more than Richard III ever did, and no one can doubt that on seizing the throne he conducted fevered searches, as Buc claims in his *History*. Clearly he desperately wished to proclaim them killed, but feared being proved wrong. The closest he came to a public statement was in the Act of Attainder which his Parliament passed in 1485. Here, in a catch-all phrase, he mentions 'shedding of infants' blood' (a standard accusation against a 'tyrant', says Dr Kincaid):

> The unnaturall, mischeivous, and grete Perjuries, Treasons, Homicides and Murdres, in shedding of Infants blood, with manie other Wronges, odious Offences, and abominacons ayenst God and Man, and in espall oure said Soveraigne Lord, committed and doone by Richard late Duke of Glouc', callinge and nameinge hymself, by usurpacon, King Richard the IIId.

It is impossible to sort out exactly what the fifteenth-century syntax intends to convey, and despite Bertram Fields's manful attempts, we cannot conclude that the positioning of the word 'Treasons' close to the phrase 'in shedding of Infants blood' necessarily means the one qualifies the other.[4] We must remember that in this same parliament, Richard was convicted of treason because he resisted 'King' Henry's invasion of England. Moreover, if Henry was truly referring to regicide, would a reigning king be reduced to the derisory term 'infant'?

This catalogue of Richard's crimes irresistibly calls to mind Edward IV's declaration of royal title by his first Parliament in 1461, which stated that the country had been afflicted with 'unrest, inward war and trouble, unrighteousness, shedding and effusion of innocent blood,' etc. A similar comparison has been drawn with the terms of a letter to Richard III from Oxford University congratulating him on the suppression of the October rebellion, without which 'they would have seen their children die by the edge of the sword' the writer avouches. This is sheer hyperbole in the same vein, and we need not trouble to identify precisely which children were referred to.

Even had Henry intended to hint at Edward V and the former Duke of York as 'infants', their murder seems curiously devoid of significance overshadowed as it is among a list of crimes of which he asserts the most specially heinous are those committed against himself.

Nevertheless, the likelihood that Henry VII was unaware of the boys' fate does not preclude the possibility that members of his faction secretly arranged their despatch without his knowledge. Had this been the case, it would obviously be better to keep him in perpetual ignorance.

* * *

Before we leave Henry Tudor to his reign of aloofness, disorder, misery, oppression, spying, hangings and miserly extortion of his unhappy subjects, as Paul Murray Kendall summarizes it,[5] there are a few curious events worth mentioning. The first is his treatment of Robert Stillington, Bishop of Bath and Wells.

Stillington was so important to Henry, says Kendall, that on the very day of Bosworth he issued a warrant for the bishop's arrest. Within five days he had been hunted down and captured. Taken as a captive to York en route to the king's justice in London, Stillington was in such a parlous state of health that the York city fathers insisted he remain to rest and recover. In Henry's first parliament he was declared guilty of unspecified 'horrible and heinous offences imagined and done' against the king.

But Henry pointedly avoided bringing Stillington to trial. Instead he pardoned him. According to a report in the *Hilary Term Year Book, Henry VII Appendix No 75*, the Lords in Parliament and Justices in the Exchequer met to discuss Richard's *Titulus Regius* and concluded 'the Bishop of Bath made the Bill' (a fact asserted by Ambassador Eustace Chapuys in 1534). These law lords had every intention of summoning Stillington before them so that they could examine him, yet Henry refused, thus preventing any further investigation.

His refusal, and the full pardon that accompanied it, represented a strange decision if Stillington's offences sprang from fabricating a story which defamed one king and deposed another. Such an investigation would also have offered another opportunity for Elizabeth Woodville to vindicate herself and her offspring, had the accusations against her marriage been spurious as asserted by so many historians. For despite *Titulus Regius* and its repeal, Stillington's precontract claim still remained to be tested in canon law; yet the new king's decree prevented it.

What reason existed for Henry to frustrate the wishes of the lords and justices, other than the fear that investigations would confirm the illegitimacy of his wife? After all, he had no way of knowing the truth of the matter.

Professor Anthony Pollard has said on television that 'no one believed' what Stillington said (which was manifestly not the case), and that Henry VII merely wished to start his reign with a clean slate and put away old quarrels. However, any similar actions in our own century would attract a different explanation: 'cover-up' would be the conclusion, not 'clean slate'. Moreover, hauling an elderly cleric the length of England and clapping him in prison hardly sounds like putting away old quarrels.

Another question arises in connection with Henry VII's union with Elizabeth of York, which took place on 18 January 1486, four days after proceedings were initiated for a dispensation before the papal legate, and two days after it was issued. Evidently the path had been cleared by Bishop John Morton, with considerable presumption, during the nine months he spent at the Holy See between January and September 1485. Presumably he also laid the foundations for Pope Innocent VIII's remarkable support for Henry after his seizure of the crown. Again one wonders what Richard was doing all the while, and why he failed to prevent his enemies monopolizing the ear of the pope.

The question that springs to mind concerns Henry's earlier, even more presumptuous dispensation which was secured for the hoped-for marriage as long ago as 27 March 1484, apparently under the auspices of the Bishop of Brittany.[6] Perhaps it slipped through unnoticed, thanks to the furtive way Henry and his anticipated bride were described as *Henricus Richemont* and *Elisabet Plantagenata*. For Elizabeth Woodville to have been a party seems highly unlikely, especially as she had spent February negotiating with Richard for her family to emerge from sanctuary. The suspicion that it was a unilateral move on Henry's part is reinforced by the redundant second dispensation two years later: there was absolutely no need to go through this process a second time, unless to disguise that a first had been granted.

The new dispensation was confirmed by Pope Innocent on 2 March 1486, in a document which boldly described Elizabeth of York as 'the eldest daughter and undoubted heiress of the late Edward IV': a tribute to the skill of Bishop Morton who had evidently convinced the pope that her parents' marriage was valid and (even more importantly) that her two brothers were dead.

C.S.L. Davies notes that the papal bull which followed, dated 27 March 1486, 'pronounced *ipso facto* excommunication against anybody challenging the marriage, or Henry's right to the throne (which, it was stressed, did not depend on the marriage)'. The move, Davies emphasizes, was significant: 'Direct papal intervention of this sort in English secular affairs was extremely unusual. ... Henry evidently thought papal sanction a useful political weapon. The bull was translated, printed and distributed through the realm.'[7] It was this bull which also addressed Henry by the titles he had awarded himself, so the combination of the two papal missives effectively did the king's propaganda work for him.

Henry postponed his queen's coronation as long as possible while pursuing all these attempts to consolidate his title to the

crown, presumably at the same time searching everywhere
for the missing princes. Eventually it was pressed on him, and
Elizabeth was crowned in November 1487, more than two years
after Bosworth.

Her husband absented himself from the coronation, in line with
current etiquette which dictated that a crowned king or queen
should not attend coronations or funerals of other crowned heads.
Margaret Beaufort seems to have excluded herself as well, but
elected to play a very visible role at Elizabeth's prior procession
by barge from Greenwich to the Tower. She was also the
principal lady present after the queen at the mass on the morning
following the coronation, and sat with her when she kept estate
in the parliament chamber. During the coronation itself Margaret
watched with Henry behind a specially erected lattice stage, and
for the banquet in Westminster Hall 'there was made a goodly
stage out of a window on the left side of the hall', latticed and
decorated with Arras cloth 'that they might prively at ther Pleasur
see that noble Feste and Service'.[8]

Elizabeth Woodville, as etiquette demanded, was also absent
from the coronation. But there is no mention of her at any of the
other events or in the private viewing party behind the lattices.
Other absentees from the queen's family included the Marquess of
Dorset. Which brings us to the curious circumstance of Elizabeth
Woodville's deprivation.

She had initially been treated well enough by her new son-in-
law, had been restored to her title and dignity as queen dowager,
received properties in satisfaction of her dower, and stood
godmother to his first son, Arthur, born 20 September 1486.
Yet the following February, not long after news of the rising in
favour of the pretender later known as 'Lambert Simnel', she was
deprived of all her property. A great council of lords, convened
by the king to deal with the unrest, granted everything to her
daughter the queen, and sent her away to Bermondsey Abbey.
This was 'on the unlikely grounds,' says her recent biographer
David Baldwin, 'that she had imperilled his cause by surrendering
her daughters (including Henry's intended bride Elizabeth) to
King Richard some three years earlier'.[9] It is a difficult proposition
to credit.

A rather lame explanation is that she gave up her lands voluntarily
for reasons of ill health. But Baldwin argues convincingly that 'it

would have been unthinkable for someone in the Queen Dowager's position to willingly reduce herself to relative poverty'. Neither is there any evidence that she was unwell at this period (she died only in 1492), 'and illness is not a very plausible explanation given that her personal involvement in the management of her properties ... could have been as considerable or as minimal as she wanted'. He contrasts Elizabeth's low profile with the elevated status of Margaret Beaufort, who was not only conspicuous during the subsequent coronation of Henry's queen, but appeared resplendent with 'a riche coronnall' on her head during the Christmas festivities that followed. Elizabeth Woodville, he concludes, 'was undoubtedly being punished for something'.

Horace Walpole was emphatically of the same opinion, citing Francis Bacon, Henry VII's admiring biographer who wrote that Elizabeth's deprivation 'being even at that time taxed for rigorous and undue, makes it very probable there was some greater matter against her.'[10] Bacon added that once consigned to Bermondsey Abbey she was so deeply tainted with treason that 'it was almost thought dangerous to visit her, or see her'.[11]

This conclusion is not undermined by Henry's proposal for her to marry James III of Scotland, which was made as long ago as July 1486 before Elizabeth lost favour. It might have been diplomatically impossible to renegotiate the clause, or perhaps he considered Scotland far enough distant for her to be effectively isolated. In any case the marriage never took place.

Polydore Vergil, trying to make sense of the deprivation, thought the real complainants were those very nobles sitting in judgement on her: 'because of her inconstancy, [Elizabeth] came to be much hated, and she suffered, leading a miserable life from then on'. Her punishment was 'an example to others to keep faith'. Below for comparison are extracts from the early manuscript version of his *Anglica Historia*, and the printed edition of 1534, which were reproduced in an article by Anne Sutton and Livia Visser-Fuchs.[12] Note the oblique references to Henry Tudor's marriage, which confirm my arguments in chapter 8.

Manuscript, *c.*1513:

[Elizabeth had] broken her promise to those ... who had, at her own most urgent entreaty, forsaken their own English property and fled to Henry in Brittany, the latter having pledged himself to marry her elder daughter Elizabeth ... it had not been for want of effort on her part that the marriage had not failed to come about.

We can see in this version she begged the rebels to join forces with Henry, but it was he, not Elizabeth, who made the marriage pledge.

Printed edition, 1534:

Going completely against the drift of the agreement formed against Richard, she drew away from those nobles who left behind, at her request in particular, all the lands they had in England, fled to Henry ... and demanded from him an oath by which he obliged himself to marry her eldest daughter. It was no thanks to her that this did not fail.

Here again, although Elizabeth encouraged the rebels, it was not she but they who compacted with Henry for him to marry her daughter. The distinction may seem small, but it is nonetheless significant: Elizabeth did not contract her daughter to Henry and then go back on her word. On the contrary, the nobles complain that she nearly scuttled *their* plan for the marriage.

There is no certainty, say Sutton and Visser-Fuchs, that the reasons given by Vergil 'were those of the council rather than his own retelling of Elizabeth's past history of political expedients'. Despite this uncertainty, they cannot subscribe to the school of thought which conjectures that Elizabeth's real crime was to support 'Lambert Simnel'. This idea, suggested by David Baldwin, is widely held. But Sutton and Visser-Fuchs observe: 'why should [Vergil] not have added this detail if he had known or suspected it?' They assert that the transfer of Elizabeth's estates was not unusual, and indeed was to be expected.

[A queen was] entitled to a substantial dower, which was likely to be made up from the same estates as had been held by the previous queen. ... The endowment of Elizabeth of York, daughter of Edward IV, with full honours as queen, may have been high among the demands of the lords summoned together by Henry, and fits very well with their concern to pardon and

bring into the fold men, such as Lovel, who were still dissident.
As the dowager, Elizabeth could only expect the much reduced
estate of a queen dowager.

Moreover the choice of Bermondsey, they argue, was not really
an unpleasant one, being only a short boat journey from three
royal palaces.

One would be rash to disagree with Anne Sutton and Livia
Visser-Fuchs, whose scholarship is beyond question. Yet Elizabeth
seems to have been deprived of considerably more than merely
estates, going by her will which clearly indicates that she died in
penury. She received a modest annual cash allowance from Henry
(400 marks from May 1488 later increased to £400, less than the
700 marks she received from Richard III), and Baldwin suggests
it was not always paid promptly. He also queries how much of it
went directly into the monks' coffers for her upkeep.[13]

As to the possibility that Elizabeth supported or wished to
support 'Lambert Simnel' perhaps Vergil failed to put this idea
forward simply because everyone carefully avoided mentioning it
to him. The implications, after all, were staggering: it would have
meant that, even if the pretender was merely a stalking-horse,
Elizabeth was prepared to believe that at least one of her sons
was still alive. From this the deduction follows that she never had
evidence of their death in 1483.

In another clear demonstration of Henry's suspicion at the time
of this rising, her eldest son, the Marquess of Dorset, was confined
to the Tower of London and held until it was over.[14]

A cool relationship between Elizabeth and her son-in-law is
not at all unlikely. Though a good politician, even she might have
found it difficult to keep up appearances with a man who had not
only used the reported death of her sons to catapult himself to
power, but had buttressed his usurpation with the claim that she
had promised him her daughter.

But why would she support an extremely dicey attempt to
depose the king and, with him, her own daughter and grandson?
Perhaps we might reconsider the argument (see chapter 9) that the
boy called 'Lambert Simnel' by Henry VII was not the low-born
impostor he was made out to be, but Edward V returning and
dying in an attempt to claim his kingdom. The Irish chronicles
gave the age of the youth who started the rebellion as at least

fifteen, and Vergil changed his description of him from 'boy' to 'adolescent', whereas Henry described his (possibly substitute) captive after the battle as ten years old. Edward's sixteenth birthday fell in November 1486.

Of course, any idea that Elizabeth harboured thoughts of her sons being alive will immediately torpedo five centuries of certainty that they were murdered. Yet the hard fact of her 1484 reconciliation with Richard III cannot be ignored, and was thrown in her face at the time of her deprivation. It needs only one reliable piece of evidence that she supported the cause of 'Lambert Simnel', and history will be stood on its head. Whilst on the subject, it is equally diverting to conjecture how different England's history would be if 'Perkin Warbeck' had conquered Henry VII and reigned as Richard IV. How many historians would protest that he was an impostor and that the real Richard had died in the Tower?

From Henry's telltale behaviour when confronted with pretenders, it seems he was genuinely in two minds yet afraid to discover the truth. Vergil claims that the king had given orders at the battle of Stoke that he wanted the Earl of Lincoln, leader of the 'Simnel' rebellion, captured alive so that he could learn more about the conspiracy. Bacon said that Henry was sorry for the earl's death, 'because from him he might have known the bottom of his danger'. Yet after Stoke he failed to punish those who killed Lincoln, neglected to conduct any public investigation into the rebellion and apparently did not interrogate anyone who could give him information.

Most importantly, why did Lincoln not lead an uprising in favour of himself, when he would have been Richard III's clear successor? Again the obvious answer is that one or both of Edward IV's sons survived.

Further indications of Henry's uncertainty are the lengths to which he went to establish the identity of 'Piers Osbeck'. Ann Wroe, author of *Perkin: a Story of Deception*, says that Henry's payments for spies follow 'Perkin's' movements almost exactly, even during his pre-pretender years. If Henry had known the boys were dead, he would surely never have bothered.

Henry, 'A dark prince and infinitely suspicious,' as Bacon described him, seems to have allowed precious few people into his charmed inner circle. Although appointed chamberlain, Sir

William Stanley appears not to have been among them. A recent study by Tim Thornton suggests a lack of trust on Henry's part and a lack of power on Stanley's, coupled with resentment at not being awarded the earldom of Chester. Thornton is ready to credit the charge for which Stanley was executed – and which has long puzzled historians – i.e. that he supported the challenge of 'Perkin' for Henry's crown (see p. 193).[15]

A perpetual prey to insecurity, the Tudor dynasty pursued a policy of liquidating any Plantagenet offspring they could get their hands on who had any proximity to the throne. Perhaps Henry VII's most craven act was the judicial murder of the young Earl of Warwick whom he had kept imprisoned for a dozen or more years. William Hutton, in *The Battle of Bosworth Field* (1788), wrote 'The destruction of Warwick by Henry was as vile a murder as that of Edward the Fifth.' There is a difference, of course: we don't know that Edward V ever *was* murdered.

* * *

'On 20 August 1485 the Yorkshire squire Robert Morton drew up his will,' Michael K. Jones relates. 'Morton was "going to maintain our most excellent King Richard III against the rebellion raised against him in this land".'[16]

Such was the perception of an ordinary Englishman who was called to defend king and country against Henry Tudor's invading forces. Robert Morton did not expect posterity to read his words and was not trying to make a political point. It was a simple statement of loyalty as he prepared to face the hideous realities of mediæval warfare in the name of his king.

His outlook was shared by the majority of his compatriots, especially those from northern parts who for many years had lived under Richard's justice and fought under his banner. But mostly what concerned people like Robert was food on the table and peace in the realm. They had no vote, they wielded no power, and they were not the stuff of history books.

Had there existed such a device as a referendum in 1485, ordinary people were not so dissatisfied with Richard III that they would have voted for a takeover by Henry Tudor, a virtual foreigner who, having fled the realm in 1471, was unknown to England's rank and file population.

Unfortunately, since history is written by the winning elite (and those who ride their coat-tails), the views of ordinary mortals enjoy little house room. Thus this book has attempted to step outside conventional academic opinion which relies too heavily on narratives that could well be biased, sectarian, opportunistic, ill-informed or perhaps, as with Polydore Vergil, more spinned against than spinning.

Jeremy Potter, in *Good King Richard?*, challenges the view of historians like Ross and Hanham who call it a gross distortion to claim the Tudor writers invented the wickedness of Richard III.[17] Ross, for example, says they 'were building upon a foundation of antagonism to Richard III which antedated his death at Bosworth'. This is undeniable, Potter concedes,

> but it is also true that the Tudor writers were selective in their foundation and chose to build exaggeration upon exaggeration, untruth upon untruth. Rumour, gossip and the reports of adversaries are frail evidence, even if contemporary ... [for] there were contemporaries who disliked and mistrusted every king of England in the fifteenth century (and most of those before and since). It would have been astonishing if, for instance, there had been no rumours that Richard had had his nephews put to death, but they tell us nothing about what actually occurred. ... In moving behind the Tudor myths to ascertain the truth, Professor Ross seems to place too much reliance on records which are sparse, partial, fragmentary, untrustworthy and by no means necessarily representative.

Referring to the 'naughty game' of selectivity which our historians so disparage, Potter comments, 'If sufficient of the evidence were hard, this would be a trick quickly exposed, but much of it is so soggy that the gates of selectivity leading to a wonderland of speculation are, if not wide open, at least temptingly ajar.'

So the enigma of Richard III continues to attract independent thinkers who can conceive of more than one way to interpret events, and who are unafraid of espousing heretical or unfashionable theories about the reign of a king who has been too often stigmatized by unsupported assumption.

Paul Murray Kendall is unabashed in lauding Richard's achievements:

> In the course of a mere eighteen months, crowded with cares and problems, he laid down a coherent programme of legal enactments, maintained an orderly society, and actively promoted the well-being of his subjects. A comparable period in the reigns of his predecessor and of his successor shows no such accomplishment.[18]

If one is making comparisons, there is another aspect often overlooked. To gain the throne of England, Richard took the lives of four opponents, all of them committed players in the great game of power. By contrast, Edward IV's path to the throne encompassed the deaths of tens of thousands, and Henry VII's, thousands more at Bosworth Field. Unlike the four magnates executed in 1483, the overwhelming majority of those maimed and slaughtered in 1461 and 1485 had no active involvement in politics and had never conspired against anyone. They were ordinary Englishmen, just like Robert Morton, and like him they died a bloody death in a quarrel that was not theirs.

15

Reappearances

To return to my remarks in Chapters 9 and 10, we have Richard as king faced with a dilemma: what to do about the sons of Edward IV, now recognized as illegitimate, but still figureheads for brewing civil strife? I have made clear my doubts that he did away with them. If the argument is that their deaths offered him security, no security existed unless he produced proof. And then their sisters would become heirs – held beyond his reach in sanctuary, with rebel plots afoot to steal them away to breed more infant figureheads. And what about Clarence's son? Ahead of Richard in the succession, with the barrier of his father's attainder much easier to ignore than bastardy. Yet this little boy remained safely cared for during Richard's lifetime. I speak nothing of his humanity towards these children, for the verdict of history affords the slandered Richard no such virtue. But I do speak of the practical options open to him as King of England, which afforded solutions far more prudent than the simplistic conclusion that, because the princes needed to be removed from public access, his only choice was to eliminate them.

Sadly the 'murder' theory has lost none of its detective-story attraction. For the media – social and commercial – the princes and their fate are merely fruit for speculation (or even certainty): cardboard cut-outs frozen in time with the caption '1483'. But we who aspire to write biographically have a commitment to engage with the boys themselves, and those around them, as flesh-and-blood people: fifteenth-century people with lives conditioned by the times they are living through, and their families' times before them.

If we revisit for a moment the realities of those times, we will recall the undercurrents, still bubbling below the surface, of the civil strife of York versus Lancaster. And if we raise our eyes to England's international relations, these were dominated by age-old hostilities with France, exacerbated under Yorkist rule by England's alliance with Burgundy, the breakaway power that France sought to subdue. The York family, when their boys were threatened at home, had found safety in the Low Countries: a bond that was cemented by the marriage of Richard's sister Margaret with Duke Charles of Burgundy. And then there was York-friendly Ireland. One of the charges Edward IV laid against his executed brother George of Clarence was that Dublin-born George had schemed to foment trouble by spiriting his son over there.

But by 1483 the picture had changed. Shortly before Edward IV's death a newly strengthened Louis XI had repudiated his peace treaty with Edward, who had immediately responded with preparations for war. A matter of weeks later he was dead, with France sabre-rattling against an England bereft of international allies and led by an inexperienced 12-year-old boy. The Woodvilles had lost no time in moving in to demote Richard, England's military supremo, from his constitutional office as Protector and Defender of the Realm.

Margaret of York, Duchess of Burgundy, wife to Duke Charles of Burgundy, stepmother to his daughter Mary and mother-in-law to Mary's husband King Maximilian I.

As Richard travelled to Westminster to face an ominous confrontation, he would have given long and hard thought to leaving his family in the turbulent North, particularly his little son of under seven years old. It is inconceivable that he would not have mapped out a potential escape route and safe destination for him.[1] Where better than over the sea?

It was documented in the 1480s that Richard was considered to have a very good brain, and discharged with distinction the responsibilities loaded on him by his brother the king. He was a leader of men and strategic thinker. And when determining a plan of action for his brother's sons, he was capable of conceiving the risky but strategically optimal ploy of constructive ambiguity. The theme of this chapter – reappearances – suggests that Richard's ploy was successful in concealing and protecting the lives of his nephews. He would recognize the risk of exposing his own reputation to suspicion, but he could scarcely have imagined his death at the hands of the Tudors and the litany of accusations their partisans would heap on his mildly irregular shoulders.

Thomas More, though the originator of the entire story of murder at the hands of James Tyrell, reported nevertheless that it was only one version he had heard: he even recorded doubts over whether the princes died during Richard's lifetime, as did Polydore Vergil and Francis Bacon. So the certainties of some of today's historians were not certainties 500 years ago.

Thus it was scarcely unfounded quixotry that led Philippa Langley to instigate searches for evidence of their survival, any more than with her famously successful search for King Richard's lost grave. This chapter is indebted to the new information she has brought to light thanks to a much more thorough scrutiny of little-known documents, having marshalled together numbers of like-minded researchers willing to co-ordinate their expertise towards a shared aim.

In view of the complexities of mediæval relations between England and her near neighbours, it is not surprising that searches in European archives, undertaken by specialists familiar with them, have proved the most fruitful.[2] Considerable effort and expertise are demanded to comb through collections of old manuscripts – whether civic records and accounts, or letters, diaries, recollections and jottings – rather than quoting the neatly catalogued (and reprinted) materials relied on by modern history. Those manuscripts in foreign vernaculars are much less likely to be consulted by non-natives. And such sources have provided evidence that countervails the hitherto prevailing mantra that Richard III ordered the killing of the princes.

Specialist knowledge always triumphs over the superficial, as proved by the team gathered by Philippa in her quest for King Richard's grave. After a lifetime of study and research I was myself invited to become a member, having published my assertion in the first edition of this book (2008) that Richard's grave-site in Leicester 'would now probably lie beneath the private car park of the Department of Social Services'.[3] Many historians and archaeologists who considered themselves experts assumed that the church of the Franciscans lay under built-up areas, impossible to excavate, and that a jeering mob desecrated his grave and threw his remains into the river Soar, which was a myth underpinned by nothing more substantial than tales of villainy penned by Tudor dramatists. It remains a source of amazement that our team – which included published historians and researchers and two PhDs, all specialists on this monarch – should have been dismissed as 'amateurs'. And this by persons whose acquaintance with Richard III was so superficial as to publish a wrong date of birth for him, among other howlers, at his reburial service.

Philippa's latest project brought together distinguished international researchers who knew precisely what they were looking for, spent months and years trawling through relevant records, and managed to locate evidence in fifteenth-century sources which had not only been overlooked and misread, but in one case deliberately disregarded. Dismiss them as 'amateurs' at your peril! The information I am privileged to offer in this chapter draws heavily on the revelations newly brought to public notice by Philippa Langley in book form and on Channel 4; readers seeking fully detailed sources will find them in her publication *The Princes in the Tower: Solving History's Greatest Cold Case*. However, a word to the wise: this is not a slavish copy, and our conclusions may not always chime. My commentary is informed by my own ideas, many of which were conceived in the 1990s when I first started writing this book.

I will begin with some known facts about the young pretender crowned as King Edward in Ireland on 27 May 1487, who led an invading seaborne army in June 1487 to challenge Henry VII for the throne of England, culminating in the battle of Stoke. Researchers with eyes raised beyond the realm of England are aware that preparations for this armada were recorded extensively in the archives of the Low Countries from where, on 15 May 1487, the generously funded fleet with its armed force set sail for Ireland from Middelburg in Zeeland.

Very few remaining British and Irish documents of the day have survived the wholesale eradication engineered by Henry VII, but four sources agree that the pretender crowned in Dublin was named 'King Edward' by his supporters and by his own hand. They include (1) a patent issued in Ireland by the king in the name 'Edwardus' (further discussed below); (2) an account of the battle of Stoke recorded in the *Heralds' Memoir*, 'And there was taken the lad that his rebels called king Edward';[4] and (3) a memorandum of the City of York, written in June 1487, which reports that 'the Lord Scropes of Bolton and Upsall ... came on horseback to Bootham Bar, and there cried *King Edward*'.[5] In addition, (4) the York records also report that he named himself King Edward in a letter that same June.[6]

What posterity has offered in opposition to these recorded facts is the fog of confusion created by Henry VII to discredit Edward's identity and counteract the danger to his recently gained throne. As with all the pretenders who plagued his reign, the official stories given out by the Tudor king varied in their details. By November 1486 rumours were already being voiced concerning plots in support of a pretender known by the name of Edward. At that time, the overall spin put about by Henry VII's government alleged that this individual was impersonating young Edward, Earl of Warwick, Clarence's son. Common gossip outside the realm of England followed this official lead and called him the son of Clarence.

Later on, government propaganda identified him as an inconsequential boy called 'Lambert Simnel' who had been groomed for the impersonation, but this masquerade seems cobbled together in retrospect. There were suspicious mismatches between the ages of 'King Edward', 'Simnel' and Edward of Warwick. Such official attempts at misdirection were needed because when the royal pretender Edward was mentioned in Ireland he was being taken very seriously indeed. The *Annals of Ulster* reported after Bosworth that there remained but one young man alive of the former blood royal;[7] and in 1487 they identified the heir of York as being in exile with the Earl of Kildare when the 'great fleet' in Edward's support came to Ireland that year.[8]

The anxious Tudor king was said by his protégé Bernard André to have sent an interrogator to Ireland in the person of a herald 'who could easily divine' his *bona fides*. This was apparently John Yonge, Falcon Pursuivant, some time after Michaelmas 1486:

'But the lad, schooled with evil art …' says André, 'very readily replied to all the herald's questions. In the end, thanks to the false instructions of his sponsors, he was believed to be Edward's son [son of Edward IV] by a number of Henry's emissaries, who were prudent men, and he was so strongly supported that a large number had no hesitation to die for his sake.'[9]

Meanwhile, Henry VII maintained the official line that this was an impostor posing as Clarence's son.[10] It was a convenient cover story in that they were both named Edward, and furthermore the Tudor king could produce and exhibit the real Earl of Warwick at will. He was in this happy position because not long after Bosworth he had incarcerated little Warwick in the Tower of London (where in 1499 he committed the unspeakable act of manufacturing a pretext to execute him).[11]

To Henry VII's chagrin, he had no way of controlling the post-Bosworth rumours that revolved around Edward V and Richard of York, whose possible survival dogged much of his reign. Indeed, he would have been heartily relieved if he'd known they had been eliminated by Richard III, because that would have saved him the chore of eliminating them himself. He knew that the rebels who challenged him as an interloper were fully prepared to overlook flaws in the Plantagenet line. Back in 1483 Edward IV's flouting of Church law, rendering his offspring illegitimate, had been an insurmountable obstacle when set against the rights of an heir, in the person of Richard III, whose claim was legitimate under the age-old rules of succession. But once the crown had been seized by this Tudor of questionable heritage, the position was wholly changed: his opponents would rally behind any challenge mounted by a disenfranchized Plantagenet of the previously ruling house of York. And in January 1486 Tudor himself had repealed the 1484 Act of Succession (*Titulus Regius*), which had previously sealed the barrier to the succession of Edward IV's offspring.

He was right to be nervous, as even his own tame historian, Polydore Vergil, in discussing the pretender of 1486–87, recorded that 'a report prevailed among the common people that the sons of Edward the king had migrated to some part of the earth in secret, and there were still surviving'.[12]

I will here remind readers of my suggestion in Chapter 9 that in 1483 it would have been a simple matter for King Richard to arrange waterborne transport for his nephews from the Tower of London with its ready access to the Thames and the open sea. And that, to preserve anonymity, the boys would have to be separated at an early stage.

In the summer of 1483, with Woodville-led rebellion being whipped up aimed at restoring Edward V, the most urgent priority would have to be an immediate, concealed route and destination for the elder brother.[13] And Richard's arrangements appear to have worked well, because although there are various clues suggesting Edward's travels between 1483 and 1486 (before he made Ireland his base), so far his whereabouts in those years are unconfirmed. He would surely not have been sent directly to Ireland during Richard's reign, for Ireland would have been the first overseas location for anyone to look.

Despite the blackening of Richard's name that led the world to condemn him as a blood-soaked murderer, any cool and rational appraisal of the situation must allow that with all his resources as King of England – including the availability of shipping under the control of his High Admiral John Howard, Duke of Norfolk – Richard could certainly have arranged two necessary evacuations offshore. Relocating the younger brother would need more careful oversight due to his youth, but in the case of Edward V the arrangements could have been more swift and less complicated. I have thought long and hard about whether young Edward himself may have been less than co-operative. But I conclude that, with ten years of single-minded education at Ludlow preparing him to wield power, he would have been alert to the obvious necessity for King Richard, once enthroned, to oust a rival king whom rebels were setting up to depose him. Offered an escape route rather than less palatable alternatives, he would certainly have preferred exile. The present evidence that he and his brother were protected, and survived, suggests Richard was not an uncle they feared.

There are indications that Edward V's survival was on the lips of many people before he appeared in Ireland. Henry VII's biographer Bernard André, whom we met earlier, asserted that 'inasmuch as he [the boy] was thought to be a scion of Edward's stock, the Lady Margaret [of Burgundy] wrote him a letter of summons. By stealth he quickly made his way to her, with only a few men party to such a great act of treason.'[14] Whether or not André had stumbled upon fact, it demands little imagination to suppose a hideaway on the Continent to account for at least part of the time.

In support of this scenario, I would call attention to certain activities of intermediaries in 1484–85 as described above in Chapter 9. For example, Margaret of Burgundy's chaplain, Goguet, together with another of the Goguet family, who were undoubtedly carrying materials in secret between the duchess and her brother Richard III, under safe-conduct, which stipulated 'without any search'. In the same connection we have the seafaring Sir Edward Brampton, who in 1484 was awarded £100 annually by Richard for unknown services due to commence from Easter 1485. Brampton would later play another role in connection with Richard of York.

Even more indicative is Richard III's warrant for Sir James Tyrell, 'the king's councillor and knight of his body' sent over the Channel on the king's business in 1484–85 with the financial assistance of the Mayor of Dover. At the same time that the helpful mayor was being reimbursed in January 1485, Tyrell was appointed commander of the castle at Guînes, part of the English-ruled Calais territory, and received the vast, unexplained payment of £3,000. Cash awards of this magnitude were almost unheard of. For centuries James Tyrell's name has been inextricably linked with the fate of Edward IV's sons, not as their saviour but as their killer; and he is not alone to have been accused of guilt (or guilty knowledge) by the busy pen of Thomas More.[15]

Later in this chapter we will encounter the parallel story of young Richard of York which happily sheds a little light on how Edward was spirited away in 1483; but I would caution readers, as I always do, not to think of the brothers as somehow joined at the hip. Richard, at barely nine years old, would have needed elaborate precautions, including chaperoning, to keep him safe when travelling incognito at his tender age. On the other hand there was the advantage that, having grown up close to his parents, he would be more accepting of arrangements made on his behalf by people long familiar to him at court.

The impetus behind the public emergence of Edward V to claim England's crown was undoubtedly the arrival of Henry Tudor as the victor of Bosworth in August 1485, together with the demise of Richard III and his closest aides who were either killed or scattered.

Edward had now reached his majority (he was fourteen the previous November), and several prominent figures among the Yorkist-supporting Irish were ready to promote him.

Wherever the prince may have been concealed, there is documentary evidence that he was in Ireland in 1486 and claiming to be king, even before his recorded coronation in Dublin in May 1487. This is the evidence I promised to return to: it consists of the record of a royal patent granted and sealed there in the name of Edwardus, by the Grace of God King of England, France and Ireland, and witnessed by his supporter and enabler, the Earl of Kildare, on 13 August in King Edward's first regnal year.

In the lead-up to her publication of *The Princes in the Tower*, I discussed this at length with Philippa Langley and compared some recorded attributions of its year of origin being 1487 (2 Henry VII), made not on the basis of evidence but on mere assumption. Historians have found nothing assigning the Irish writ to August 1487 (*after* the reign of King Edward had been extinguished at Stoke Field), nor to the juvenile Edward V in 1483, nor to the Tudor child-king Edward VI; so these alternatives can be ruled out. And no one has been rash enough to suppose that its date was 13 August 1484 or 1485. Furthermore, a King Edward styling himself King of Ireland is otherwise wholly unknown, as is Kildare being styled Lieutenant. This king is uniquely claiming direct rule over Ireland with the assent of Kildare and his fellow supporters. So the obvious date is 1486, when Irish records corroborate the pretender Edward's presence in Ireland.

There are some who espouse the idea that the patent's royal author was Edward, Earl of Warwick but they are hindered by two huge impediments: that Ulster records describe him as a 'young man' at this time, whereas Warwick was aged eleven; and that little Warwick was currently incarcerated in the Tower of London.

It also remains to address various assertions that King Edward inexplicably assigned himself the regnal number 'VI',[16] which is another topic much discussed. Regrettably I must disagree with John Ashdown-Hill who claimed that the record of Edward's letter to the city of York, mentioned above, points to his usage of the regnal number VI.[17] This has not been 'ignored by historians' but in fact rightly discounted, because it is an inscription by a third party and cannot be assumed to indicate what King Edward's supporters thought. It was not customary for a king to refer to himself by a regnal number, so Edward's *letter*, as transcribed, contains merely the usual formula 'By the King'. The comment in the York House Book 'calling hymself King Edward the vj' was a fifteenth-century *annotation* to introduce the *copy* of Edward's letter written into the city records.[18] This annotation signifies no more than the understanding or belief of the city's recorder who wrote it. York's response to the letter was not welcoming, so Henry VII's official spin, that this King Edward was an impostor masquerading as Clarence's son, had clearly been effective. There survives no first-hand document using any regnal number – least of all any that emanated from the pretender himself – and none was carried by the coins minted in Ireland upon his coronation.

It has also been claimed that a document in a fifteenth-century Irish Exchequer Memoranda Roll gives this as his regnal number; but the original Latin MS is destroyed and the only near-reliable record (from the 1820s, written by William Lynch, a clerk in the Rolls Office) is an English translation, either a repertory or an abstract, which clearly puts slashes either side of the words '/1 Ed 6/'.[19] The added slashes are important, and more than likely indicate this as a later interpolation or interlineation – no such marks occur around other regnal years noted by Lynch on the same page. There is no internal indication whether the entry was engrossed in 1487 or 1488, so it would be reasonable for a clerk to clarify the year by adding an interpolation. It could have been added at any time from the 1480s to the 1800s.

With the repeal of *Titulus Regius*, and his bastardy no longer on the statute books, it was open to a returning King Edward V to challenge the present incumbent and regain the throne, as discussed on pp. 325–6 (Chapter 14). Indeed, according to Polydore Vergil, when his forces arrived in England they announced they had 'come to *restore* [*ad restituendum*] the boy Edward, recently crowned in Ireland, to the kingdom': *se venisse ad restituendum in regnum Edwardum puerum nuper in Hybernia coronatum*. This sentence repeats exactly the same assertion made by Vergil some pages earlier, 'to *restore* the boy to the kingdom': *pro restituendo puero in regnum*.[20]

In support of his challenge, an invasion fleet had been prepared in the Low Countries, instigated by Yorkist supporters including Richard III's close friend Francis, Viscount Lovell, and led by John de la Pole, Earl of Lincoln, who, significantly, abandoned his own claim to the throne to promote this returning King Edward. Formed with the active supervision and financial backing of Richard's sister Margaret, Dowager Duchess of Burgundy, its seasoned German military commander was Martin Schwartz, who had already fought on behalf of Burgundy. The mustering army consisted mainly of German Landsknechte, much favoured in battle by Margaret's son-in-law King Maximilian, together with soldiers from the country's southernmost maritime county of Zeeland. Situated on the coast of the North Sea, Zeeland's port of Arnemuiden, in the municipality of Middelburg, would see the armada's departure on 15 May; from there they navigated south through the Channel, around the point of Cornwall and then northward to Ireland.

On arrival they joined Edward's Irish supporters to crown him in Dublin cathedral on 27 May 1487[21] after which, preparatory to his invasion of England, a Parliament was held (though Henry VII prudently expunged all records thereof). Fortunately the *Annals of Ulster* survive to record that he 'was exiled at this time with the Earl of Kildare'.[22] Augmented by Irish reinforcements, the fleet made landfall in England on 4 June in north Lancashire, close to Furness Fells. Twelve days later, on 16 June, King Edward's bid for the crown came to an end at the battle of Stoke.

These are the bare bones of the 1487 operation to regain the throne for the house of York, and it is by no means certain what happened to Edward after Stoke Field. Of more immediate importance is our quest to establish his identity as Edward V. His threat to Henry VII had certainly raised sufficient alarm for the Tudor Great Council (Sheen, February 1487) to resolve, surprisingly, on the deprivation of Elizabeth Woodville.[23] At the time of this denial of resources to the mother of Henry's queen, it was – and still is – suspected that she had shown indications of support for this pretender. If the Great Council in their wisdom did not dismiss the possibility of opposition to the Tudor king by the mother of a returning Edward V, neither should we. Especially as her eldest son, the Marquess of Dorset, was arrested at the same time and held in the Tower.

Meanwhile, Henry VII's story about the pretender being a counterfeit Edward of Warwick remained the official line in England. But surviving sources in the Habsburg Netherlands, or at least those that documented the pretender with any confidence, usually disregarded any imposture and described him as the real thing: 'the son of Clarence'. One example relating to Edward's invasion is a Dutch record of costs in the accounts of Margaret of

Burgundy's household, incurred for a large body of men to assist the 'duke' of Clarence (Warwick's title, had his father not been attainted);[24] elsewhere the record more accurately identifies him as 'her brother's son and by right succession and honour entitled to the crown of England'.[25]

Another example is the Danzig Chronicle of Caspar Weinreich, which in two places records the gathering of the fleet in 1487 and their departure for Ireland to support the pretender who was waiting there: '... *qwam uber ausz Sehelandt vil schiffe in Irlandt zu hulffe dem jungen her ... des duc Klarens son ... entgegen konig Ritzmundt ...*' Weinreich is interesting in that he offers a different identifying name for 'Clarence's son' in two places, though nowhere does he call him 'Edward' or 'Warwick'. In both places Weinreich evidently wrote a name beginning with the capital letter 'J' (pronounced as English 'Y'); but sadly his manuscript doesn't survive, and its sixteenth-century transcriber, Bornbach, is known to have 'improved' Weinreich's work which he culled from a number of notebooks.[26] So in one place he has interpreted Weinreich's writing as the name 'Jores' and in another, 'Jorgen', probably taking two stabs at the same word. My tentative suggestion is that, in ignorance of Weinreich's familiarity with fifteenth-century English affairs, Bornbach failed to recognize that the original was the author's way of writing the name '*Jork/Jorke*' ('York') at a time when spelling and handwriting were inconsistent. If so, Weinreich could have been identifying the pretender as a scion of that house of York which he knew had occupied the English throne for over twenty years of his seafaring lifetime.[27]

An indicative Flemish report also exists in the city accounts of Malines (Mechelen) for 1487, in which Clarence's son is mentioned as the recipient of a gift of wine,[28] demonstrating the esteem in which he was held in Flanders. This was noted in my Chapter 9, though I originally cited a source that gave the wrong year;[29] thankfully the diligent research of Nathalie Nijman-Bliekendaal now places this gift in its correct year of 1487, on the occasion of 'the procession of St Rumbold and of the Holy Sacraments', for which the relevant entry reads: '... Also 8 stopen of wine presented to the son of Clarentie from England ...' The Malines archivist has confirmed that the mistake was a misreading of the annual accounting period, and the relevant procession was on 18 April 1487, at a time when preparations were in train for the invasion force being gathered some 50 miles north in Zeeland. To be clear, this entry doesn't make certain the identity of the recipient of the wine: its importance is to demonstrate how widely the Yorkist pretender was identified as the 'son of Clarence' in the Low Countries.

However, in an amazing breakthrough, a key piece of evidence has now been discovered that positively identifies the boy who would be king in 1487, not as Clarence's son but as an altogether different nephew of Margaret of Burgundy: Edward V.

It derives not from the seagoing Low Countries but from Lille, now part of inland France, in the archives of the Département du Nord. Lille is very close to the present-day Belgian border, and in the fifteenth century was one of the principal cities in the Burgundian county of Flanders. Thanks to the researches of Albert Jan de Rooij, another of Philippa Langley's European team, the Archives Départementales have yielded a document that provides incontrovertible evidence that the young man supported by Margaret was officially identified not only by her but also by her son-in-law Maximilian, King of the Romans, as (in translation) 'her nephew and son of the late King Edward IV, who was expelled from his dominion'.[30]

This document, dated 16 December 1487, is a proof of payment written in French, found among the accounts of the 'Recette de l'Artillerie' (Maximilian's famous artillery). It constitutes a receipt for the payment of 120 livres made by Laurens le Mutre, councillor and receiver of 'The Artillery of the King of the Romans and his Son the Archduke [Philip]'.[31] Le Mutre had paid one Jehan de Smet, a merchant and woodworker living in Malines, for supplying 400 long pikes to Maximilian in June 1487. The receipt states explicitly that the pikes were taken away by King Maximilian himself and delivered to one of his leading and most trusted courtiers, Jan van Bergen, Lord of Walhain.

The receipt specifies that the pikes were intended for the Yorkist rebellion of 1487 described above, for which we know the great armada left Zeeland on 15 May 1487. It states the purpose of the expedition in detail, and identifies the person in whose name it was mounted: 'the son of King Edward'. Translated into modern English the receipt reads as follows:

[These pikes were] to be distributed among the German-Swiss pikemen, who were then under the command of my lord Martin de Zwarte, a knight from Germany, to take and lead across the sea, whom Madam the Dowager sent at the time, together with several captains of war from England, to serve her nephew – son of King Edward, late her brother (may God save his soul), [who was] expelled from his dominion – and obstruct the King of the aforementioned England in his activities.

The significance of the document lies in the authentication of this transaction by signature of a litany of impeccable witnesses. It was not only drawn up for Laurens le Mutre, but also witnessed, signed and dated by another key official from the Burgundian Habsburg Court, Florens Hauweel, one of Maximilian's own secretaries. Furthermore, the receipt is countersigned at the bottom where a brief statement is inserted and signed by two other high-ranking officials, re-confirming its accuracy and certifying that the payment and distribution of the weapons has actually taken place 'in the manner contained and extensively described in the receipt above'. This appended statement represents an accounting procedure to ensure the reliability and accuracy of the Artillery's financial statements. The signatories are Lienart de la Court, Chamberlain and Master of the Artillery, and Andrieu Schaffer, controller/ quartermaster of the Artillery.

Maximilian I, Habsburg King of the Romans from 1486, ruled Burgundy after his co-ruler (wife Mary) died in 1482.

With this amount of high-level scrutiny by three leading officials of the Burgundian court, including a secretary to King Maximilian, the likelihood of error is virtually nil. Just as unlikely is the possibility that misinformation was purposely inserted into a purely internal accounting instrument that was never intended for public gaze. Clearly Maximilian and Margaret of Burgundy were amassing armaments for the challenge to Henry VII that took place in May–June 1487, led by the young man who was named King Edward, and who had indeed been ejected from his domain after being deposed four years earlier. Thus we have the identity of Edward V, son of Edward IV, recorded in writing by order of King Maximilian and the Duchess of Burgundy.

This is the first document we have that departs from the almost universal European habit of naming the pretender as the son of Clarence. This had been a useful misdirection, in this story of counterfeits, that would have been politic for Margaret to foster for as long as possible (I mention this in the knowledge that Edward had a younger brother whose later life may also have been secretly known to Duchess Margaret). So the more obfuscation, the better.

There was already speculation around a certain pampered little boy known as Jehan le Sage, who had been in her care at Binche for some years.[32] Jehan was said to have been about five when he arrived in 1478, the year Clarence had been brought down by his fatal plotting, and I have suggested that Jehan may possibly have been a natural son of Duke George, secretly sent to be brought up by his childless sister away from public gaze. Certainly the idea took hold on the Continent that Clarence's son was leading an army against Henry VII, assisted by the Tudor king's own official story that this was who the pretender ('impostor') of 1486–87 was claiming to be. The opportunity for Margaret to foster ambiguity about his presence at her court was too good not to make use of, especially if this offered Yorkists a welcome rallying centre.

In the years from mid-1483 to mid-1485 there would have been need to conceal the expatriate Edward V to prevent his becoming a figurehead for Richard III's rebels. I suggest that the serendipity of speculation around Jehan and his royal connections could have been used to divert attention from any other youthful visitor of noble bearing who might crop up within Margaret's purview. Jehan eventually disappeared from records at the end of 1485: a prudent moment, after the Tudor accession, for him to be quietly moved out of reach. Then Edward V was reported in Ireland soon afterwards and any subterfuge could be dropped once he had gained a protective network of Irish supporters at his back.

The theme of counterfeit continues even after Stoke, where some commentators say that King Edward was killed, some that he was helped to escape, and Henry VII's official line was that 'the impostor Lambert Simnel' was set to work in the royal household as a kitchen-hand. To complicate matters, nearly every chronicler gives a different estimate of the pretender's age. The alleged age of the kitchen-hand is absurdly young, and the fact of his survival contributes to disbelief that anyone would ever have taken this lad for a king. Now that we have specialist researchers combing little-known archives, there may well be more revelations to come.

★ ★ ★

Our next reappearance is that of the younger prince, Richard of York. In an equally amazing discovery in the Gelderland Archives (regional archives of Guelders, based in Arnhem), a manuscript was found in 2020 by researcher Nathalie Nijman-Bliekendaal that apparently represents a narration of his own story by young York himself.[33]

As is so often the case with mediæval manuscripts, what survives is a copy. Anyone familiar with research will not be alarmed by this, and indeed scribes in their day could be relied upon to make very faithful copies, especially those employed by people in high authority. Though neither dated nor signed, the archives have dated the copy to about 1500 with the aid of internal evidence, and it is written in a typical late fifteenth-century hand.

This is not the first time its remarkable detail and seeming authenticity have been noticed, along with its inventory of credible names, locations and descriptions of witnesses not encountered elsewhere. A Gelderland correspondence from the 1950s is on file in which the enquiry of a previous researcher is promptly stifled by a university professor with the blinkered reply that surely everyone already knows about the 'false York Perkin Warbeck'. And, indeed, the lad known as 'Perkin' is one of the most famous pretenders of all time, alleged by Henry VII to be a certain Piers Osbeck, son of a boatman of Tournai. But this alleged imposture as Richard, Duke of York, has always been open to question. Even Sir George

Buc, who found that Richard III might have had 'reasons of state' for having his nephews killed, nevertheless refused to believe he did – and firmly declared that the pretender dismissed as 'Perkin' was the younger son of Edward IV.[34] But once again conventional history has followed the easy path of believing Henry VII's official pronouncements, ignoring this lad's astonishingly widespread acceptance among the royal houses of Europe, his promotion by the King of Scotland, and the support of thousands who were willing to fight and die for him.

In a nutshell, the newly rediscovered Gelderland document is a detailed narrative in the first person by 'The Duke of York, son and heir of King Edward the Fourth', describing how he fared after he and his brother were moved from their apartments at the Tower of London. Its opening lines chime with the more condensed proclamation which was issued on his behalf in Scotland in September 1496, saying 'wee in oure tender age escaped by godes might out of the tower of London and were secretlie conveyed over the sea into other divers countries, there remayninge certaine years as unknowne'.[35]

It contains disappointingly little about Edward V, but gives enormous detail, much of it hitherto unknown, about Richard's travels over several years up to the time of his arrival at the court of his aunt Margaret of Burgundy in Malines in late 1492/early 1493, when it was evidently written down at his dictation.

The first detailed analysis of the new-found Gelderland document appears in Langley's *The Princes in the Tower*, undertaken for The Missing Princes Project, where it is reproduced in full.

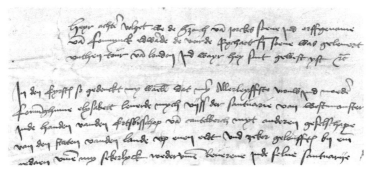

Opening lines of Richard of York's Gelderland MS (*c.*1493).

It records Richard's reception by the Burgundian court, when an account of his recent history would have been dictated, written out and several copies made for those who needed to be assured of his identity. It is beyond dispute, says the analysis, that in the years following his arrival in the Burgundian Netherlands Richard was unreservedly recognized as the son of Edward IV and rightful heir to the English throne after the calamity of Stoke Field. Evidence also reveals that to regain his kingdom he received military and financial support, not only from King Maximilian but also from Albert of Saxony, and Engelbert II of Nassau, who held leading military and administrative roles in Maximilian's service: 'Both lent to Richard of England quite astonishing sums of 30,000 gold florins and 10,000 golden écus respectively,' which Richard undertook to repay once he became sovereign ruler of England.

Writing of his adventures, Richard begins with his departure from the Westminster Abbey sanctuary in May 1483 (16 May is the known date). His mother Elizabeth Woodville had insisted on remaining there with her underage children in silent reproach when the King's Council had declared a protectorate during the twelve-year-old Edward V's minority, overturning her family's plan for him to take immediate power to rule in his own right. Richard says he was 'delivered ... into the hands of the Archbishop of Canterbury' upon his promise of being safely returned – a fact we know from the contemporary report of Domenico Mancini who was in London at the time.[36]

The archbishop took him 'to my uncle of Gloucester. And so I was brought to my brother who was already there, in the Tower of London.' He then recollects several men (?knights and squires) 'who were waiting for us there, of whom I think I remember that johan norijssche [John Norris] was one, and William tyrwijte [Tyrwyth or Tyrwhite] another'. The Missing Princes Project researchers have established that men of these names were esquires of the body to Edward IV.

'On the first night,' Richard continues, these guards were relieved: 'they took leave of us with great melancholy and sadness. To these guards my brother often said melancholic words.[37] Among other things he said and prayed my uncle of Gloucester to have mercy on him, for he was just an innocent.' In the entire account, these are the only references to Richard, Duke of Gloucester, later Richard III.

Next, the Gelderland narrative continues that 'we were delivered to Brackenbury, and then to Sir James Tyrell, and then to the Duke of Buckingham, by whose orders we were separated'. All these named individuals were trusted associates of Gloucester/Richard III at that time. He had appointed Robert Brackenbury his treasurer in 1479 and at the same time Sir James Tyrell his Chamberlain. On 17 July 1483, just before Richard left on progress as king, Brackenbury was appointed Constable of the Tower (he was knighted in 1484); and Sir James Tyrell had been given a combination of great responsibilities upon Richard's accession, being made a Knight of the Body, Master of the Horse and Master of the Henchman.

The Duke of Buckingham needs no introduction. Though he was later suborned to rebellion, he was trusted implicitly by Richard at this time. If Vergil is correct in relating that Buckingham went to his estates at the beginning of August, we may deduce that the two princes came into his hands before the end of July. However, Vergil is not always reliable.

Three more names of men follow, one of whom was very probably Miles Forest, accused by Thomas More of murdering the princes.[38] They had been given orders to take young Richard to 'a room in a place where the lions are kept. There I was for such a long time that Lord Howard, later made Duke of Norfolk, came to me and encouraged me.' The lions of the royal menagerie were housed at the Lion Tower, at the western entrance to the Tower estate, reached via a drawbridge. This seems to have offered a secluded location for the younger prince to be concealed for an unspecified period, which probably seemed a very long time to a boy accustomed as he was to courtly life.

Presumably Edward V had already been very promptly relocated, under the necessity of removing him from London where he was too easy a target for rebels who were scheming to restore him to the throne. We have already discussed the attempt to abduct the princes,[39] and the role of John Howard, Duke of Norfolk, Earl Marshal of England, in bringing the culprits to justice. As one of the foremost shipowners in the country, Norfolk is entirely believable as the organizer of a seaborne evacuation; and, having secured the safe transit of the elder boy, he would now be concerned to make appropriate arrangements for his nine-year-old brother. The Gelderland narrative states that Norfolk then brought along two men, 'hinrijck Parcij' and 'thomas Parcij', who would play a significant part in the young prince's future. 'They swore by honour and oath to Duke Howard … to hide me secretly' for a number of years. 'Then they shaved my hair and put a poor and drab skirt (rockesgen) on me,' then transferred him from the Tower to the adjacent wharf area of St Katherine's, present-day St Katherine's Docks, just a few minutes' distance along the Thames. From here they took a rowing boat out to 'a small narrow ship already waiting'.

These circumstantial details of names and places are impressive and easily credible. What is more, exhaustive searches by The Missing Princes Project have managed to identify the presence of a Thomas and Henry Peirse/Peirs/Percy in Bedale in April 1483 at the manorial court of Francis Lovell. Lovell was Richard III's chamberlain and a particularly close friend from younger days. There was no more loyal lieutenant for him to entrust with the secret whereabouts of the princes, and it may well be that Lovell's knowledge of this precious secret was what prompted his king to exclude him from his knightly company at Bosworth. He remained faithful to the cause, and we have met him as one of the leaders of Edward V's attempt on the Tudor throne in 1487. The Peirses of Bedale would have been closely connected to Lovell and probably numbered among his retainers; thus it is fair to assume, in the absence of any more likely candidates, that these were Richard of York's travelling companions.[40]

Richard of York's wide-ranging travels under their supervision on the continent of Europe are enumerated in his narrative from place to place, and their first destination was the densely populated city of Paris, which they reached after making landfall at the busy port of Boulogne. Norfolk would have known Paris well from his many mercantile contacts and diplomatic missions. So in Paris they stayed 'for a long time: till the moment I was noticed by English folks there', when it was time to make themselves scarce. Many wanderings are then described, first to Chartres, and thereafter ever northwards to Rouen, Dieppe and elsewhere in France, then farther north to Hainault, where they entered Burgundian territory. Other destinations would now centre on the Low Countries, including Malines, Antwerp, Bergen op Zoom, all the while heading north. Presumably there had been contact with Richard's aunt, Duchess Margaret; but if she was already preoccupied with the safeguarding of an incognito Edward V (or a commitment to do so when needed), then to harbour another prince herself would have elevated the level of risk. Such risk became considerably greater, of course, following

King Richard III's death at Bosworth, whereupon the new Tudor king would have turned his eyes toward Burgundy in his need to extinguish opposition.

Eventually Richard of York's party moved westward to Zeeland on the coast, and halted in Middelburg. It may be, if any part of the notorious 'Perkin Warbeck confession' is to be believed, that he was lodged in Middelburg with a merchant between Christmas 1486 and Easter 1487 (Easter Day was 17 April) – perhaps a trusted agent of his aunt? During this time the gathering of Edward V's armada had commenced, and it would have been inconceivable to risk both princes in the same place at the same time. So Richard's next move was to take ship to Portugal in the company of Sir Edward Brampton's wife.[41]

In his Gelderland narrative he awaits Lady Brampton's readiness and then sails with the Peirses to Lisbon. The death of Norfolk beside his king at Bosworth must have been a major blow to whatever plans had been set for young Richard's safekeeping, and it seems that whoever was now directing operations needed some token to prove that it was genuinely the young prince who was being carried overseas. Richard rather charmingly mentions that he is recognizable by his playing the clavichord, a small keyboard instrument of delicate tone that could be folded up and easily transported. This tends to enhance the *bona fides* of the narrator, as skills on such an instrument chime with his upbringing at the Edwardian court, and would be incongruous for the alleged 'son of a boatman' of Henry VII's propaganda machine.[42] We may imagine that he gained solace from this pastime during his wanderings.[43]

From Portugal, probably as soon as he was able, Richard sent Thomas Peirse to England with messages for his mother, Elizabeth Woodville: presumably reassurances of his safety, but also commiseration on the fate of his brother at Stoke. Tragedy then struck closer to home when his other guardian, Henry Peirse, fell ill of the plague and died. The plague made its appearance in parts of Portugal between about 1488 and 1491, and Richard's sixteenth birthday would fall in mid-1489.[44] This was his age of majority by royal standards, and Henry Peirse had already received advice, it seems, as to Richard's next actions: 'he told me that when he died I would have to travel to Ireland to the lords of Kyldare and Desmond, and also told me how I should rule the country.'

In 1491 Richard made his way back north to Brittany, where he found a ship bound for Ireland. He did not name the shipmaster, but was confident at the time of his narration that the man would testify to his true identity.[45] In Ireland, by at least November that year, 'I found several of my acquaintances, among them the lord of Kyldare ... and many others. There I was recognized for who I was and treated as such.'

In yet another twist to the tale, he adds what happened after his welcome in Ireland: '... my cousin the King of France contacted me,' he says, 'and made a firm promise to assist and help me to claim my rights. However, when I arrived in France I found the opposite.' The *volte-face* by Charles VIII that put paid to their alliance was due to his negotiating the Treaty of Étaples with Henry VII, which precluded either party from supporting the other's claimants, rebels or traitors. Margaret of Burgundy was now the one safe haven near at hand: 'So I left, and went to my dearest aunt, the Duchess of Burgundy: she recognized my rights and honesty. And by the grace of God, I received help, honour and comfort from my dear friends and servants, so that in a short time I will obtain my right to which I was born.'

The assertion 'I will obtain my right' brings Richard's narration right up to the present (around end 1492–early 1493), expressing his hopes for the future with the help of his aunt.

At this time, on 25 August 1493, Margaret is known to have confirmed his arrival in a letter to Queen Isabella of Spain, citing the testimony of the Irish Earls of Desmond and Kildare: 'At last the Duke of York himself came to me out of France, seeking help and assistance. ... I indeed for my part, when I gazed on this male remnant of our family – who had come through so many perils and misfortunes – was deeply moved ... I embraced him as my only nephew and my only son.'[46]

This letter was Margaret's attempt to enlist Isabella to their cause, and it was supported by Richard's recorded 'Dendermonde letter' of the same date to the Spanish queen, signed Richard Plantagenet, recounting some of his experiences in brief.[47] Comparison of this with the Gelderland manuscript shows that where the same events are recounted they are almost identical, suggesting that they were set down at about the same time. Of course, there are problems with the contents of the letter, especially the anomaly which declares the brothers had been 'handed over to a certain lord to be killed', and that Edward had died 'a pitiable death'. But it must be appreciated that Isabella was not yet a supporter, and it could not be expected that any letter would be kept confidential. There was the possibility that she would share its contents with Henry VII – which, indeed, she did.

Richard would have realized the good sense behind keeping the brothers' movements separate and their enemies guessing. By withholding details from Isabella, he was protecting anyone in England who had assisted him or his brother but who yet remained in Henry VII's favour, since any clues to their identity would have led to their downfall.[48] As we have seen, even Sir William Stanley was sent to the block for voicing the possibility that this lad might be the genuine article.[49]

Probably Richard was advised, when writing to outsiders, to scotch any lingering hopes for his brother Edward V; such hopes would do nothing but queer the pitch for the prospects of a King Richard IV, now the standard-bearer for York. As detailed earlier in Chapter 9, far from the Tudor fable of the humble boatman's son, the returning Richard of York garnered substantial support and belief in his royal identity among several of Europe's heads of state. The sad end to his attempt upon England's throne is, alas, only too well known.

In reflecting on this final chapter of reappearances, I am reminded how many times as a biographer I have wished my subject had written a diary. Amazingly, Richard of York did the equivalent when he set down his Gelderland testimony detailing when and how he and his brother were quietly moved out of the Tower where tradition says they died. It may be thought that these revelations cost him some concern since the many details, especially the names of those who had helped him at risk of their lives, had never previously been recorded. In this document we are at last regaled with enough specifics of identifiable persons, places and dates to answer at last the sterile (and unproven) voice of authority that claims the princes never survived the reign of Richard III. The crux of such argument has always been why, if their deaths were so necessary to secure his crown, it was never allowed to be known; whereas, in sending them to safety, secrecy was paramount. Facts do not cease to be facts because they are ignored.

In 1493 Richard of York revealed these facts because, now the die was cast, those who were enlisted to support his bid for the throne needed to know the full truth. And truth is the daughter of time, not of authority.

Appendix

Principal Sources

Because it is important to understand the origin and nature of sources on which books like this rely, there follows a compendium, grouped chronologically, of principal sources used herein (excluding official documents and collections of letters). Thumbnail sketches assist in evaluating factors such as their reliability, when they were written and for whose consumption.

It was routine to flatter a patron and pander to his prejudices, so we must always enquire whether the writer had a particular audience in mind. If not, there was still room for personal prejudice and partisanship.

It was also routine to plagiarize other works without acknowledgement, adding embellishments and passing off the result as one's own. Therefore, even plain statements of what appear to be historical facts must be assessed for reliability, asking whether the information is likely to be first-hand or derived from elsewhere. Sources are listed in four categories:

(1) *Commentaries dating from Richard's lifetime*
(2) *Personal reminiscences after Richard's reign*
(3) *Tudor 'histories'*
(4) *Post-Tudor investigations*

(1) *Commentaries dating from Richard's lifetime*

There are no useful contemporaneous books or chronicles, but there are letters, official records, household accounts and the like. There is also an important, lengthy report by Domenico Mancini.

De Occupatione Regni Anglie Per Riccardum Tercium Libellus by Domenico Mancini (*c.*1434–*c.*1500)

A hostile source, but immensely significant because contemporary. This Italian cleric had come to England probably in late 1482. He was on a fact-finding (or spying) mission on behalf of his patron Angelo Cato, Archbishop of Vienne, who was in turn physician and close councillor to England's enemy, the French King Louis XI. Mancini left England very soon after Richard's coronation and wrote up his account before December 1483.

It seems unlikely that Mancini knew English and, not moving amid inner royal or government circles himself, he must have relied heavily on what he was told. He provides no physical description of Richard III, and shows no sign of personal acquaintance with anyone connected with him.

Mancini asserted that Richard had been aiming to seize power from the moment of Edward IV's death. Although he almost certainly harboured no personal malice against any of the protagonists, he clearly knew that a negative picture of England would please his French masters.

Mancini's information seems to have come from sources predominantly hostile to Richard and the entire house of York, as would be expected from France's history of supporting Lancaster. His reportage was only as accurate as his anonymous informants; any contacts provided by his patron would almost certainly have been of like mind. Only one informant is named: Edward V's physician John Argentine, who was probably with the young king at Ludlow and Stony Stratford as well as at the Tower.

Despite the hostility which led Mancini to report (even before Richard III's coronation) that there were suspicions of Edward V's death, the Italian was scrupulous enough to declare that at the time of writing he had been unable to ascertain the truth of the matter.

The manuscript was found and published in the 1930s by C.A.J. Armstrong, with his own translation and commentary, both being symptomatic of an era when the fifteenth century was not widely studied, and when Thomas More's essay on Richard III was considered authoritative. Armstrong employed the resoundingly condemnatory tropes of his day, with the result that Latinists ever since have realized that mistranslated words and concepts were attributed to Mancini's pen. In particular the title adopted by Armstrong contained a most unwelcome mistranslation of the word *occupatione* – rendered as 'usurpation' when applied to Richard III – whereas when applied to Henry VI he rendered it as 'occupation'. In terms of mediæval Latin usage, the strongest translation would be 'seizure', and some Latinists have preferred 'taking'. Mancini himself did not accuse Richard of usurpation.

Armstrong espoused an oddly back-to-front idea, which I refute, that the contents of Mancini's report could not have informed other writers/chroniclers on whose works historians have based their opinions. Thus Mancini is often cited, when it chimes with later writings, as 'proof' of their accuracy. When the opportunity arose in 2020 I published my own edition of Mancini with a new translation, analysis and up-to-date historical notes. My new translation has now been adopted for all quotations within this book.

The Rous Roll (English version) by John Rous (1411–1491)

Rous was a chantry priest, chaplain of the chapel of St Mary Magdalen at Guy's Cliff, near Warwick, which was founded by Richard Beauchamp, Earl of Warwick. He enjoyed the patronage of both the Beauchamp and Neville earls. Rous wrote two versions of his 'History of the Earls of Warwick' between 1477 and 1485 – one Roll in English and one Roll in Latin. The English version survives in the British Library and was written during Richard III's lifetime. Rous is believed to have intended it for the queen, so it was complimentary towards Richard; for example it contains the following words:

> The moost myghty prynce Rychard, by the grace of God kynge of Ynglond ... all avarice set asyde, rewled hys subiettys in hys realme ful commendabylly, poneschynge offenders of hys lawes, specyally extorcioners and oppressors of hys comyns, and chereschynge tho that were vertues, by the whyche dyscrete guydynge he gat gret thank of God and love of all his subiettys

ryche and pore and gret laud of the people of all othyr landys a
bowt hym.

Rous evidently still had possession of the Latin version when
Henry VII seized the throne, and he proceeded to recast it to suit
the Tudor stance (the revised manuscript is preserved in the College
of Arms, see below). He was unable to retrieve and alter the English
original, so both copies can be compared, most instructively, as
examples of how important it suddenly became in 1485 to expunge
anything favourable to the former king. The standard edition is
The Rows Roll, edited by William Courthope in 1859, which was
reproduced in 1980 with an introduction by Charles Ross.

(2) *Personal reminiscences after Richard's reign*

Written after the king's death, these are records of events of
Richard's day which the writers may have witnessed. They may
be personal recollections, or copies of written notes made by
others. Most would be geared to finding favour with the ruling
Tudor house, which from the start encouraged vilification of the
late king. As well as applying the same criteria of believability
(did they really know, or were they just recounting popular
stories?), another aspect to be aware of is that these reminiscences
are written with hindsight, so they often incorporate knowledge,
perceptions or assumptions accrued since the events they mention.

The Crowland Chronicle (Ingulph's Chronicle of the Abbey of Crowland)

This contained work by several successive chroniclers, recording
topics of concern to the Abbey of Crowland (or Croyland) in
Lincolnshire, together with matters of interest in the world at
large. The section covering Richard's reign occurs towards the
end of the Second Continuation. The contents seem to have
been supplied to the abbey by an outside source and written into
the chronicle around the death of the abbot in October 1485,
two months after Bosworth. The edition principally quoted in
this book is the most recent available: *The Crowland Chronicle
Continuations: 1459–1486* edited by Nicholas Pronay and John Cox,
published in 1986.

Much of the manuscript was destroyed or severely damaged by a fire in 1731, but fortunately an edition in the original Latin had been published by William Fulman of Oxford in 1684. Although its accuracy cannot be established in total, Pronay and Cox have compared the Fulman edition with such of the manuscript as survives, and declared it to exhibit careful work of a remarkably high standard. The original manuscript was of course compiled by monkish scribes, who may themselves have made errors and quite possibly inserted some elements in the wrong sequence.

Differing views have been expressed over the years as to who originated the information recorded in the Second Continuation. Clues earlier in the text have been taken to refer to a doctor of law who under Edward IV went on diplomatic missions and held the status of *conciliarius* (a councillor or an official who had sworn the councillors' oath). He may have retained the same position in the early post-Edwardian council, and seems initially to have been privy to what transpired in many council proceedings; however, Pronay and Cox observe that from the beginning of Richard's reign 'many writers have commented on the apparent decline in the quality of political information, which seemed to them to come from a more distant vantage point than before, and a corresponding decline in the confidence with which he is writing'.

In a hunt for the identity of the originator, many historians have expended energy advocating their preferred candidates at the expense of analysing the noticeably variable quality of the information supplied to the abbey. In the past Richard III's chancellor John Russell, Bishop of Lincoln, has been touted as author. But there are several aspects, including its pettifogging tone, that make Russell a somewhat unlikely originator, especially of material pertaining to Richard's reign for whose policies he shared some collective responsibility. Pronay and Cox favour a senior Chancery official such as Dr Henry Sharp, since the author is evidently familiar with Chancery and with drawing up legal documents. Sharp's status seems to have declined after Richard III's accession and to have improved under the regime of Henry VII.

With all its faults, the continuation is the most authoritative source we have for Richard's reign, written by someone with inside information, and the only near-contemporaneous record of events in and near the capital that carries anything like the authenticity of a first-hand account. Setting aside the all-too-evident speculating and moralizing, the author is generally to be believed on matters about which he was in a position to record objective facts. But he held strong, often prejudiced views which not infrequently coloured his recollections. He also made assumptions which cannot be substantiated. From the death of Edward IV onwards he increasingly favours the Woodville party and is disapproving of Richard.

The Rous Roll (Latin version)

As mentioned above, John Rous changed his coat to suit the political climate of the day, and when Henry VII took the throne he retrospectively edited the Latin version of his Roll by the simple means of taking a knife and doing a cut-and-paste job. He excised complimentary textual references to Richard, instead describing him as merely *infelix maritus* (unhappy husband) of Anne Neville, and interposed her first husband, Edward of Lancaster, between images of Anne and Richard. This doctored version currently resides in the College of Arms, London.

Historia Regum Anglie (BL Cotton MS Vespasian A XII)

Another work by John Rous, recounting his version of the general history of England, produced ?1490 (long enough after Bosworth for him to leave a blank instead of writing the year which he had obviously forgotten). Rous evidently felt his revised Latin Roll (above) cast too little odium on Richard, so he proceeded to remedy the situation in the relevant portion of this *History of the Kings of England*, dedicated to King Henry VII.

Again Rous tailored his narrative to suit the Tudor view, taking the opportunity to blacken Richard's name with a litany of crimes and murders. In his grotesque tale of a baby with teeth and hair emerging after two years in the womb, we see the basis for the monster-figure of later Tudor writings. As Alison Hanham comments in *Richard III and his Early Historians*, his account 'suggests the fullness of malice', possibly because he believed Richard poisoned Queen Anne.

It might have been a valuable contemporaneous text had it not consisted of (in Hanham's words) 'a rag-bag of gleanings' from 'a busy-minded man who loved gossip'. His isolation in Warwick also means his reliability is limited to events arising from local knowledge. The complete Latin text was published by Thomas Hearne as *Joannis Rossi Antiquarii Warwicensis Historia Regum Angliae* in 1745 (available online); part of the text is translated in Dr Alison Hanham's *Early Historians*.

Historical Notes of a London Citizen (College of Arms MS2 M6)
A fragment brought to light in 1980 by Professor Richard Firth Green and published in *English Historical Review* in 1981. This is the commonplace book of a London merchant, recording the sort of views that were current in London. The notes form part of a miscellaneous sixteenth-century collection of papers and appear to be copies, made about 1512–13, of fifteenth-century originals. The nearest clue to date appears in a reference to Elizabeth of York in the present tense regarding her marriage to Henry VII, which may have been written by 1487 or at least before her death in 1503. Two extracts are of interest: the first deals with the Hastings treason plot and the second mentions Harry, Duke of Buckingham as possibly responsible for or instigating the murder of Edward V and his brother.

Chronicles of Jean Molinet (1435–1507) edited by J.A. Bouchon in *Collection des Chroniques nationales françaises* (Paris, 1827–8)
The Frenchman Jean Molinet served the Dukes of Burgundy, and was the continuator of the *Chroniques de ce Temps* begun by Georges Chastellain. His account, written in about 1500, is more confused and unreliable than that of Philippe de Commynes. He claims, *inter alia*, that Richard III plundered the churches.

Memoirs of Philippe de Commynes (1447–1511)
Philippe de Commynes was a valued councillor at the court of the French King Louis XI in Richard III's reign, having defected from Louis's enemy Charles of Burgundy. He wrote the first six books of his *Mémoires* between 1488 and 1504, at the behest of that same Archbishop Cato who commissioned Mancini to write his report. Unlike Mancini, de Commynes was a politician and man of the world. He drew personal conclusions from the events he recounted, and was not above colouring his reflections to suit his own purposes, such as when he took pains to characterize Charles

of Burgundy as mentally deranged. Nevertheless, although he might be unreliable as to detail, his position at Court depended on being well-informed on foreign affairs so the occurrences he recounts are broadly based on events as he understood them. De Commynes's Book 6 deals with matters of interest concerning our period (in various editions, including a translation by Michael Jones, 1972). Originally printed and reprinted between 1524 and 1548, the *Mémoires* were published in full in Paris in 1924–5, edited by J. Calmette and G. Durville.

The author tends to overdramatize what he has heard of goings-on in England ('The Duke of Gloucester had his two nephews murdered and made himself king. ... All his late brother's loyal servants, or at least those he could capture, were killed on his orders'). In one of three different versions of the fate of the 'princes in the Tower' he cites the Duke of Buckingham as their murderer. The memoirs were used by Edward Hall in compiling his *Union of the Two Noble Families* (below).

British Library MS Cotton Vitellius A.XVI

A chronicle dating from the early part of Henry VII's reign which is known simply by its B.M. shelf reference. It is alone in openly asserting that 'King Richard ... put to death the two children of King Edward, for which cause he lost the hearts of the people'. It appears to share common sources with the *Great Chronicle* and Fabyan's *New Cronycles* (below), but the charge does not appear in those accounts even though they may have been written later. Charles Ross comments in the introduction to his *Richard III*: 'In some respects the penny-plain narrative of Vitellius A.XVI may be preferred to the more prejudiced version of the *Great Chronicle*.' The Vitellius manuscript was published in 1905 in *Chronicles of London* edited by C.L. Kingsford, of which a facsimile edition was published in 1977.

The New Cronycles of England and France (aka The Chronicle of Fabyan or The Concordaunce of Historyes or Fabyan's Chronicle)
by Robert Fabyan (*c*.1450–1513)

Originally completed in 1504, may have been extended during his retirement; probably circulated in manuscript long before first publication (1516). Fabyan was a learned alderman of the city of London, sheriff in 1493, and freeman and master of the Drapers'

Company. He was apparently present in London during the reigns of Edward IV and Richard III. However, Alison Hanham (*op. cit.*) feels his presence 'need have little to do with the authenticity of the work ascribed to him'. Research by M.T.W. Payne (Harlaxton Symposium, 2011) suggests Fabyan started on this in the 1490s after his continuation of the *Great Chronicle* (below), although the two contain differences. Fabyan notes that before Richard's accession he was so 'loved and praised' that many would have 'jeoparded life and goods with him'. He makes no mention of witchcraft and withered arms, and in his report of Shaw's sermon (which he could have heard in person) there is nothing about Edward IV being illegitimate. The standard edition is that edited by Henry Ellis, published in 1811.

The Great Chronicle of London

Payne (see above) argues that Robert Fabyan found this chronicle in need of completion in the 1490s and continued it up to 1496, when he decided to concentrate on his *New Cronycles*. Then in retirement he returned to continue the London story to 1512. Both Thomas More and Richard Grafton knew it well (or its sources), the latter using it in his *Continuation of Hardyng's Chronicle*. It gives an eyewitness account of Edward V's entry into London on 4 May 1483, but becomes inaccurate in recording later events, with internal contradictions and mistakes in facts and chronology: e.g. (referring to 1484) 'After Easter much whispering was among the people that the king had put the children of King Edward to death, and also that he had poisoned the queen his wife.' This chronicle received its first modern publication in 1938, edited by A.H. Thomas and I.D. Thornley.

(3) *Tudor 'histories'*

These invariably reflect the orthodox Tudor view that Richard III was a villainous usurper who was justly deposed by the heroic Henry Tudor. They claim to provide authoritative information, but contain many discrepancies.

A lost Latin manuscript castigating Richard III by John Morton
(*c*.1420–1500)
Probably written in the 1490s. Morton was Henry VII's Cardinal
Archbishop of Canterbury (Bishop of Ely during the reign of
Richard III) and a long-time supporter of the Tudor-Beaufort
camp. Often ignored or discounted by traditional historians,
the erstwhile existence of such a manuscript is confirmed by
scholars who have studied those early seventeenth-century
writers that were prepared to challenge the Tudor demonization
of Richard III. In particular it has been held by Dr A.N. Kincaid
and others that Sir William Cornwallis's defence of Richard (see
below) was prompted by Morton's hostile tract.

There was also a suggestion, going back at least to 1596 (Sir
John Harington in *The Metamorphosis of Ajax*), that Morton's book
was the original of Thomas More's *History of King Richard the
Third*, which More was supposed to have merely copied. Though
a popular theory for some years, and vehemently espoused by Sir
Clements Markham in 1906, this notion no longer carries weight.
The likelihood is that More did not so much copy it as base the
bulk of his work on its contents.

Sir George Buc was another member of Harington's literary
group, which included Harington's friend Sir Edward Hoby
who also had knowledge of the Morton manuscript. In Buc's
own notes handwritten between 1604 and 1611 and found in one
of his books (Francis Godwin's *Catalogue of the Bishops of England*,
now in the Bodleian Library), he described Morton's manuscript
as being in the possession of the Roper family, which Buc later
confirmed in his *History of King Richard the Third* (see below):
'This book was lately in the hands of Mr Roper of Eltham, as
Sir Edward Hoby (who saw it) told me.' Buc's text also states
categorically that Morton's book 'came after to the hands of
Mr More'.

It is understandable that More would have taken for granted
what was written by his former mentor. We may perhaps also
be permitted to guess that More's inexplicable abandonment of
his *Richard III*, unfinished, after a decade spent intermittently
honing and polishing it to the heights of literary excellence,
might have resulted from a gradual realization that it
was based on a work whose assertions, when scrutinized,
appeared questionable.

Readers are invited also to consider Henry Tudor's penchant for commissioning writers (Bernard André, Polydore Vergil) to produce official narratives that legitimated him and vilified the Ricardian régime. He might well have been following the advice and example of John Morton.

Historia Regis Henrici Septimi by Bernard André (1450–*c*.1521)

Henry VII's official biographer and poet laureate wrote his *Life of Henry VII* in about 1502 at the express request of the king (Cott. MSS Dom A xviii). Charles Ross (*op. cit.*) describes it as 'Elegant toadyism to a royal paymaster'. André was a blind poet from Toulouse who did not reside in England until after the accession of Henry Tudor, to whose suite he was attached and whose fortunes he followed. He was in no position to conduct independent research, and merely parroted whatever he was told, making his patron the glowing hero of his tale. He says 'Richard ordered the princes to be put to the sword' but offers no candidate for the task, and the supposed confession by Sir James Tyrell is not mentioned. Available online at www.philological.bham.ac.uk/andreas.

Anglica Historia by Polydore Vergil (*c*.1470–1555)

This was a relatively scientific undertaking in terms of its attempt to reconstruct the history of England and her people from the earliest times. Vergil arrived in London from Italy in about 1502 and came to the notice of Henry VII, who encouraged him by a formal request to write his massive *Anglica Historia* which eventually emerged in the form of thirty-six books. The printed texts date from 1534 onwards, but a manuscript version was ready by 1512–13 (although this was subject to government scrutiny). Books 23–25 cover the reign of Richard III, and it is interesting to note that of the fifty-four pages therein, there are very few in which Henry Tudor fails to be mentioned. An incorrigible editorializer and moralizer, Vergil takes it as his thesis that Tudor was predestined by God to be the saviour of the English nation; consequently all his facts after about 1400 are neatly lined up behind this theme.

While it would be an injustice to Vergil to claim that he was a mere propaganda hack for the Tudor party, nevertheless it is evident that his sources were close to royal circles and the only records made available to him would have been official and approved. Vergil himself complained of the paucity of written records dating from the late fifteenth century (perhaps because they were withheld or destroyed?), and admitted relying to a considerable extent on oral sources. Among these, a chronicler would search long and in vain to find anyone still alive who was likely to offer an impartial view of events of Richard's reign, let alone someone openly prepared to support Richard in conversations with Henry VII's protégé.

There is no escaping the long shadow cast by the Court when it came to Vergil's choice of what to put down in print. In Alison Hanham's words: 'he was not altogether guiltless of suppressing truth and suggesting falsities'. Other phrases that occur in her analysis of Vergil include 'discreet omission', 'minor omissions and distortions', 'fiction has sometimes been disguised as historical relation' and 'does seem deliberately to lie (or at any rate prevaricate)'. When it came to awkward facts that did not suit the prevailing Court climate, Hanham points to Vergil's decisions often being dictated by expediency.

Thus, while we cannot dismiss Vergil out of hand, we have to acknowledge he is a tainted source. Where he becomes very useful is in his detailed, almost blow-by-blow knowledge of the movements of Henry Tudor and his supporters during 1483–85. Even so, facts and dates are sometimes skewed to show them in the best light. By contrast with this intimate knowledge obviously obtained from the horse's mouth, Vergil's observations on Richard, and his claim to understand the innermost workings of his mind, must be taken with a large pinch of salt. Nevertheless he manages one or two comments favourable to Richard.

Since Vergil gives no sources for his pronouncements, we must conclude that his text is too greatly affected by expedient, and contains too much of what Dr Hanham calls 'general gossip or artistic enlargement' to be fundamentally reliable, unless we have good reason to believe otherwise.

Books 23–25 cover the reigns of Henry VI, Edward IV and Richard III. The J.B. Nichols edition of Book 25, *Richard III*, is accessible on the website of the Richard III Society's American Branch (www.r3.org).

The History of King Richard the Third by Thomas More (1478–1535)

More was born in 1478, knighted in 1521 and executed by Henry VIII in 1535. This is a work of literature which has been taken as history for nearly 500 years, evidently thanks to the deference in which Thomas More's reputation for probity is held. It has been described as of paramount importance in forming the traditional (Tudor) picture of Richard III.

Master More probably started writing his narrative somewhere around 1515, and went back to make numerous changes in later years (clues in the texts suggest that he was working on it in the 1520s, perhaps even after 1527). But it was never a finished manuscript, and during More's lifetime he exhibited no desire for it to be published. Indeed it is evident, from the five different surviving versions in English and in Latin, that it never satisfied him.

It was first published after his death by Richard Grafton in 1543, in the guise of a 'continuation' (compiled by Grafton) to *The Chronicle of John Hardyng*, so that from the very first edition it acquired its erroneous label as an historical chronicle. More's nephew William Rastell published a different version in 1557, inventing the title '*History*' and claiming that his was more authentic, whereas the 1543 version was 'very much corrupt in many places'. However Alison Hanham (*Richard III and his Early Historians*), has made a convincing case that both versions were by More himself, penned at different times and moreover, that Grafton's 1543 version was probably a revised and extended text produced after the earlier manuscript found by Rastell (which the latter thought, in all honesty, was the definitive version).

It is the belief of many scholars, Dr Hanham among them, that More was no more intent on writing a work of history than was Shakespeare in his play *Richard III*. Like Shakespeare, More was attracted by a character of theatrical proportions, which he could portray as evil made flesh. He had no personal knowledge of King Richard, and relied on information gleaned from others—notably from John Morton, who wrote a tract vilifying the late king (see above), and in whose household More spent some of his early years.

It is reasonable to assume that More took what Morton wrote and used it as his starting-point. The work became a vehicle for his elegant style and trenchant wit, emerging as an outstanding piece of dramatic literature. Suffice to say here that criticisms of More's frequent inaccuracies, blatant bias and fabrication of 'facts' generally miss the point that the author was only distantly interested in what actually happened. He never intended to write a history of events, and cannot be blamed for failing to do so.

Hence we should not take More too seriously, enticing though it is to believe his vivid narratives and anecdotes, especially because in many places there is a kernel of truth that can be corroborated by reference to other sources. However, even where he admits of genuine doubt in his own text, More invariably chooses whichever stance supports his essential characterization of Richard as the personification of evil.

We know More had access to Polydore Vergil's manuscript (by 1514 Vergil had completed a draft covering events up to 1513), and to several other chronicles of which some survive. Therefore, the discerning historian will preferably look for facts in those other works, not in Thomas More's satirical drama.

The Chronicle of John Hardyng (1378–1465)

This was essentially a time-serving chronicle in doggerel verse written by John Hardyng, a northerner and aspiring antiquary who had fought at Agincourt. He was still writing his chronicle in Edward IV's reign at the age of eighty-six, constantly revising it to flatter changing patrons. It was published by Richard Grafton in 1543 (reprinted 1812 ed. Ellis). Obviously Hardyng himself never wrote of Richard III so the supposed 'continuation' about Richard inserted by Grafton was lifted wholesale from other relevant writings – Polydore Vergil and, for the first time, Thomas More. Grafton used a version of More that probably contained that author's most up-to-date revisions and when More's narrative abruptly broke off during his account of the Buckingham-Morton conspiracy, Grafton reverted to Vergil's text for the remainder of his 'continuation' to Hardyng. This text was later used by Edward Hall.

The Union of the Two Noble and Illustre Famelies of Lancastre and Yorke by Edward Hall (or Halle) (*c.*1498–1547)

This was first published by Richard Grafton in 1548 with a second edition in 1550. Hall was a sixteenth-century lawyer and judge, and according to Paul Murray Kendall (in *The Great Debate*) an ardently loyal subject of Henry VIII: 'It is Hall's fervid work via Holinshed's *Chronicle* (in the second edition of 1587), that William Shakespeare exuberantly dramatized in his *Richard the Third* (about 1593)'.

Charles Ross (in *Richard III*) confirms Hall's work was framed as a fulsome eulogy of the Tudor régime. 'This histrionic approach … suited Shakespeare well, and was heightened by Hall's exuberant and highly charged style and his lavish embellishment of his sources to strengthen dramatic effect.' For example, Henry Tudor, appearing before Bosworth, 'seemed more an angelical creature than a terrestrial personage'.

Hall reproduced Thomas More's account of Richard's seizure of the throne in its entirety, taken from Grafton's continuation to *The Chronicle of John Hardyng* (above), and for the remainder relied on Polydore Vergil and the London Chronicles, occasionally contributing a few unique facts of his own. He also copied from the *Memoirs* of Philippe de Commynes (section 2 above).

The 1809 edition with the title *Hall's Chronicle* (Johnson: London)was edited by Henry Ellis and includes the variant material from 1548, and also has a useful editorial introduction. A facsimile edition of the 1550 was published in 1970 under the original title (using the spelling Halle). Hall's account comes to an end in 1532 and he died in 1547.

The Pastime of People by John Rastell (*c.*1475–1536)
Written in 1529. A compiler and collator, Rastell was no historian but quoted from existing chronicles and common gossip. His list of different ways in which Edward IV's sons are said to have been killed is extensive, yet despite being Thomas More's brother-in-law he makes no mention of More's Tyrell story. This and the next two publications follow the standard Tudor line and cannot be taken as reliable sources; they are merely derivations of those mentioned above, with the additional caveat that they tend to record as fact many calumnies of Richard III reported elsewhere only as rumour.

A Chronicle at Large (Richard Grafton, *c.*1511–1572)
Another derivative work (1568) from this publisher of several Tudor chronicles who took advantage of his position to plagiarize

many sources. He makes the following comment about Richard: 'if
he had continued Lord Protector the realm would have prospered,
and he would have been praised and beloved'. (Reprinted Johnson:
London, 1809.)

Chronicles of England by Raphael Holinshed (*c*.1529–*c*.1580)
Published in 1577 and 1587, essentially derived from other
chronicles, the second edition was used extensively as a source by
Shakespeare. Holinshed's account of Richard III is very much a
copy of Edward Hall in form and content.

(4) Post-Tudor investigations

In the last quarter of the sixteenth century, mainly owing to the
loss of written records brought about by Henry VIII's dissolution
of the monasteries, a movement grew up devoted to preserving
documents of antiquity. The scholarly 'College or Society of
Antiquaries' was founded in 1586, with members who included
historians like John Stow together with lawyers, archivists,
heralds (e.g. William Camden) and collectors (e.g. Sir Robert
Cotton). They built up priceless libraries and threw themselves
into the task of reassessing the annals and chronicles which had
hitherto been accepted unquestioningly as the authentic history
of England. Many new and valuable publications ensued, which
influenced the views of later writers.

The Annales or Generall Chronicle of England by John Stow
(*c*.1525–1605)
Published in 1580, 1592 and repeatedly into the 1600s. A member
of the College of Antiquaries, Stow built up a large library of
historical material for his own interest and analysed his sources
critically. His colleague John Speed asserted that Stow believed
the princes had not been murdered but were living incognito
beyond the sea. 'Stow's entry into the world of scholarship,'
says A.N. Kincaid in his Introduction to Buc's *History* 'was
impelled by a dissatisfaction with Grafton's adopting wholesale
and without documentation accounts from his chronicler
forebears ... though his *Annales* still lean toward reliance on
the older chronicles, his use of them is acknowledged, and they

are supplemented and often contradicted by [his] references to public records.' Such works, says Kincaid,

> began, though only slightly, to liberalize the view of Richard. Stow was apparently making investigations, as we can see from Buc's *viva voce* references to him, and finding many of the charges unjustified. In his *Survey*, he describes Richard's accession as an election, not a usurpation, and in his *Annales* he lists Richard's good works. This is as far as he goes in his published writings, but as Buc's *History* shows, his private researches went much farther.

The Encomium of Richard III by Sir William Cornwallis (*c.*1579–1614)

Published in 1616 but written earlier. In separate analyses of *The Encomium*, Professor W.G. Zeefeld in 1940, followed by J.A. Ramsden and A.N. Kincaid in 1977, held that Cornwallis wrote his defence of Richard as a direct response to John Morton's tract which gave a hostile account of Richard III and his reign.

The Morton manuscript was erroneously thought by some, including Zeefeld, to be the real original of More's *History of King Richard the Third*, but this idea is no longer current. 'Interest seems to have existed among a group of literary men,' wrote Kincaid, 'all of whom were aware of a pamphlet by Bishop Morton on which More's history is based.' References by Sir John Harington in 1596, and Sir George Buc *c.*1604–1611, show that Morton's tract was still in circulation in the 1590s and early 1600s. Cornwallis, as a member of their group and with other useful connections, would have had the opportunity to read it for himself and thus closely address the allegations it contained. These allegations parallel those found in More's *Richard III* including the fiction of 'Elizabeth Lucy', Richard's supposed accusation of his mother's adultery, and his desire to marry his niece. Cornwallis seeks not so much to rebut them as to justify Richard's actions.

In their introduction to Cornwallis (ed. Kincaid, 1977), Ramsden and Kincaid state: 'our theory is that Cornwallis came across the original Morton tract and set out to refute it, probably afterwards turning his work into something like a paradox'. This afterthought manifests itself in the final words, 'yet, for all this, knowe I hold this but as a Paradoxe'. However, there is doubt as to whether Cornwallis even wrote these words, which occur not in the original but in later versions: the *Encomium* circulated through many hands and underwent many transformations by people who copied it and passed it on with their own additions and amendments. Moreover, Cornwallis was a successful master of the paradox form, in which the *Encomium* has been adjudged a failure by classical standards, so the words attempting to categorize it as such could well have been added by some other hand.

The History of King Richard the Third by Sir George Buc (1560–1622/3)

A vindication of Richard written in 1619 by Sir George Buc (aka Buck), Master of the Revels to King James I; it was stolen and published in corrupted form by his great-nephew in 1646. The great-nephew's name was, conveniently, George Buck and he passed the work off as his own. As late as 1973 this corrupt version was still being republished, despite A.N. Kincaid having undertaken the mammoth task of editing the original manuscript, much damaged by fire, in a version as faithful as possible to the original (published 1979). Until this date, Sir George's book had been largely discounted as an unreliable source thanks to the interferences, errors and excisions of his great-nephew, which removed references to the original author's careful personal research. Over the course of 400 years, historians consistently attacked Buc on the basis of this diluted and mutilated version without troubling to check its authenticity.

Sir George Buc, well reputed and 'one of the most exemplary scholars of his era' (Kincaid), was almost certainly a member of the College of Antiquaries and thus observed their scrupulous and critical use of sources. He was assisted by some of the most eminent antiquaries of the age including John Stow, then a much older man. Dr Kincaid states that 'Buc was ... writing at a time when and among a group of scholars to whom documentation was an increasingly important issue,' and maintains that, in contrast to his Tudor predecessors, he exercised critical judgement in his use of secondary sources. A salient feature is the author's repeatedly stated conviction that the downfall and concomitant vilification of Richard III were engineered by John Morton, later Henry VII's chancellor. Buc was evidently familiar with Morton's anti-Richard tract, to the extent that he twice quotes Morton as a direct source for information that does not appear in More. Dr Kincaid's new, revised edition of Sir George Buc's *History* was published in 2023.

Even in its corrupted form, the *History* was influential in calling attention to *Titulus Regius*, the *Crowland Chronicle* and other original documents, and led several subsequent historians to caution against wholesale belief in More and the Tudor writers.

Notes

- The calendar year is deemed to start on 1 January. The Julian calendar applies, since the Gregorian calendar was not introduced until 1582 (and not adopted in England until 1752). Fifteenth-century dates can be converted to the modern calendar, and thus aligned with modern seasons, by the removal of nine days: e.g. instead of 22 August, the battle of Bosworth would have fallen on 31 August had a corrected calendar been in effect, and Richard III's birthday would have fallen on 11 October.

- Modernized and anglicized versions of proper names are preferred except where original sources are quoted *verbatim*. Fifteenth-century spelling was inconsistent, often whimsical, and to adopt a spelling such as Wydeville for Woodville would necessitate such absurdities as Tydder for Tudor.

- Maiden names for women are preferred, where known.

Notes and References

The place of publication is London unless otherwise stated.

Abbreviations

Buc	Sir George Buc, *The History of King Richard the Third* (1619), ed. Arthur Kincaid (2023)
CCR	*Calendar of Close Rolls*
CPR	*Calendar of Patent Rolls*
Commynes	Philippe de Commynes, *Memoirs*, ed. J. Calmette and G. Durville (Paris, 1924–5)
Crowland	*The Crowland Chronicle Continuations: 1459–1486*, ed. N. Pronay and J. Cox (1986)
EHR	*English Historical Review*
Harley 433	*British Library Harleian MS 433*, ed. R.E. Horrox and P.W. Hammond (Upminster and London, 1979–83)
Mancini	*Domenico Mancini: de occupatione regni Anglie*, ed. Annette Carson (Horstead, 2021)
Molinet	Jean Molinet, *Chroniques de Jean Molinet 1474–1504*; in *Collection des Chroniques nationales françaises*, ed. J.A. Buchon, 5 vols (Paris, 1827–8)
Rot. Parl.	*Rotuli Parliamentorum, ut et petitiones et placita in Parliamento*
Rous	John Rous, *Historia regum Anglie*, tr. Hanham, *Richard III and his Early Historians 1483–1535*, pp. 118–24 (Oxford, 1975)
TNA:PRO	The National Archives: Public Record Office
Vergil	Polydore Vergil, *Anglica Historia, Books 23–25*, J.B. Nichols (1846)

1: Poisoned?

1 Rosemary Horrox, *Richard III: A Study of Service* (Cambridge, 1989), p. 89.
2 Richard E. Collins, 'The Death of Edward IV', Part II of *Secret History*, J. Dening and R.E. C ollins (Suffolk, 1996).
3 Paul Murray Kendall, *Richard III* (1973), p. 160.
4 P.W. Hammond and Anne F. Sutton, *The Road to Bosworth Field* (1985), p. 14, where the antiquary John Stow is also quoted as having ascertained Richard's height from people who had seen him.
5 Livia Visser-Fuchs, 'What Niclas von Popplau really wrote about Richard III', *The Ricardian*, June 1999.
6 Michael K. Jones, *Bosworth 1485: Psychology of a Battle* (Stroud, 2002), p. 73.
7 *Harley 433*, vol. 2, pp. 108–9.
8 John Ashdown-Hill and Annette Carson, 'The Execution of the Earl of Desmond', *The Ricardian*, 2005.

2: The Politics of Power

1 Rous, p. 118.
2 *Vita Henrici VII*, p. 23, in *Memorials of King Henry VII*, ed. J. Gairdner (Rolls Series 10, 1858), www.philological.bham.ac.uk/andreas.
3 Rosemary Horrox (personal communication 27 February 2015); 9 May starts the formal listing of Edward V's grants under the signet in BL Harleian MS 433. The earliest written references occur in commissions of the peace, TNA C 66/551, m.8*d*.
4 Charles Ross, *Edward IV* (1975), p. 426.
5 Andrew Kettle, 'Parvenus in Politics: the Woodvilles, Edward IV and the Baronage 1464–1469', *The Ricardian*, 2005.
6 Three quotations in Keith Dockray, 'Edward IV: Playboy or Politician?', *The Ricardian*, December 1995.
7 Livia Visser-Fuchs, 'The Danzig Chronicle, 1461–1495', *The Ricardian*, December 1986.
8 E.W. Ives, 'Andrew Dymmock and the Papers of Antony, Earl Rivers, 1482–3', *BIHR*, vol. 41 (1968), pp. 216–29.
9 York Records, *Extracts from the Municipal Records of the City of York*, ed. R. Davies (1843; repr. 1976), pp. 142–3. Horrox, in *Richard III*, p. 90n, says the same early report apparently reached Exeter.

3: Plot and Counter-Plot

1 Mancini, pp. 56–7; R. Horrox, 'Financial Memoranda of the Reign of Edward V: Longleat Miscellaneous Manuscript Book II', *Camden Fourth Series Miscellany XXIX*, vol. 34 (Royal Historical Society, 1987), pp. 202–3, 211.

2 Rosemary Horrox, *Richard III: A Study of Service* (Cambridge, 1989), pp. 102–3.

3 *Ibid.*, p. 109.

4 Paul Murray Kendall, *Richard III* (1973), p. 165.

5 Gordon Smith, 'Stony Stratford: The Case for the Prosecution', *Ricardian Bulletin*, Spring 2004.

6 Vergil, p. 173.

7 Michael Hicks, 'Richard Duke of Gloucester: The Formative Years', in John Gillingham (ed.) *Richard III: A Medieval Kingship* (1993), p. 37.

8 Colin Richmond, '1483: The Year of Decision' in Gillingham, *Richard III*, pp. 43–8.

9 *Rot. Parl.* vol. iii, p. 343.

10 John Ashdown-Hill, 'The Lancastrian Claim to the Throne', *The Ricardian*, 2003. It is argued by Ian Mortimer that Henry invoked the name of Henry III in order to claim the throne as that king's heir *male*. But this creates inconsistencies, most importantly undermining Henry's own *matrilineal* claim to the crown of France. Note also that when Richard of York placed his (successful) case before Parliament in 1460 challenging the Lancastrian succession, part of his evidence was to refute the Crouchback myth by reciting the names of each of Henry III's sons in proper order and giving their exact dates of birth (*Rot. Parl.* vol. v, 1439–1467/8, p. 375).

11 Buc, pp. 280–1.

12 *CPR, 1405–8*; Excerpta Historica, ed. S. Bentley (1831), pp. 152–3.

13 Michael K. Jones and Malcolm G. Underwood, *The King's Mother: Lady Margaret Beaufort, Countess of Richmond and Derby* (Cambridge, 1992), p. 24.

14 Ralph A. Griffiths and Roger S. Thomas, *The Making of the Tudor Dynasty* (Stroud, 1993), pp. 28–9.

15 Jones and Underwood, *The King's Mother*, p. 117.

16 *Ibid.*, pp. 60, 61.

17 *Ancient Correspondence*, XLV, no. 236.

18 Court of Common Council, City of London Corporation (LMA COL/CC/01/01/009), Journal 9, 23 May 1483.

4: A Shadow over the Succession

1 A.J. Carson, *Richard Duke of Gloucester as Lord Protector and High Constable of England* (2015), Appendix X, pp. 101–6.

2 Michael Hicks, *Richard III* (Stroud, 2000), pp. 113–4.

3 Louise Gill, *Richard III and Buckingham's Rebellion* (Gloucester, 2000), p. 52.

4 Charles Ross, *Edward IV* (1975), p. 402.

5 For a full study of Richard's powers and authority see A.J. Carson, *Richard Duke of Gloucester as Lord Protector and High Constable of England* (2015). Gill is mistaken in stating (*Richard III*, p. 57) that Earl Rivers was Constable of England at this time. The office had been held by Richard of Gloucester since 1469.

6 Rosemary Horrox, *Richard III: A Study of Service* (Cambridge, 1989), p. 85.

7 Ross, *Edward IV*, p. 396.

8 The ensuing comments and extracts concerning marriage and canon law are necessarily abridged. Readers wishing to understand the legal niceties should consult the publications quoted.

9 John Ashdown-Hill, 'Edward IV's Uncrowned Queen', *The Ricardian*, December 1997. Much of what follows about Lady Eleanor has been culled from Dr Ashdown-Hill's research.

10 Commynes, vol. 2, pp. 232, 305. Stillington had not yet been made bishop, so he was Canon Stillington at the time.

11 John Ashdown-Hill, 'Lady Eleanor Talbot: New Evidence, New Answers, New Questions', *The Ricardian*, 2006.

12 H.A. Kelly, 'The Case Against Edward IV's Marriage and Offspring', *The Ricardian*, September 1998.

13 Mary O'Regan, 'The Precontract and its Effect on the Succession in 1483', *The Ricardian*, September 1976.

14 R.H. Helmholz, 'The Sons of Edward IV: A Canonical Assessment of the Claim that they were Illegitimate' in P.W. Hammond (ed.), *Richard III: Loyalty, Lordship and Law* (1986).

15 From C. d'O. Farran, 'The Law of Accession', *Modern Law Review*, vol. 16 (1953), p. 144.

16 Hicks, *Richard III*, p. 118. Presumably his illegitimate mediæval kings are not English.

17 David Baldwin, *Elizabeth Woodville* (Stroud, 2002), p. 7.

18 G.M. Trevelyan, *History of England* (1966), p. 113.

19 B.P. Wolffe, *Yorkist and Early Tudor Government* (1960), p. 6.

20 Muriel Smith, 'Reflections on Lady Eleanor', *The Ricardian*, September 1998.

21 Ashdown-Hill, 'Lady Eleanor Talbot: New Evidence'.

22 *Harley 433*, vol. 1, p. 16.

23 A.J. Carson, 'Convocations Called by Edward IV and Richard of Gloucester in 1483: Did They Ever Take Place?', *The Ricardian*, 2012, pp. 35–45.

24 *Stonor Letters and Papers, 1290–1483*, ed. C.L. Kingsford (1919), ii, pp. 159–60.

25 *York Records*, pp. 149–50.

5: Battle Lines are Drawn

1 Vergil; *The Great Chronicle*; Fabyan's *New Cronycles*; Rous, pp. 121–2.

2 M.H. Keen, 'Treason Trials under the Law of Arms', *Transactions of the Royal Historical Society*, 5th series vol. 12, 1962, p. 93.

3 Richard Firth Green, 'Historical notes of a London citizen, 1483–1488', *EHR*, vol. 96, July 1981.

4 Michael Hicks, *Richard III* (Stroud, 2000), p. 114.

5 Alison Hanham, *Richard III and his Early Historians 1483–1535* (Oxford, 1975), p. 41 (source of the memorandum: TNA:PRO SC 1/53/19).

6 *Stonor Letters*, ii, 161.

7 Alison Hanham, *Richard III*, pp. 168–70.

8 Charles Ross, *Richard III* (1981), p. 80.

9 *Ibid.*, p. 87.

10 Hicks, *Richard III*, p. 114.

6: 'This Eleccion of us the Thre Estates'

1 James Gairdner, *History of the Life and Reign of Richard the Third* (Cambridge, 1878).

2 Appendix to Robert Henry's *History of Great Britain* (1823), vol. 12.

3 Michael K. Jones, *Bosworth 1485: Psychology of a Battle* (Stroud, 2002); Livia Visser-Fuchs, '"By just computation of the time": Edward IV's Phantom Bastardy', *The Ricardian*, 2018, pp. 15–28.

4 *Calendar of Letters and Papers Foreign and Domestic of the Reign of Henry VIII*, VIII, p. 281.

5 Rosemary Horrox, 'Richard III and London', *The Ricardian*, September 1984.

6 Anne F. Sutton, 'Richard III's "tytylle & right": A New Discovery', *The Ricardian*, June 1977.

7 Charles Ross, *Richard III* (1981), p. 91.

8 Alison Hanham, *Richard III and his Early Historians 1483–1535* (Oxford, 1975), p. 47.

9 C.S.L. Davies, 'Bishop John Morton, the Holy See, and the Accession of Henry VII', *EHR*, January 1987, p. 20.

10 J. Ashdown-Hill, 'The Elusive Mistress', *The Ricardian*, 1999.

11 M. Barnfield, S. Lark, 'Paternity of Lady Lumley', *The Ricardian*, 2016.

12 John Ashdown-Hill, 'The Elusive Mistress: Elizabeth Lucy and Her Family', *The Ricardian*, June 1999.

13 Bertram Fields, *Royal Blood* (New York, 1998), pp. 109–17.

7: Witchcraft and Sorcery

1 H.A. Kelly, 'English Kings and the Fear of Sorcery', *Medieval Studies*, vol. 39, 1977, p. 207.

2 *Ibid.*, p. 214.

3 Christina Hole, *Witchcraft in England* (1990), pp. 57, 58.

4 *Ibid.*, p. 148.

5 *Ibid.*, p. 115.

6 *Ibid.*, p. 69.

7 Kelly, 'English Kings', p. 224.

8 W.E. Hampton, 'Roger Wake of Blisworth', *The Ricardian*, March 1976.

9 Hole, *Witchcraft*, p. 117.

10 David Baldwin, *Elizabeth Woodville* (Stroud, 2002), p. 199 n. 22.

11 Michael Hicks, *Edward V* (Stroud, 2003), p. 42. He details various such chronicles p. 208n, and mentions that two sources claimed to know the identity of the officiating priest, p. 41.

12 W.E. Hampton, 'Witchcraft and the Sons of York', *The Ricardian*, March 1980.

13 *Rot. Parl.*, vi, p. 273 ('Nandyk' has metamorphosed into 'Vandyke').

14 Michael Hicks, *Richard III* (Stroud, 2000), p. 124.

15 Rosemary Horrox, *Richard III: A Study of Service* (Cambridge, 1989), p. 113.

16 Alison Hanham, *Richard III and his Early Historians 1483–1535* (Oxford, 1975), p. 169.

17 Hole, *Witchcraft*, pp. 30–1.

18 John Ashdown-Hill, 'Richard III: The Monster Myth and its Meaning', *Medelai Gazette*, April 2006.

19 Rous, p. 120.

8: Dynastic Manoeuvrings

1 Jeremy Potter, *Good King Richard?* (1983), p. 213.
2 Michael Hicks, *Edward V* (Stroud, 2003), p. 169.
3 John Stow, *The Annales or Generall Chronicle of England* (1615), p. 460.
4 Michael Hicks, 'Unweaving the Web: The Plot of July 1483 against Richard III and its Wider Significance', *The Ricardian*, September 1991, citing Thomas Basin, *Histoire de Louis XI*. ed. C. Samaran, vol. 3, *Les Classiques de l'histoire de France*, vols 26, 29, 30 (Paris, 1972), p. 234.
5 Society of Antiquaries MS 77, ff. 71^v, 73$^{r&v}$, 75^v, 76^r; Howard Household Books, part 2, pp. 416, 419, 420, 423, 424.
6 Ralph A. Griffiths and Roger S. Thomas, *The Making of the Tudor Dynasty* (Stroud, 1993), p. 83.
7 Rosemary Horrox, 'Richard III and London', *The Ricardian*, September 1984; Louise Gill, *Richard III and Buckingham's Rebellion* (Gloucester, 2000), p. 63; Rosemary Horrox, *Richard III: A Study of Service* (Cambridge, 1989), p. 169.
8 Michael K. Jones and Malcolm G. Underwood, *The King's Mother: Lady Margaret Beaufort, Countess of Richmond and Derby* (Cambridge, 1992), p. 125; Horrox, *Richard III*, p. 150.
9 Bill Hampton, '"Our trusty and welbeloved servant and squire for oure body", Nicholas Baker alias Spicer', *The Ricardian*, 2003.
10 Gill, *Richard III*, p. 64.
11 Griffiths and Thomas, *Making of the Tudor Dynasty*, p. 91.
12 *Ibid.*, p. 102.
13 Buc, pp. 163, 184. N.B. In the younger Buck's 1646 version it is Edward IV whose death they were plotting, which confirms the persistence of the rumour that he was poisoned.

9: The Disappearance of the Princes

1 The term 'princes' is used for convenience, since they have been known as such for centuries.
2 *Harley 433*, vol. 2, p. 2 (originally thought to be 14 men).
3 A.J. Pollard, *Richard III and the Princes in the Tower* (Stroud, 1991), chapter 5.
4 Bertram Fields, *Royal Blood* (New York, 1998), p. 189.
5 David Baldwin, *The Lost Prince: The Survival of Richard of York* (Stroud, 2007).
6 Jeremy Potter, *Good King Richard?* (1983), p. 85.

7 John Ashdown-Hill, 'The Death of Edward V: New Evidence from Colchester', *Essex Archaeology and History*, vol. 35, 2006. A later deletion, deeply excised, has been made between the words *Edwardi* and *quinti*, where (as shown to Dr Ashdown-Hill by my calligraphy) it might have once read *Bastardi*. Use of the formulaic phrase 'Edward the Bastard' continued in some documents, but would have been unacceptable under Henry VII. If this is the missing word, its significance may be reflected in the subsequent *nuper filii* (the bastard whose status was lately 'son' of Edward IV).

8 *The Maire of Bristowe is Kalendar*, ed. L. Toulmin Smith, 1872.

9 See also endnote 3 of Postscript below.

10 Livia Visser-Fuchs, 'Danzig Chronicle, 1461–1495', *The Ricardian*, December 1986. A similar chronicle compiled by Jan Allertsz, recorder of Rotterdam, reports that Richard 'killed two of his brother's children, boys, or so he was accused', but this report was written after 1485.

11 C.A.J. Armstrong, *The Usurpation of Richard III* (1989).

12 Charles Ross, *Richard III* (1981), p. xlv.

13 Potter, *Good King Richard?*, p. 76.

14 Armstrong, *op. cit.*, note 91, p. 128.

15 With acknowledgements to John Ashdown-Hill.

16 Barrie Williams, 'Rui de Sousa's Embassy and the Fate of Richard, Duke of York', *The Ricardian*, June 1981.

17 De Barante, *Ducs de Bourgogne*, vol. 10, no cxiii, pp. 213–4.

18 Maaike Lulofs, 'Richard III: Dutch Sources', *The Ricardian*, June 1984.

19 Para 54, www.philological.bham.ac.uk/andreas.

20 *Anglica Historia*, Liber XXVI. This literal translation from Halsted's *Richard III* (1844, Vol II, p. 181n) is of Latin in Vergil's 1546 and 1555 editions.

21 A.N. Kincaid, 'George Buck senior and George Buck junior: a literary historical mystery story', *The Ricardian*, March 1978.

22 Buc, pp. 138–44.

23 Sir Francis Bacon, *The Historie of the Reigne of King Henry the Seventh*, 1622 (first edition), p. 4 and 19–20.

24 *Harley 433*, vol. 2, p. 187.

25 *Harley 433*, vol. 2, p. 191.

26 Audrey Williamson, *The Mystery of the Princes* (Gloucester, 1978), p. 122.

27 *Harley 433*, pp. 129, 178.

28 Ann Wroe, *Perkin, a Story of Deception* (2003), p. 22, citing CCR EIV/EV/RIII, p. 370, CPR EIV/EV/RIII, p. 481.

29 Gordon Smith, 'Lambert Simnel and the King from Dublin', *The Ricardian*, December 1996. Re regnal number 'Edward VI' see chapter 15.

30 B.L. Harleian MS 283, ff. 123v–124v.

31 Christine Weightman, *Margaret of York, Duchess of Burgundy 1446–1503* (Gloucester, 1989), p. 145. Formerly attributed to 1486.

32 Wroe, *Perkin*, p. 516.

33 Richard Firth Green, 'Historical notes of a London citizen, 1483–1488', *EHR*, vol. 96, July 1981.

34 Ashmolean MS 1448–60, f. 287, which bears the signature of Humphrey Llwyd.

35 A.S. Marques, *Ricardian Bulletin*, Winter 2006, Autumn 2008: Livro de Apontamentos (1438–1489) (Códice 443 da Colecção Pombalina da BNL), Imprensa Nacional – Casa da Moeda, Lisboa, 1983. If Sir Edward Woodville was the purveyor of this information – the veracity of which he could not have known first-hand – it is likely that his 1486 mission to negotiate a marriage between the royal houses of Portugal and England required him to come equipped with a suitable story to reassure his hosts that the princes were safely dead.

36 Commynes, book 6, chapter 2.

37 Molinet, vol. 2, p. 402.

38 P.W. Hammond and W.J. White, 'The Sons of Edward IV: A Re-examination of the Evidence on their Deaths and on the Bones in Westminster Abbey' in P.W. Hammond (ed.), *Richard III: Loyalty, Lordship and Law* (1986), p. 110.

10: Bones of Contention

1 L.E. Tanner and W. Wright, 'Recent Investigations regarding the fate of the Princes in the Tower', *Archaeologia* LXXXIV, 1935. This and other seventeenth-century references are examined in detail by, *inter alia*, Helen Maurer 'Bones in the Tower: A Discussion of Time, Place and Circumstance', *The Ricardian*, December 1990 (Part 1), March 1991 (Part 2), and by John Morgan in *Have the Princes' Bones Been Found in the Tower?* (1962).

2 Louis Aubery du Maurier, *Mémoires pour servir à l'histoire de Hollande* (Paris, 1680), pp. 214–5, quoted in Maurer, Part 1.

3 *Catalogue and Succession of the Kings, Princes, Dukes, Marquesses, Earles, and Viscounts of this Realme of England* (2nd edition, 1622) p. 33. The

discovery was not mentioned in Brooke's 1st edition (1619), nor by Buc, who knew only the story of the unfortunate ape. Contrary to Maurer's suggestion, Buc would have gained nothing by misreporting so significant an event as the discovery of dead children at the Tower whilst writing his great work in <1619–20.

4 See note 1.

5 Personal correspondence (Dr Geoffrey Parnell, Dr William J. White and Historic Royal Palaces); Plantagenet Somerset Fry, *The Tower of London* (1990), pp. 15–16.

6 P.W. Hammond and W.J. White, 'The Sons of Edward IV: A Re-examination of the Evidence on their Deaths and on the Bones in Westminster Abbey' in P.W. Hammond (ed.), *Richard III: Loyalty, Lordship and Law* (1986), pp. 104–47.

7 Personal letter to the author, 3 March 2004.

8 M.A. Rushton, CBE, LLD, MD, OdontD, FRCS, FDS, Professor of Dental Medicine, University of London: 'The Teeth of Anne Mowbray', *British Dental Journal*, vol. 119, 1965, pp. 358–9.

9 A.C. Aufderheide and C. Rodriguez-Martin, *The Cambridge Encyclopedia of Human Paleopathology* (1998), p. 409.

10 A.S. Hargreaves and R.I. MacLeod, 'Did Edward V suffer from histiocytosis X?', *Journal of the Royal Society of Medicine*, vol. 87, February 1994, pp. 98–101.

11 Molinet, vol. 2, p. 402.

12 Buc, p. 140.

13 Michael Hicks, *Edward V* (Stroud, 2003), pp. 137, 146.

14 *Ibid.*, pp. 65–6 (although the dates and locations of Christmas celebrations are erroneous); Ross, *Edward IV* (1975), p. 280.

15 Hicks, *Edward V*, pp. 176, 191.

16 William White, 'Whose Bones?', *Ricardian Bulletin*, Winter 2003, pp. 19–20.

17 Hammond and White, 'Sons of Edward IV', pp. 125, 143n.

18 *Ibid.*, p. 126.

19 Paul Murray Kendall, *Richard III* (1973), notes pp. 497–8.

20 *Ibid.*, pp. 406–7.

21 Ross, *Richard III* (1981), pp. 233–4.

22 A.R. Myers, 'The Character of Richard III', *History Today*, 1954, iv.

23 Theya Molleson, 'Anne Mowbray and the Princes in the Tower: a study in identity', *The London Archaeologist*, vol. 5, Spring 1987; summarized and updated in Paul Bahn (ed.), *Written on the Bones: how human remains unlock the secrets of the dead* (Newton Abbott, 2003).

24 John Ashdown-Hill, 'The Missing Molars: A Genealogical
    Conundrum', *The Ricardian*, September 1998.

25 Hammond and White, 'Sons of Edward IV', note 101.

11 : The October Rebellion

1   CPR 1476–1485, pp. 465–6, TNA:PRO C 66/556 m 7d.

2   *Harley 433*, vol. 1, pp. 3–4.

3   TNA:PRO C 81/1392/6.

4   Sir William Cornwallis, *The Encomium of Richard III*, ed. A.N. Kincaid
    (1977), p. 25.

5   Buc, pp. 59–63.

6   Williamson, *The Mystery of the Princes* (Gloucester, 1978), p. 87.

7   Ralph A. Griffiths and Roger S. Thomas, *The Making of the Tudor
    Dynasty* (Stroud, 1993), p. 96.

8   Buc, pp. 60–1.

9   Michael K. Jones and Malcolm G. Underwood, *The King's Mother:
    Lady Margaret Beaufort, Countess of Richmond and Derby* (Cambridge,
    1992), p. 64.

10 Louise Gill, *Richard III and Buckingham's Rebellion* (Gloucester,
    2000), p. 64.

11 A. Bouchard, *Les Grandes Croniques de Bretaigne* (Caen, 1518),
    f. ccviii^r, followed by B.A. Pocquet du Haut-Jussé, *François II, Duc
    de Bretagne et l'Angleterre* (Paris, 1929), p. 252, cited by
    C.S.L. Davies, 'Bishop John Morton, the Holy See, and the
    Accession of Henry VII', *EHR*, January 1987, p. 14.

12 Charles Ross, *Richard III* (1981), p. 105.

13 *Ibid.*, pp. 109–10.

14 *Ibid.*, p. 112.

15 Horrox, *Richard III*, p. 151.

16 *Ibid.*, p. 171.

17 Jeremy Potter, *Good King Richard?* (1983), p. 46.

18 Ross, *Richard III*, p. 119; Bellamy, *The Law of Treason*, p. 193

12 : Brave Hopes

1   Crowland, p. 133.

2   *Harley 433*, vol. 2, pp. 48–9.

3 Sharon Turner, *The History of England During the Middle Ages* (1830).

4 Buc, p. 254.

5 Anne F. Sutton, 'A Curious Searcher for Our Weal Public' in P.W. Hammond (ed.), *Richard III: Loyalty, Lordship and Law* (1986), pp. 72–3.

6 P.W. Hammond and Anne F. Sutton, *The Road to Bosworth Field* (1985), pp. 182–4.

7 Anne F. Sutton, 'Richard III's "tytylle & right": A New Discovery', *The Ricardian*, June 1977.

8 S.B. Chrimes, *English Constitutional Ideas in the Fifteenth Century* (Cambridge, 1936), pp. 123–6.

9 R.H. Helmholz, 'The Sons of Edward IV: A Canonical Assessment of the Claim that they were Illegitimate' in P.W. Hammond (ed.), *Richard III: Loyalty, Lordship and Law* (1986).

10 Jeremy Potter, *Good King Richard?* (1983), pp. 22, 53.

11 Alison Hanham, *Richard III and his Early Historians 1483–1535* (Oxford, 1975), p. 16.

12 Bertram Fields, *Royal Blood* (NY, 1998), pp. 162–3. He also made history by using English for the ancient coronation oath.

13 Paul Murray Kendall, *Richard III* (1973), p. 284.

14 Turner, *History of England*, lib. v, pp. 18–22.

15 *The Union of the Two Noble and Illustre Famelies of Lancastre & Yorke,* editions of 1548 and 1550 collated as *Hall's Chronicle* (London, 1809), p. 698.

16 Myers, 'The Character of Richard III'.

17 Charles Ross, *Richard III* (1981), chapter 7.

18 *Ibid.*, pp. 143–4.

19 *Ibid.*, pp. 100, 113.

20 Rosemary Horrox, *Richard III: A Study of Service* (Cambridge, 1989), pp. 151–2.

21 Carson, *Protector and Constable*, p. 67. The exact wording of this oath is not recorded.

22 C.S.L. Davies, 'Bishop John Morton, the Holy See, and the Accession of Henry VII', *EHR*, January 1987, p. 10.

23 Rous, p. 123.

24 Michael K. Jones, *Bosworth 1485: Psychology of a Battle* (Stroud, 2002), chapter 5.

25 Ralph A. Griffiths and Roger S. Thomas, *The Making of the Tudor Dynasty* (Stroud, 1993), pp. 86, 102, 106.

26 *Ibid.*, pp. 124–5; Molinet, vol. 2.

27 Jones, *Bosworth 1485*, pp. 123–5 (letter from Charles VIII to the town of Toulon, where Tudor is described as '*fils du feu roi Henry d'Angleterre*' [spelling modernized]). For full text see: Alfred Spont, 'La marine française sous le règne de Charles VIII', *Revue des questions historiques*, new series, 11 (1894), p. 393.

28 British Library Harleian MS 787, f.2.

29 *Harley 433*, vol. 3, pp. 124–5.

13 : Barbarians at the Gates

1 The Latin in this passage is problematical, and I am grateful for second opinions from scholars including Dr Lesley Boatwright of the Richard III Society. As a result, I have chosen Dr Alison Hanham's translation in *Richard III and his Early Historians 1483–1535* (Oxford, 1975), pp. 52–3.

2 Again the Latin presents problems. There are alternative readings depending on whether the Latin verb is *indicavit* ('he declared') or *iudicavit* ('he judged'). *Indicavit* makes better sense.

3 Crowland (Pronay and Cox), pp. 173–5.

4 Translation from Alison Hanham, *Richard III*, pp. 52–3.

5 *The Great Chronicle* and Commynes report her murder. Vergil's list of accusations, including poisoning, is echoed by Hall and others.

6 Translation from P. W. Hammond and Anne F. Sutton, *The Road to Bosworth Field* (1985), pp. 202–3.

7 Peter D. Clarke, 'English Royal Marriages and the Papal Penitentiary', *EHR*, September 2005.

8 'The Marriage of Lady Anne Neville and Richard Duke of Gloucester', *Ricardian Bulletin*, December 2016, pp. 46–52; see also 'Edward of Middleham's Birth', *Ricardian Bulletin*, September 2016, pp. 53–5. The best indication of the latter's death in 1484 is given by John Rous (see Appendix), writing within 5–6 years of the occurence, saying that Edward died *tempore Paschali*, 'at Easter-tide' (Rous, p. 123). Easter Sunday in 1484 fell on 18 April.

9 Marie Barnfield, 'Diriment Impediments, Dispensations and Divorce: Richard III and Matrimony', *The Ricardian*, 2007.

10 Michael Hicks, *Anne Neville, Queen to Richard III* (Stroud, 2006), p. 205.

11 Buc, p. 191. This letter was altered by Buc's great-nephew (see Appendix p. 370) on p. 128 of his 1646 published version, where the words 'in body and in all' were omitted; an omission which has been

misconstrued by a number of writers including Alison Weir who has since published a revised view in her book *Elizabeth of York* (Cape, 2013). Dr Kincaid's square brackets reproduced in this extract from his edition of Sir George's original text serve to indicate that the words they enclose are missing from the autograph MS. They have been supplied after consulting early scribal copies of Sir George Buc's *History*, which are in accord as to the missing words. The square brackets are used because even though these manuscripts are in complete agreement, no *guarantee* can be offered that the seventeenth-century scribal copies are 100 per cent accurate. Nor, for that matter, is it *certain* that Sir George's recollection of the letter itself was accurate down to the last word. Nor need we necessarily accept the construction he placed on it.

12 Alison Hanham, 'Sir George Buck and Princess Elizabeth's Letter: A Problem in Detection', *The Ricardian*, June 1987, pp. 398–400.

13 Arthur Kincaid, 'Buck and the Elizabeth of York Letter: a Reply to Dr Hanham', *The Ricardian*, June 1988, pp. 46–9.

14 *Ibid.* p. 49, as adapted to conform with 2023 edition, p. 191.

15 Barrie Williams, 'The Portuguese Connection and the Significance of "the Holy Princess"', *The Ricardian*, March 1983; Domingos Mauricio Gomes dos Santos, *O Mosteiro de Jesus de Aveiro* (Lisbon, 1963). The Portuguese scholar António S. Marques confirms (personal correspondence, April 2015) that this report appears among recollections of the Holy Princess penned by the nun, Sister Margarida Pinheiro, who was a constant presence in Joana's life and attended her deathbed. Margarida reported on events in which she was closely concerned, some of which she probably witnessed first-hand.

16 *The History of King Richard the Third* (ed. Kincaid), p. 331.

17 Translation from Alison Hanham, *Richard III*, pp. 52–3.

18 A.J. Salgado, Álvaro Lopes de Chaves, Livro de Apontamentos (1438–89), Códice 443 da Colecção Pombalina da B.N.L., Lisboa, 1983, p. 255.

19 Hanham, *Richard III*, p. 134. See K.B. McFarlane, *EHR*, vol. 78 (1963), pp. 771–2; *Cal. Papal Registers*, XIV, 1484–92.

20 Michael K. Jones, *Bosworth 1485: Psychology of a Battle* (Stroud, 2002), pp. 149–50 and note 13 p. 212. Also TNA:PRO E404/79.

21 Buc (p. 290, note 105/22–25) quoting Hall, p. 421.

22 James Petre (ed.), *Richard III: Crown and People* (1985), pp. 24–31; A.J. Carson (ed.), *Finding Richard III* (Horstead, 2014, 2015), pp. 16, 20, 23.

23 L. Pidgeon, 'Who Killed Richard III?', *Ricardian Bulletin*, December 2012, pp. 48–9.

24 'The Scoliosis of Richard II', *The Lancet*, 2014, Vol. 383: p. 1944; www.thelancet.com/journals/lancet/article/PIIS0140-6736(14)60762-5/fulltext.

14: Postscript

1 Buc, pp. 82, 87–9.

2 Ann Wroe, *Perkin, a Story of Deception* (2003), p. 140.

3 I am grateful to John Ashdown-Hill for pointing out that a requiem mass was observed in the Vatican for 'Edward King of England' on 23 September 1483 (C.S.L. Davies, 'A Requiem for King Edward', *The Ricardian*, September 1991, pp. 102–05). It cannot be assumed, however, that Edward V was meant, else how could Mancini, writing nearly three months later, claim to be ignorant of whether he had died? Davies himself inclines to the view that this was more likely a delayed requiem for Edward IV. (N.B. Any such mass would not obviate the need for one at home.)

4 Bertram Fields, *Royal Blood* (New York, 1998), p. 194.

5 For a spirited account of Henry VII's duplicitous career see Jeremy Potter, *Good King Richard?* (1983), pp. 117–19. Sir Francis Bacon described Henry VII as 'a sanguinary, sordid and trembling usurper'.

6 Peter D. Clarke, 'English Royal Marriages and the Papal Penitentiary', *EHR*, September 2005.

7 C.S.L. Davies, 'Bishop John Morton, the Holy See, and the Accession of Henry VII', *EHR*, January 1987, p. 15.

8 I am grateful to Joanna L. Laynesmith for this information.

9 David Baldwin, *Elizabeth Woodville* (Stroud, 2002), p. 121.

10 Horace Walpole, 'Historic Doubts on the Life and Reign of King Richard III' in *Richard III: The Great Debate*, ed. P.M. Kendall (1965), p. 207.

11 Sir Francis Bacon, *The History of the Reign of King Henry the Seventh* (1971), p. 60.

12 Anne F. Sutton and Livia Visser-Fuchs, 'The "Retirement" of Elizabeth Woodville and her Sons', *The Ricardian*, September 1999, pp. 561–5.

13 Baldwin, *Elizabeth Woodville*, p. 132–3.

14 *The Anglica Historia of Polydore Vergil*, A.D. 1485–1537, ed. D. Hay (1950), p. 21.

15 Tim Thornton, *Cheshire and the Tudor State, 1480–1560* (Woodbridge, 2000).

16 Michael K. Jones, *Bosworth 1485: Psychology of a Battle* (Stroud, 2002), p. 133. Morton was not related to Bishop Morton.

17 Jeremy Potter, *Good King Richard?* (1983), pp. 250–1.

18 Paul Murray Kendall, *Richard III* (1973), p. 319.

15: Reappearances

1 Note that as soon as the Woodvilles began gearing up for rebellion, Richard moved the little Earl of Warwick into the household of his wife, Duchess Anne (Warwick's aunt), and the boy was honoured and cared for as long as Richard lived.

2 In particular Albert Jan de Rooij and Nathalie Nijman-Bliekendaal.

3 *Richard III: The Maligned King*, Chapter 13, p. 270, in editions of 2008, 2009.

4 BL Cotton MS. Julius B.XII, p. 117 (1488–90).

5 York House Book B6, f.98–99v.

6 York House Book B6, f.97r.

7 U1485.22.

8 U1487.12.

9 *De Vita atque Gestis Henrici Septimi Historia*, www.philological.bham.ac.uk/andreas (para. 54).

10 For the record, an 'impostor' is a counterfeit, whereas a 'pretender' is a person who claims to be the rightful sovereign.

11 Even King James I was heard to deplore the execution of Warwick: Buc, *The History of King Richard the Third*, p. cxxx.

12 Vergil, 1546 and 1555 editions: *quod in vulgus fama valeret, filios Edouardi regis aliquo terrarum secreto migrasse, atque ita superstites esse*, etc. In his 1534 edition he had written *quod in vulgo essent, qui suspicarentur filios Edouardi regis aliquo terrarum secreto migrasse, atque ita superstites esse*; thus in the earlier version he had stated that 'there were those among the common people by whom it was suspected'. In the later versions it was no longer merely 'suspected' but 'a report prevailed among the common people'. In 1662 Francis Bacon (in his *Historie of the Raigne of King Henry the Seventh*) echoed this report in his references to the so-called 'Lambert Simnel' conspiracy, saying (p. 4) 'neither wanted there even at that time secret Rumours and whisperings (which afterwards gathered strength and turned to

great troubles) that the two young Sonnes of King Edward the Fourth, or one of them (which were said to be destroyed in the Tower) were not indeed murthered but conveyed secretly away, and were yet living: which if it had beene true, had prevented the Title of the Lady Ellizabeth.' Then, on pp. 19–20: 'And all this time it was still whispered every where, that at least one of the Children of Edward the Fourth was living.'

13 Chapter 9 of this edition, pp. 189ff. See also my book *Richard III: A Small Guide to the Great Debate* (2023), under the heading 'Survival theories revisited'. The purpose of separation was not only to preserve anonymity, but to ensure neither boy could know whether the other was still living, and thus could not inadvertently betray his whereabouts.

14 *De Vita atque Gestis Henrici Septimi Historia*, www.philological.bham. ac.uk/andreas (para. 54).

15 Among others, John Green, Robert Brackenbury, William Slaughter, Miles Forest, John Dighton, an unnamed page and unnamed priest: More, ed. Sylvester, pp. 85–8.

16 The formula for adoption of Edward's regnal number had already been promulgated in 1483 as 'fifth of that name after the conquest' (*Edwardus quintus eo nomine a conquestu Angliæ*). To adopt a different regnal number would be to undermine the solemn oaths of allegiance which had been sworn to him under that name.

17 *The Dublin King* (2015, 2017), chapter 2, esp. pp. 42–4.

18 York House Book B6, f.97r.

19 College of Arms Phillips MS 15175, p. 304.

20 Vergil, *The Anglica Historia A.D. 1485–1537*, ed. with trans. Denys Hay, London 1950, pp. 14, 22.

21 The spurious date of Thursday 24 May given for this coronation by Henry VII's Parliament has been proved by Langley to be wrong, perhaps deliberately to obscure that the coronation did take place, as was traditional, on a Sunday.

22 U1487.12.

23 Vergil gave conflicting accounts of this: see full account in Chapter 14 above, pp. 322–5.

24 Warwick was also referred to as 'Clarence' by Sir George Buc, writing in 1619, p. 154.

25 The National Archives, The Hague, the Netherlands, Grafelijkheidsrekenkamer, Margaret of York's Domain Account Voorne, reg. nr access: 3.01.27.02, inv. nr 3337. Annual account from January 1487.

26 Stenzel Bornbach. ed., APG 300, R/LI,q, 32, pp. 57–76, 135–46, extracts translated by Livia Visser-Fuchs, 'English Events in Caspar Weinreich's Danzig Chronicle 1461–1495', *The Ricardian* (December 1986), pp. 310–20, though her translation renders both names as 'George'. This is unlikely, as elsewhere when Weinreich means 'George' he actually writes 'George'.

27 Naming the house of York would chime with Weinreich's repeated use of '*konig Ritzmundt*' rather than 'King Henry', showing that he thought in terms of the king's Richmond title. If he actually wrote '*... zum konige zu sein, bei seinem namen [Jork/Jorke] und den Ritzmundt zu vertreiben*' I suggest this would mean he was writing of this challenger in the name of the house of York seeking to overthrow the 'house of Richmond'. Since these were Weinreich's personal notes, he had no need to concern himself finding out the pretender's forename.

28 *City Account Mechelen 1486–1487* (folio 153r and further). 'Gifts with the procession of Saint Rumbold and of the Holy Sacraments.'

29 Previously dated 1486, now corrected to 1487. See pp. 194–5 above.

30 Archives départementales du Nord, Lille: B 3521, nr 12456.

31 Maximilian I, son of the Holy Roman Emperor Frederick III, married (in August 1477) Mary of Burgundy, the only child of Charles the Bold (d. January 1477). Mary was the step-daughter of the Dowager Duchess Margaret of Burgundy, who was sister to the brothers Edward IV, Richard III and George of Clarence. At this time Maximilian was known by the title King of the Romans.

32 Described in Chapter 9 above, see p. 195.

33 Gelders Archief, 0510 'Diverse Charters en Aanwinsten', nr 1549: *Verhandelingen over de lotgevallen van Richard van York, ca 1500.*

34 Buc, *op. cit.*, produces supporting testimonies pp. 160ff. See also p. 173: 'For the Flemish, French and Wallons acknowledge no such noble young man to have been bred in Warbeck or in Tournay, but make honourable mention of a young son of the King of England who was brought to the Duchess of Burgundy, his aunt, being then in Flanders, and how he was in France and in other kingdoms.'

35 From a near-contemporary copy of Richard of York's proclamation, Griffith Collection, National Library of Wales, Carreglwyd Estate Archive, Series 1/695 (1496), located/transcribed by Dr Judith Ford; see also Judith Ford, 'Richard of England's Proclamation', *Ricardian Bulletin* (March 2022), pp. 46–51.

36 *Domenico Mancini de occupatione regni Anglie* (ed./trans. Carson, 2021), pp. 62–3.

37 Cf. *ibid.*, pp. 64–5.

38 These three named men have almost certainly been correctly identified. Halneth Mauleverer was an usher to the Chamber for Edward IV, and William Poche a Yeoman of the Crown who held office at the Tower of London. Miles Forest became newsworthy in 2021 when Prof. Tim Thornton named a later generation of Forests at the court of Henry VIII.

39 Chapter 8 above, pp. 153–5.

40 'That they were trusted servants is apparently demonstrated by Thomas's father, Peter Peirse (*c.*1440s–1510) who acted as the king's standard bearer at Bosworth': Philippa Langley, *The Princes in the Tower*, pp. 202–3.

41 Brampton had a long record of being trusted by the Yorkist kings, and had seen service with the Duke of Norfolk in Edward IV's Scottish wars.

42 We know that ambassador Rui de Sousa heard Richard sing as a child: such accomplishments were prized at court, where, unlike his brother, he had been kept with his mother rather than undergoing the more usual knightly apprenticeship. I have always thought this gentler upbringing manifested itself in Richard's later tenderheartedness when it came to leading men into the brutal realities of war.

43 There exists a curious French version of 'the confession of Perkin Warbeck' which has an appendix absent in the English version, containing a completely different account of his childhood. It alleges that he was educated in the cathedral choir school in Tournai where he was taught the manicordium (an early precursor of the clavichord): Archives Courtrai, Collection Jacques Goethals-Vercruysse MSS, inv. III, ff. 188v–189r. This was just one of probably countless rumours swirling around Henry VII's cynical execution of the young pretender who so discomfited him, probably picking up on Richard's known penchant for the clavichord. Of course no reliance can be placed on any version of the extorted official 'confession', especially in light of its trumped-up circumstances which aroused condemnation at the time and for centuries afterwards.

44 The Setubal testimonies of 1496 revealed that the pretender had been in Portugal for more than three years (through 1490), not just one year as the official 'confession' alleged: Wroe, *Perkin: A Story of Deception*, pp. 24, 525–8.

45 The official 'confession' mentions a Pregent Meno as that Breton shipmaster. By then Meno had apparently turned king's evidence.

46 Bibliothèque Nationale de France, Fonds Espagnol 318, f. 83.
   Examined at length in Wroe, *Perkin*, pp. 126–130.
47 BL Egerton MS 616, f. 003r, trans. Dr Betty Knott; see Weightman,
   Margaret of York, p. 172. Both his and Margaret's letters were written in
   less-than-perfect Latin, presumed to be that of a clerk.
48 Such concerns must be remembered also in relation to testimony such
   as Brampton's later statements.
49 There was also, since Stoke Field, the young man 'Lambert Simnel'
   who had been taken into the Tudor king's service; whoever he was,
   his life hinged on being thought to be a counterfeit.

Select Bibliography

The place of publication is London unless otherwise stated.

André, Bernard, *History of the Life of Henry VII* www.philological. bham.ac.uk/andreas

Armstrong, C.A.J., *The Usurpation of Richard III* (Gloucester, 1989)

Ashdown-Hill, J., *Eleanor, the Secret Queen* (Stroud, 2009)

Ashdown-Hill, J., *The Last Days of Richard III* (Stroud, 2010, 2011)

Bacon, Sir Francis, *The Historie of the Reigne of King Henry the Seventh* (1622)

Baldwin, D., *Elizabeth Woodville: Mother of the Princes in the Tower* (Stroud, 2002)

Baldwin, D., *The Lost Prince: The Survival of Richard of York* (Stroud, 2007)

Baldwin, D., *Stoke Field* (Barnsley, 2006)

Barron, C. and Saul, N. (eds.), *England and the Low Countries in the Late Middle Ages* (Stroud, 1995, 1998)

Basin, Thomas, *Histoire de Louis XI*, ed. C Samaran (Paris: *Les Classiques de l'histoire de France*, 1972)

Bellamy, J.G., *The Law of Treason in England in the Later Middle Ages* (Cambridge, 1970)

Bray, G. (ed.), *Records of Convocations (Canterbury 1313–1509)*, (2006)

British Library Harleian Manuscript 433, ed. R.E. Horrox and P.W. Hammond, 4 vols (Upminster and London, 1979–83)

Buc, Sir George, *The History of King Richard the Third (1619)*, ed. Arthur Kincaid (Society of Antiquaries, 2023)

Calendar of the Carew Manuscripts at Lambeth (1868) [includes *The Book of Howth*]

Calendar of Close Rolls

Calendar of Letters etc between England and Spain, ed. G.A. Bergenroth (1862)

Calendar of Papal Registers, 1484–92 (1955)

Calendar of Patent Rolls, 1441–1509, 8 vols (1908–16)

Carson, A.J., *Richard III: A Small Guide to the Great Debate* (Horstead, 2023)

Carson, A.J. (ed.), *Finding Richard III: The Official Account of Research by the Retrieval and Reburial Project* (Horstead, 2014)

Carson, A.J., *Richard Duke of Gloucester as Lord Protector and High Constable of England* (Horstead, 2015)

Carson, A.J. (ed./trans.), *Domenico Mancini: de occupatione regni Anglie* (Horstead, 2021)

The Cely Letters, 1472–1488, ed. A. Hanham (Early English Text Society 273, 1975)

Chrimes, S.B., *English Constitutional Ideas in the Fifteenth Century* (Cambridge, 1936)

Chronicles of London, ed. C.L. Kingsford (1905; repr. Gloucester, 1977) [three London chronicles including B.L. MS Cotton Vitellius A. XVI]

Chronicles of the White Rose of York, ed. J.C. Giles (1843; repr. Gloucester, 1974) [includes *Hearne's Fragment*, the *Historie of the Arrivall* and Warkworth's *Chronicle*, all in modernized spelling]

Collins, R.E., 'The Death of Edward IV', in Part II of *Secret History*, J. Dening and R.E. Collins (Suffolk, 1996)

Commynes, Philippe de, *Memoirs*, ed. J. Calmette and G. Durville (Paris, 1924–5)

Cornwallis, Sir William, *The Encomium of Richard III*, ed. A.N. Kincaid (1977)

Crawford, A., *Howard Household Books* (Stroud, 1992)

The Crowland Chronicle Continuations: 1459–1486, ed. N. Pronay and J. Cox (1986)

Cunningham, S., *Richard III: A royal enigma* (Richmond, 2003)

Dockray, K., *Richard III: A Source Book* (Stroud, 1997)

Edwards, R., *The Itinerary of King Richard III 1483–1485* (1983)

An English Chronicle of the Reigns of Richard II, Henry IV, Henry V and Henry VI Written before the Year 1471, ed. J.S. Davies (1856)

Excerpta Historica, ed. S. Bentley (1831, 1833)

Fabyan, Robert, *New Chronicles of England and France*, ed. H. Ellis (1811)

Fields, B., *Royal Blood* (New York, 1998)

Fry, P.S., *The Tower of London* (1990)

Gainsford, Thomas, *The True and Wonderful History of Perkin Warbeck* (Harleian Miscellany vol. 6, 1745)

Gairdner, J., *History of the Life and Reign of Richard the Third* (Cambridge, 1878, rev. 1898)

Gairdner, J., *Letters and Papers Illustrative of the Reigns of Richard III and Henry VII*, 2 vols (Rolls Series 24, 1861, 1863)

Gill, L., *Richard III and Buckingham's Rebellion* (Stroud, 1999, 2000)

Gillingham, J. (ed.), *Richard III: A Medieval Kingship* (1993)

Grants from the Crown during the Reign of Edward V, ed. J.G. Nichols (1854)

The Great Chronicle of London, ed. A.H. Thomas and I.D. Thornley (1938; repr. Gloucester, 1983)

Griffiths, R.A. and Thomas, R.S., *The Making of the Tudor Dynasty* (Stroud, 1985, 1993)

Hallam, E. (ed.), *Chronicles of the Wars of the Roses* (Surrey, 1997)

Halsted, C., *Richard III* (1844; repr. Gloucester, 1980)

Hammond, P.W. (ed.), *Richard III: Loyalty, Lordship and Law* (1986)

Hammond, P.W. and Sutton, A.F., *Richard III: The Road to Bosworth Field* (1985)

Hanham, A., *Richard III and his Early Historians 1483–1535* (Oxford, 1975)

Hicks, M., *Edward V* (Stroud, 2003)

Hicks, M., *Richard III* (Stroud, 2000)

Hole, C., *Witchcraft in England* (1990)

Horrox, R., *Richard III: A Study of Service* (Cambridge, 1989)

Impey, E. (ed.), *The White Tower* (Yale University Press, 2008)

Jones, M.K., *Bosworth 1485: Psychology of a Battle* (Stroud, 2002)

Jones, M.K. and Underwood, M.G., *The King's Mother: Lady Margaret Beaufort, Countess of Richmond and Derby* (Cambridge, 1992)

Kendall, P.M., *Richard III* (1955, 1973)

Kleyn, D.M., *Richard of England* (Oxford, 1990)

Langley, Philippa, *The Princes in the Tower: Solving History's Greatest Cold Case* (Cheltenham, 2023)

Lapper, I. and Parnell, G., *Landmarks in History, The Tower of London: A 2000-Year History* (2000)

Lyne-Pirkis, R.H.G., *Regarding the Bones Found in the Tower*; speech by modern anatomist given to Richard III Society, 27 February 1963

Mancini, Domenico, *de occupatione regni Anglie*, see Carson, A.J.

Mandrot, Bernard de, ed., *Journal de Jean de Roye connu sous le nom de Chronique Scandaleuse, 1460–1483*, Tome II (Paris, 1896, repr. Wentworth Press, 2019)

Markham, Sir Clements, *Richard III: His Life & Character* (1906; repr. Bath, 1973)

Molinet, Jean, *Chroniques de Jean Molinet 1474–1504*, in *Collection des Chroniques nationales françaises*, ed. J.A. Buchon, 5 vols (Paris, 1827–8)

More, Thomas, *History of King Richard the Third* [*Chronicle of John Hardyng* with Grafton continuation, as published by Richard Grafton in 1543], in *Richard III: The Great Debate*, ed. P.M. Kendall (1965)

More, St Thomas, *The History of King Richard III* [William Rastell version, 1557] and Selections from the English and Latin Poems, ed. R.S. Sylvester (New Haven, 1976)

Morgan, J., *Have the Princes' Bones Been Found in the Tower?*, summary by teacher of Constitutional History in the Law School of Melbourne University, 1962

Paston Letters, ed. J. Gairdner (Gloucester, 1983)

Paston Letters & Papers of the Fifteenth Century, ed. N. Davis, 2 vols (Oxford, 1971, 1976)

Petre, J. (ed.), *Richard III: Crown and People* (1985)

Pollard, A.J., *Richard III and the Princes in the Tower* (Stroud, 1991, 1993)

Potter, J., *Good King Richard?* (1983)

Register of Archbishop Thomas Bourchier, Canterbury

Register of Bishop John Alcock, Worcester

Register of Bishop John Russell, Lincoln

Ross, C., *Edward IV* (1975)

Ross, C., *Richard III* (1981)

Rotuli Parliamentorum, ut et petitiones et placita In Parliamento, ed. J. Strachey, 6 vols (1767–77). Also published as *The Parliament Rolls of Medieval England*, ed. Chris Given-Wilson *et al.* [Windows CD-ROM] and on the internet by subscription www.sd-editions. com/PROME/ (Scholarly Digital Editions, 2005). Rolls covering 1455–1504 ed. R. Horrox.

Rous, John, *Historia regum Anglie* (BL Cotton MS Vespasian A XII) [for translation of section relating to Richard III, see Hanham, A., *Richard III and his Early Historians*]

Rymer, T., *Foedera Conventiones…*, 20 vols (1704–35)

Snyder, W.H. (ed.), *The Crown and the Tower* (New York/Gloucester, 1981)

Stonor Letters & Papers, 1290–1483, ed. C.L. Kingsford (1919)

Storey, R.E., *The End of the House of Lancaster* (Gloucester, 1986)

Storey, R.E., *The Reign of Henry VII* (1968)

Stow, John, *The Annales or Generall Chronicle of England* (1615)

Trevelyan, G.M., *History of England* (1966)

Tudor-Craig, P., *Richard III*, Catalogue of National Portrait Gallery Exhibition (1973)

Turner, S., *The History of England during the Middle Ages* (1830)

Vergil, Polydore, *Anglica Historia* (1555 edition) www.philological. bham.ac.uk/polverg

Vergil, Polydore, *The Anglica Historia of Polydore Vergil, A.D. 1485–1537*, ed. D. Hay (1950)

Walpole, Horace, *Historic Doubts on the Life and Reign of King Richard III*, ed. P.W. Hammond (Gloucester, 1987)

Walpole, Horace, *Historic Doubts on the Life and Reign of King Richard III*, in *Richard III: The Great Debate,* ed. P.M. Kendall (1965)

Weightman, C., *Margaret of York, Duchess of Burgundy 1446–1503* (Gloucester, 1989)

Williamson, A., *The Mystery of the Princes* (Gloucester, 1978)

Wilson, S., *The Magical Universe* (London/New York, 2000)

Wroe, A., *Perkin: A Story of Deception* (2003)

York House Books 1461–1490, ed. L.C. Attreed, 2 vols (1991)

York Records, Extracts from the Municipal Records of the City of York, ed. R. Davies (1843; repr. 1976)

Journals

Archaeologia [journal of the Society of Antiquaries of London]

British Dental Journal

Bulletin of the Institute for Historical Research

English Historical Review

History [journal of the Historical Association]

History Today

Journal of the Royal Society of Medicine

The London Archaeologist

Medieval Studies

The Ricardian [journal of the Richard III Society]

Ricardian Bulletin [published by the Richard III Society]

Textile History

Transactions of the Royal Historical Society

Index